Historical Dictionary of Ethics

Harry J. Gensler
Earl W. Spurgin

*Historical Dictionaries of Religions,
Philosophies, and Movements, No. 91*

The Scarecrow Press, Inc.
Lanham, Maryland • Toronto • Plymouth, UK
2008

SCARECROW PRESS, INC.

Published in the United States of America
by Scarecrow Press, Inc.
A wholly owned subsidiary of
The Rowman & Littlefield Publishing Group, Inc.
4501 Forbes Boulevard, Suite 200, Lanham, Maryland 20706
www.scarecrowpress.com

Estover Road
Plymouth PL6 7PY
United Kingdom

British Library Cataloguing in Publication Information Available

Library of Congress Cataloging-in-Publication Data

Gensler, Harry J., 1945–
  Historical dictionary of ethics / Harry J. Gensler, Earl W. Spurgin.
    p. cm. — (Historical dictionaries of religions, philosophies, and
movements ; no. 91)
  Includes bibliographical references.
  ISBN-13: 978-0-8108-5763-6 (hardcover : alk. paper)
  ISBN-10: 0-8108-5763-4 (hardcover : alk. paper)
  eISBN-13: 978-0-8108-6271-5
  eISBN-10: 0-8108-6271-9
  1. Ethics—History. 2. Ethics—Dictionaries. I. Spurgin, Earl W. II. Title.
  BJ71.G46 2008
  170.9—dc22   2008020022

♾™ The paper used in this publication meets the minimum requirements of
American National Standard for Information Sciences—Permanence of
Paper for Printed Library Materials, ANSI/NISO Z39.48-1992.
Manufactured in the United States of America.

HISTORICAL DICTIONARIES OF
RELIGIONS, PHILOSOPHIES, AND MOVEMENTS
Jon Woronoff, Series Editor

1. *Buddhism*, by Charles S. Prebish, 1993
2. *Mormonism*, by Davis Bitton, 1994. *Out of print. See no. 32.*
3. *Ecumenical Christianity*, by Ans Joachim van der Bent, 1994
4. *Terrorism*, by Sean Anderson and Stephen Sloan, 1995. *Out of print. See no. 41.*
5. *Sikhism*, by W. H. McLeod, 1995. *Out of print. See no. 59.*
6. *Feminism*, by Janet K. Boles and Diane Long Hoeveler, 1995. *Out of print. See no. 52.*
7. *Olympic Movement*, by Ian Buchanan and Bill Mallon, 1995. *Out of print. See no. 39.*
8. *Methodism*, by Charles Yrigoyen Jr. and Susan E. Warrick, 1996. *Out of print. See no. 57.*
9. *Orthodox Church*, by Michael Prokurat, Alexander Golitzin, and Michael D. Peterson, 1996
10. *Organized Labor*, by James C. Docherty, 1996. *Out of print. See no. 50.*
11. *Civil Rights Movement*, by Ralph E. Luker, 1997
12. *Catholicism*, by William J. Collinge, 1997
13. *Hinduism*, by Bruce M. Sullivan, 1997
14. *North American Environmentalism*, by Edward R. Wells and Alan M. Schwartz, 1997
15. *Welfare State*, by Bent Greve, 1998. *Out of print. See no. 63.*
16. *Socialism*, by James C. Docherty, 1997. *Out of print. See no. 73.*
17. *Bahá'í Faith*, by Hugh C. Adamson and Philip Hainsworth, 1998. *Out of print. See no. 71.*
18. *Taoism*, by Julian F. Pas in cooperation with Man Kam Leung, 1998
19. *Judaism*, by Norman Solomon, 1998. *Out of print. See no. 69.*
20. *Green Movement*, by Elim Papadakis, 1998. *Out of print. See no. 80.*
21. *Nietzscheanism*, by Carol Diethe, 1999. *Out of print. See no. 75.*
22. *Gay Liberation Movement*, by Ronald J. Hunt, 1999
23. *Islamic Fundamentalist Movements in the Arab World, Iran, and Turkey*, by Ahmad S. Moussalli, 1999
24. *Reformed Churches*, by Robert Benedetto, Darrell L. Guder, and Donald K. McKim, 1999
25. *Baptists*, by William H. Brackney, 1999
26. *Cooperative Movement*, by Jack Shaffer, 1999

Contents

Editor's Foreword

Of all the branches of philosophy, the one that ordinary people hear the most about is ethics. That is also the one that masses of men and women, including experts in other areas, think they know the most about. That is usually a mistake since ethics in many ways is harder to pin down and comprehend than logic, aesthetics, or even metaphysics. Worse, a person's own view of ethics tends to blot out countless alternative views, leaving many of them poorly understood or utterly ignored. This should make the latest addition to the philosophies sub-series particularly welcome, if only people would admit their limits and find out more about the subject, which is hopefully the case. This volume provides, among other things, information about major ethical issues, significant schools of thought, outstanding philosophers, and basic terminology. It does so not by pontificating or deciding for the reader what is right and wrong but by showing the range of alternatives proposed by various experts. Also, and this is a big plus, while rooted in the "Western" study of ethics it also includes the insight and wisdom of other cultures, including Buddhism, Daoism, Hinduism, Islam, and Judaism.

This *Historical Dictionary of Ethics*, like other volumes in the series—some of which should serve as excellent partners with it—starts with a chronology, showing just how far back the roots of ethics lie and tracing its evolution and expansion to the present day. The introduction demonstrates why ethics is so important, why it has attracted some of the greatest minds, and how it has affected generation after generation despite the fact that many once unquestionable ideas have since become disputed or cast aside. Just how up-to-date it is should be evident from the issues dealt with in the dictionary section, including some at the top of the contemporary agenda, ranging alphabetically from abortion to capital punishment, euthanasia, happiness, homosexuality, justice, racism, privacy, sexism, terrorism, and war. It also includes entries on philosophers, such as Aristotle and Mary Wollstonecraft, that cover a wide range of periods and approaches in the history of ethics. The bibliography, not usually the most important section, certainly is worthy of attention since this book can be only a first step toward a better understanding of ethics while the many titles it lists can take readers further and further.

This book was written by Harry J. Gensler and Earl W. Spurgin, both professors of philosophy at John Carroll University in Cleveland, Ohio. Dr. Gensler is interested in logic and ethics and may be familiar to readers as the author of the recently published *Historical Dictionary of Logic*. This is hardly his first book on ethics, since he has already written *Formal Ethics* and *Ethics: A Contemporary Introduction* as well as many articles and papers. Dr. Spurgin, besides his work in philosophy, is director of the university core curriculum. His interest in ethics revolves around, among other things, business ethics, which is a newish but rapidly advancing field, it having previously been assumed that business and ethics somehow did not go together. This expands their circle of interests and their combined knowledge; and their need to explain ethics to students and business persons enhances their ability to communicate what often seem, until examined closely, to be deceptively simple concepts.

Jon Woronoff
Series Editor

Preface

Ethics (moral philosophy) is the philosophical investigation of questions about morality. It formulates and defends answers to questions such as these: What are the basic principles of right and wrong? What is ultimately good or worthwhile in life? What constitutes virtue and good character? What would a just society be like? What do "good" and "ought" mean? Are there moral truths and moral facts? How can we know or rationally defend beliefs about right and wrong? Like most areas of study, ethics has a long history and has grown more complicated over the years.

This book is an encyclopedia of ethics. It introduces the central concepts of the field in a series of brief, nontechnical "dictionary entry" articles. These deal with a wide range of topics about ethics, including its history, branches, vocabulary, controversies, and relationships to other disciplines. Following the series guidelines, *Historical Dictionary of Ethics* tries to be useful for specialists (especially ethicists in areas outside their subspecialties) but understandable to students and other beginners.

The major part of this book is the dictionary section, with 283 entries. While these are arranged alphabetically, there is also an organization based on content. Six very general entries start with "**ethics:**" and serve mainly to point to more specific entries; together they point to *all* the substantive entries in this dictionary. The six "**ethics:**" entries are:

- **ethics: metaethics** points to entries on the nature and methodology of moral judgments, like **cultural relativism, emotivism, ideal observer theory, impartiality,** and **knowing right from wrong.**
- **ethics: normative** points to entries on general principles about how we ought to live, like **consequentialism, double effect, egoism, justice, moral agent, rights, social contract,** and **utilitarianism.**
- **ethics: applied** points to entries on specific moral issues or areas, like **abortion, bioethics, business ethics, disability ethics, paternalism, racism, sexual ethics, stem-cell research,** and **war.**
- **ethics: history** points to entries on historical periods and figures, like **Aristotle, David Hume, medieval ethics, G. E. Moore, Jean-**

Paul Sartre, Peter Singer, and **twentieth-century ethics.**

- **ethics: interdisciplinary** points to entries relating ethics to science, world religions, and other parts of philosophy, like **anthropology, Biblical ethics, biology, epistemology, Hindu ethics, logic, psychology,** and **sociobiology.**
- **ethics: miscellaneous** points to entries that do not fit neatly into the other categories, like **autonomy, feminist ethics, free will, prisoner's dilemma,** and **weakness of will.**

The entries vary in length from a sentence or two to several pages.

The front of the book has two important parts:

- A chronology lists many significant events in the history of ethics.
- An introduction provides an overall view of ethics and a broader context for the dictionary entries.

The back of the book has a substantial bibliography on related readings.

While this book is predominantly on Western ethics, it has entries on **Buddhist ethics, Confucius, Daoist ethics, Hindu ethics,** and **Islamic ethics.** The authors' background and the available literature regrettably are weak in such areas. As **globalization** intensifies, it may be advisable to have a separate *Historical Dictionary of Non-Western Ethics.*

Writing a brief *Summa Ethica* like this is difficult, because ethics is so vast and complicated. It is humanly impossible to succeed completely; the authors ask your forgiveness for any omissions or inaccuracies and hope that you find this book useful—either to get a quick fix on some particular topic or to explore in a broader way the fascinating field of ethics.

To sum up: ethics studies how we ought to live—and this book tries to provide a clear, basic introduction to a very broad range of ethical topics.

Chronology

1,000,000 BC   Fred Flintstone helps a stranger who was robbed, beaten, and left to die. He says, "It is *good* to help him." Moral thinking is born!

c. 1780 BC   The Babylonian Code of Hammurabi gives penalties to 282 kinds of wrongdoing; a typical rule states "If a man puts out the eye of another, his eye shall be put out." The rules are given as the king's invention to protect the weak; but the king's wisdom is from the gods.

c. 1500–1200 BC   The Vedas are composed and become the sacred writings of Hinduism. They teach a cosmic order about how we are to live; we suffer if we violate this order, since the good or evil that we do to others will come back to us (karma). The Hindu golden rule says to do nothing to others which would cause you pain if it were done to you.

c. 1000 BC   The Jewish Scriptures formulate the Ten Commandments, which list the chief duties to God and to human beings. The rules state what to do in a direct way, without qualifications, like "You shall not kill."

600–400 BC   Ancient Greek interest in reasoning grows: geometry develops, philosophers debate metaphysics, and Sophists debate politics.

c. 563–483 BC   Siddhārtha Gautama (Buddha) achieves enlightenment. He teaches compassion, the golden rule (we are not to hurt others in ways that we would find hurtful), and karma (the good or evil that we do to others will come back upon us). His five precepts tell us to abstain from killing or harming sentient beings, from stealing, from adultery, from lying, and from intoxicating drinks and drugs.

c. 551–479 BC   Confucius's *Analects* likely is the world's first extended treatise on ethics. It consists of proverbs, anecdotes, and brief dialogues. Confucius sums up his teaching in the golden rule: "Do not do to others what you do not wish them to do to you."

c. 490–420 BC Protagoras, a Sophist, proposes that justice is what accords with local customs; he draws the conservative conclusion that our thinking about what is just must conform to local standards.

c. 470–399 BC Socrates, the father of Western philosophy, uses the dialogue method to investigate ethics and the good life. He opposes Sophists who use verbal tricks instead of seeking the truth. Socrates pursues the life of reason even though it leads to his conviction and death, purportedly for corrupting the youth of Athens.

450–300 BC Three minor schools say that the good life is one of bodily pleasure (Cyrenians), one of virtue and of indifference to pleasure and pain (Cynics), or unknowable (Skeptics).

c. 428–347 BC Plato argues for an objective good based on reason and the theory of forms. He contends that being just toward others benefits us because it promotes the health, harmony, and good of our soul.

c. 400–200 BC Laozi's mystical *Dao Te Jing* becomes the classic text of Daoism, a competitor of Confucianism and Buddhism in China. Our moral duty is to follow nature in an instinctive way; we do badly when we bind ourselves to social convention or strict rules.

384–322 BC Aristotle's *Nicomachean Ethics*, the first systematic treatment of ethics in the West, argues that the good life is one of virtue, whereby we exercise in an excellent way the rational powers that make us distinctive as human beings.

372–289 BC Mencius, Confucius's disciple, argues that humans have an innate concern for others that can either grow or wither, depending on social influences and personal effort, but can never totally disappear. So morality grows out of something that is part of our nature.

366–280 BC Zeno of Citium founds the Stoic school of philosophy; other early members include Cleanthes and Chrysippus. The Stoics believe that the good life is one of virtue, which brings inner happiness; we should be indifferent to social conventions and misfortunes that we cannot control. To be virtuous is to follow the natural moral law that is accessible to every person's reason.

c. 341–270 BC   Epicurus argues that the good life is what brings the greatest balance of pleasure over pain for oneself. In practice, he advocates a simple, relaxed, leisurely life where we pursue social and mental pleasures (like friendship and study) and try to avoid pain.

100 BC–200 AD   Roman Stoic thinkers (the orator Cicero, the statesman Seneca, the ex-slave Epictetus, and the emperor Marcus Aurelius) propose a natural moral law, accessible to everyone's reason, that leads us to be just and considerate toward everyone and follow the golden rule.

c. 99–55 BC   Lucretius preaches Epicureanism to a Roman audience.

c. 4 BC–30 AD   Jesus Christ, believed by his followers to be divine, proclaims the love of God and neighbor and the golden rule to be the basis of how we should live. Like Socrates, he was put to death.

c. 120   The Christian Athenian philosopher Aristides defends Christianity to the Roman Emperor. Aristides argues for belief in God as the world's designer and mover, claims that Christianity is religiously and morally superior to polytheism, and protests religious persecution.

c. 160   The Christian thinker Irenaeus argues for free will, which he sees as presupposed by moral praise and blame. He also proposes an approach to the problem of evil; God created the first humans weak and imperfect, and intended life to be a significant, free struggle against evil in which we gradually grow toward moral and spiritual maturity and eternal happiness.

c. 205–270   Plotinus's *Enneads* founds Neoplatonism, which builds on Plato's metaphysical and mystical elements. All of reality emanates (or flows) from a supreme reality called "the One" and leads, through a series of levels, to the lowest level, the material world. Neoplatonism becomes the dominant Christian philosophy; it tends to accentuate Christianity's other-worldly strains and to devalue life's material and bodily aspects.

354–430   Augustine of Hippo combines Christian and Neoplatonic ideas. He argues that our highest happiness is to be found in God. His ethics claims that the soul is to rule the body, reason is to rule the soul, and the unchangeable (God and his law) is to rule reason. In short, "Love, and do as you will."

524   Boethius's *The Consolations of Philosophy* argues for the compatibility of human freedom and divine foreknowledge. After Boethius, European Christians do little creative work in philosophy until the 11th century.

570–632   Muhammad purportedly receives from the Angel Gabriel the Quran and the mission to convert his people from immorality and paganism. The Muslim golden rule says that true believers will desire for others what they desire for themselves.

c. 800–1200   The Arab world dominates in philosophy. Some Arab philosophers are Christian, but most are Muslim. Works of Aristotle that are as yet unknown in the West are translated into Arabic. Aristotle's virtue ethics influences Muslim ethics.

1079–1142   Peter Abelard presents an ethics that emphasizes our inner motivation and intention to follow God's will.

c. 1175–1253   Robert Grosseteste translates Aristotle's *Nicomachean Ethics* into Latin. This long-lost work is now available, with other lost writings of Aristotle, to the Christian West. Soon Aristotelianism replaces Neoplatonism as the dominant perspective of Christian philosophers.

1224–1274   Thomas Aquinas, the most influential thinker of the Middle Ages, defends a two-level natural-law ethics: his moral philosophy, knowable by natural reason, follows Aristotle, while his moral theology adds further elements based on Christian revelation.

1266–1308   John Duns Scotus emphasizes the will over the intellect; he claims, with Platonic Christian thinkers but against Aquinas, that our final end is not knowing God, but rather loving him.

c. 1285–1349   William of Ockham becomes one of the few important Christian philosophers to give a clear endorsement of the divine command theory. Since good is what God wills, Ockham acknowledges that God could have set up the moral norms so that stealing and hatred were good.

1313–1905   Confucian ethics is part of the civil service exam in China.

1492   Christopher Columbus's travels begin a new era of globalization.

1513   Niccolò Machiavelli suggests that rulers, while appearing to be ethical, adopt ethical means only if doing so furthers their interests.

1600–1800   There is much debate among Enlightenment thinkers about whether morality is based on reason (as argued by Francisco Suárez, Hugo Grotius, Henry More, Ralph Cudworth, Samuel Pufendorf, John Locke, Samuel Clark, Joseph Butler, Thomas Reid, Richard Price, and Mary Wollstonecraft) or on feelings (as argued by the Earl of Shaftesbury, Francis Hutcheson, Jean-Jacques Rousseau, Adam Smith, and David Hume).

c. 1612   The Jesuit Francisco Suárez argues that Spanish colonization is wrong because it violates the natural rights of sovereign peoples.

c. 1625   Hugo Grotius, in an attempt to discourage the frequent wars of his time, appeals to natural rights and international law.

1651   Thomas Hobbes's *Leviathan* argues that morality and government are based on a social contract that egoist humans, to further their interests and prevent social chaos, would agree to in the state of nature.

1673   Samuel Pufendorf's *On the Duty of Man and Citizen according to Natural Law* gives a detailed account of our duties that owes much to Hobbes but remains in the natural law tradition. One of our duties is to act out of respect for the equal dignity of all humans, an idea that becomes influential during the Enlightenment.

1690   John Locke's *Two Treatises of Government* gives a social-contract defense of representative government. Unlike Hobbes, Locke argues that humans are not pure egoists and that there are natural moral standards that do not depend on human conventions.

1729   Joseph Butler's *Fifteen Sermons Preached at the Rolls Chapel* criticizes Hobbes's view of humans as pure egoists. He instead proposes that four things motivate us: particular impulses (like hunger and pride), self-love, benevolence, and conscience.

1739   David Hume's *A Treatise of Human Nature* argues that ethical judgments are based on feelings and not reason. Reason is and ought only to be the slave of the passions. He argues for natural virtues, which directly promote the good of others, and artificial virtues (like keeping promises), where a social practice promotes good.

1751   David Hume's *Enquiry Concerning the Principles of Morals* repackages his idea that humans have a natural sympathy for others and that morality requires that we take a general point of view common with others.

1758   Jean-Jacques Rousseau's *Discourse on the Origin of Inequality* argues, against Hobbes, that our egoist tendencies come from civil society rather than human nature; humans by nature are good.

1759   Adam Smith's *Theory of Moral Sentiments* argues for ideal observer theory and makes sympathy the basis for morality and virtue.

1762   Jean-Jacques Rousseau's *On the Social Contract* begins: "Man was born free, but he is everywhere in chains." His solution is direct democracy; we can be free in civil society only if laws are determined by the general will.

1764   Thomas Reid's *An Inquiry into the Human Mind on the Principles of Common Sense* defends commonsense morality against David Hume's skepticism and subjectivism.

1776   The American *Declaration of Independence* echoes ideas from John Locke: "We hold these truths to be self-evident, that all men are created equal, that they are endowed by their Creator with certain unalienable Rights, that among these are Life, Liberty and the pursuit of Happiness.—That to secure these rights, Governments are instituted among Men, deriving their just powers from the consent of the governed."

1776   Adam Smith's *The Wealth of Nations* defends capitalism; his "invisible hand" image (that individuals pursuing their own interest in a free market will tend to maximize the social good) has influenced many contemporary economists, philosophers, and politicians.

1785   William Paley argues that, since our duties depend on God's will and God desires our happiness, our duty is to do whatever brings about the greatest amount of happiness (a view later called utilitarianism).

1785 Immanuel Kant's *Groundwork of the Metaphysic of Morals* argues that ethics is based on pure reason. The highest motive is to do our duty simply because it is the right thing to do. The basic principle of morality is that we are to act only on a maxim that we can will to be universal law.

1789 Jeremy Bentham's *An Introduction to the Principles of Morals and Legislation* defends utilitarianism: we are to do whatever has the best total consequences as measured by the pleasures and pains of all those affected.

1790 Mary Wollstonecraft's *A Vindication of the Rights of Man* defends the ideals of the French Revolution. As rational beings, we all have a right to that degree of civil and religious liberty that is compatible with a similar right of every other individual.

1792 Mary Wollstonecraft's *A Vindication of the Rights of Woman* argues that, since the inherent rationality of humans of both sexes is basically equal and the same, women should have the same educational, political, and employment rights as men.

1808 James Mill, the father of John Stuart Mill, meets Bentham and becomes a political activist for the utilitarian movement.

1821 Georg Wilhelm Friedrich Hegel's *Philosophy of Right* sees history as progressing toward higher forms of society and freedom. What at one time brings progress later becomes a constraint that needs to be overcome. Eventually we will reach a society where community interest coincides with self-interest.

1836 Ralph Waldo Emerson founds the transcendentalism movement, which sees introspection as an access to eternal moral truths. His movement attracts individuals who promote abolitionism, women's suffrage, and experiments in communal living.

1836 Arthur Schopenhauer focuses on suffering, which he sees as pervasive. The moral imperative is to sympathize with all who suffer and to reduce suffering, which can in part be done by minimizing desire. Since the distinction between persons is an illusion, we should have the same concern for others that we have for ourselves.

1840   Pierre-Joseph Proudhon's *What is Property?* advocates anarchy and socialism. His idea that property is theft influences Karl Marx. Later, Proudhon rejects Marx's advocacy of collective ownership and violent means to obtain it. Proudhon hopes for small communities with no centralized government and a society based on cooperation instead of coercion.

1845   William Whewell's *The Elements of Morality* bases ethics on commonsense intuitions, which first have to be made consistent with each other. It defends norms about benevolence, justice, truth, purity, and order. Whewell became John Stuart Mill's main opponent.

1848   Karl Marx and Friedrich Engels's *Communist Manifesto* calls workers to action. It tells them that historical necessity will eventually produce a stateless, classless, communist society.

1859   John Stuart Mill's *On Liberty* argues that society should not interfere with the acts of an individual unless these harm someone else.

1861   John Stuart Mill's *Utilitarianism* becomes the classic statement of utilitarianism. It argues that, while all pleasures are intrinsically good, higher pleasures are more valuable than lower pleasures. Our duty is to do whatever maximizes the sum-total of everyone's good.

1865–1872   American slaves are granted freedom, citizenship, and (for males only) the right to vote.

1867   Volume 1 of Karl Marx's *Das Kapital* claims that capitalists take for themselves a product's "surplus value" that the workers actually create. Friedrich Engels later adds volumes 2 and 3.

1869   John Stuart Mill's *On The Subjection of Women* criticizes the treatment of women.

1871   Charles Darwin's *Descent of Man* explains the place of ethics in an evolving world. He argues that animals with social instincts would develop a moral sense when their intellectual powers develop. Human morality is evolving from a limited tribal concern to a higher, universal concern for all that is summed up in the golden rule.

1872 Mikhail Aleksandrovich Bakunin quarrels with Marx about whether the state should fade away quickly (Bakunin's view) or only after socialism was achieved (Marx's view). As an anarchist, Bakunin thinks government is unnatural, violates our freedom, and brings many evils.

1874 Henry Sidgwick's *The Methods of Ethics* argues that commonsense morality, although often vague and inconsistent, is at its core utilitarian. He sees utilitarianism and egoism as based on self-evident principles.

1876 Francis Herbert Bradley's *Ethical Studies* follows Hegel and criticizes Mill. Its "My Station and Its Duties" sees duties in light of specific social roles instead of in general terms that apply to everyone.

1879 Herbert Spencer's *The Data of Ethics* teaches Social Darwinism. Evolution is a struggle where the strong survive and overcome the weak. Human life rightly follows this same pattern, whereby stronger individuals, corporations, classes, and nations dominate weaker ones.

1879 William Clifford's "The Ethics of Belief" says it is wrong always, everywhere, and for anyone, to believe anything on insufficient evidence.

1882 Leslie Stephen's *The Science of Ethics* tries to establish a somewhat utilitarian ethics on natural facts about evolution.

1883–1885 Friedrich Nietzsche's four-part *Thus Spake Zarathustra* argues that we, like other animals, have evolved with the will to power as our basic motivation. In repressing this, Christianity violates our nature.

1886 Friedrich Nietzsche's *Beyond Good and Evil* distinguishes the *slave morality* of the lower classes, a conformism that emphasizes concern for others, with the *master morality* of the nobles, which leads us to create our own values and promote our own power and advancement.

1889 Franz Brentano's *The Origin of the Knowledge of Right and Wrong* proposes that moral judgments express positive or negative emotions, but that these can be correct or incorrect in a basic, unanalyzable way; we know what is intrinsically good by intuition, not by empirical evidence or proof. Other continental philosophers of his era who took the same general approach include Nicolai Hartmann, Hans Reiner, and Max Scheler.

1890   "The Right to Privacy" by Samuel Warren and Louis Brandeis begins the current ethical discussion about privacy. It argues that law recognizes a "right to be let alone" that protects individuals' beliefs, thoughts, desires, and the like from public disclosure.

1896   The Dewey School at the University of Chicago provides a laboratory for testing John Dewey's ideas about education and psychology.

1897   William James's "The Will to Belief" responds to Clifford (1879). James claims that it is morally permissible under certain conditions to believe even when we lack strong evidence.

1900   John Dewey's *The School and Society* advocates less authoritarian schools and more experiential learning.

1903   G. E. Moore's *Principia Ethica* sets the stage for 20th-century ethics by arguing that attempts to define "good" in empirical terms commit the naturalistic fallacy. "Good" is indefinable, and basic moral principles are based on intuition instead of proof. Moore's ideal utilitarianism says we ought to do whatever maximizes good consequences, where many things other than pleasure are good in themselves.

1912   H. A. Prichard's "Does Moral Philosophy Rest on a Mistake?" argues, against Moore, that duties can be as self-evident as the goodness of consequences.

1916   Max Scheler's *Formalism in Ethics and Non-Formal Ethics of Values* attacks Kantian formalism and defends an intuitive approach to intrinsic value.

1917   The Russia revolution embraces Marxism. The Soviet Union (U.S.S.R.) is formed in 1922, and many other countries adopt Marxism.

1920   American women gain the right to vote.

1922   Ludwig Wittgenstein's *Tractatus Logico-Philosophicus* limits legitimate language to science and mathematics. Ethics, while important, cannot be expressed; it is transcendental and cannot be put into words.

1922   Martin Buber's *I and Thou* distinguishes *I-It* relationships (where we regard our neighbor as a thing to be used) from *I-Thou* relationships (where we more deeply communicate with and appreciate the other).

1926   Nicolai Hartmann's *Ethics* presents a phenomenology of value; value is known by an emotional intuition of essences.

1926   Ralph Perry's *General Theory of Value* defines "good" as "the object of a positive interest (desire)" and "right action" as "action that promotes a harmony of interests."

1930   W. D. Ross's *The Right and the Good* defends and further develops Moore's intuitionism. Ross also attacks utilitarianism and proposes seven self-evident prima facie moral duties, such as the duty to keep promises.

1934   The American anthropologist Ruth Benedict claims that ethics is relative to culture and that "morally good" means "socially approved."

1936   A. J. Ayer's *Language, Truth and Logic* defends *logical positivism*: any genuine truth claim has to be either analytic (true by definition) or empirically testable. Ayer uses this to argue for *emotivism*: moral judgments are expressions of feeling, like "Boo" and "Hurrah," instead of truth claims. The sole function of ethical philosophy is to tell us that ethical concepts are pseudo-concepts and therefore unanalyzable.

1938   John Dewey's *Experience and Education* cautions against sacrificing subject matter in order to please students. Dewey thinks some of his followers have gone too far in promoting experiential learning.

1939–1945   Nazi genocide kills six million Jews, one of the greatest moral atrocities of all time.

1942   Albert Camus's *Myth of Sisyphus* asks how we can live in an absurd world devoid of inherent moral significance.

1943   Jean-Paul Sartre's *Being and Nothingness* argues that we are radically free and responsible for our actions. We create our own values and the meaning of our lives. Determinism is "bad faith" since it denies our freedom and thus relegates us to the status of mere things.

1944   Charles Stevenson's *Ethics and Language* gives a more detailed analysis of ethical language from the emotivist perspective.

1945–1946   Former Nazi leaders are tried as war criminals in Nuremberg, Germany. The world learns about exterminations, genocide, and inhumane medical experiments.

1946   Jean-Paul Sartre's *Existentialism and Humanism* argues that we create our own values and that no theory is specific enough to tell us what to do in concrete situations; but he also demands that a kind of universality guide our actions: in choosing for ourselves we choose "for all."

1947   Simone de Beauvoir's *The Ethics of Ambiguity* presents an existentialist ethics. She argues that, while we must freely create our own values, the authentic approach is to respect the freedom of others to do likewise.

1947–1948   Led by Mahatma Gandhi and his policy of nonviolent resistance, India achieves independence from British colonial rule. India officially outlaws the caste system. Gandhi, who opposed the caste system and preached universal justice and love, is assassinated. Colonial empires across the world began to break down.

1948   The United Nations by a 48–0 vote (but with South Africa, Saudi Arabia, and six Soviet nations abstaining) passes an extensive *Universal Declaration of Human Rights*.

1949   Aldo Leopold's *A Sand County Almanac* inspires environmental ethics by advocating a *land ethic*: the land is a complex structure of living things that should not be seen merely as a tool for human use.

1949   Simone de Beauvoir's *The Second Sex* treats womanhood in an interdisciplinary way and calls for an end to sexist oppression.

1950   Norbert Wiener's *The Human Use of Human Beings: Cybernetics and Society* discusses social and ethical aspects of computer technology.

1950   Stephen Toulmin's *An Examination of the Place of Reason in Ethics* gives a rule-utilitarian analysis of the moral language game.

1950 The mathematician Albert Tucker creates the prisoner's dilemma, a game-theory story where two prisoners can do better for themselves if they cooperate instead of pursuing their own interests individually.

1951 The economist Kenneth Arrow shows by a purely logical argument that every possible voting system has flaws.

1951 Hannah Arendt's *The Origins of Totalitarianism* discusses anti-Semitism, imperialism, and the rise of Nazi and Soviet totalitarianism.

1952 R. M. Hare's *The Language of Morals* argues that moral judgments are a kind of prescription or imperative (like "Do this"), a view called prescriptivism. Ethicists devote much attention to moral language.

1952 Roderick Firth's "Ethical Absolutism and the Ideal Observer" proposes that calling something "good" means that we would desire it if we were ideally rational.

1953 Ludwig Wittgenstein's *Philosophical Investigations*, in a shift from his previous work, sees language as diverse, with many different language games being legitimate. Ethicists are encouraged to study the rules of the ethical language game.

1954–1975 The U.S. wages war in Vietnam. As the war becomes increasingly unpopular, a generation of youth in the West becomes radicalized and rejects the establishment. North Vietnam eventually wins and unifies the country under a Marxist regime.

1955 C. I. Lewis's *The Ground and Nature of the Right* presents the fundamental rational imperative as "Be consistent in thought and action." We are to act as if we were to live out in sequence our lives and the lives of those affected by our actions.

1958 Kurt Baier's *The Moral Point of View* defends a *rationalized attitudes* approach to making moral judgments.

1958 Philippa Foot's "Moral Arguments" argues for naturalistic constraints on what could count as "good" or "moral."

1958   Elizabeth Anscombe's "Modern Moral Philosophy" inspires contemporary virtue ethics by arguing that utilitarian and Kantian theories ignore important areas of the moral life such as virtues, emotions, moral character, moral education, and wisdom.

1959   Richard Brandt's *Ethical Theory* gives a widely acclaimed analysis of the main options in normative ethics and metaethics. It introduces the terms "act utilitarianism" and "rule utilitarianism."

1961   Marcus Singer's *Generalization in Ethics* revitalizes the "What if everyone did that?" argument.

1962   Rachel Carson's *Silent Spring* helps to make environmental ethics a formal academic discipline by addressing how pesticides harm humans and wildlife.

1963   Hannah Arendt's *Eichmann in Jerusalem: A Report on the Banality of Evil* discusses the trial of the Nazi war criminal who organized the genocide. Eichmann emerges as a somewhat ordinary person who acted not out of ideology or hatred but out of unthinking conformism.

1963   Martin Luther King is jailed in Birmingham, Alabama, for an illegal civil rights march. From jail, he writes a letter defending his policy of nonviolent civil disobedience and calling for an end to segregation. King is assassinated five years later.

1963   President John Kennedy appeals to the golden rule in calling for the end to segregation and racism in the United States. Kennedy is assassinated later that year. The following year, the government passes a Civil Rights Act to enforce desegregation.

1963   R. M. Hare's *Freedom and Reason* argues that the logic of "ought" supports golden-rule reasoning: I am inconsistent if I think I ought to do A to X, but I do not desire that A be done to me in an imagined reversed situation. He applies this idea to problems of racism.

1963   William Frankena's *Ethics* is a brief but thorough and influential ethics textbook. Among other things, it argues for a moderate emotivism that includes much moral rationality.

1964 William Hamilton's "The Genetic Evolution of Social Behavior" proposes looking at evolution in terms of the survival of the fittest genes (not the fittest individuals or groups), an idea that leads to sociobiology and its stress on *kin altruism* and *reciprocal altruism*.

1965 Ayn Rand's *The Virtue of Selfishness* argues for ethical egoism. Society would be better off if we all promoted our own interests instead of sacrificing them for the sake of others.

1965 David Lyons's *Forms and Limits of Utilitarianism* argues that many forms of rule utilitarianism collapse into act utilitarianism.

1965 Richard Brandt's "Toward a Credible Form of Utilitarianism" proposes a form of rule utilitarianism that he claims is credible and does not collapse into act utilitarianism.

1965 The U.S. Supreme Court in *Griswold v. Connecticut* decides that states cannot prohibit the sale of contraceptives because this violates marital privacy. It thus recognizes a Constitutional right to privacy.

1966 Ayn Rand's *Capitalism: The Unknown Ideal* argues that capitalism is the best economic system; if capitalism were allowed to operate freely, it would bring a prosperity that benefits everyone.

1967 Pope Paul VI's *Humanae Vitae* argues that the inherent natural purpose of intercourse is to procreate life; he concludes that the use of the birth-control pill is wrong. Catholics praise or criticize this conclusion.

1968 Albert Carr's "Is Business Bluffing Ethical?" argues that business is like a game with special rules distinct from morality. The objections that follow help business ethicists frame their discipline.

1968 Paul Ehrlich's *The Population Bomb* addresses the harm to our planet caused by increasing human population.

1969 The Hastings Center is established as the first bioethics study institute, helping to mark the birth of bioethics as an academic discipline.

1970   Jürgen Habermas's *Toward a Rational Society* critically analyzes contemporary society. It sympathizes with responsible student protests against authoritarian institutions.

1970   Simone de Beauvoir's *The Coming of Age* deals with the elderly and our responsibilities toward them.

1970   Thomas Nagel's *The Possibility of Altruism* argues that ethical judgments are objective. We all regard the fact that A would benefit *us* as a reason in favor of A; but then we must also regard the fact that A would benefit *others* as a reason in favor of A.

1970   The first Earth Day highlights environmental issues.

1970   The U.S. establishes the Environmental Protection Agency, which is concerned with areas like pesticide control and clean air and water.

1971   Frances Moore Lappé's *Diet for a Small Planet* addresses diet, proteins, world hunger, and a responsible use of the earth's resources.

1971   Georgetown University's Kennedy Institute of Ethics is established for the academic study of bioethics.

1971   Robert Trivers's "The Evolution of Reciprocal Altruism" argues that organisms that mutually benefit each other will tend to develop a kind of altruistic concern for each other.

1971   John Rawls's *A Theory of Justice* uses social-contract notions to defend liberal democratic ideas. The principles of justice are principles that people would agree to if they were rational but did not know their specific place in society (whether rich or poor, black or white, and so forth). On this basis, Rawls argues for two principles of justice, the first about human rights and the second about the distribution of wealth. His views are much discussed over the next several years.

1971   The first volume of *Philosophy and Public Affairs* appears. It has articles on applied ethics by prominent philosophers such as Judith Jarvis Thomson ("A Defense of Abortion"), Thomas Nagel ("War and Massacre"), Richard Brandt ("Utilitarianism and the Rules of War"), R. M. Hare ("Rules of War and Moral Reasoning"), Peter Singer ("Famine, Affluence, and Morality"), and Baruch Brody ("Thomson on Abortion"). Applied ethics continues to grown as an academic discipline.

1972 The first philosophy conference on environmental ethics is held at the University of Georgia; its proceedings are published in *Philosophy and Environmental Crisis* (1974).

1973 Arne Næss's "The Shallow and the Deep, Long-Range Ecology Movement" advocates *deep ecology*: all living things have value in their own right, independent of their usefulness to humans. Richard Routley (now Sylvan) similarly argues that our failure to see the intrinsic value of the natural world is merely a human prejudice.

1973 J. J. C. Smart and Bernard Williams's *Utilitarianism: For and Against* debate act utilitarianism.

1973 Jürgen Habermas's *Legitimation Crisis* argues that the modern state is subject to crises that come from its failure to meet the competing demands of rationality, democracy, and cultural identity.

1973 The U.S. Supreme Court legalizes abortion in the Roe v. Wade decision. Philosophers praise or condemn the decision.

1974 Françoise D'Eaubonne's *Le féminisme ou la mort* advocates *ecofeminism*: the male approach leads to the domination of both women and the environment.

1974 John Passmore warns that radical theories of environmental ethics have less chance of public acceptance than do appeals to the Judeo-Christian notion of humans as stewards of the natural world.

1974 Robert Nozick's *Anarchy, State, and Utopia* argues that people are entitled to any goods that they gain in a just way, even if some have more goods than others. Governments act wrongly if they try to redistribute such goods. Only a minimal libertarian state is justified.

1974 The first business ethics conference is held at the University of Kansas. Some see this as the formal birth of the academic discipline.

1974–1978   A national commission in the U.S. leads to the *Belmont Report*, which gives three ethical principles to guide research on human subjects: respect for persons, beneficence, and justice.

1975   Peter Singer's *Animal Liberation* becomes the "bible" of the animal liberation movement; the book sells 500,000 copies and contributes to the improved treatment of animals.

1977   Ronald Dworkin's *Taking Rights Seriously* argues that rights set boundaries that the state cannot cross to promote social utility. Rights promote liberalism by letting individuals be free to pursue their own conceptions of the good life.

1977   J. L. Mackie's *Ethics: Inventing Right and Wrong*, while admitting that moral judgments intend to assert independent moral facts, argues that there are no such moral facts; so all moral judgments are false. Ethicists debate the issue of moral realism: "Are there moral facts?"

1977   Gilbert Harman's *The Nature of Morality* argues that the best explanation of our experiences requires scientific facts but not moral facts. So it is reasonable to accept scientific facts but not moral facts.

1978   Alan Gewirth's *Reason and Morality* tries to derive the central principle of ethics by pure logic. His principle of generic consistency says that all agents must act in accordance with their own and all other agents' generic rights to freedom and well-being.

1978   The growth of bioethics is marked by the *Encyclopedia of Bioethics* (sponsored by Georgetown's Kennedy Institute of Ethics), the anthology *Contemporary Issues in Bioethics* (edited by Tom Beauchamp and LeRoy Walters), and, in the following year, the textbook *Principles of Biomedical Ethics* (by Tom Beauchamp and James F. Childress).

1979   Business ethics comes of age with three new anthologies: Vincent Barry's *Moral Issues in Business*, Tom Beauchamp and Norman Bowie's *Ethical Theory and Business*, and Thomas Donaldson and Patricia Werhane's *Ethical Issues in Business: A Philosophical Approach*.

1979   Peter Singer's *Practical Ethics* applies utilitarianism to a range of practical issues. It is best known for its permissiveness about infanticide:

"Killing a disabled infant is not morally equivalent to killing a person. Very often it is not wrong at all."

1979 Richard Brandt's *A Theory of the Good and the Right* argues that moral concepts are confused and need replacement rather than analysis; he proposes a definition of "rational desire" that would replace "good" and not presuppose any preexisting moral facts.

1980 John Finnis's *Natural Law and Natural Rights* gives a classic restatement of natural law ethics in contemporary terms.

1980 Peter Singer's disciple Henry Spira places a full-page ad in the New York Times showing how Revlon tests cosmetics by pouring toxic chemicals on the eyes of rabbits. Spira demands that Revlon fund research into alternative tests not involving animals; these tests turn out to be more accurate and less expensive, besides avoiding pain to animals.

1981 Alasdair MacIntyre's *After Virtue* argues that virtues are habits or dispositions that are needed to achieve excellence in social practices and to obtain goods internal to those practices. In giving community interest priority over individual rights, MacIntyre expresses the communitarian criticism of liberal views such as those of John Rawls.

1981 R. M. Hare's *Moral Thinking* argues for a preference utilitarianism: we ought to maximize the satisfaction of everyone's desires. Seeking to defuse objections to utilitarianism based on intuitions, Hare claims that utilitarianism works only on the "rational level" of moral thinking, not on the day-to-day "intuitive level" whereby we follow the moral intuitions most useful to have instilled in us.

1981–1984 Lawrence Kohlberg's *Essays on Moral Development* proposes that people, regardless of culture, all develop in their moral thinking through a series of six stages. We start by thinking in terms of punishments and rewards; later we rely on social conventions; still later, if we progress far enough, we evaluate moral beliefs using justice, consistency, and concern for the equal dignity of every person. Ideas from Kant, Hare, and Rawls are used to explain the highest stage.

1982 Carol Gilligan's *In a Different Voice* claims, against Kohlberg, that there are two mature ways to think about morality: justice and caring. Men tend to think of morality in terms of justice, principles, rights, and duties; women tend to appeal to caring, feelings, personal relationships, and responsibilities. While Christina Sommers and others criticize Gilligan's views, others develop care and feminist approaches further.

1982   Single-authored textbooks in business ethics appear: Richard De George's *Business Ethics* and Manuel G. Velasquez's *Business Ethics: Concepts and Cases.*

1983   Stephen Darwall's *Impartial Reason* argues that rationality requires not just coherence and ends-means rationality but also impartiality.

1984   Nel Noddings's *Caring: A Feminine Approach to Ethics and Moral Education* argues for a feminist ethics.

1984   Derek Parfit's *Reasons and Persons* questions the common belief in a "self" that persists through time. He proposes the Humean/Buddhist view that what we misleadingly call the "self" is merely a collection of experiences; he shows how this alters the choice between self-interest and an impersonal concern for good results wherever they occur.

1984   R. Edward Freeman's *Strategic Management: A Stakeholder Approach* argues that corporations must consider the interests of not only shareholders but also *stakeholders* (those affected positively or negatively by corporations).

1985   Deborah Johnson's *Computer Ethics* is the first textbook to deal with moral issues about computers.

1985   Bernard Williams's *Ethics and the Limits of Philosophy* argues that morality is too complex to be captured by any systematic theory. He advocates a return to the ancient Greek question, "How do I live well?"

1986   Thomas Nagel's *The View From Nowhere* explores the subjective/objective tension. How can we balance the fact that we exist in a specific time and place, with a specific history and set of influences, with our thirst for beliefs and attitudes that transcend subjectivity and see the world from a vantage point that is "nowhere in particular"?

1986 James Griffin's *Well-Being* takes well-being to be what we would desire if we were rational, argues for limits in measuring it, and considers the extremes of egoism and equal respect for everyone's well-being.

1986 David Gauthier's *Morals by Agreement* presents a Hobbesian ethics enriched by game theory (especially the prisoner's dilemma). Morality is an agreement between self-interested individuals for mutual benefit. Gauthier notes that the resulting morality may not protect the rights of the weak (including animals and the handicapped).

1986 Ronald Dworkin's *Law's Empire* argues that the state has legitimate authority only when it treats its citizens equally and allows them to pursue their own conceptions of the good life.

1988 Environmental ethics comes of age with Holmes Rolston's *Environmental Ethics* and Mark Sagoff's *The Economy of the Earth*.

1988 Jeffrie Murphy and Jean Hampton, in their *Forgiveness and Mercy*, present conflicting views on the ethics of forgiveness.

1988 Geoffrey Sayre-McCord's *Essays on Moral Realism* anthologizes different perspectives on the moral realism debate.

1988 David McNaughton's *Moral Vision* argues that there are moral facts that we can discover. Morality is not just about attitudes or constructions; instead, it attempts to learn the truth about how we ought to live, a truth that does not depend on what we think or feel.

1989 David Brink's *Moral Realism and the Foundations of Ethics* defends *Cornell realism*. There are objective moral facts about right and wrong, not dependent on human thought or attitudes. While not reducible to other kinds of fact, these moral facts are about the natural, empirical world. Since it is possible to have no desire to be moral, moral beliefs are not intrinsically motivating.

1989 J. Baird Callicott's *In Defense of the Land Ethic: Essays in Environmental Philosophy* develops Aldo Leopold's land ethic.

1989 Thomas Donaldson's *The Ethics of International Business* is the first systematic work on international business ethics.

1989   Michael Stocker's *Plural and Conflicting Values* argues that it does not harm moral rationality to accept several incommensurable basic goods.

1989   Shelly Kagan's *The Limits of Morality* considers and rejects two commonsense ideas often used to criticize consequentialism: (1) Morality rules out some actions (like harming the innocent) even if they would bring about a greater good. (2) Morality does not require us to maximize the overall good when this involves great personal cost.

1990   Allan Gibbard's *Wise Choices, Apt Feelings* defends *expressivism*: moral claims express feelings or attitudes, not objective facts. Moral claims can be assessed as rational or not; to call something rational is to express one's acceptance of a system of norms that permits it. Gibbard advocates a way to form moral beliefs that goes beyond consistency and being clear about the facts; we must also partly adjust our attitudes to those of other people in order to promote social cooperation.

1991   The Soviet Union (U.S.S.R.) dissolves. Russia rejects Marxism.

1991   The U.S. Federal Sentencing Guidelines for Corporations becomes law. Many corporations create a corporate ethics officer position, designed to ensure compliance with ethical and legal standards and to prevent scandals that would hurt a company's reputation.

1992   Paul Ricoeur's *Oneself as Another* connects our self-identity with the narratives we create about ourselves, where we see ourselves as if we were another person. The heart of morality is to see another as oneself, which involves the golden rule.

1993   Barbara Herman's *The Practice of Moral Judgment* defends a Kantian ethics that emphasizes practical reason. She thinks Kant has often been misunderstood. For example, Kant's virtuous person is not one who lacks caring feelings and acts only from duty, but rather one who acts from good human motives (like caring feelings) but whose commitment to do the right thing will carry the day even when these motives are absent.

1993   Elizabeth Anderson's *Value in Ethics and Economics* says that not everything is a commodity; some things cannot be assigned a price. She offers a pluralistic account of value and criticizes a cost-benefit approach to issues like the environment and commercial surrogate motherhood.

1993 Richard De George advances international business ethics with his *Competing with Integrity in International Business.*

1993 John Rawls's *Political Liberalism* considers justice in pluralistic societies where people differ radically in religion and philosophy. Principles of justice can be based on an "overlapping consensus," where they rest on different grounds for different people.

1993 The Parliament of the World's Religions, at the urging of Catholic theologian Hans Küng, adopts a "Declaration for a Global Ethic" that teaches the common core values of the world religions.

1993–1996 Frances Myrna Kamm's *Morality, Mortality* (2 volumes) gives a comprehensive, non-consequentialist analysis of moral issues involving death and killing.

1994 Half a million Tutsis are killed in the small African country of Rwanda. Despite global agreements to stop genocide, the world powers do nothing to stop it. In 1998, U.S. President Bill Clinton goes to Rwanda to apologize for his lack of action.

1994 Jürgen Habermas's *Justification and Application: Remarks on Discourse Ethics* rejects theories that deny ethical truths and those that aim at impartiality by focusing on a solitary individual's reasoning instead of on a rational discussion that involves all affected parties.

1994 Samuel Scheffler's *The Rejection of Consequentialism* finds problems with the view that we ought always to do what has the best consequences and with the view that we ought sometimes not to do what has the best consequences. He searches for a compromise.

1995 Michael Smith's *The Moral Problem* examines three plausible but apparently incompatible beliefs: moral judgments are objectively true or false, they give reasons to act, and only desires give reasons to act. Smith points to an ambiguity in "reasons to act": *motivating reasons* move us to act, and *normative reasons* justify the rightness of an act. While normative reasons need not move us to act, they would do so if we were rational.

1996 Christine Korsgaard's *The Sources of Normativity* defends Kant's approach to morality. She sees the source of authoritative obligations in autonomy, which is our capacity as reflective, rational beings to impose principles on ourselves and act in a principled way.

1996   Harry Gensler's *Formal Ethics* studies moral consistency principles about things like ends-and-means, believing-and-acting, impartiality, and the golden rule (formulated as "Treat others only as you consent to being treated in the same situation"). He argues that consistency principles are useful for various approaches to ethics and can be defended in different ways (for example, as self-evident truths, as reflecting our feelings, or as constructs to promote social harmony).

1996   Jeffrey Wattles's *The Golden Rule* gives an extended historical and religious analysis of a moral principle that is widely shared across different eras, cultures, and religions.

1998   Bernard Gert's *Morality: Its Nature and Justification* argues that rational people would construct moral rules to help them live together, that these would include 10 specific rules (such as not to kill or hurt others), and that these rules cover most cases but leave many issues undecided. Gert answers criticisms against earlier versions of his view.

1998   Thomas Scanlon's *What We Owe to Each Other* defends a version of the social contract theory. The moral life involves our willingness to restrict our actions by social rules that can be justified to all. Accordingly, Scanlon proposes (roughly) that an act is wrong if and only if it would not be permitted by social rules that can be justified to all.

1998   Simon Blackburn's *Ruling Passions* defends *expressivism*: moral claims express feelings or attitudes, not objective facts. He argues that this view would not destroy the moral life and that it allows us to speak in a meaningful *quasi-realist* way of "moral truth" and "moral knowledge."

1999   Three books break new ground in business ethics: John Boatright's *Ethics in Finance*, Norman Bowie's *Business Ethics: A Kantian Perspective*, and Thomas Donaldson and Thomas Dunfee's *Ties that Bind: A Social Contracts Approach to Business Ethics*.

1999   About 50,000 people protest a meeting of the World Trade Organization in Seattle, holding signs like "Stop exploiting workers" and "WTO hurts the environment."

1999   John Rawls's *The Law of Peoples* addresses international justice. While Rawls argues for universal human rights, restrictions on war, and some aid to poorer nations, he opposes applying principles of economic equality on an international basis.

1999   Rosalind Hursthouse's *On Virtue Ethics* shows how virtue ethics can motivate us to act, guide us in difficult decisions, and connect with emotions. While her approach is Aristotelian, she finds Kant congenial to virtue ethics and in many ways close to Aristotle.

1999   Timothy Chappell's *Understanding Human Goods* argues that ultimate goods are what ultimately motivate us. People who repeatedly ask "Why do I want this?" until they can answer no more will arrive at fairly similar lists of ultimate goods. These goods cannot be measured on a common scale; so the idea of "maximizing total value" is senseless. While we are morally free to pick which basic goods we want to emphasize in our lives, it is always wrong to violate a basic good (for example, by murder, which violates the basic good of life).

2000   Thomas Carson's *Value and the Good Life* examines views like hedonism, rejects independent facts about intrinsic value, and argues for determining the good life on the basis of what it would be rational or correct to prefer. He argues that the most plausible form of this view would appeal to God's perfect rationality.

2001   John Hare's *God's Call: Moral Realism, God's Commands, and Human Autonomy*, after examining contemporary alternatives, argues for basing ethics on God's will.

2001   Philippa Foot's *Natural Goodness* argues that "good" refers to what fulfills a biological life form. A tree has *good roots* if these enable it to fulfill what it is to be a tree. Similarly, to be a *good human* is to fulfill what it is to be a human, which is to be rational in practical affairs. Foot's Aristotelian approach attempts to overcome the fact/value distinction.

2001   Michael Slote's *Morals from Motives* defends a virtue ethics based more on Hume than on Aristotle. Right actions are those that come from virtuous motives, especially caring about the well-being of others.

2001 Terrorists on 11 September crash hijacked planes against the World Trade Center in New York and the Pentagon in Washington, killing 3,000 people. People debate about how to respond. How diverse groups can live together becomes a key moral challenge of the 21st century.

2002 Thomas Nagel's *Concealment and Exposure* argues for a private sphere not subject to public surveillance and control. People need aspects of life that are free from public scrutiny.

2002 Corporate ethics scandals such as Enron and WorldCom lead the U.S. Congress to pass the Sarbanes-Oxley Act. Companies must adopt ethics codes for senior financial officers and hold these officers criminally liable for the fairness and accuracy of financial statements.

2004 John Broome's *Weighing Lives* examines how to make decisions that involve weighing the value of one life against the value of another. For example, a patient might decide whether to have an operation, or a couple might decide how many children to have. Broome tries to construct a mathematical model for answering such questions.

2004 Jonathan Dancy's *Ethics without Principles* argues for the particularist view that mature moral thinking does not need moral principles. We need moral sensitivity to the concrete situation; plausible rules are vague and can lead us to error if we lack sensitivity. He argues that there are moral facts that we discover but not invent.

2007 William Sullivan and Will Kymlicka's *The Globalization of Ethics* considers various globally influential traditions of ethical thought and argues for a tempered optimism in the attempt to set minimal global standards for the treatment of persons and cooperation across cultures.

2007 The world's climate experts, at the Intergovernmental Panel on Climate Change, say global warming is very likely caused by humans and may lead to massive food shortages and other catastrophes if it continues. How humanity can come together and learn to live in harmony with nature becomes a key moral challenge of the 21st century.

Introduction

A key dialogue in *Star Wars* led the young idealistic Jedi knight Anakin Skywalker to become the evil emperor Darth Vader (from *Episode III: Revenge of the Sith*, 2005, directed by George Lucas).

> Chancellor: Remember back to your early teachings. "All who gain power are afraid to lose it." Even the Jedi.
>
> Anakin: The Jedi use their power for good.
>
> Chancellor: Good is a point of view, Anakin. The Sith and the Jedi are similar in almost every way, including their quest for greater power.
>
> Anakin: The Sith . . . think inward, only about themselves.
>
> Chancellor: And the Jedi don't?
>
> Anakin: The Jedi are selfless. They only care about others.

Is good a "point of view"? Are we all ultimately selfish? Ought we to care about others? *Star Wars* raises important issues. Unfortunately for the galaxy, though, it does not pursue these issues in a rigorous way.

In Plato's dialogues, raising an issue is just a beginning. From there, the characters (often including Socrates) try to clarify proposed views and look for objections. Had Socrates been in the *Star Wars* dialogue, he would have examined carefully the "Good is a point of view" aphorism. To the philosophically sophisticated, this vague aphorism suggests views like cultural relativism or subjectivism, which become less plausible when we examine them carefully. Had Socrates been in the dialogue, would Anakin Skywalker still have been corrupted into becoming the evil Darth Vader? Perhaps not.

The Importance of Ethics

Ethics is important because choices are important. Our choices make a difference to our planet and galaxy—and to our lives and the lives of our friends, students, customers, families, and nation. Our choices grow out of deeper beliefs about good and bad, right and wrong—beliefs that often are implicit, confused, and poorly examined. The study of ethics pushes us to be clearer about these beliefs and to examine arguments for or against them. Ethics helps us to be more rational about the framework that we use in making choices.

Ethics is important also because of how it connects with other disciplines. Many areas of life—like politics, business, medicine, education, and religion—raise special questions about values, for example, about the duties of a chancellor toward the citizens. And many areas of study—like anthropology, biology, and psychology—raise factual questions that are relevant to ethics, for example, about the extent to which cultures differ in their ethical thinking. Since values are so important to human existence, every area of study has to come to grips with them in its own way; and thus every area of study connects, in some way, to ethics.

So the importance of ethics lies (1) in helping us to understand and improve the framework that we use for making choices and (2) in connecting to other disciplines. In addition, many people find the field of ethics to be intrinsically interesting and stimulating.

Ethics (Moral Philosophy)

To do *philosophy* is to reason about the ultimate questions of life—questions such as: Is there a God? Are our actions free or determined? Are humans completely explainable in material terms? How and what can we know? What is the nature and methodology of moral judgments? What principles ought we to live by?

Other disciplines can deal with beliefs about ultimate questions; we can study the history of such beliefs, their psychological causes or stages, how they can be understood using religious faith, or how they are treated in movies (like *Star Wars*) and literature. Philosophy, in contrast, deals with ultimate questions by reasoning about them, by debating the merits of alternative answers. We first try to clarify the question. Then we consider the range of possible answers. We criticize each one as forcefully as we can, trying to uncover problems; and we eliminate views that lead to absurdities. We look for the most adequate of the remaining views. If we cannot completely resolve the issues, at least we can hope to arrive at a well-considered answer.

Ethics (also called *moral philosophy*) is the philosophical investigation of questions about morality. Ethics commonly divides into three areas:

- Metaethics: the nature and methodology of moral judgments.
- Normative ethics: general principles about how we ought to live.
- Applied ethics: specific moral issues like lying or abortion, or areas like business or medicine.

This introduction briefly sketches these areas, the history of ethics, and some areas outside philosophy that deal with morality (including science and world religions).

Metaethics

Metaethics studies the nature and methodology of moral judgments. It asks questions like: What do "good" and "ought" mean? Are there moral truths and moral facts? How can we know or rationally defend beliefs about right and wrong?

A metaethical view often has two parts. One part is about the nature of moral judgments; this often includes a definition of "good" or "ought." The other part is about methodology; this tells how to select moral principles. For example, cultural relativism takes "good" to mean "socially approved"; it tells us to determine our moral principles on the basis of what is accepted in our society. This view makes morality relative to culture. As the Chancellor in the *Star Wars* dialogue put it, "Morality is a point of view"; something may be good (socially approved) in the Jedi culture but bad (socially disapproved) in the Sith culture, and there is no sense in asking which side is right. Many ethics teachers like to begin with cultural relativism because it sounds sophisticated and appeals to many beginning college students; but the view self-destructs when we see what it logically entails. The entry on cultural relativism has a longer discussion of its pros and cons. (To keep this introduction brief, it will not go into the pros and cons of the various views.)

Another view, subjectivism, defines "X is good" as "I like X"; this makes moral judgments relative to the feelings of the individual. If the Chancellor says "This is good" and Anakin says "This is bad," each is making claims about how he feels. As with cultural relativism, we cannot ask which side is right; moral judgments just describe feelings, and people may differ in their feelings. Subjectivism, like cultural relativism, does not allow for significant reasoning about values.

The ideal observer approach tries to combine feelings with reason. It takes "X is good" to mean "We would desire X if we were ideally rational," where being rational is being informed, consistent, impartial, and so forth. Moral judgments are not about our actual feelings but rather about how we would feel if we were ideally rational observers. On this view, Anakin and the Chancellor should work to resolve their moral differences by trying to be as rational as possible (which includes being factually informed and impartially concerned with everyone's good) and then determining what they favor.

The divine command approach sees morality as based on religion: "X is good" means "God desires X." We would determine what is good by determining what God desires, perhaps by appealing to the Bible, the church, prayer, or reason. If Anakin followed this approach, he would perhaps follow the subtle urgings of "the Force" about what he is to do.

Intuitionism sees morality as based on self-evident principles, norms that are built into us and need no further support. Accordingly, the American Declaration of Independence begins by claiming that it is a self-evident truth that we all have the unalienable right to life, liberty, and the pursuit of happiness. On this view, Anakin and the Chancellor would need to search inside themselves for the truths about how to live.

Some views are more skeptical. The error theory holds that all moral beliefs are false. Moral beliefs make claims about an objective realm of values which in fact does not exist; so there cannot be moral facts or moral knowledge. Perhaps the Chancellor would like this error theory. Or perhaps he would prefer emotivism, which holds that moral judgments are exclamations that express feelings: "X is good" means "Hurrah for X!" Since moral judgments express feelings instead of truth claims, again there cannot be moral truths or moral knowledge.

Moderate emotivism, while it agrees that moral beliefs are essentially emotional, insists that emotions can be rationally appraised to some extent. Moral emotions can be rationally criticized if they are inconsistent, based on ignorance or factual errors, or show bias. If people were completely rational in their moral beliefs and emotions, they would substantially or perhaps completely agree on their moral beliefs.

Prescriptivism, while also denying independent moral facts, goes further in asserting the rationality of ethics. It holds that moral judgments express imperatives (like "Do this") about how I want people to live that, under pain of inconsistency, must be applied in a similar way to similar cases. So my moral beliefs express at the same time how I am to live toward others and how they are to live toward me. This subsumes impartiality under consistency and leads to a golden-rule requirement: I am inconsistent if I think I ought to enslave you but yet I do not desire that I be enslaved in similar circumstances. To form my moral beliefs in a rational way involves understanding the facts (especially about how my actions affect others), imagining myself in the place of the other person, and seeing if I consistently want my moral beliefs to be followed when I imagine the roles of the parties switched (which involves the golden rule).

Popular today is a generic *rationalized attitudes* approach to knowing right from wrong, along the lines of prescriptivism, moderate emotivism, or ideal observer theory. To pick out our moral principles, we would try to be as rational as possible (informed, imaginative, consistent, and so forth) and then determine what our attitudes are about how we want people to live. This approach can be defended from various perspectives (as based on social conventions, personal feelings, divine commands, self-evident truths, and so on). Proponents argue that this approach gives a helpful and plausible methodology for reasoning about right and wrong which is consistent with different underlying views about the nature of moral judgments. If Anakin followed this approach, he could answer the Chancellor's statement "Good is a point of view" by saying "Yes, it is the point of view that we would favor if we were rational about the matter."

Normative Ethics

Normative ethics studies general principles about how we ought to live. It defends answers to questions like: What are the basic principles of right and wrong? What things are ultimately good or worthwhile in life? What would a just society be like? What are the basic human rights? What makes someone a good person? What are the main virtues and vices?

There are two basic approaches to normative ethics:

- Consequentialism: We ought always to do whatever maximizes good consequences; it does not in itself matter what kind of thing we do.

- Non-consequentialism: Some kinds of action (such as lying or killing the innocent) are wrong in themselves, and not just wrong because of their consequences.

Most normative theories follow one of these approaches. Consequentialism comes in various forms. Egoism says we ought to do whatever maximizes good consequences for ourselves; the Chancellor in *Star Wars* likely holds egoism since he implies that Jedi and Sith both think only about themselves. Utilitarianism, in contrast, says we ought to do whatever maximizes good consequences for everyone, where "everyone" may include all sentient beings, animals as well as humans. Intermediate views are possible, for example, that we ought to consider only our group (our family, city, nation, race, galaxy, or whatever) or that we ought to consider everyone but ourselves (which may be Anakin's view).

Another issue is how to gauge the value of consequences. Hedonism adopts a pleasure/pain criterion; the only thing good in itself is pleasure and the avoidance of pain. So hedonistic egoism says we ought to do whatever maximizes the balance of pleasure over pain for ourselves; and hedonistic utilitarianism says we ought to do whatever maximizes the total balance of pleasure over pain for everyone. The Chancellor seems to think the good is power; assuming that he is an egoist, he would hold that we ought to do whatever maximizes our own power. Pluralism says many things are worthwhile for their own sake, including perhaps knowledge, freedom, life, virtue, friendship, and pleasure; so pluralistic utilitarianism says we ought to do whatever maximizes these things for everyone. The preference view says anything desired for its own sake is intrinsically good; so preference utilitarianism says we ought to maximize as far as possible the satisfaction of everyone's desires.

How do we decide between these and other normative views? Depending on the metaethical view we adopt, we would appeal to moral intuitions (intuitionism), feelings (subjectivism or emotivism), God's will (divine command theory), rationalized attitudes, or whatever. Utilitarianism has been defended and criticized on all these grounds.

Utilitarianism comes in *act* and *rule* forms. Hedonistic act utilitarianism says we ought to do whatever individual action maximizes the balance of pleasure over pain for everyone. We could apply this norm either directly or indirectly. To apply it directly, first determine your options; maybe you could do A or B. Then estimate the likely pleasure/pain consequences of each option on affected parties. If we could put these into numerical units, using positive numbers for pleasure and negative ones for pains, we could sum the numbers and go with the option that has the highest total; if option A gives a total of 25 units of pleasure (counting everyone) while option B gives only 20 units, then we ought to do A. In practice, since we do not know how to put them into numbers, we just weigh the pleasures and pains in our minds and judge intuitively which option maximizes the balance of pleasure over pain. Since it would be too tedious to reason out every choice this way, for routine choices it is more useful to apply utilitarianism indirectly, by using "rules of thumb" about what kinds of action tend to have good or bad results. Stealing, for example, tends to have bad results; so, unless circumstances are peculiar, we just assume that stealing will not have the best consequences. But any moral rule should be broken when it has better consequences to do so.

Rule utilitarians are unhappy with seeing moral rules as "rules of thumb" which we should violate if we judge it useful to do so. They say this would lead to moral chaos, whereby people would kill the innocent when they thought this had a slight gain in good consequences. To avoid this problem, rule utilitarians consider the consequences of rules instead of individual actions. We ought to follow the rules that would have the best consequences for society to adopt and follow. They argue that the most useful rule about killing would be very strict, outlawing killing in all but a few clearly specified cases (like self-defense) and not permitting you to kill your sick father and give his money to charity when you judge that this would have the best consequences.

Non-consequentialists think rule utilitarianism does not go far enough. They say killing innocent persons is wrong in itself; it is not wrong just because forbidding such actions happens to be a useful rule for society to have. Some non-consequentialists say it is always wrong to intentionally kill an innocent human being; others add exceptions, perhaps for cases like mercy killing. Non-consequentialism is the general view that some kinds of action are wrong in themselves, and not wrong just because of bad consequences. Such kinds of action may be exceptionlessly wrong or may just have some independent moral weight against them. A major issue is which moral rules to accept and how stringently each is to be applied.

Many non-consequentialists think most of our basic duties are prima facie duties (they hold other-things-being-equal). Suppose you promise to do something for someone; then you have some duty to do as you promised. How strong is the duty? The duty to keep our promises is stronger than a utilitarian "rule of thumb"; we cannot set the duty aside just because it has slightly better consequences to do so. But the duty is not exceptionless either, since it could be overridden by a stronger duty (maybe the duty to save someone's life requires that we break a promise).

Non-consequentialists see some duties as stronger than others. The duty not to harm others, for example, is stronger than the duty to do what has good consequences for others; it is not in general right to harm one person in order to help another. And many of our duties are relational; we have specific duties to X if we made a promise to X, harmed X, or were helped by X, or if X is our spouse, child, or friend. Thus many of our duties are based on our relationships to others; our duty is not just to maximize the sum-total of good consequences, regardless of who benefits.

Non-consequentialism and rule utilitarianism can have fairly similar practical implications, but the theoretical basis is different. Rule utilitarians would justify a strict (but not exceptionless) duty of promising on the grounds that such a rule has good consequences for society. Non-consequentialists can accept this but would add that breaking your word is in itself an evil thing to do.

Further topics include justice, rights, and virtues. For act utilitarians, a just society is one that is set up to maximize the sum-total of benefits for its members, rights (like the right to life) are based on strong rules of thumb about what brings good consequences, and virtues are habits that maximize good consequences for everyone. For non-consequentialists, justice and human rights are not to be violated on utilitarian grounds, and virtues (like honesty) are habits to do what is right for its own sake.

Applied Ethics

Applied ethics studies specific moral issues like abortion or lying, or areas like business or medicine.

Ethicists disagree about abortion as much as does the general population; with ethicists, however, the positions are more carefully defended. On one extreme, some say killing a human fetus is seriously wrong in itself, with no exceptions; on the other extreme, some say killing a fetus or infant that has not gained rational self-awareness is not wrong in itself, although it may be wrong if, for example, it brings distress to the parents. Intermediate views say a serious right to life emerges at birth or at some point during pregnancy (perhaps when the zygote cannot split or fuse with another, when the fetus exhibits brain waves, when it looks human, or when it could live apart from the womb); some say the right to life emerges gradually, so that more reason is needed for a later abortion or infanticide than an earlier one. While many defend abortion on consequentialist grounds, as often the option with the best consequences, others argue on rule utilitarian grounds that a strong rule against killing (including abortion and infanticide) would have the best consequences for society to adopt.

While many attack abortion on non-consequentialist grounds (saying that an actual or potential human person has a strong right to life), others argue on non-consequentialist grounds that a fetus's right to life has to be weighed against the personal cost to the woman—and that we have no obligation to preserve the life of another at great cost to ourselves unless we have voluntarily assumed this obligation.

With abortion and other issues, we should not look to professional ethicists to provide us with easy, agreed-upon answers. Rather, they give us a range of carefully defended alternatives to help us think out issues for ourselves in a more reflective way.

Business ethics studies moral issues about the practice of business. It deals with issues like the following: Are capitalism, private property, and a free market justifiable—or are there better alternatives? Do corporations have social responsibilities toward the general public, or are they responsible only to maximize their shareholders' wealth within the bounds of law? Can a corporation as such have moral responsibility for its actions, or does the notion of moral responsibility apply only to individual human beings? What counts as wrongfully deceptive advertising? Are corporations responsible for harm done by defective products even when they take reasonable care to ensure that the products are safe? What are the rights of employees? Can corporations fire employees at will, or do employees have a right not to be fired without just cause? Does a corporation have a duty not to discriminate racially or sexually, even if it does business in countries where this is accepted? If a corporation produces products in poorer countries using cheap labor, what wages should they pay these workers? What duties do corporations have toward environmental issues like pollution and global warming? Should government encourage responsible business practices more by regulations or by market incentives?

Bioethics studies moral issues about medicine and biology. It deals with issues like the following: Should patients always be told the truth about their illnesses, or should information be withheld that may devastate and harm patients? Should physicians tell patients what they judge to be the best treatment, or should they present the pros and cons of various options and let patients decide? Is it right to conduct medical experiments on humans without their informed consent? Can prisoners or the poor who get rewards for participation in experiments give genuine informed consent?

To what degree should information about patients be kept confidential? Should physicians give life-saving treatment that violates the religious beliefs of patients or their parents? Is it right for physicians to assist in the suicide of a terminally ill patient? Are passive euthanasia (withholding of life-extending treatment, such as a respirator) or active euthanasia (direct killing, such as by lethal injection) permissible? Is it ethical for a physician who opposes abortion to refuse a legal abortion to a woman who wants one when no other doctors are available? Is healthcare a universal right that society should provide for, or does this lead to undesirable socialized medicine? Further issues deal with surrogate pregnancy, killing frozen embryos, aborting defective fetuses, genetic engineering, stem-cell research, hospitalizing the sick against their will, drug testing, rising medical costs, medical school admissions, and a slew of related legal issues. There are also subfields, such as nursing, dental, and pharmaceutical ethics.

Important also are political philosophy and moral education, and issues about academic freedom, animals, computers, the disabled, the environment, future generations, killing, pornography, poverty, punishment, racism, sex, sexism, terrorism, war, and so on—where the list of important issues that are discussed grows day by day.

Ancient Ethics

Ethics deals with a range of issues, from the nature of morality and the basic moral norms down to concrete moral questions. Besides this issues approach, there is also an historical approach that studies historical periods and figures. So we now turn to the history of ethics (as you read these sections, you might want to consult the chronology on page xiii).

In ancient Greece, Socrates began moral philosophy as we know it today. While he claimed to teach no ethical doctrine, he taught people to think carefully about ethical issues. He taught them to think clearly, to look for objections to proposed views, and to search for beliefs that could be held consistently after careful examination. He used dialogues to push others to explore and test their ideas. Yes, there was moral thinking before Socrates. Religious and social traditions taught norms of right and wrong, as did political leaders; and Sophists discussed moral issues, often using verbal trickery. But perhaps no one before Socrates subjected moral questions to such rational scrutiny.

Plato, who was Socrates's star pupil, did have an ethical doctrine. The

Good is a pattern we grasp with our minds, an abstract Form, like the perfect circles of geometry. The norm of right and wrong is within us: things are good insofar as they follow the pattern of Good that our minds grasp. Ethics is objective and not dependent on religion: something is not good because the gods love it; instead, the gods love it because it is already good. If we know the Good, we will act rightly. The good life is a life based on virtue, especially the virtue of wisdom, whereby the lower parts of the soul are controlled by the highest part, which is reason. Wisdom leads us to be just, which is to give to everyone their due; the unjust pursue an illusory self-interest that in the end hurts them by disorienting their souls. The good life brings pleasure; pleasure is not the goal of the good life but rather is a byproduct of acting rightly.

Aristotle, who was Plato's star pupil, had an ethical doctrine of his own. The Good is that which we all seek. We find the Good not by rational introspection, as in Plato, but rather by observing why people do things. People act for many reasons; a doctor might act to promote the health of patients. But why is health good? If we push such questions far enough, we see that we all act, ultimately, for the sake of happiness. But what is happiness? Happiness is not pleasure or honor, but rather to live well, to use in an excellent way—in a way that accords with virtue—our rational powers, for it is reason that makes humans distinctive. Since reason involves both thinking and doing, there are intellectual virtues about thinking as well as moral virtues about doing. A virtue is an intermediate between extremes; so the virtue of courage falls between the vices of foolhardiness (too much confidence) and cowardice (too little confidence). The intermediate is determined by practical reason, which picks the proper means to the end. To gain virtue and thus happiness, it is not enough just to know what is good, since we might not act accordingly; instead, we need to form our character and gain virtue by practice, by acting in a virtuous way until virtue becomes part of us. The highest form of the good life, and the most pleasurable, is the study and contemplation of the highest truths.

There followed further ancient moral thinkers of some significance. Epicurus taught that the good was pleasure but that we reach pleasure through moderation. Stoics like Cicero, Seneca, Epictetus, and Marcus Aurelius believed in an ordered world and a natural law of right and wrong that governs all peoples as citizens of the world. Neoplatonists like Plotinus argued that happiness requires a withdrawal from the material toward a mystical grasp of the Good.

Medieval Ethics

Augustine was the most influential Christian thinker in the first thousand years after Biblical times. He tried to combine the best elements from Greek philosophy (especially Plato and Neoplatonism) with Christian faith. He saw God as our supreme good and our journey on earth as a search for God. He summed up his ethics as "Love, and do as you will"; central are love of God, in which our ultimate happiness consists, and love of neighbor for the sake of God. Evildoing comes from disordered desire, where we submit to lower impulses; the correct order is for the soul to rule the body, reason to rule the soul, and the unchangeable Good (God and his law) to rule reason. While much of Augustine's thought is religious, his secular contributions have also been influential, such as his views about what factors are needed for a war to be just.

Thomas Aquinas was the most important medieval philosopher. His theme was the harmony between human reason (especially as explained by Aristotle) and Christian faith: while reason gives us some truths about God and morality, divine revelation builds on these and gives us much more. Aquinas's thinking about morality divides into two parts. (1) His moral philosophy mostly follows Aristotle, but with additions from the Stoics and others. Moral norms, called "natural laws," are knowable to everyone through natural reason; the basic laws, like "Good is to be done and promoted, and evil avoided," are self-evident. We recognize goods by looking at human inclinations; there are goods of the body and goods of the mind. Moral norms promote our natural human happiness and need to be internalized in virtues (good habits). While our minds can be perverted by passion or vice, we cannot be blinded completely to the basic moral norms. (2) Aquinas's moral theology requires Christian revelation; it adds further norms, called "divine (revealed) laws," and gives a religious context for morality. The natural moral law is part of God's plan for the world. God formed our minds so our reason can know the natural moral laws, which are also his commands and lead us toward our final end. Our ultimate happiness is the contemplation of God in the afterlife. Promoting this end are three theological virtues: faith (believing in God and what he has revealed), hope (trusting in God and his promises), and love (unselfishly serving God and doing good and not harm to his creatures).

William of Ockham in the late middle ages became skeptical of the faith-reason synthesis of Aquinas and others; Ockham advocated believing in God on the basis of faith alone. He rested morality purely on God's will;

good is what God wills, and God could have set up the moral norms in the opposite way from how he did (so that stealing and hatred, for example, were good). Ockham was one of the few important Christian philosophers to clearly endorse divine command theory. Many later Protestant thinkers accepted Ockham's approach to ethics, which tended to place morality on the turf of theologians rather than philosophers; most Catholic thinkers adopted Aquinas's Aristotelian view, which based ethics on right reason but also added theological elements.

Modern Ethics

The Renaissance and Enlightenment gave philosophy a more secular direction away from the religious orientation of the middle ages. Thomas Hobbes proposed that morality is a construct to further human cooperation. Humans by nature are amoral egoists. If we imagine a "state of nature" without social rules, we thus imagine a hellish state where unrestrained self-interest leads people to kill, steal, and do whatever else will promote their lives, thereby making life miserable for everyone. Rational egoists in such a state would agree in a "social contract" to behave in a civil way toward each other; this is how moral rules would originate in an amoral world. To enforce the contract, these egoists would agree to obey an absolute monarch who punishes them if they break the rules. Thus absolute monarchy is based on the consent of the governed.

John Locke, Samuel Pufendorf, Joseph Butler, David Hume, and Jean-Jacques Rousseau lined up to criticize Hobbes. In the debate that followed, they (or at least some of them) argued that humans by nature have some altruistic motivation and access to moral truths, the state of nature would not be as bad as Hobbes paints it, many evils come from society and not human nature, punishment is an inferior and ineffective motive for following the moral law, and democracy is superior to monarchy. Many opponents of Hobbes, however, continued to use the social contract idea.

There also began a debate about whether morality was based on reason or feelings—a debate that continues today. Defenders of reason included Ralph Cudworth, Henry More, Samuel Clark, Joseph Butler, Richard Price, Thomas Reid, and Mary Wollstonecraft. These intuitionist thinkers, who admired Plato, saw moral principles as independent, objective truths that the mind grasps in a direct intuitive way, as the mind grasps mathematical axioms. They especially wanted non-Hobbesian principles that would move us from a concern for ourselves to a concern for others. So More proposed as self-evident the idea that if it is good for X to be happy, then it must be doubly good for X and Y to be happy. Clark proposed as self-evident the idea (later called universalizability) that what is right or wrong for someone to do to me must thereby be right or wrong for me in a like case to do to that person. These rationalists were opposed by thinkers who based ethics on feeling (the "moral sense" approach); these included the Earl of Shaftesbury, Francis Hutcheson, Adam Smith, and, most famously, David Hume. Also struggling with the egoism/benevolence problem, they tended to base ethics on *benevolent* feelings. Shaftesbury argued that we get greater personal satisfaction by following other-regarding feelings than by being selfish. Hutcheson argued that benevolent feelings would lead us to favor whatever promotes "the greatest happiness for the greatest number," a view later called utilitarianism.

David Hume argued that moral beliefs must be based on feeling since they can move us to act and only what is based on feeling can move us to act. No series of external facts can ever by themselves lead to a moral belief: we cannot deduce an "ought" from an "is" (an idea later called "Hume's law"). Moral beliefs are about how we feel, not about external facts. We also need reason since we need to understand something before our feelings can judge it; but reason alone is not enough. Some object that Hume's view would lead to social chaos since people would lie, cheat, and steal whenever they felt like it. Hume countered that we have benevolent as well as selfish feelings, and that moral beliefs express benevolent feelings. A moral term like "vicious" (unlike a personal term like "my enemy") assumes a general point of view that moves beyond personal biases; if we use reason to understand the facts and then see how we feel from the standpoint of impartial benevolence, we will largely agree on our moral beliefs and have all the "objectivity" needed for social life to work.

Immanuel Kant, in contrast, based ethics on reason. Since the purest motive is to do our duty just because it is the right thing to do, basing ethics on self-interest debases our dignity as moral beings. Since basic moral laws must hold of necessity for every rational being, they cannot rest on personal feelings or on contingent facts about human nature. So basic moral laws do not rest on self-interest, feelings, or facts about the sensible world. Nor do they rest on moral intuitions, as proposed by earlier rationalists. Instead, moral laws rest on a consistency test. To test a moral maxim, we ask whether we can consistently will that everyone follow it (and thus act that way toward us); we reject the maxim if we cannot will this. So moral laws express our autonomous will and are the outcome of rational choice. What is self-evident in ethics is that moral beliefs are to be submitted to the universal-will test, that we are to act only on a maxim that we can will to be a universal law. This test leads to exceptionless duties when the contrary maxim could not exist as a universal law; so we ought *never* to make a promise that we do not intend to keep (since as rational beings we support the practice of promise keeping and yet as makers of deceitful promises we do what would destroy this practice). The test leads to looser duties when the contrary maxim could exist as a universal law but we would not will it as such; so we have a duty to help others in need, but we can to some extent choose how and whom to help (the practice of never helping others could exist but we would not will it to since we need help ourselves). We can express the universal-law test more loosely as "Treat humanity, whether yourself or another, as an end-in-itself and not only as a means"; we act wrongly when we use people as mere things, as mere tools to promote our own desires.

Nineteenth-Century Ethics

As the 19th century drew near, a utilitarian tradition started in England. Jeremy Bentham proposed that we ought always to do whatever maximizes the total balance of pleasure over pain for those affected by our action. We are to add *amounts* of pleasure; the mindless pushpin game is as valuable as poetry if both give equal pleasure. The utilitarian John Stuart Mill disagreed with Bentham on this. Mill thought higher (intellectual) pleasures were more valuable than lower (bodily) pleasures, even if the amount of pleasure is the same; we know this because those who have experienced both find that they prefer the higher pleasures. Mill preferred the "inductive" view that bases ethics on our desires or preferences to the "intuitive" view that bases it on self-evident principles (and seems to consecrate our prejudices). We know that only pleasure (happiness) is good in itself because it is the only thing that people desire for its own sake; and so we ought to bring about as much of it as we can. The utilitarian Henry Sidgwick disagreed with Mill on method. Sidgwick thought that, quite apart from Mill's claims about what people desire, the fact that people desired something would not show that it was good (since people might desire bad things). Instead, he took it as self-evident that pleasure is good. He also accepted as self-evident "It is rational to prefer a greater good in the future to a lesser good now," "Everyone's good is equally important," and "Rational beings ought to aim at the general good." He thought commonsense moral intuitions fit well with utilitarianism.

The 19th century also brought a series of thinkers who connected ethics with larger historical processes. Georg Wilhelm Friedrich Hegel saw history as the progress of Absolute Spirit, a progress that brings increasing freedom and will lead to a society that reconciles community interest with self-interest. Karl Marx radicalized this idea. For Marx, history is driven by materialistic forces that will lead through class struggles to the classless society. While conventional ethics is economically determined, imposed by the rich to solidify their power, a true ethics would lead us toward the classless society that brings freedom to all and ends the miseries of the working class. The opposite view, Social Darwinism, saw evolution as a struggle where the strong survive and overcome the weak. Human life follows and ought to follow this same pattern; so it accords with nature and is right that strong individuals, businesses, social classes, and nations struggle for supremacy and overcome the weak. Friedrich Nietzsche had similar ideas. He thought humans, like other animals, evolved with the will to power and domination as their basic motivation; Christianity and utilitarianism, which preach a morality suitable only for slaves, thus violate our nature and lead to frustration. Charles Darwin himself applied evolution differently to morality. He thought humans were social animals, like wolves, and thus have an inbred tendency to help each other; this promotes the survival of the group. While human sympathy at first was limited to one's own clan or tribe, in time, as our rational powers evolved and developed, we started to extend our sympathies more widely, to all humanity, including its weakest members, and even to animals.

Twentieth-Century Ethics and Beyond

G. E. Moore began 20th-century ethics with a vigorous and influential defense of intuitionism. He claimed that most philosophers, from Aristotle to Mill and the evolutionists, based their ethics on a simple mistake—that of defining "good" in factual terms, as perhaps "desired" or "more evolved." Such definitions are wrong, since we can consistently imagine bad things being desired (or being more evolved). So attempts to infer moral conclusions from factual premises fail. If we know moral truths, then some moral knowledge must rest not on further premises but rather on direct intuition. Moore thought we know intuitively that various kinds of things (not just pleasure) are intrinsically good and that our duty is to maximize good results (utilitarianism).

While most British ethicists for a time followed Moore's intuitionism, many saw his utilitarianism as clashing with our intuitions. W. D. Ross argued that we clearly sometimes ought to keep our word even when breaking it has slightly better total consequences; he defended a set of self-evident prima facie duties. In the U.S., empirical approaches to ethics still dominated, with the pragmatists William James, John Dewey, C. I. Lewis, and Ralph Perry; Perry defined "good" as "the object of a positive interest (desire)" and "right action" as "action that promotes a harmony of interests." Bertrand Russell gave up Moore's intuitionism when the American George Santayana criticized its absolutizing of moral intuitions. As time went on, many thinkers became skeptical about moral intuitions, as they seemed to vary so much.

In 1936, A. J. Ayer proclaimed that ethical judgments are emotional exclamations: "X is good" means "Hurrah for X!" There is no ethical truth or ethical knowledge; there are only ethical feelings. Ayer rested his case on logical positivism, a science-is-everything view that claimed that any genuine truth claim has to be either analytic (true by definition) or empirically testable. "X is good" fails the logical positivism test, since it is neither analytic nor empirically testable; so "X is good" cannot be a truth claim. By now logical positivism has long since died, abandoned even by Ayer; but yet few today appeal to considerations, like the "self-evident moral truths" of Moore and Ross, that are not either analytic or empirical.

For the next few decades, moral philosophy in English-speaking countries focused mainly on analyzing moral language. Charles Stevenson gave a more detailed emotivist analysis. Philippa Foot argued for linguistic constraints on what could count as "good" or "moral." Stephen Toulmin gave a rule-utilitarian analysis of moral language, while Roderick Firth gave an ideal-observer analysis. Kurt Baier and William Frankena claimed that moral judgments, even if essentially emotional, could be criticized if they were based on incomplete or faulty information or were biased.

Even Nazi moral atrocities committed during this period did little to move moral philosophy in English-speaking beyond its focus on moral language. But eventually philosophers broadened their interests to substantive moral issues. R. M. Hare's *Freedom and Reason* (1963) pointed in the new direction. While ethics was still about analyzing language, its goal was to give us tools to think better about moral issues, tools like universalizability and the golden rule, which Hare applied to the problem of racism (which Martin Luther King was then confronting).

Two events of 1971 pointed to an expansion of interest beyond the analysis of moral language. First, John Rawls's *A Theory of Justice* used social-contract notions to attack utilitarianism and defend liberal ideas about human rights and the distribution of wealth. Rawls's Harvard colleague Robert Nozick quickly published an opposing libertarian view; communitarians later objected that both Rawls and Nozick overemphasize the rights of individuals at the expense of the historical values of the community. There followed much debate on political philosophy, justice, and human rights. Also in 1971, the first volume of *Philosophy and Public Affairs* was published with articles on applied ethics by philosophers such as Judith Jarvis Thomson, Thomas Nagel, Richard Brandt, R. M. Hare, Peter Singer, and Baruch Brody. Applied ethics became very important over the next several years, embracing areas like business ethics, bioethics, animal rights, environmental ethics, racism, and sexism.

There was also a rebirth of normative theory. Richard Brandt introduced the terms "act utilitarianism" and "rule utilitarianism"; philosophers debated which view was better and whether either was acceptable. R. M. Hare defended preference utilitarianism and a higher synthesis between act and rule utilitarianism. Peter Singer applied utilitarianism in a radical way to practical issues, including animal rights and infanticide.

Lawrence Kohlberg, a psychologist who was unhappy with the relativism of many social scientists, did research to support the idea that humans naturally develop toward higher forms of moral reasoning (which he described using Kant, Hare, and Rawls). He concluded that people of every culture develop in their moral thinking through a series of six stages; we all as young children begin thinking of morality in terms of punishment and reward, and we gradually move toward a purer justice perspective. However, Carol Gilligan claimed, against Kohlberg, that there are two mature ways to think about morality: justice and caring. Men tend to think of morality in terms of justice, principles, rights, and duties; women instead tend to appeal to caring, feelings, personal relationships, and responsibilities. This sparked debate and the growth of feminist ethics.

J. L. Mackie encouraged the rethinking of metaethical issues. While admitting that moral language asserts independent moral facts, he argued that there are no such moral facts; so all moral judgments are false. There followed much debate about moral realism and the existence of moral facts. Richard Brandt argued that moral concepts were confused and need replacement rather than analysis; he proposed a notion of "rational desire" that would replace "good" and not presuppose preexisting moral facts.

Elizabeth Anscombe and Alasdair MacIntyre encouraged the growth of virtue ethics and a debate about the role of virtue in ethical theory. Other hot topics include social cooperation between egoists (often involving the prisoner's dilemma), the evolutionary origins of ethics (sociobiology), natural law and divine command approaches, various Kantian approaches, and so on. At the present time, ethics in English-speaking countries is very diverse and not reducible to a few key trends or issues.

So far, this section has dealt with ethics in the analytic tradition dominant in English-speaking countries. There also is much ethical thinking in the continental tradition that has been popular on the continent of Europe. Unfortunately, although this is starting to change, the two traditions grew up in relative isolation from each other. There are interesting parallels and contrasts between the two traditions, and there is much that each tradition can learn from the other.

Phenomenologists Franz Brentano, Nicolai Hartmann, and Max Scheler based ethics on emotions, which they saw as being correct or incorrect in a basic, unanalyzable way; something is intrinsically good if it is correct to have positive emotions toward it for its own sake. Like Moore and Ross of the analytic tradition, they rejected empirical definitions of "good" and claimed that we know objective facts about what is intrinsically good by intuition, not proof. On the opposite side, atheistic existentialists Albert Camus, Simone de Beauvoir, and Jean-Paul Sartre rejected moral facts and struggled about how to live in an absurd world devoid of inherent moral significance. Like emotivists and prescriptivists of the analytic tradition, they thought we must create our own values. Jewish thinkers Martin Buber and Emmanuel Levinas based ethics on our encounter with the Other—the finite Thou of our neighbor and the infinite Thou of God. With Buber, we can have either an I-It relationship with our neighbor (where we regard the other as a thing to be used) or an I-Thou relationship (where we enter into deeper communication and appreciation). The Christian Paul Ricoeur wrote much about religious ethics, the meaning of life, and the golden rule. Political thinkers Simone Weil and Hannah Arendt reflected on the evils of Nazi totalitarianism. Weil based values on God and claimed that every human being is sacred and deserving of respect. Arendt wrote of the "banality of evil": Nazis committed atrocities not out of hatred but in an unthinking, conformist way, whereby they isolated themselves from thinking morally about the human significance of their actions. Jürgen Habermas and other critical theorists analyzed social phenomena, often borrowing from Marx, and criticized views that reject ethical truths and ethical rationality. They based ethics on Kantian rational discourse, whereby people discuss issues in an informed, impartial, consistent, and free manner. This is much like the *rationalized attitudes* approach, except that it is explicitly dialogical (which Socrates would have appreciated). So there you have a 10-page sketch of the history of Western ethics. There has been much debate about values over the years, and many differences in opinion; but there is nearly unanimous commitment to Socrates's insistence that we subject beliefs about values to rational scrutiny. What will the future bring to moral philosophy? There will likely be new approaches to old issues, for example, how to ground practical moral norms on reason or feelings (or some combination of these) and how to understand concern for others and impartiality. The last word has not been written about such matters, and the debate is not closed. There will likely be new issues too. Influences from outside philosophy are bound to be important, especially the growth in science/technology and globalization.

Beyond Philosophy

This introduction so far has addressed mostly philosophers and philosophy, but values are important to everyone and to all aspects of life. Politicians, preachers, and journalists speak of values. Many complain about our obsession with material things and sex, and the neglect of family and community values. Parents struggle with how to teach right and wrong to children. There is debate about areas like abortion and animal rights, and sometimes violent demonstrations. Immigrants wrestle with how to relate to Western values and practices. The public calls for the removal of professors who raise unpopular ideas about areas like infanticide or racial equality. People doing business in foreign countries try to cope with local norms, for example, about truth-telling and politeness. Movies like *Star Wars* portray moral issues and struggles. The terrorist attacks on the United States of 11 September 2001 raise issues about international relations; do we need more guns or more mutual understanding? And threatened disasters from global warming raise questions: can humanity cooperate and moderate its consumption for the sake of future generations?

Three areas outside philosophy have a very strong impact on values: science (including technology), religion (including non-Western religions), and globalization. This book has multiple entries on these areas.

Science tries to understand different aspects of the world; in doing so, it gives essential background information for thinking about values. Anthropology, biology, and psychology raise questions such as these: How much do cultures differ in their ethical thinking? Are there cultural universals? Are humans motivated only by their own personal pleasure? How much of our motivation and ethical thinking is innate (from our biological makeup) and how much is learned (from socialization)? How and why did evolution give us the capacity for moral thinking? Is science compatible with the belief in free will? Is one race or sex genetically superior? How do children develop in their moral thinking as they grow up? Do males and females develop differently in their moral thinking?

The growth of technology, which science has spurred, has had a great impact on values. Technology raises new ethical issues, for example, about atomic weapons, genetic engineering, stem-cell research, and Internet privacy. Technology can be part of the problem (as in global warming) or part of the solution (as new grains can help with world hunger), or both. Technological advances in transportation, communication, and the Internet have "shrunk" the planet and brought people of diverse religious and cultural backgrounds in contact with each other; the resulting globalization raises new problems and new opportunities.

Another great influence is religion. Religion tries to situate people into a larger context, often in relation to the supernatural, and says much about values and the meaning of life. Judaism and Christianity, which both teach "Love your neighbor as yourself," have had a major influence on Western values; their moral influence often continues even with those who discard the Judeo-Christian belief system. Elsewhere, other religions and quasi-religions predominate, especially Buddhism, Confucianism, Daoism, Hinduism, and Islam, but also many smaller religions; each of these has a moral tradition about what is important in life and how people are to live.

Airplanes, television, telephones, and the Internet have made the world "smaller." Large companies have become multinational. Immigration has made neighbors out of people from different parts of the globe. Eastern religions come to the West, and Western religions go to the East. In all these ways, we have increasing contact with people from other parts of the world with different traditions about values.

Is there a possibility of a global ethics, a consensus across the globe about core values? Many are skeptical about this. They say there is a Western ethics and an Eastern ethics, and the two clash on central issues. They point to the terrorist attacks of 11 September 2001 as confirming this incompatibility. The East is more mystical, and believes in things like jihad, reincarnation, nirvana, karma, and Dao—beliefs alien to the West.

Others say it is a gross oversimplification to speak of either Western ethics or Eastern ethics as a unified system. The history of Western ethics presents a wide range of different views about the nature of morality and concrete moral issues. Similarly, Eastern ethics is not a unified system. In China, which differs much from India or the Arab world, there were traditionally three competing schools of thought: Confucianism, Buddhism, and Daoism. Of these three, Confucianism is perhaps closest to mainstream Western thinking. Daoism, whose classic text starts by saying that the Dao that can be put into words is not the true Dao, is the most mystical and alien to the West; but there are similar sayings in the West, such as the statement of Ludwig Wittgenstein, who was one of the most influential 20th-century analytic philosophers, that ethics cannot be expressed, that it is transcendental and cannot be put into words. Some claim that the same variety of views that occur in the West often occur in the East, and vice versa, although not necessarily in the same proportion.

Mahatma Gandhi (Hindu), the Dalai Lama (Buddhist), and many others contend that, despite differences in customs and traditions, the core moral ideals of all religions are the same. All the major, and most of the minor, religions of the world teach the golden rule and concern for the well-being of others. Admittedly, these groups do not always live up to their ideals; and all have sub-groups that de-emphasize these core teachings. Many claim, however, that the best hope for world peace and harmony is for people to follow these core teachings of their own individual traditions.

In many ways, this is the most intriguing and demanding period in the entire history of ethics. There is a merging of peoples and cultures, and other forms of globalization, that affect ethics. There also is a technological transformation that will generate new problems and perhaps provide new solutions to old problems. These and other trends over the coming decades may reshape ethics more than in any previous period.

The Dictionary

– A –

ABORTION AND INFANTICIDE. The **killing** of the unborn and of infants. These two beginning-of-life issues are conveniently discussed together because both raise the question of when there emerges a strong **right** to life and whether the two types of killing are morally equivalent. There is much dispute about such matters.

Many argue on **consequentialist** (**egoist** or **utilitarian**) grounds that aborting an unwanted fetus often has the best consequences. Abortions can avoid financial burdens, disgrace to an unwed mother, and disruption to school or career. The child-to-be has less chance for happiness when these problems or probable birth defects exist. And abortion provides a second chance to prevent a birth when contraceptives fail.

Peter Singer says those who defend abortion on such grounds ought to defend infanticide in similar cases. An older fetus and a newborn have similar capacities; and **disabilities** are often clearer after birth. Singer's *preference utilitarianism* makes a strong right to life depend on a desire to continue living, which presupposes a concept of the self. So a developing child has a strong right to life only when it attains rational self-awareness; before this, killing an unwanted infant or fetus is in itself no more morally serious than killing an unwanted frog.

Some critics say we can have as good consequences without killing; we need better social support for unwed mothers and poor families, better adoption practices, wiser use of contraceptives, artificial wombs, and so on. Children with disabilities grow up to be just as happy as others; disabilities can bring families together and give them a sense of purpose. In addition, abortions and infanticides can harm women psychologically and promote callous attitudes toward human life.

Others object that utilitarianism relies on guesses—since we cannot know whether killing the fetus or baby would have better total consequences. Many say utilitarianism is inhumane, since it justifies killing any innocent human (whether fetus, infant, handicapped, or elderly) when this brings even a tiny increase in good consequences.

Rule utilitarianism works differently, since it asks what *rule* about killing (including abortion) would have the best consequences for society to adopt. Some claim it would have the best long-range consequences if society adopted a strict rule against killing (including against abortion); others dispute this.

Non-consequentialists typically appeal to a general principle about killing and use this to draw conclusions about abortion and infanticide. Principles (1) to (5) have been proposed, sometimes with qualifications about rape, incest, deformed babies, or protecting the mother's life:

(1) Infanticide and abortion are both wrong.
(2) Early abortion is permissible, up to such and such a point; infanticide and late abortion are wrong.
(3) Abortion is permissible at any point, but infanticide is wrong.
(4) Abortion and infanticide are both permissible; the child gains a right to life when it achieves rational self-awareness.
(5) Since the growth of a fetus into a child is a gradual process, there is no "point" at which killing becomes wrong; instead, the seriousness of killing gradually increases. A young fetus can be killed for almost any reason; a child who is x years old can be killed for almost no reason.

These principles often are defended by appealing to moral **intuitions**, despite the fact that intuitions here vary greatly. Some first appeal to the principle that it is seriously wrong to kill innocent *human life* (sometimes with qualifications, for example about **euthanasia**) and then argue that "human life" in the relevant sense begins at (1) conception, (2) some intermediate point during the pregnancy (perhaps when the zygote cannot split or fuse with another, when the fetus exhibits brain waves, when it looks human, or when it could live apart from the womb), (3) birth (at which point the newborn enters into various social relationships), or (4) when the child develops rational capacities—or (5) that human life emerges gradually. Some claim instead that a fetus, while not a human person, ought not to be killed because it is a *potential human person*.

Judith Jarvis Thomson, in her influential paper "A Defense of Abortion," accepts something like the sliding-scale principle (5). She adds that the fetus's (increasing) right to life has to be weighed against the personal cost to the woman; she appeals to this principle:

(6) One who has voluntarily assumed no special obligation toward another person has no obligation to do anything requiring great personal cost to preserve the life of the other.

A woman who voluntarily gets pregnant in order to have a baby assumes a special obligation toward the fetus's life. One who gets pregnant involuntarily by rape or contraceptive failure, however, has not voluntarily assumed any special obligation and has much less obligation toward the fetus's life; here abortion can be justified relatively easily. Critics often attack (6), claiming that not all special obligations are voluntarily assumed and that people have a special obligation toward their offspring whether or not they voluntarily assume it.

The clash of principles in these arguments brings up a more basic question: "How should we pick out our moral principles?" How we answer this depends on our metaethical perspective. Intuitionists appeal to moral intuitions; but intuitions on this issue vary greatly. **Cultural relativists** follow their society's norms. **Subjectivists** and **emotivists** go with their feelings; for them, you just think about the issue and then follow what you feel. Those who go by **divine commands** appeal to religion and God's will. The **Bible** does not directly mention abortion and can be interpreted either way on this issue; but the first Christian source after the Bible, the *Didache*, is explicitly against both abortion and infanticide. Catholic teaching has strongly condemned abortion, but many other churches are more divided on the issue.

Some argue, appealing to the *rationalized attitudes* approach (*see* **knowing right from wrong**), that **golden rule** consistency favors the belief that abortion is wrong in at least most cases. They argue that most people will not be consistent if they hold that abortion is normally permissible since they will not consent to the idea of themselves having been aborted in normal circumstances. But this argument, even if it succeeds, will still leave some details unresolved.

Many **feminist ethicists** defend a right to abortion; they appeal to a woman's right over her own body, the contingent value of fetal life, a woman's need to control reproduction in order to plan her life in an autonomous way, or the right of women to social equality with men (who can be **sexually** active without fearing that they may have to care for a baby). But not all feminists agree. When the National Organization for Women (now.org) became pro-abortion, many left the organization and established Feminists for Life (feministsforlife.org). The pro-life feminist Sidney Callahan (whose husband Daniel is pro-choice) argues that human life begins at conception, that its value is intrinsic (not contingent), that responsible **autonomy** recognizes this, that killing is not a proper means to social equality, that easy abortion legitimizes male irresponsibility toward fatherhood, and that abortion is psychologically harmful to women (who by nature are oriented more toward nurturing than toward violent solutions to problems). To show the injustice of abortion, she uses the original position of **John Rawls**; if we were selecting the moral rules for society and did not know our position in it (including whether we were a fetus about to be aborted), we would choose a rule that protects our life against being aborted. The diversity of women's views on abortion is well symbolized by the fact that Norma McCorvey, who was "Roe" in the Roe v. Wade Supreme Court decision legalizing abortion in the United States in 1973, later changed her mind and came to oppose abortion.

   Whether abortion is wrong differs from the issue of whether it ought to be legal. Some think abortion is wrong but ought to remain legal, since abortions would still take place (and in less safe conditions) even if they were illegal. The legality question raises issues about the proper role of the state (*see* **political philosophy**). *See also* BIOETHICS; DOUBLE EFFECT; MEDIEVAL ETHICS; MORAL PATIENT.

ABSOLUTISM. See EXCEPTIONLESS DUTIES.

ACADEMIC FREEDOM. The freedom of teachers and students to explore ideas without undue restriction by government, religion, and the academy. Academic freedom allows professors in their teaching and research to investigate and share matters they find intellectually interesting. It also allows students to study the areas they wish, and to develop and express their own ideas.

   Academic freedom began in **medieval** universities, which were free to choose their faculties and set admission and study requirements; but these schools often censured teachers and students on grounds of religious orthodoxy. Academic freedom as we know it today received an important boost in the early 1900s with the development of academic tenure; this system guarantees job security, except for cases like gross incompetence, for professors who survive a probationary period. The main purpose of tenure is to promote academic freedom. Tenured professors need not conform to ideas approved by government, religion, school administrators, or wealthy donors. Instead, professors can pursue, without fear of losing their jobs, ideas that are outside the mainstream but may turn out to benefit society.

Academic tenure was born a few decades after **John Stuart Mill**'s defense of free speech. Mill argues that society should not control speech because we gain by hearing deviant opinions. If a deviant opinion is true, we gain by learning about it; if it is false, we gain by coming to understand better the truth of the mainstream view. So society benefits by free speech, as does the university. To see how restricting ideas can be harmful, consider Galileo Galilei, who in the early 17th century developed the Copernican, sun-centered view of the universe that we now take for granted. Galileo was persecuted by the Inquisition and by church leaders; some of his important writings were forbidden to be published. This inhibited our understanding of the universe and the rise of science.

Academic freedom has limits. It may be against the law for a professor to make a point in a classroom using a loaded gun. School officials may stop a teacher who devotes an entire philosophy course to chemistry; the course title and description limit what can be taught. Likewise, students may pursue areas of their choice, but they must meet certain requirements if they wish to graduate; they also must meet the requirements of the particular courses they choose to take.

So-called "political correctness" raises questions about academic freedom. Some professors and students who advocate ideas that others view as **racist** or **sexist** claim that they are pressured to conform to "correct" ideas. They complain that their academic freedom is compromised since they cannot freely express their views without fear of repercussion. Others argue that requiring people to express their ideas in sensitive and respectful ways is no threat to academic freedom. It merely allows us to engage more people in the pursuit of ideas, thereby contributing to the social good that academic freedom promotes.

Advances in information technology raise questions. The Internet lets us find much information quickly; but it also raises issues about which ideas we are free to use and which are the intellectual property of others (*see* **computer ethics**).

Ethicists, while disagreeing about details, agree that academic freedom is important and should be protected by society. It seems necessary in order for society to progress intellectually, morally, and economically. *See also* POLITICAL PHILOSOPHY.

AESTHETICS. Raises issues like those of metaethics (*see* **ethics: metaethics**). We can ask what "beauty" means, whether there are objective truths about beauty, and how we can know or defend beliefs about what is beautiful. Perhaps calling something "beautiful" just describes or expresses our feelings (**subjectivism** or **emotivism**). Or perhaps there are socially accepted standards about what is beautiful that we must follow (**cultural relativism**). Or perhaps we need to accept what a critic with refined and educated sensibilities would judge (**ideal observer theory**). Or perhaps we intuit a thing's beauty or general principles about beauty (**intuitionism**). Or perhaps our language about beauty asserts objective facts about beauty while in reality there are no such facts (**J. L. Mackie**'s *error theory*).

Some claim that our theory about "**good**" should match our theory about "beautiful," since the concepts are so close. Others take a more objective approach to ethics than to aesthetics; they argue that the areas differ in important ways. For example, **social contract** and **golden rule** reasoning work better in ethics than in aesthetics; and ethical principles are easier to formulate than aesthetic ones. *See also* EPISTEMOLOGY; MOORE, G. E.; OUGHT; REID, THOMAS; PHILOSOPHY AND ETHICS; PLATO; SUPERVENIENCE; UTILITARIANISM.

AFFIRMATIVE ACTION. *See* DISCRIMINATION.

ALTRUISM. Sometimes "altruism" is used as equivalent to **benevolence**, which is about doing **good** and not harm to others. Sometimes "altruism" is understood in a different way, as about doing good to others when this harms (or at least does not benefit) oneself; this raises the issue of how benevolence relates to self-interest (*see* **egoism**). *See also* BUTLER, JOSEPH; HOBBES, THOMAS; LOVE YOUR NEIGHBOR; RAND, AYN; SOCIOBIOLOGY.

ANCIENT ETHICS. Moral ideas of some sort likely go back to the beginnings of the human race; even primitive tribes had customs and sayings about how their members should live. As time went on, norms were formulated and discussed by religious leaders, politicians, poets, dramatists, parents, and ordinary people. But this is not yet moral philosophy, which involves a rational debate about moral questions.

Two factors contributed to the rise of moral philosophy in ancient Greece. First, rapid democratization and urbanization led to a questioning of the old values. Second, there was much interest in reasoning, especially in geometry and metaphysics. The Sophists tried to reason about values; but they did so poorly, often using clever ways to persuade rather than to seek the truth. Many Sophists were skeptical about ethics; Protagoras (c. 490–420 BC) saw **justice** as nothing more than what accords with local customs and drew the conservative conclusion that our moral thinking must conform to local standards. **Socrates** (c. 470–399 BC) started moral philosophy and introduced a dialogue method. His dialogue partner would begin with a claim, like "**Good** is what the gods desire" or "Justice is what serves the interest of the stronger party." Socrates would ask questions about the claim, and the partner would answer; there would be clarifications, arguments, objections, and responses. The method seeks out beliefs that can be held consistently after a careful examination. Socrates, even though he had no developed ethical doctrine of his own, taught the life of reason; he taught people to think long and hard about ethical issues.

Plato (c. 428–347 BC), a student of Socrates, used dialogues and arrived at a more complex ethical doctrine. According to Plato, goodness is something objective that we can grasp with our minds, just as we grasp the perfect circles of geometry. If we know the Form of the Good, we will pattern our lives after it and act rightly; evil actions come out of ignorance. The good life is one of harmony, where the higher rules the lower, where reason and the Form of the Good rule desires and emotions. The good life is characterized by four cardinal **virtues**: *wisdom* is excellence in thinking, *temperance* is the rational control of our desires, *courage* is the rational control of our emotions (especially fear), and *justice* is the correct ordering of the parts of the soul, whereby reason guides the other parts. The good life is pleasant but not aimed at pleasure (which is lower); injustice brings disharmony and thus distress to the soul.

Aristotle (384–322 BC), a student of Plato, based his ethics on an empirical method closer to what is used in **biology**. If we study humans, we find that they act for reasons and that these reasons form a hierarchy; we all act, ultimately, for the sake of **happiness**. But what is happiness? Aristotle argues that it is not pleasure or honor; instead it is a life where we exercise most excellently our highest and most distinctive capacity, which is reason. Reason has two uses: to think and to act. So there are two sorts of excellence we should pursue: those of thinking (intellectual virtues) and those of acting (moral virtues). A virtue is a mean between extremes, as determined by practical reason; so being courageous is to fear danger just enough, while being cowardly is to fear too much and being foolhardy is to fear too little. The good life is to live according to the virtues, which are instilled by practice and not just knowledge. The highest form of the good life is the contemplation of the highest truths; but this is too high for most people. After Aristotle came three approaches of lesser note. The Cyrenians saw bodily pleasure as the good. The Cynics claimed that the good life was one of virtue and of indifference to pleasure and pain; extreme Cynics defied social conventions and chose to live free "according to nature" in the forest like dogs. The Skeptics contended that, since we know nothing, we do not know what the good life is; extreme Skeptics would not answer questions but would merely grunt.

Of greater import was Epicurus (c. 341–270 BC), who was a hedonistic **egoist**; the good life is what brings the greatest balance of pleasure over pain for oneself. He advocated a relaxed, leisurely life where we pursue social and mental pleasures (like friendship and study) and avoid pain. We should limit our desires to simple things that are easily attainable; pursuing pleasures like lust and greed brings more pain than pleasure. Despite the common meaning of "epicure," Epicurus did not favor gourmet food and fine wines. But he did advocate withdrawing from public life, which he thought brings little pleasure. Lucretius (c. 99–55 BC) later preached Epicureanism to a Roman audience.

Even more important were the Stoics, a school founded by Zeno of Citium (366–280 BC); other early members of the school include Cleanthes (c. 331–232 BC) and Chrysippus (c. 280–206 BC). The early Stoics did much work in logic and epistemology, and they believed in a rational cosmic order. They held that the good life is one of virtue, which brings inner happiness; we should be stoically indifferent to social conventions and to misfortunes that we cannot control. To be virtuous is to follow the **natural moral law** that is accessible to every person's reason. While Greek Stoics advocated withdrawing from public life, the later Roman Stoics encouraged people to engage in the affairs of the world. Roman Stoics include the orator Cicero (106–43 BC), the statesman Seneca (c. 4 BC–65 AD), the ex-slave Epictetus (c. 55–135), and the emperor Marcus Aurelius (121–180). They taught the importance of discipline and virtue, the duty to be just and considerate toward everyone, and the **golden rule**. They saw themselves as citizens of the world and believed in universal moral equality. The Roman Stoics had a major influence on Western values.

Plotinus (c. 205–270) founded Neoplatonism. His philosophy, which develops the mystical side of Plato and may have been influenced by Hinduism, sees all reality as emanating (or flowing) from a supreme reality called "the One." Between "the One" and the material world were intermediates, like spirit (nous), soul (psyche), and lower gods. Happiness and the good life require withdrawing from matter toward a mystical grasp of the Good. Plotinus had a major influence on **Christian** theologians and mystics, who adapted his ideas to monotheism (*see* **medieval ethics**). This entry is about ancient **philosophical** ethics in the West. There was also much ancient **religious** ethical reflection in the East and West; *see* **Biblical ethics, Buddhist ethics, Confucius, Hindu ethics, Jewish Ethics,** and **Taoist ethics**. *See also* POLITICAL PHILOSOPHY.

ANIMALS. The chief issue here is whether we have duties to nonhuman animals and, if we do, then what these duties are.

Some ethicists, such as **Immanuel Kant**, think we have no *direct* duties toward animals, since we have direct duties only toward rational beings (*see* **moral patient** and **social contract**). We may still have *indirect* duties toward animals. Harming a dog may be wrong if it makes the dog's owner suffer; and torturing a dog may be wrong if it makes us less sensitive to human pain. But if secretly torturing a dog brings pleasure to a sadist and no pain to humans, then there can be no moral objection to it. Most people find this view implausible.

René Descartes thought animals were incapable of feeling pleasure and pain. But this view is difficult to accept since humans and animals are so much alike in their nervous systems and pain behavior.

Some **utilitarians**, including **Jeremy Bentham** and **Peter Singer**, hold that an equal amount of pleasure/pain, regardless of what human or animal experiences it, has the same value/disvalue and ought to be weighed equally in our moral decision making. So your daughter's pain ought to be given the same consideration as an equal pain of your pet dog. Some argue for a stricter view, that animals have a **right** not to be treated merely as a means to promote human goals, even when the human gain exceeds the animal pain.

A moderate view is possible. **W. D. Ross** claimed that, while we have duties toward everyone, we have greater duties toward some (e.g., our friends, benefactors, or children) than toward others; and our duty not to harm others is greater than our duty to do good to them. If we extend this view to our treatment of animals, we could say that (1) we have duties about the well-being of animals, but lesser duties than we have about the well-being of humans; and (2) our duty not to cause animals pain is greater than our duty to bring them pleasure. From this, we might argue for a moderate principle about animal treatment: "It is wrong to bring animals great suffering in order to promote trivial interests of humans."

Even this moderate principle would have a major impact on how we treat animals. For many years, companies tested cosmetics in ways that were cruel to animals—for example, by dropping noxious chemicals on the eyes of rabbits. Henry Spira, a follower of Singer, brought this to people's attention; it seemed like a clear case of bringing animals great suffering to promote trivial interests of humans. Partly through Spira's efforts, there now are laws protecting animals used in experiments, to ensure that these animals are treated as humanely as possible. Animals raised for food are not as well protected.

Some vegetarians argue that eating meat (1) harms our health (clogging our arteries and making us obese), (2) aggravates world hunger (since more resources are needed to produce animal protein than vegetable protein), (3) harms the environment (especially since the meat industry's heavy use of fossil fuels promotes global warming), and (4) harms animals (especially those raised in factory farms). **R. M. Hare** thinks these arguments are overstated; he advocates a "demi-vegetarian" policy of eating only a small amount of meat, taken from animals raised under humane conditions. He claims that this (1) is at least as healthy as eating no meat, (2) is better for world hunger than vegetarianism (since some hilly or arid land is suitable for grazing but not farming), (3) does little harm to the environment, and (4) is in the interest of farm animals who are raised in a happy manner (since otherwise they would not exist). If meat is labeled as to its source, demi-veg buying habits can discourage cruel farming practices and thus produce considerable good for animals.

Some suggest that we add two categories to the "Nutrition Facts" box found on most foods. An environment-resources category would say, for example, that producing the one-pound steak took five pounds of grain, 2500 gallons of water, and a gallon of gasoline, and had such and such results that may contribute to global warming. An animal-treatment category would say, for example, that the chicken was raised in a factory farm with half a square foot of space. As it is now, people do not know the environmental and cruelty costs of the food they eat.

There is also an issue about whether animals are capable of moral thinking. **Charles Darwin** thought that, while morality is the most important difference between humans and other animals, other social animals have less developed analogues of human morality. For example, some animals show great concern for the welfare of their offspring, even to the point of risking their own safety. Darwin thought human morality works by rationalizing instincts that are present in all social animals. *See also* BIOETHICS; BIOLOGY; BUDDHIST ETHICS; ENVIRONMENTAL ETHICS; EUTHANASIA; GOOD; HINDU ETHICS; JOHN STUART MILL; MORAL AGENT; SCIENCE; SOCIOBIOLOGY.

ANSCOMBE, ELIZABETH (1919–2001). British philosopher born in Ireland who worked in ethics and philosophy of mind. She studied at Cambridge under Ludwig Wittgenstein; later she assumed the chair he had held and provided translations of and commentaries on his work. Her "Modern Moral Philosophy" (1958) contributed to the growth of **virtue** ethics and her *Intention* (1957) contributed to action theory. She was influenced by Wittgenstein, **Aristotle**, **Thomas Aquinas**, and Catholicism, to which she converted while an undergraduate.

Anscombe rejected **utilitarianism** and **Kantianism**; she thought they were too legalistic and ignored moral aspects of life such as virtues, emotions, moral character, **moral education**, and moral wisdom. Rather than seeking a fundamental principle about how we ought to act, in the manner of **John Stuart Mill** or Immanuel Kant, she argued that we should approach ethics as did **ancient** and **medieval** thinkers, especially Aristotle and Aquinas. We should begin with a robust concept of **happiness** or human flourishing. Then we should pursue questions such as: What is the **good** life? How should I live? What sort of person should I be? How do I become the person I should be? These focus on actions, intentions, and **responsibility**. These are practical issues one faces in one's daily, ethical life and they are not answered by legalistic notions of principles and duties.

Anscombe's first published work, in 1939, addressed the **justice** of World **War** II. Since then, she has written much on topics of applied ethics (*see* **ethics: applied**), such as nuclear deterrence and **euthanasia** (*see* **bioethics** and **killing**). She defended Pope Paul VI's **natural law** argument against the birth control pill and other forms of artificial birth control; this argument, in *Humanae Vitae* (1967), is based on the idea that the inherent natural purpose of **sexual** intercourse is to procreate.

Catholicism's influence on Anscombe's ideas also is evident in her defense of **double effect**: the principle that under certain conditions it is permissible to do something with a morally good intended effect and a morally bad unintended side effect. This principle figures prominently in the Catholic Church's position on matters such as **abortion** and killing. Double effect allows the removal of a pregnant woman's cancerous uterus even though it will kill her fetus, but it does not allow the direct killing of a fetus to perform an abortion.

ANTHROPOLOGY. Raises questions like these about ethics: How much do cultures differ in their ethical thinking? Can we judge the morality of one culture to be higher or more rational than another, or are all moralities equal? How much of our ethical thinking is learned (from socialization) and how much is innate (from our **biological** makeup—*see* **sociobiology**)? What ethical duties do anthropologists have toward the indigenous peoples they study? Can we get valuable insights about ethical problems by learning how other cultures deal with these problems?

Some thinkers—like **Ruth Benedict, J. L. Mackie,** and Edward Westermarck—emphasize how greatly societies disagree on issues like **sexual ethics, racism,** slavery, **sexism, abortion,** infanticide, and human sacrifice; they often conclude, rightly or wrongly, that there are no objective moral standards (*see* **cultural relativism, knowing right from wrong,** and **relativism**). Others—like Ralph Linton and Clyde Kluckhohn—emphasize the large agreement between cultures on areas like fairness, honesty, family life, and gratitude; they argue for *cultural universals* that are shared by all or most societies but take on different forms in different cultural contexts. Joyce Hertzler and others claim that the **golden rule** and related principles (*see* **benevolence** and **love your neighbor**) are almost universal across the different cultures of the world. And **Lawrence Kohlberg** claims, based on transcultural studies, that people of all cultures go through the same stages of moral thinking, although cultural differences can favor or retard the development of higher ethical thinking. *See also* HUMAN RIGHTS DECLARATION; NORMATIVE/DESCRIPTIVE; PSYCHOLOGY; SCIENCE.

APPLIED ETHICS. *See* ETHICS: APPLIED.

AQUINAS, THOMAS (1224–1274). Italian monk who was the dominant thinker of the **medieval** era, of Catholic philosophy, and of the **natural law** approach to ethics. Aquinas wrote two comprehensive treatments of philosophy and theology: the *Summa Theologica* and the *Summa Contra Gentiles*. His central theme is the harmony between human reason (especially as explained by **Aristotle,** whose main works had just been rediscovered) and Christian faith (based on the **Bible** and church Tradition): while reason gives us some basic truths about **God** and morality, divine revelation builds on these and furnishes other truths that exceed the powers of reason.

Most medieval thinkers, including Aquinas, accepted the difference between philosophy and theology; for example, they debated whether reason (philosophy) could show that the world had a beginning in time, or whether this could only be based on revelation (theology). Correspondingly, Aquinas's thinking about morality has two parts, which we might call his "moral philosophy" and his "**moral theology**":

- Aquinas's *moral philosophy* mostly follows Aristotle. Its norms, called "natural (moral) laws," are knowable from natural reason and do not require Christian revelation (which Aristotle lacked).
- Aquinas's *moral theology* requires Christian revelation. It adds further norms, called "divine (revealed) laws," and a larger religious context for viewing reason's natural laws.

Reason and revelation should not conflict if approached correctly; they overlap in their conclusions, since both teach many of the same norms (e.g., that stealing is wrong). Aquinas thinks this redundancy is helpful; those who lack the time or ability to think out moral issues rationally are still able to follow Biblical norms.

Aquinas's moral philosophy borrowed four key ideas from Aristotle: (1) all our voluntary actions are directed toward ends and ultimately a final end; (2) **happiness** is the final end, since it is desirable for its own sake, self-sufficient, and attainable; (3) choice involves picking means to this final end; and (4) an agent needs a moral character developed through habits of choice (**virtues**) to realize this happiness.

Aquinas sees the first principles of natural law, like those of speculative reason, as "self-evident," in that their subject contains their predicate; but those who do not grasp the notions might not see the self-evidence. The first principle of natural law is that **good** is to be done and pursued, and evil avoided. If we take this to imply that we ought to seek the neighbor's good too, and avoid bringing harm to the neighbor, then the norm to **love your neighbor** is a consequence. Aquinas argues that our reason naturally apprehends as *good* anything to which we are naturally inclined; these goods include those common to all beings (like self-preservation), those common to all animals (like **sexual** intercourse and raising offspring), and those peculiar to rational beings (like knowing about God and living in society). Similarly, we naturally apprehend that we ought to act reasonably and have reason direct our inclinations.

While all our voluntary actions aim at some (at least apparent) good, we sometimes act for lower instead of higher goods. The basic principles of natural law are unchangeable and known to all; but their applications are not known by all and can vary with circumstances. Our practical reason can be perverted by passion, vice, or an evil disposition; but we cannot be completely blinded to the basic principles of natural law.

Human laws ("positive laws") can be set up to promote the good. Aquinas defined "law" in a generic sense as an "ordinance of reason for the common good, made by him who has care of the community, and promulgated." Civil laws and customs can rightly vary from place to place, so long as they do not violate the natural law. Civil rules that violate the natural law are unjust and thus not genuine laws at all.

What makes an action bad is that it moves us away from our ultimate goal. To promote this goal, we need virtues (good habits). Aquinas borrowed his four cardinal moral virtues from Greek philosophy:

- *Wisdom* (*prudence*) is governing ourselves by reason, whereby we understand how we ought to live and we act on this.
- *Courage* is facing danger and fear with proper confidence.
- *Temperance* is rationally controlling our desires and emotions.
- *Justice* is dealing fairly with others.

These virtues can be acquired by effort, as Aristotle described. For an act to be totally good, both what is done and why it is done must be good (*see* **praiseworthy**).

So far, none of this involves Christian revelation. When we add the latter, we move into moral theology.

Aquinas's moral theology sees the whole structure of natural law as part of God's larger plan for the world (his "eternal law"). Natural moral laws, besides being norms based on reason, are commands of God. God created our minds in such a way that we can **know right from wrong**. So the universe is purposeful, we are here for a reason, and **responsible** living requires that we live in accord with this.

Based on his Christian faith, Aquinas argues that Aristotle's description of happiness is incomplete. Yes, there is such a thing as *natural happiness*, which consists in a proper and excellent use of our rational facilities (intellect and will) and which brings us a degree of fulfillment. Beyond this is a greater *supernatural happiness*, which consists in the contemplation of God, the beatific vision, in the afterlife.

This supernatural happiness is the activity of our highest faculty (knowledge) toward the highest object (God); it will bring ultimate fulfillment and is the highest end of all our actions. The Bible gives us religious laws revealed by God. These laws direct us to our supernatural end; they also serve to reinforce and clarify the natural moral law and purify our motivation. To the four cardinal moral virtues mentioned above, Christianity adds three theological virtues—and claims that the greatest of these is love:

- *Faith* is believing in God and what he has revealed.
- *Hope* is emotionally trusting in God and his promises.
- *Love* is unselfishly striving to serve God and do good and not harm to his creatures.

So moral theology builds on moral philosophy, adding elements from Christian revelation to what can be known on the basis of reason.

Aquinas did much work in what today is called *applied ethics* (*see* ethics: applied). For example, he used ideas from **Augustine** to formulate a classic just **war** doctrine. Aquinas argues that war can be just if it is waged by a legitimate authority, for a just cause (like self-defense), and with proper intention (for example, to promote the good and not just self-interest or cruelty). Just war theorists have added further elements over time, for example, that war must be the last resort, the harm done must be proportionate to the good obtained, innocent civilians cannot be targeted directly, and prisoners of war must be treated humanely. Today much of the secular world accepts similar principles.

There has been much interest in Aquinas's ethics by recent thinkers, such as **Elizabeth Anscombe**, Alan Donagan, **John Finnis**, Peter Geach, **Alasdair MacIntyre**, Ralph McInery, and Eleonore Stump. *See also* DOUBLE EFFECT; PUFENDORF, SAMUEL; WHY BE MORAL QUESTION.

ARENDT, HANNAH (1906–1975). Jewish philosopher who examined totalitarianism and **political philosophy**. She grew up in Germany, where she wrote a doctoral dissertation under Karl Jaspers on **Augustine**. She was influenced by the phenomenological method of Martin Heidegger, with whom she had a love affair. When the Nazis assumed power, she fled to Paris and then New York. She worked for Jewish organizations and taught at the New School for Social Research.

Her *The Origins of Totalitarianism* (1951) discusses anti-Semitism, imperialism, and the rise of Nazi and Soviet totalitarianism. With the breakdown of traditional civil and religious structures, there emerged a new form of absolute government that relied on **terror** and ideology. The terror was defended by a story that helped people understand their place in history, a Nazi story about **racial** superiority or a **Marxist** story about the inevitable march toward the classless society. With ideology driving powerful nations, the future became increasingly more frightening, unpredictable, and insane.

Arendt went to Jerusalem in 1961 to report for *The New Yorker* magazine on the trial of Adolf Eichmann, the Nazi war criminal who organized the genocide. Her *Eichmann in Jerusalem: A Report on the Banality of Evil* (1963) described what took place. The defense claimed that Eichmann had not killed anyone himself, that he just followed orders, that he did nothing illegal, that Israel acted illegally in taking him from Argentina and putting him on trial, that he was just a "cog in a machine," and that he ought not to be made into a scapegoat. Examination revealed that Eichmann was sane and fairly normal; he had no personal hatred for Jews and little interest in Nazi ideology, and he personally found the killing so nauseating that he kept himself distant from it. He was just following orders, carrying them out as an efficient manager. He did not reflect much on the morality of what the Nazi state was doing; that was not his job. Insofar as morality was concerned, his duty was to obey the commands of the Führer, Adolph Hitler, which had the force of law; had Eichmann disobeyed, he would have had a bad **conscience**. Arendt described how he went to the gallows with dignity and calmness.

Arendt was attacked for her report, which seemed to downplay the evil of the mass murderer. But downplaying evil was not her intention. She wanted instead to understand accurately what happened, so the world could keep it from happening again. Arendt wrote of the "banality of evil." Most Nazis committed atrocities not out of hatred but out of an unthinking conformism; they isolated themselves from thinking morally about the human significance of their actions.

Her postscript counters Eichmann's defense. Israel, as the Jewish state, had the right to try him, since the offense had been committed against the Jews. The penal and military codes of Germany and most other countries agree that clearly criminal orders must not be obeyed.

Arendt explains how Hitler started by killing the incurably ill, and then those who had heart and lung problems (*see* **euthanasia** and **disability ethics**); she fears that future societies may be tempted to kill all those whose intelligence is below a certain level. She also points out how totalitarian governments demand absolute obedience and discourage **autonomous** moral thinking.

She was led to reflect on moral thinking, the kind of thinking that Eichmann and others did not do. She saw moral thinking not in terms of deducing conclusions from accepted moral premises, like "Thou shalt not kill" or "Obey your superiors" (since these may be in doubt), but rather as using processes like role reversal, where we **imagine** ourselves in the place of our victims, and an **impartial** standpoint, where we think things through together in a public forum from the standpoint of everyone, in the manner of **Immanuel Kant**. She saw genuine moral thinking not as a prerogative of the few but as something that everyone is capable of doing or avoiding. Arendt had a major influence on **Jürgen Habermas**. *See also* GOLDEN RULE; HARE, R. M.; RESPONSIBILITY; TWENTIETH-CENTURY ETHICS.

ARISTOTLE (384–322 BC). **Ancient** Greek philosopher who studied at **Plato's** Academy. Before founding his own Athenian school, the Lyceum, he tutored Alexander the Great for three years. He worked extensively in philosophy (ethics, logic, metaphysics, and **political philosophy**), science (biology, chemistry, physics, and psychology), and other areas (history, literary theory, and rhetoric). He had a major influence on the development of Western thought, especially in the Middle Ages; **Thomas Aquinas** called him simply "the philosopher." Aristotle's *Nicomachean Ethics* was the first systematic ethical treatise in the Western world and is the basis of much recent **virtue ethics**.

Aristotle moves away from Plato's idea that there is one Form of the **Good** and adopts the view that there are many goods. For humans, these goods are the observed goals of our various rational activities, why we do things; these goods form a hierarchy determined by the associated activities. Running shoes (good A) are subordinate to exercise (good B) because running-shoe manufacturing (activity A) is subordinate to running (activity B). No company would manufacture running shoes if no one ran. There is one good at the top of the hierarchy, *eudaimonia*, for the sake of which we seek all other goods.

According to Aristotle's teleological conception of the universe, each thing has a function. To be a good thing of its kind, a particular thing must perform its function well. A good racehorse is one that performs well in races. Likewise, humans have a function, which involves reason, and a good human must perform rational activities well; in

Aristotle's terms, our function is to achieve *eudaimonia*.

The Greek word *eudaimonia* is usually translated as "**happiness**," though that can be misleading. We often use "happiness" to refer to something akin to a sensation or feeling, whereas for Aristotle it is a condition or state of character. *Eudaimonia* for Aristotle really means "living well" or "rational activity that accords with virtue." This is our highest good and that which allows us to fulfill our function; we achieve happiness, in the Aristotelian sense, when our characters are such that our activities conform to virtue.

A virtue is a *golden mean* between vices of excess and deficiency. The virtue of bravery falls between the vices of foolhardiness (excessive confidence) and cowardice (deficient confidence). The mean is determined by practical reason, which picks the proper means to the end. There are intellectual virtues (about thinking) and moral virtues (about acting). We achieve happiness when we live according to virtue.

For Aristotle, our characters are in some sense up to us. We are not born with virtues or vices, nor do we acquire these simply by learning what they are. Instead, we form our character through practice, through repeatedly choosing to live in a way that accords with the virtues until these become habitual.

Although our characters are in some sense up to us, we are not left alone and unguided. Society's **praise**/blame and rewards/**punishment** play an important role by giving us incentive to practice the virtues and avoid the vices. But society can only provide incentive; it still is up to us to choose and practice the virtues.

Society should limit its praise/blame and rewards/punishment to our voluntary acts. Only those acts show our characters, and thus only they are subject to society's influence. Voluntary acts have their origin within the agent, whereas involuntary acts have their origin outside the agent. Involuntary acts fall into two categories, depending on whether they result from force or from ignorance. By "force," Aristotle means actual force such as when a gust of wind blows one into another person. He excludes duress, such as when a gun is held to your head to coerce you into doing something; you still can refuse and take the bullet. Since the choice is there, society can influence our acts through praise/blame or reward/punishment. Ignorance lessens our **responsibility** only if the ignorance is not culpable (such as when we step on a child but had no reason to think that the child was under our feet). If a drunk driver runs over a pedestrian that the driver does not see, but does not see because the driver is drunk, then the driver's ignorance is culpable since it resulted from the driver's drunken state; Aristotle would not exclude such a driver from blame and punishment.

Aristotle gives an important role to society because he sees the social good as more important and more difficult to achieve than the individual good. Thus politics, the study that aims at the societal good, is the highest and most noble of practical concerns.

Aristotle moves away from **Socrates**'s view that one will always do what one knows is right—so all bad acts result from ignorance. Aristotle thinks one can know what is right but fail to do it because of either impetuosity or weakness. With impetuosity, one's feelings prevent deliberation; with weakness, one deliberates but then feelings cast aside the result of the deliberation.

Like Plato before him, Aristotle rejects the hedonistic view that pleasure is the good; but he does not exclude pleasure from the good life. Happiness will allow some pleasures, but not all. Since each activity has a pleasure that accompanies it, we must judge pleasures by looking at these activities. Pleasures that accompany desirable (virtuous) acts are a part of happiness while those that accompany undesirable (vicious) acts are not.

For Aristotle, then, we live the good life by developing virtuous characters. This good life is most complete if we engage in study, especially the contemplation of the highest truths. Study best enables us to conform to virtue and appreciate the pleasures that accompany virtues.

Aristotle begins his ethics by saying that the good is that at which all things aim, thus connecting good with desire. Whether or not this is a strict definition (*see* **naturalism** and **natural law**), Aristotle has been an inspiration to later thinkers who place the foundations of ethics in sense experience, as opposed to pure reason. *See also* CONFUCIUS.

ARROW, KENNETH (1921–). American social scientist known for *Arrow's theorem*, which says roughly that every voting system is flawed. Suppose your department is deciding between candidates A, B, and C. Three people show up to vote. Your ranking is A-B-C (A first, then B, then C). One of your colleagues ranks the candidates B-C-A, and the other ranks them C-A-B. So most prefer A to B, most prefer B to C, and most prefer C to A. Who wins is then determined by how the voting procedure is set up. Suppose you first take two candidates and have everyone vote, and then have the winner go against the remaining candidate. Then the candidate not in the first vote will win. If you first decide between A and B, then A will win; but then A will go against C, and C will win. Note that the argument here is logical, not empirical.

AUGUSTINE (354–430). Aurelius Augustine, Bishop of Hippo in North Africa, was the most influential Christian thinker in the first thousand years after Biblical times. Born of a pagan father and a Christian mother, he became a firm Christian only later; he spent much of his life as a spiritual seeker. He struggled intellectually and morally, fathering an illegitimate child. He credits the beginning of his conversion to reading Cicero. He later turned to Neoplatonism, and then to Christianity; his mature thought was a Christian Neoplatonism. He saw his life as a search for **God**, and he saw the human condition in these terms too: God is our supreme **good** and our hearts are restless until we find him, either here on earth or ultimately in the afterlife.

Augustine summed up his ethics as: "Love, and do as you will." Central here is love of God, shown in commitment and obedience. We are to **love our neighbor** not for the neighbor's sake, but for the sake of God. (Not all Christian thinkers would follow Augustine on this or many other points.) We are not even to love ourselves for our own sake, but only for God's sake; it is a perversion to act morally in order to avoid punishment (*see* **why be moral question**). The focus of our lives and our actions has to be God, in whom our true **happiness** lies. God is the eternal and unchangeable, and to seek and love him fulfills morality and the Scriptures.

Augustine's notion of God has Platonic overtones. Loving God involves a passion and mystical devotion that brings to mind **Plato**'s love of Beauty or the Good, or Plotinus's love of "the One" (*see* **ancient ethics**)—a love that involves rising above material concerns. God is seen as unchangeable, as beyond time. Critics question whether this unchangeableness is compatible with the **Bible**, which portrays God as involved in history in a temporal way, as remembering the past and planning for the future.

Humans, for Augustine, are composed of body and soul; while both are good, the soul is higher. The soul is to rule the body, reason is to rule the soul, and the unchangeable (God and his law) is to rule reason. *Good will* is a will whereby we desire to live upright and honorable lives, attain the highest wisdom, and follow what is unchanging; good will has value beyond wealth, honor, or physical pleasure. Evildoing comes from *inordinate desire*, where we submit to material impulses, following our lower parts; it comes from enjoying material things as ends-in-themselves instead of using them to promote higher ends, and ultimately God, who alone is to be enjoyed as an end-in-itself.

When Augustine was a Manichaean, he believed that there were two supreme uncreated deities—one good and one evil—and that evil came from the evil deity. When he became a Christian, he gave this up in favor of believing in one supreme, all-powerful, all-good God. But if such a God exists, why is there evil in the world? Augustine answers that evil comes from the sin of free creatures. **Free will** is a great gift, even though it makes us able to neglect the eternal and do evil, since it makes good will possible; without free will, moral **praise**/blame and reward/**punishment** would be unjust. All evil is either sin or penalty for sin; the penalty can be either sin's natural result (as hateful people make themselves miserable) or sin's punishment (as God punished the original sin of Adam and Eve, who were created perfect, by sending moral weakness, disease, and death into the world). Augustine's view of evil has two metaphysical elements. First, evil merely is a lack or deficiency in a being that is otherwise good; a being that possessed no goodness at all could not exist. Second, the world has greater value because it has a range of created beings, from higher to lower; thus even lower beings contribute to the value of the world.

Augustine later became involved in a controversy with the Pelagians and perhaps retracted some of his ideas on free will. Martin Luther (1483–1546), who rejected human free will as violating God's sovereignty, saw Augustine as rejecting free will. Whether this is a correct interpretation of Augustine is much disputed.

Augustine made many contributions to ethics. He was perhaps the first to point out that the literal formulation of the **golden rule**—"If you want X to do A to you, then do A to X"—has absurd implications. Imagine that you want X to challenge you to get drunk; then, according to the formula, you ought to challenge X to get drunk. To avoid this problem, Augustine suggested that we understand the golden rule as "Do unto others *whatever good things* you want done to yourself."

Augustine's ideas on **suicide**, while not original, have been influential. He saw suicide as forbidden by the Biblical commandment "You shall not **kill**"; suicide is wrong because it violates our natural self-love, hurts the community, and usurps a right that belongs only to God (who owns our lives). Critics dispute these reasons and point out that the Bible contains no clear prohibition of suicide.

Also important are Augustine's ideas on **sexual** intercourse (which he saw as justified only in marriage and only when oriented toward procreation—every other sexual expression is wrong), **war** (where he built on the "just war" approach of Cicero and **Aristotle**), and law (where he claimed that an unjust law is no law at all and has no binding force—*see* **natural law**). Augustine was very influential in the **medieval** era and was often quoted by **Thomas Aquinas**. Augustine also had a strong influence on several recent continental thinkers, including **Hannah Arendt**, Albert Camus, and Jean-François Lyotard. *See also* MEDIEVAL ETHICS.

AUTONOMY/HETERONOMY. Autonomy is being self-governed, while heteronomy is being governed by outside forces. Ethicists agree that some persons are incapable of autonomy: children have not achieved the rationality and maturity needed for autonomy, the senile have lost this rationality, and the insane and mentally disabled are unable to develop this rationality. Such cases aside, ethicists tend to support autonomy, often on the grounds that a society of autonomous citizens is more likely to advance morally and economically. Examples of atrocities perpetrated by those who say they "just followed orders" show why ethicists tend to favor autonomy (*see* **Hannah Arendt**).

Ethicists disagree about the precise nature of autonomy. Libertarians such as **Robert Nozick** tend to treat autonomy/heteronomy simply as being free/unfree from physical and legal constraints that prevent one from acting as one chooses. Other philosophers believe autonomy requires more than the absence of physical and legal constraints; to be autonomous, one must conform one's behavior to a moral law that one creates oneself (*see* **Immanuel Kant** and **Jean-Jacques Rousseau**). For such thinkers, autonomy is not the freedom to do as you please, but rather the capacity to author and follow moral demands. For Kant, the mere freedom to do as you please is heteronomy; an enslavement to inclinations is like an addict's enslavement to heroin. We become autonomous only when we break free from inclinations and conform to the moral law. Rousseau further argues that physical and legal constraints can help one become autonomous; one can be "forced to be free." Libertarians would see such force as unjustified **paternalism**.

Many conceptions of autonomy fall between the two extreme views just described. Many today see the libertarian "freedom from physical and legal constraints" view as inadequate, but do not want to accept Rousseau's "forced to be free" view or Kant's idea that we "create the moral law." Autonomy for many thinkers is the ability to think for oneself about life decisions and moral issues in a reasonable way and to act accordingly, without undue interference from others; so keeping information from people could hinder their autonomy since it hinders their ability to think things through in a reasonable way.

Autonomy relates to many areas of applied ethics (*see* **ethics: applied**). **Bioethics** pays much attention to patient autonomy; *informed consent* is about providing patients with information they need to make autonomous decisions about their healthcare. In **business ethics**, employee **privacy** in part deals with whether the autonomy of employees is threatened when their personal matters are known to employers. Many ethicists see privacy as valuable because it is needed for one to develop a life that is autonomous instead of just conforming to the will of others. *See also* EUTHANASIA; SUICIDE.

AXIOLOGICAL LOGIC. *See* LOGIC.

AYER, A. J. (1910–1989). Alfred Jules Ayer was a British philosopher whose *Language, Truth and Logic* in 1936 introduced **logical positivism** to the English-speaking world. He argued for an **emotivist** interpretation of moral judgments, seeing these as expressions of feeling, like "Boo" and "Hurrah," instead of truth claims.

– **B** –

BAD. *See* GOOD.

BEAUVOIR, SIMONE DE (1908–1986). French existentialist and **feminist** philosopher. She was a lifelong companion of **Jean-Paul Sartre**.

Her *The Ethics of Ambiguity* (1947) presents an existentialist ethics with Sartrean themes. The "ambiguity" is that we are both things and people. As things, we have a history and context, and are subject to laws of nature. As people, we can choose freely, within limits, what to make of our lives. There are no external, objective values telling us how to choose; such values could exist only if there were a **God** to issue **divine commands** or define a *human nature* to which we must conform (*see* **natural law**). Beauvoir thinks there is no God; so we are on our own and must create our own values. But we can act *authentically* (truthfully) or in *bad faith* (which denies our **responsibility** to choose and thus our personhood). Examples of bad faith are the "serious man," who dishonestly conforms to inherited standards as if they were objective, and the "nihilist," who correctly sees that the world is in itself meaningless but cowardly refuses to create a meaning through his actions. A more authentic approach is to choose freely some way to live, but in a way that respects the freedom of others to do likewise and thus promotes the conditions (like the defeat of Nazism) needed to exercise freedom. If this argument works (and critics raise doubts), then existentialism avoids "the anarchy of personal whim" and instead leads to an ethics of humanistic concern for others.

Beauvoir's *The Second Sex* (1949) was her greatest work and a classic of feminist ethics. This massive book treats womanhood in an interdisciplinary way, using **biology**, history, **psychology**, mythology, and **Marxism**. It analyzes the female as child, adolescent, prostitute, lesbian, and mother. A common theme is the **sexist** oppression of women. Our culture understands "human" in male terms; womanhood is seen as "the other sex" and is given an inferior role-definition that women are expected to satisfy. The "myth of the eternal feminine" gives a complex structure of conflicting roles for women, like responsible mother and seductress. As an atheistic existentialist, Beauvoir believes that there is no preexisting *nature* or role-pattern that woman must fulfill; she says "One is not born, but rather becomes, a woman." So women must freely choose what to make of their own lives. Women also need to support social and **political** structures (like child care and equal education and employment) that help to promote this.

Beauvoir's *The Coming of Age* (1970) was a massive work about the elderly, who are often ignored or treated in a dehumanized way; but old age can be a time of meaningful and creative activity. Beauvoir describes the situation of the elderly in two ways: from outside observation and from the inside (what it is like to be old and to be treated in certain ways). This area of aging and the elderly deserves much more attention by philosophers and by society.

BENEDICT, RUTH (1887–1948). Influential American **anthropologist** who specialized in native American cultures. Benedict claims that what is considered "normal" varies greatly between societies. So trances and **homosexuality**, while "abnormal" in many cultures, are tolerated and have important social functions in some other cultures. What a culture considers "normal" is encouraged to continue; in time, it becomes a cultural "**good**."

Benedict is known for advocating **cultural relativism**; she claims that ethics is relative to culture and that "morally good" is synonymous with "socially approved." Yet she seems to contradict her own theory when, after World War II, she called **racial** segregation a sickness (and thus bad) while admitting that it was socially approved (which on her theory would make it good). She appealed to anthropological studies against the view that one race is better than another; she argued that all races would be represented if we picked the top third of all humans in physical, intellectual, or moral excellence. She appealed to the U.S. to promote the human dignity of all its citizens and to work against racial and other stereotypes. *See also* RELATIVISM.

BENEVOLENCE. The duty to do **good** and not harm to others. A large part of ethics deals with benevolence in some way.

Here are a few key questions about benevolence:

- Do we have a stronger duty to promote the good of those who are close to us, such as friends and relatives, or an equal duty to promote everyone's good? (*See* **impartiality**.)
- Is benevolence summed up in the **utilitarian** idea that we ought to maximize the sum-total of good consequences for everyone? Or is the duty not to harm (*non-maleficence*), as **W. D. Ross** claims, stronger than the duty to do good (*beneficence*)?
- How are we to understand this "good" that we are to do to others and this "harm" that we are to avoid doing to them? Can we harm others only by causing them pain? Or can we harm them in other ways too, such as breaking a promise made to them that they never discover?
- Can we be *overly benevolent*, by being so concerned for others that we neglect ourselves? Do we have duties to ourselves too?
- Are all benevolent actions motivated by a deeper **egoism**?
- Do we have a natural orientation toward benevolence?
- Does benevolence always or usually promote our self-interest?
- Is benevolence our only duty? Is **justice** a distinct duty?

Some distinguish *beneficence* (doing good to others) from *benevolence* (intending the good of others); others use these terms interchangeably.

While this entry focuses on the benevolence principle, there is also a **virtue** of benevolence: a disposition to care about the good of others and to act accordingly. *See also* ALTRUISM; ANTHROPOLOGY; BUTLER, JOSEPH; GOLDEN RULE; HUME, DAVID; LOVE YOUR NEIGHBOR; MEDIEVAL ETHICS; RAND, AYN; SIDG-

WICK, HENRY; SOCIOBIOLOGY.

BENTHAM, JEREMY (1748–1832). English philosopher who gave the first systematic account of **utilitarianism** and inspired the British utilitarian movement of the 19th century. He influenced **James Mill**, who applied Bentham's principles to social and **political** issues, and **John Stuart Mill**, who became the most influential utilitarian.

According to Bentham, we should choose the act with the best consequences, which are measured in terms of the pleasures and pains of all those affected. Suppose I am planning a trip to Zion National Park for myself and Molly, we can stay in either the lodge or a backcountry tent, and no one else is affected by the choice. On Bentham's view, we might evaluate the alternatives this way (using positive numbers for pleasure and negative numbers for pain):

	Lodge	Tent
Molly	+100 units of pleasure (+150 from being in the park, −10 from traveling, −40 from knowing I prefer the tent)	+50 units of pleasure (+150 from being in the park, −10 from traveling, −90 from backcountry hardships)
Myself	+70 units of pleasure (+200 from being in the park, −30 from traveling, −100 from not being in the tent)	+110 units of pleasure (+200 from being in the park, −30 from traveling, −60 from knowing Molly prefers the lodge)
Total	+170 units of pleasure	+160 units of pleasure

We should choose the lodge, because it has the greatest total pleasure, even though I would get more pleasure from the tent option.

Critics object that such calculations are impossible; we cannot know what pleasures/pains would result and how these go into numbers. Moreover, the choice is oversimplified by assuming that it only affects two people. Others may be affected too, such as a couple who would be unable to get a room or tent site depending on our choice, or store owners who would benefit from our purchasing camping supplies.

Perhaps units of pleasure and pain should not be taken literally. Bentham is aware that it may make only metaphorical sense to speak of actual numbers. He believes we can weigh pleasures and pains, and such weighing is the only sensible way to determine how we should act. Although I cannot accurately put numbers to the matter, I know that more pleasure would be produced for Molly and myself if I choose the lodge. Also, no matter how vague it might be, I do have some idea of the pleasures and pains for others who might be affected.

This weighing of pleasure and pain is complicated by such factors as their likelihood, duration, and extent. We are to consider the probability of various pleasures and pains occurring (this gives rise to the contemporary **decision theory** notion of *expected utility*), how long they will last, and how many people will be affected.

John Stuart Mill criticized Bentham for focusing on the *quantity* of pleasure and ignoring its *quality*. Mill claimed that *higher* pleasures (like enjoying poetry or a symphony) are more valuable than *lower* pleasures (like the pushpin game or watching "American Idol"), even if the quantity of pleasure were the same in both cases. But Bentham could deny the latter claim. He could argue that, while the pleasures of pushpin and poetry would be equal if their quantities were the same, in fact the higher pleasures are more intense and longer lasting; thus we get a greater quantity of pleasure from poetry than from pushpin.

Although Bentham contributed to ethical theory, he was more concerned with social and legal reform. Seeing the British legal system as fraught with problems, he devised simpler and more humane approaches based on utilitarian principles. He was especially concerned with prisons. He thought the **punishment** for a crime should be the exact amount of pain needed to deter criminals and others from committing similar crimes. Punishing too little will bring more pain for future victims of crimes; punishing too much is cruel and unnecessary. Bentham designed a model prison that he believed would produce the desired results by inflicting just the right punishments on prisoners. Despite spending considerable time and money on the concept, he was unable to win approval for his model. Because of this and other failures, Bentham became disillusioned with the ability of politicians and government officials to enact reform. *See also* GOOD.

BIAS. To be biased is to violate **impartiality**.

BIBLICAL ETHICS. The Bible is an account, through the eyes of faith, of **God**'s involvement in human history and humanity's response. While it does not contain systematic ethical treatises, there is much of moral significance in its stories, heroes, sermons, prayers, exhortations, controversies, and proverbs.

While the **Jewish** Law in the Old Testament is said to contain 613 precepts, the most important of these are the Ten Commandments (from Exodus 20:1–17 and Deuteronomy 5:6–21); we can divide the commandments into four groups:

Duties to	1.	I am the Lord your God who brought you out of slavery in Egypt. You shall not worship false gods.
God	2.	You shall not take God's name in vain.
	3.	Keep holy the Sabbath.
Duties to	4.	Honor your father and mother.
family	6.	You shall not commit adultery.
Duties to	5.	You shall not **kill**.
anyone	7.	You shall not steal.
	8.	You shall not bear false witness.
Duties to	9.	You shall not covet your neighbor's wife.
yourself	10.	You shall not covet your neighbor's goods.

While the Bible recognizes other duties (for example, gratitude and reparation), these 10 are especially important.

The first group gives duties toward God. Other duties toward God include faith, hope, and love; obedience; and prayerful responses of praise and thanksgiving. Duties to other people are indirectly duties to God since they express obedience to him and concern for his creatures.

The second group gives duties to one's family, seen in traditional terms as a husband, wife, and children. For a family to flourish, the bond between husband and wife must be strong; adultery is forbidden since few things can destroy a family so quickly. Further duties between spouses include affection, communication, and avoiding physical and mental cruelty. Children are to honor their parents; this involves obedience, and later friendship, and even later caring for parents in their old age. Parents are to care for their children and help them grow into caring and **responsible** adults; later, they are to provide emotional support for their adult children through life's difficulties. There also are duties to brothers and sisters, to members of an extended family, and to members of other social units (like villages and the nation).

The third group gives duties that we have to anyone. We are not to kill, steal, or lie. Other duties are to show respect and politeness toward others, help those in need, and show gratitude and reparation.

The last group gives duties to ourselves. The duty not to covet is the duty to avoid bad desires, whether these be to steal or commit adultery (or to kill or lie or hate). We also have a duty to improve ourselves and to live our lives in the wisest way that we can.

Also important in the Old Testament are the call to social **justice** by the prophets (Isaiah 1:11–17), Nathan's use of a similar-case **universalizability** story to get King David to realize his errors (2 Samuel 12:1–13), the commandment to **love one's neighbor** as oneself (Leviticus 19:18), and the **golden rule** (Tobit 4:15) and its application to aliens ("Do not oppress aliens; you know how it feels to be an alien from when you were aliens yourself in Egypt"—Exodus 23:9).

The word "testament" in a Biblical context means "covenant," "treaty," or "agreement." The Old Testament was the agreement between God and the Jewish people, whereby God would be their special guide and protector and they in turn would worship and obey God. Christians see the New Testament as an extension of this, whereby the agreement is between God and all humanity.

The most important norms of the New Testament are the love norms and the golden rule:

- You shall love the Lord your God with all your heart and mind and soul and strength. This is the greatest commandment. The second is similar: You shall love your neighbor as yourself. On these depend the law and the prophets. (Matthew 22:36–40)
- Do unto others as you would have them do unto you. This is the summary of the law and the prophets. (Matthew 7:12; *see also* Luke 6:31)

These express the deeper basis behind the norms of the Old Testament, which is here referred to as the "the law and the prophets" (the Torah and the prophetic writings).

Also important in the New Testament are the beatitudes (like "Blessed are those who suffer persecution for the sake of doing right, for theirs is the kingdom of heaven"—Matthew 5:3–10), the good Samaritan parable (Luke 10:29–37), loving your enemies (Matthew 5:38–48), Jesus's example ("As I have loved you, so you are to love one another; this is how people will know that you are my disciples"—John 13:34–5), St. Paul's poem about love ("Love is patient and kind, it is not jealous or pompous"—1 Corinthians 13:1–13), and St. Paul's statements about how nonbelievers can know the moral law ("The demands of the law are written in their hearts"—Romans 2:13–5).

The Bible can appeal to higher motives (unselfish love and gratitude to God) or lower motives (**punishments** and rewards); this is fitting, since it has to appeal to a wide range of people. The Bible shows a gradual development toward higher approaches to morality.

The Bible has no explicit metaethics (*see* **ethics: metaethics**); so it does not discuss **Plato**'s *Euthyphro* question: "Is a good thing good because God desires it? Or does God desire it because it is already good?" (*see* **divine command theory**). But it says much on **impartiality** (partiality being condemned) and **consistency** (especially between beliefs and actions—Luke 13:14–17) in making moral judgments.

It would be wrong to think the Bible provides clear-cut answers on all moral issues. Many issues are not discussed; for example, the Bible does not mention **abortion** (although the earliest Christian document after the Bible, the *Didache*, condemns abortion and infanticide). And on many issues, like pacifism, divorce, and **homosexuality**, the Bible can be interpreted in different ways. So pacifists appeal to passages like "You shall not kill" and "Turn the other cheek" in favor of their view that killing even in self-defense is wrong; those who defend **war** appeal to passages like "David slew the Philistines and the Lord gave him a great victory." *See also* AQUINAS, THOMAS; AUGUSTINE; MEDIEVAL ETHICS; MORAL THEOLOGY; NATURAL LAW; RACISM; RICOEUR, PAUL.

BIOETHICS. The study of moral issues in medicine (*medical ethics*) and **biology**. These issues range from broad questions, such as "How ought healthcare to be distributed in society?" to more specific questions, such as "May prisoners be used in biological experiments?" Bioethics has become increasingly important in the last 50 years, as medical science advances and ethicists give greater emphasis to practical issues (*see* **ethics: applied**).

The roots of bioethics lie in the ancient world. The Greek physician Hippocrates (c. 460–377 BC), sometimes called "the father of medicine," promulgated principles of conduct for physicians and for teachers and students of medicine. His ideas have been influential; even today, many graduating medical students take his Hippocratic Oath, in the original or a contemporary form. The oath directs physicians to act for the benefit of sick patients, avoid doing them harm and injustice, respect their **privacy**, and share medical knowledge with others.

The physician/patient relationship raises several issues. For example, should patients always be told the complete truth about their illnesses? Some argue that physicians may withhold information that would harm a patient. Suppose that Mary is diagnosed as having a painful disease that took her father's life; if Mary learned about her disease, she would be devastated and unable to cope. Some think physicians may withhold this diagnosis from Mary, or perhaps wait until a better way is found to tell her, such as through her family. Others say this is unacceptable **paternalism** since it limits Mary's information supposedly for her own good. Mary needs to be given full information so she can make **autonomous** choices about her life.

Sometimes there is more than one possible treatment. A physician may think it better to treat John's testicular cancer by a surgical removal of the testes instead of by chemotherapy and radiation. Should the physician tell John only about the surgical option? Or should the physician present all the options, with pros and cons, and let John decide? Many argue that the latter approach better respects John's autonomy and is needed if John is to give *informed consent* for the treatment.

Informed consent also arises in discussions about biological experiments. Bioethicists agree that it is immoral to conduct experiments on humans without their informed consent; so the cruel Nazi medical experiments on Jews and others against their will are condemned. But what constitutes "informed consent"? Some may be unable to understand or evaluate the risks involved. Others may be pressured into volunteering by their desperate medical condition, by financial rewards (for the **poor**), or by special privileges (for prisoners). Can such people give genuine informed consent?

The ancient Hippocratic Oath saw the need for confidentiality, a need that becomes greater as information technology grows. Whereas Hippocrates's patients worried that he would speak of what he found, patients today worry about who has access to **computer** databases that contain their medical records. While some need access in order to treat patients, other access may be questionable; governments, insurance companies, employers, and estranged spouses might misuse the information. Many bioethicists argue that access should be controlled by patients or permitted only for clear medical reasons. Things become more complicated when lives are at stake. For example, all agree that confidentiality is important for psychotherapy; without it, therapy would not be effective since patients would be unwilling to share personal matters. But should a therapist keep quiet if a patient threatens another's life? Some say the risk of death takes precedence here; others say confidentiality is too important to violate, especially since therapists do not know for sure whether patients will act on their threats.

Life-saving treatments raise other issues. The Hippocratic oath tells physicians to benefit the sick and avoid harm; but what if a patient refuses life-saving treatment? Some Jehovah's Witnesses refuse blood transfusions because they equate them with the sin of ingesting blood; should a physician go against their wishes to save their lives? Most bioethicists argue, on autonomy grounds, that a physician should respect the wishes of a patient who is a competent adult. But what if the patient is a child whose parents object to life-saving treatment? Some say the wishes of the parents should be followed, but others argue that a physician is justified in giving life-saving treatment.

Another issue is physician-assisted **suicide**. Suppose John suffers from a cancer that promises a slow and painful death, and he wants the suffering to end. Is it moral for a physician to help John end his life? Some argue that this would be immoral, since it harms John and violates the **sanctity of life.** Others argue that such assistance is permissible, since it prevents suffering and respects John's autonomy.

A related issue is **euthanasia,** which is **killing** done out of mercy. Most people would approve of killing a terminally sick family pet; but is it right to kill a similarly sick human being? Suppose that Mary is in a coma with no chance for recovery; is it permissible to end her life? Most bioethicists agree that it is moral for the physician to withhold life-extending treatment (such as a respirator) if Mary's family opposes this or if Mary had previously forbidden such treatment. Such *passive euthanasia* merely allows diseases or injuries to run their courses and bring death. *Active euthanasia*, taking steps (such as a lethal injection) to end a patient's life, is more controversial. Some argue that such acts violate the physician's duty to respect the sanctity of life and to do no harm. Others argue that such acts are more humane because they end the suffering more quickly. Or suppose that the family wants Mary's life-extending treatment to continue, but the physician believes there is no hope for recovery. Some argue that the physician must follow the wishes of the family, but others think this wastes resources that could benefit patients who have a chance for recovery.

Abortion, even apart from the general issue of whether it is moral, raises significant questions. For example, are physicians obligated to perform abortions to which women are legally entitled? Suppose that the only physician in a small town believes that abortion is wrong and yet has a patient who wants one. Is it ethical for the physician to refuse to perform the abortion? Some argue that it violates one's autonomy to require one to act against one's **conscience**. Others argue that the physician's refusal violates the autonomy of patients and that any physician should be prepared to perform an abortion if no one else is available to do it. Related issues arise when pharmacists refuse, on similar grounds, to fill prescriptions for contraceptives.

Newer reproductive technologies raise ethical issues, such as the following: (1) Surrogate pregnancy involves a woman who agrees to carry a fetus to term for another couple; does this exploit the woman, often one in need of money, who acts as a surrogate? (2) Methods that help infertile couples often produce many unneeded embryos. Are such methods moral? Can the unneeded embryos be killed, or does this violate the sanctity of human life? Can the embryos be used for **stem-cell research** that promises medical advancements? (3) Couples today have greater ability to select the sex of their babies. Is this moral on the grounds that it leads to greater happiness in the family? Or does it reinforce stereotypes about the superiority of one sex over another? (4) Couples today can know more about the health of fetuses. Should couples abort fetuses they know to be defective? Some argue that this would lead to healthier and happier families and societies; others disagree and recall Nazi killing that aimed at promoting the perfect race.

Bioethicists examine issues about allocating resources for healthcare. Is healthcare a universal **right**? Should a society do what it can to give adequate care to all its members, including the **poor**? Some, objecting that this leads to **socialized** medicine, defend a **capitalistic** free-market approach to healthcare; they say the profit motive brings medical advances that ultimately help everyone. There are related issues about medical research, where the free-market approach may emphasize research on medical problems that affect the rich and powerful.

There are many other bioethical issues that cannot be addressed here, such as issues about genetic engineering, the infanticide of **disabled** infants, hospitalizing the sick or mentally disturbed against their will, testing new drugs, responsibilities toward poor patients who cannot pay, medical insurance, malpractice lawsuits, medical costs, pay scales, vegetarianism, **animal** experimentation, **environmental** issues about plants and animals, the ethical training of medical personnel, holistic medicine versus just treating diseases, medical school admissions, and a slew of related legal issues. There are also subfields, such as nursing, dental, and pharmaceutical ethics. *See also* HUMAN RIGHTS DECLARATION; SINGER, PETER; SOCIOBIOLOGY.

BIOLOGY. Raises many issues about morality. Here are some factual questions about biology that arise as we theorize about morality:

- How much of our motivation and ethical thinking is innate (from our biological makeup) and how much is learned (from socialization)? Does our genetic makeup ensure that we are motivated only by self-interest (*see* **egoism**) or by pleasure and the avoidance of pain (*see* **good**)?
- Is one race or sex genetically superior (*see* **racism** and **sexism**)?
- Do genetic differences lead males and females to think differently about morality (*see* **feminist ethics**)?
- Is **free will** compatible with biology?
- Can **animals** think morally?
- How and why did evolution provide us with the capacity for social behavior and moral thinking (*see* **sociobiology**)?

Biology has not yet given us decisive answers on such questions.

There also are normative issues about medicine and biological experimentation (*see* **bioethics**) and the metaethical issue of whether "good" can be defined in biological terms (perhaps as "what accords with evolution"—*see* **evolutionism** and **ethics: metaethics**). *See also* ENVIRONMENTAL ETHICS; SCIENCE.

BRANDT, RICHARD (1910–1997). American philosopher who taught at the University of Michigan and contributed to various areas of moral philosophy. Early in his career, to see how cultural differences affect moral thinking he investigated Hopi ethics on an Indian reservation. He concluded that reasonable people from different cultures would agree in a broad way on most moral issues but would disagree on some details, especially where rational reflection cannot overcome differences from social conditioning (*see* **relativism**). He introduced the distinction between *act* and *rule* **utilitarianism**; he later defended a form of rule utilitarianism designed to avoid act utilitarianism's implausibilities. He defended **ideal observer theory** as a **naturalistic** analysis of what we mean by terms like "good" and "right." But his *A Theory of the Good and the Right* (1979) later argued that moral concepts were confused and needed replacement rather than analysis. He gave a definition of "rational desire" to replace "good" without assuming preexisting moral facts (which he rejected); this new meaning is clearer and satisfies the purposes for which we use "good." We can justify a moral system to people by showing that they would, if fully informed, want this moral system for a society in which they expected to live. He thought we could justify a minimal **Hobbes**ian moral system to **egoistic** people and a stronger moral system to **benevolent** people.

Brandt's approach to "rational desires" gives a useful tool for various approaches to ethics. Many thinkers assume that desires cannot be appraised as rational or irrational. Brandt disagrees; he proposes that a "rational desire" is one that would survive "cognitive psychotherapy," a maximal criticism in terms of logic and a vivid exposure to facts. Suppose you have an aversion to yogurt that comes from social conditioning; although you never tried yogurt, you were told that it has bad germs, tastes awful, and is eaten only by weird people. It may be that your aversion would lessen or disappear if you learned ·more about yogurt, tried it, and understood the origin of your aversion; then your aversion would be irrational. Or suppose you have an aversion to group X because your family hated Xs, called them names, taught false stereotypes about them, and had you meet only a few atypical Xs. It may be that your aversion to Xs would diminish if you understood its origin and broadened your experience and knowledge of Xs in an open way. Cognitive therapy can be a useful tool for conquering our prejudices.

BRENTANO, FRANZ (1838–1917). German philosopher and psychologist who applied phenomenological methods to the study of intentionality. In ethics, he rejected **naturalistic** definitions and saw moral concepts as irreducible but objective; we know what is intrinsically **good** by intuition, not by proof. Moral judgments express positive or negative emotions which can be correct or incorrect in a basic, unanalyzable way. Something is intrinsically good if it is correct to have positive emotions toward it for its own sake. While Brentano appeals to emotions, his view is a form of **cognitivism**, much closer to **intuitionism** than to **emotivism**. Other continental philosophers of his era who took the same general approach to the objectivity of value include Nicolai Hartmann, Hans Reiner, and Max Scheler. The analytic thinker **G. E. Moore** saw Brentano's thinking as close to his own.

BUBER, MARTIN (1878–1965). Jewish religious philosopher and educational leader who examined dialogue and personal relationships. He grew up in Germany and joined the Zionist movement; unlike many Zionists, he hoped for Jewish-Arab cooperation and a state in Palestine that would represent and respect both groups. When the Nazis assumed power, he fled to Palestine, where he later taught at Hebrew University in Jerusalem. Buber at first was a religious mystic; later he shifted from mysticism to personal encounter. His philosophy focused on the dialogical encounter of a human person with other humans, with **God**, and with nature. He saw a lack of genuine dialogue as the source of many problems in the world. At his state funeral in Jerusalem, an Arab student organization put a wreath on his grave—symbolizing the need for understanding between peoples that Buber had come to represent.

Buber's *I and Thou* (1923) distinguishes two primordial relationships; I can deal with someone as an IT or as a THOU. Most dealings with others are I-It relationships; for example, I order spaghetti from a waitress or I learn about a candidate who applies for a job. Here the relationship is impersonal; the Other is a means to an end or an object of knowledge. Less frequent, but more special, are I-Thou relationships, where I enter into a personal dialogue with the Other, as I might do with a friend or lover. Here there is deep, mutual communication and appreciation. Buber thought there was a place for each relationship, but the I-Thou form was higher and more valuable. The I-Thou relationship is especially important for morality, which is corrupted if it hides from us the face (personal reality) of the Other.

Buber's friend Franz Rosenzweig objected that *I and Thou*, while recognizing the "Thou," neglected the "It." Buber responded that if he lived at a time when I-Thou relationships were thriving, he would have praised I-It relationships more; but he found I-Thou relationships to be weak. Buber was particularly frustrated at the weakness of the I-Thou between Jews and Arabs in Israel; he thought any genuine solution of Israel's problems had to begin with greater mutual understanding between the parties.

Buber saw every genuine I-Thou relationship with another human as giving us a glimpse into God, the eternal Thou. Toward God, our relationship must be always I-Thou, and never I-It. So Buber emphasized our personal encounter with God and deemphasized religious rules, rituals, dogmas, and organizations. Some criticized him for going too far on this. As a believer in dialogue, Buber listened to such critics and in time moderated his views. *See also* ISLAMIC ETHICS.

BUDDHIST ETHICS. Siddhārtha Gautama (c. 563–483 BC), who started the religion of Buddhism, was born a **Hindu** in northern India (now Nepal) to a royal family, where he lived in luxury. He became deeply distressed when he discovered the suffering that existed outside the palace. He turned to a life of extreme asceticism as a monk; he denied himself the pleasures of life and ate almost nothing. After several years he found this empty and turned to a "middle way" of moderation and meditation, shunning both luxury and self-denial. At age 35, he achieved *enlightenment* while sitting under a tree, and henceforth was called the "Buddha" (enlightened one). He began to remember events from a previous incarnation and understand how our deeds influence our next life. He attained wisdom, compassion, moral **virtue**, and freedom from fear, hatred, and desire. He achieved *nirvana*, which guarantees the avoidance of future suffering since he would not again be reborn into a future life. Out of compassion for others, he returned to the world and taught others his path to enlightenment.

Classical Buddhism teaches four noble truths: (1) Life involves suffering. (2) We suffer because we do not get what we desire. (3) We can avoid suffering by shunning desires; this will bring nirvana—a peaceful, happy existence now and the freedom from being reincarnated into another life after our death. (4) We can avoid suffering and achieve enlightenment through the noble eightfold path, which involves living rightly with respect to beliefs, intentions, speech, actions, employment, effort, feelings, and meditation.

Classical Buddhism teaches compassion and the **golden rule**: we are not to hurt others in ways that we would find hurtful. It teaches *karma*, that the good or evil that we do to others will come back upon us, now or in a future life. And it teaches five precepts that have us abstain from killing or harming sentient beings, from stealing, from adultery, from lying, and from intoxicating drinks and drugs.

It is difficult to generalize about "all Buddhists," since the many branches of Buddhism have radically different beliefs and practices. Most branches do not believe in gods; but some believe in many gods or one supreme **God**, and some see the Buddha as God's manifestation. Most branches do not believe in a genuine self (like **David Hume** and **Darek Parfit**, they believe that the so-called "self" is merely a collection of experiences); but some believe in a self and in something like the **Christian** idea of personal survival and heavenly bliss. Some branches are highly rational and have developed epistemological and logical systems to rival those of the West; other branches delight in paradoxes, such as the sound of one hand clapping. Some branches have highly developed belief systems, while others are agnostic about beliefs and instead stress meditation or action. Some branches involve much prayer and worship, while others are more secular. Some branches believe in one Buddha, while others believe that many Buddhas appear through time or that we are all called upon to reach a Buddha state.

Buddhists tend to be tolerant; they claim they have never fought a war to promote their religion. Buddhism is becoming popular in the West; even many Christians use Buddhist meditation techniques to promote spiritual development. The Dalai Lama, who views himself as a simple Buddhist monk but is a major Buddhist spokesperson, emphasizes the similarity in the basic moral message of all religions. *See also* DAOIST ETHICS; FORGIVENESS; GLOBAL ETHICS.

BUSINESS ETHICS. The study of moral issues involving the practice of business. These issues range from broad questions, such as whether capitalism is justified, to more specific questions, such as what behavior qualifies as sexual harassment in the workplace.

Business ethics is a contemporary area with roots in several classic works on capitalism. **John Locke** in the 17th century supported capitalism with his "labor-mixing" theory of property **rights**: one obtains rightful ownership of property when one mixes one's labor with goods not yet appropriated. (**Robert Nozick** provides a contemporary version of this view.) Then **Adam Smith** in the 18th century defended capitalism with his "invisible hand" theory: if individuals pursue their interests in a free market, the forces of competition will act to allocate society's resources in the most efficient way possible. (**Ayn Rand** uses this idea to support ethical **egoism**.) After these pro-capitalism treatises, **Karl Marx** criticized capitalism in the 19th century; he argued that capitalism exploits and alienates workers, brings crises of overproduction, reduces honored professions to the status of wage laborers, and allows owners to take for themselves value that is produced by workers. In the 20th century, Milton Friedman, winner of the Nobel Prize for economics, responded to Marxist criticisms and defended capitalism by arguing that it is necessary for a society truly to be free.

As business ethics became a distinct sub-discipline in the 20th century, it focused less on justifying capitalism and more on specific issues about capitalism and business. Many of these issues concern the corporations that dominate contemporary capitalism. One central issue is corporate social responsibility. Friedman adopted the *classical model* and argued that corporations have no social responsibility per se. Their only responsibility is to maximize the wealth of their shareholders within the bounds of law and avoiding fraud. In this way, corporations contribute to the good of society through new and cheaper products, more jobs, and greater wealth. Others, such as R. Edward Freeman, adopted the *stakeholder model* and argued that corporations must take into account their impact on society. They must consider the interests not only of shareholders but also of *stakeholders* (those affected positively or negatively by corporations). For some, this merely is a strategic concern, while for others it is a **normative** matter.

Business ethicists also have explored the moral status of corporations. Friedman argued that the corporation is an abstract entity without moral standing. Although the corporation is a "legal person," with the legal right to own property, enter contracts, and sue in courts, it is not a moral person; it is not morally **responsible** for activities undertaken in its name. Rather, individuals are responsible for what is done by their corporation, which merely is a legal umbrella for them to pursue certain common goals. Others, such as Peter French, argued that the corporation has an internal decision structure that allows us to recognize corporate intentions. Through these, we are able to place moral responsibility on the corporation itself and hold it accountable as a **moral agent** for its decisions and actions.

Consumers are one of the groups most affected by business and corporations. Business ethicists have focused on two broad areas involving consumers: marketing and product safety.

Much has been written about deception in marketing. While ethicists generally agree that deceptive marketing practices are unethical, they often disagree about what counts as deceptive. Although most let marketers make false or exaggerated claims that would not be taken seriously, they do not allow deceptive claims that would mislead a reasonable person. They disagree about what a reasonable person should or should not know. Another issue is whether advertising and other marketing practices impair our **autonomy**. Many argue that advertising dulls critical evaluation skills needed for persons to develop full autonomy; this is especially true with advertising directed at children, who are just developing autonomy. Others believe that critics overstate the impact of advertising; perhaps one's autonomy is shaped more by family and other social institutions.

With product safety, there is debate over the responsibility of businesses for harm caused by their products. Some adopt a *caveat emptor* (buyer beware) approach: consumers need to learn about and take responsibility for risks that products may involve. Others argue that this approach is unfair to customers; products often are too complex for us to determine their risks and businesses should produce products without defects. Some hold that businesses are responsible for harm caused by any defective product (*strict product liability*), while others hold that they are responsible only for harm due to negligence on their part (*due care*). Other issues arise from products, such as guns and cigarettes, that cause harm even when not defective.

With regard to employees, the central issue is employee rights. Some reject employee rights and defend *employment at will*: employees serve at the will of employers who can hire, fire, promote, and demote as they see fit. Likewise, employees are free to quit if they are unhappy with working conditions. The main argument for employment at will is that it results in an equal playing field for employers and employees. Others reject this doctrine and argue that it favors employers. Except in cases of low unemployment or highly specialized skills, employers have the advantage; it is far easier for them to replace employees who quit than it is for employees to find new jobs after being fired. To equalize the playing field, employees need some set of rights. Advocates of employee rights often include the right not to be fired without just cause, the right to privacy, the right to occupational safety, the right to unionize, the right to blow the whistle on wrongdoings, the right not to be discriminated against, and the right not to be sexually harassed.

Globalization brings further issues. As multinational corporations grow, debate arises over cultural differences. Imagine a firm doing business in a country that has radically different views about bribes or about **discrimination** (**racist** or **sexist**); should the firm follow the local practice? Consider "sweatshops" that produce products in **poor** countries using cheap labor. Some believe that this practice is a colonialism that exploits desperate people; corporations should pay a living wage to workers regardless of where they reside. Others believe that so-called sweatshops benefit the workers and countries involved; the wages are high by local standards and eventually will promote a better economy and higher standard of living for poor countries.

The **environment** raises issues. How should we reduce pollution and global warming—by government regulations or by market incentives? There is interest in the notion of *sustainable business*: how can business meet present needs while preserving resources and the environment for future generations?

Diversity is a concern. Ought corporations to promote diversity through affirmative action programs? Should women make the same as men for the same jobs? While some argue that it is not the role of business to take the lead on such matters, others argue that business is in a good position to take such a lead. This entry sketches some important issues in business ethics. New issues continue to arise. For example, recent corporate scandals have led ethicists to scrutinize accounting techniques. And the relatively new practice of corporations owning, and being beneficiaries of, insurance on the lives of their rank-and-file workers has led Earl Spurgin to charge that these corporations have an unethical conflict of interest.

Some well-known business ethicists not mentioned earlier in this entry include John Boatright, Norman Bowie, George Brenkert, Richard De George, Joseph DesJardins, Thomas Donaldson, John McCall, Patrick Murphy, Lisa Newton, Manuel Velasquez, and Patricia Werhane.

BUTLER, JOSEPH (1692–1752). English philosopher and Anglican bishop. Despite being a bishop who expressed his ideas in sermons, Butler, like other **modern ethicists**, based ethics on the natural world instead of divine revelation. His *Fifteen Sermons Preached at the Rolls Chapel* (1729) was very influential for the next two centuries and was the most commonly reprinted work in ethics in the 19th century.

Butler defends **natural law** ethics against the ideas of **Thomas Hobbes**. Both thinkers base ethics on human nature, which they see as open to empirical observation. But they differ in their accounts of human nature. Hobbes sees humans as mechanical systems driven by desire and self-interest (*see* **egoism**). For us to judge a thing to be **good** merely means that we desire it. The pre-social state of nature has no moral rules; it is a "do anything necessary to survive" world that is miserable for everyone. Our notions of right/wrong and just/unjust are based not on nature but on convention; they come from a **social contract**, enforced by **political** authority, that we agree to so we can avoid the state of nature and cooperate in ways that help us to satisfy our needs. Even when we do things that benefit others, we are motivated only by self-interest; if I stop to help a bicyclist with a flat tire, I do so only because, say, I want to feel good about myself and avoid feeling guilty—not because I care about others for their own sake.

When Butler observes our behavior, he sees something different. While he admits that we often are motivated by self-interest, he thinks Hobbes overstates this motivation. Butler sees self-interest as one motive among many; he contends that four things motivate us:

- particular impulses (like hunger, thirst, anger, and the desire for fame and possessions),
- self-love,
- **benevolence (love your neighbor)**, and
- **conscience** (our **intuitive** grasp of right and wrong).

In the natural order of things, particular impulses are to be restrained by rational self-love; so we restrain our impulse to eat six hamburgers by the thought that this would make us sick. Against Hobbes, the object of our desire is not only self-interest but also various things, such as the eating of six hamburgers, which motivate independently of thoughts about self-interest. Similarly, self-love is to be restrained by benevolence (so we keep from doing what helps us but hurts others more), and benevolence is to be restrained by conscience (seen in non-**consequentialist** terms, so we do not use evil means to help others). We are **happier** if we follow this hierarchy, including the priority of conscience, since this is part both of **God**'s plan and of our human nature.

Hobbes might object that we get satisfaction from following conscience or being benevolent, and this satisfaction is what we ultimately desire in doing such actions; since these actions are only a means to our satisfaction, we seek only our own good. Butler would reply that, yes, we do get satisfaction from doing these things. But we do not desire to do these things because of the satisfaction; instead, we get satisfaction from doing them because we first desire to do them. Hobbes has things backward; and he confuses the object of our desire (to follow our conscience) with the satisfaction we get when our desire is satisfied.

Butler believes that self-love, benevolence, and conscience usually support and reinforce each other; for example, good feelings from helping others motivate us to perform further benevolent acts. But these motivations may also conflict, as when a professor wants to go home but stays to help a struggling student who arrives late for office hours. Hobbes would say that the professor acts out of self-interest and follows the strongest desire; Butler would say that the professor is motivated by benevolence and conscience. Butler thought that conscience separates us from **animals**. Both humans and dogs have desires, but only humans can reflect on them and judge them to be right or wrong, good or bad. Butler would say that Hobbes's account of human nature is a better account of the nature of some lower animals. Hobbes ignores the capacity of conscience that makes us **moral agents** capable of **autonomous** moral thinking. The professor can reflect on the desire to go home and the desire to help the student, determine which is the right one to satisfy, and act on that judgment. We can hold the professor **responsible** for judging or acting incorrectly. If we merely were the mechanistic beings Hobbes thinks we are, the professor could not judge competing desires and we could not hold the professor responsible for judgments and actions.

Butler leaves a gap in his ethics by not explaining better how conscience works and why we should see it as part of human nature rather than as coming from a convenient political arrangement. Many think this gap comes from his theology; Butler seems to think conscience needs no explanation because it is part of God's plan to make us fit creatures for society.

Butler's ideas form a bridge between Hobbes and **David Hume**. Hume's natural sympathy for others mirrors Butler's benevolence, and Hume's **impartial** judgments mirror Butler's conscience. Both thinkers argue for a reflective capacity that is beyond the mechanistic view of Hobbes. Butler's conscience perhaps anticipates **Immanuel Kant**'s idea that moral agents create the moral law through their own reason.

$$- \text{C} -$$

CAPITAL PUNISHMENT. State-sanctioned **killing** of human beings as a form of **punishment**. The centuries-long debate about capital punishment was given new energy by the U.S. Supreme Court, which banned the death penalty in 1972 but reinstated it in 1976.

Is capital punishment morally permissible? There are three general justifications for punishment: *reform*, *deterrence*, and *retribution*. Supporters of capital punishment usually argue from deterrence or retribution since the reform approach (with roots in **Aristotle**) gives them little support; it is difficult to argue that the death penalty reforms and rehabilitates criminals.

The deterrence justification (with roots in **utilitarianism**) argues that the death penalty is needed to deter potential murderers, who fear death more than prison. Critics object on various grounds. Some claim that many criminals fear confinement more than death. Others point out that most murders and other heinous crimes are committed by irrational people and stem more from passion or mind-altering drugs than from a deliberation that considers punishments. Others argue that murder rates are not significantly lower in places with the death penalty. Still others argue that capital punishment costs much more than imprisonment in a society that allows lengthy legal appeals; without such appeals, however, a greater number of innocent people would be executed.

The retribution defense of capital punishment has its roots in **Immanuel Kant** and in the **Biblical** notion of an "eye for an eye" (which was intended to limit punishment to the harm the offender caused). Retributivists argue that punishment that fits the crime "balances the scales" of **justice** since criminals get what they deserve. So murderers need to die; justice is violated otherwise since the murderer would live while the victim's family suffer the loss of their loved one. Some critics object that the notion of "balancing the scales" is misguided and often unattainable. Should not, on this view, a murderer who has killed a member of one's family have a member of his family killed, so he can experience the same pain? And how can we restore the balance when a serial killer has killed several people? Other critics argue that retribution is mere vengeance and thus illegitimate; while vengeance, like anger, is a natural emotion, it does not give a moral basis for action. Kantians respond that retribution, rather than being mere vengeance, respectfully treats criminals as they themselves will people (others and themselves) to be treated. But critics object that murderers normally act from passion instead of from a reasoned principled approach that expresses how they will everyone to be treated.

Some oppose capital punishment on religious grounds, often appealing to the **sanctity of life**; since human life is from **God**, it is sacred and can be taken only by God. Some religious people recognize the **right** to kill when needed for self-defense, as in times of **war**, and argue that capital punishment is needed for self-defense. Others say society can defend itself from murderers by keeping them in prison.

Many object that capital punishment, as currently practiced, is unfair. People sentenced to death are often discovered, before or after their time of execution, to be innocent. And among those who commit similar crimes, African-Americans and the **poor** are statistically more likely to be given the death penalty; this may be in part because such people often cannot afford the best attorneys. Given this practical unfairness, we should not have capital punishment.

Supporters and opponents of capital punishment for the most part agree that any executions should be as humane as possible. So lethal injection, which is often believed to cause less suffering, has in many places replaced more traditional forms of the death penalty, such as the gas chamber, electric chair, firing squad, hanging, beheading, or crucifixion. Others argue that, despite being more gruesome, methods such as hanging and beheading, when carried out properly, cause less suffering because they result in quicker deaths.

There are further issues. Should insanity excuse one from the death penalty? If so, how should insanity be defined for this purpose? Should the mentally retarded (in terms of IQ) be subject to execution? As our understanding of mental illnesses and **disabilities** grows, such issues will become more complex as long as capital punishment is legal.

CAPITALISM. *See* BIOETHICS; BUSINESS ETHICS; EVOLUTIONISM; LOCKE, JOHN; MARX, KARL; NINETEENTH-CENTURY ETHICS; NOZICK, ROBERT; POLITICAL PHILOSOPHY; SMITH, ADAM; SOCIALISM; RAND, AYN.

CARE. *See* GILLIGAN, CAROL; LOVE YOUR NEIGHBOR.

CATEGORICAL IMPERATIVES. *See* HYPOTHETICAL/CATEGORICAL IMPERATIVES; KANT, IMMANUEL.

CENSORSHIP. *See* ACADEMIC FREEDOM; MILL, JOHN STUART; POLITICAL PHILOSOPHY; ROUSSEAU, JEAN-JACQUES.

CHARITY, PRINCIPLE OF. The principle, often appealed to in philosophical discussions, that we ought to interpret another's unclear ideas in such a way that they become as sensible and plausible as possible. This may involve understanding ambiguous terms one way rather than another, supplying implicit premises, or adding needed qualifications to statements. The principle of charity is part of what might be called the *ethics of thinking and rational discussion. See also* CONSISTENCY; ETHICS OF BELIEF; HABERMAS, JÜRGEN; LOGIC; LOVE YOUR NEIGHBOR.

CHRISTIAN ETHICS. *See* AQUINAS, THOMAS; AUGUSTINE; BIBLICAL ETHICS; DIVINE COMMAND THEORY; GLOBAL ETHICS; GOD; LOVE YOUR NEIGHBOR; MEDIEVAL ETHICS; MORAL THEOLOGY; NATURAL LAW.

CIVIL DISOBEDIENCE. Deliberate nonviolent lawbreaking by citizens to protest in**justice** and appeal to the conscience of the wider community. Henry David Thoreau (1817–1862), an American who refused to pay taxes as an act of protest against slavery and the **war** with Mexico, defended the idea. Mahatma Gandhi (1869–1948) used civil disobedience in India to oppose British colonial rule (*see* **Hindu ethics**), and **Martin Luther King** (1929–1968) used it in the U.S. to oppose segregation. There is a regular protest against the School of the Americas (now called "Western Hemisphere Institute for Security Cooperation"), which involves illegal trespassing on its grounds in Georgia; the school allegedly trains **terrorists** to further U.S. interests in Latin America.

King, who gave one of the clearest defenses of civil disobedience, sees the practice as one of moderation, midway between using violence and doing nothing. He and others would restrict its use to major injustices; one cannot resort to civil disobedience for minor matters.

While most philosophers today would defend civil disobedience in certain cases, some classic approaches to **political philosophy** would forbid it. **Plato**'s perfect society permits little in the way of reform by such means since the philosopher-kings know what is best for society. **Thomas Hobbes** states that one who disobeys the sovereign acts unjustly; his **social contract** yields all power to the sovereign. But **John Locke** would permit civil disobedience, since he even allows the people to dissolve a government that fails to secure their natural **rights**.

COGNITIVISM/NON-COGNITIVISM. *Cognitivism* holds that moral beliefs are *true or false* in the full and robust sense of these terms; cognitivist views include **intuitionism, divine command theory, natural law, naturalism** (including **evolutionism, ideal observer theory, cultural relativism,** and **subjectivism**), and perhaps **J. L. Mackie**'s *error theory* (which holds that all moral beliefs are false).

Non-cognitivism is the view that moral beliefs are not *true or false* in the full and robust sense of these terms; non-cognitivist views include **emotivism** and **prescriptivism.** Some non-cognitivists hold that moral beliefs are true or false in a manner of speaking, even though they do not refer to moral facts; perhaps we can say "It is *true* that act A ought to be done" if we intend this as a longer way to say (or agree with) "Act A ought to be done" or if we are just referring to the truth of the factual claims (perhaps that act A would maximize human happiness) to which we would appeal in defending our moral judgment. Some object that this sense of "true or false" is weak and misleading.

Another complication is that some emotivists and prescriptivists, like **William Frankena**, argue that we would all agree on our moral beliefs if we were ideally rational and that this leads to a kind of "moral truth"—which is defined not in terms of correspondence to an independent moral fact but in terms of what ideally rational inquirers would agree on. Perhaps such views are better viewed as cognitivist.

The *moral realism/anti-realism* distinction is somewhat related but does not coincide exactly. *Moral realism* is roughly the view that moral beliefs are robustly true or false and there are objective moral truths that we can know and discover but do not depend on human attitudes or conventions. Moral realisms include intuitionism, natural law, and evolutionism. Moral anti-realisms include cultural relativism, subjectivism, emotivism, prescriptivism, and error theory. Divine command theory and ideal observer theory are seen sometimes as realisms and sometimes as anti-realisms. *See also* ETHICS: METAETHICS.

COMMON SENSE. *See* EMOTIVISM; HARMAN, GILBERT; INTUITIONISM; KOHLBERG, LAWRENCE; MOORE, G. E.; NINETEENTH-CENTURY ETHICS; REID, THOMAS; ROSS, W. D.; SIDGWICK, HENRY; UTILITARIANISM.

COMMUNITARIANISM. *See* LIBERALISM/COMMUNITARIANISM.

COMPUTER ETHICS. The study of moral issues involving computers. The first large-scale electronic computer, the ENIAC, dates back to 1946; so computers are fairly new. Today personal computers are all around us and link us to the rest of the world by e-mail and the Internet. We increasingly carry in our pockets cell phones with computer capacities more powerful than the original ENIAC. We use such technology to write books, follow the news, do research, plan our activities, conduct business, take pictures, listen to music, watch movies, and buy products from around the world. The future promises increasing technology and greater impact on our lives.

Expanding technology sometimes gives us new and perplexing moral issues, where traditional wisdom often provides little guidance. Philosophers have become involved in this area; the first textbook, Deborah Johnson's *Computer Ethics*, appeared in 1985.

Consider intellectual property: software, books, music, movies, and so forth. Technology makes us able to pirate such items—to duplicate copyrighted or patented materials illegally. Is it right to do this? Some take piracy lightly, especially if the materials are overpriced. Others see piracy as wrongful stealing and as harmful to society; authors who are poorly compensated might not produce similar work in the future. While there are laws against piracy, the Internet resists being bound by the laws of one particular country; pirates can conduct business from places where piracy is legal or not prosecuted.

Often it is unclear what the law should be. Soon it will be possible to make the text of most books available to everyone on the Internet; this would be wonderful for research. But how can authors and publishers be compensated? What should the law be, and how can it be enforced across international boundaries? Can people all over the **globe**, coming from different cultural traditions, agree on what to do?

Other issues include how to deal with

- computer viruses, e-mail spam, and spyware;
- **privacy** in a world where technology could take this away;
- employees who surf the Web instead of doing their jobs;
- **pornography** (and its availability to children);
- job displacements due to technology;
- Internet crime (from stealing credit card numbers);
- basic politeness in Internet discussions; and
- plagiarism from Internet sources.

There also are **business** issues about computer companies and **political** issues about laws.

CONFIDENTIALITY. *See* BIOETHICS.

CONFUCIUS (c. 551–479 BC, also called Kung Fu Zi). Ancient Chinese teacher who had a great influence on the ethical thinking of the East. His *Analects* likely was the world's first extended treatise on ethics; it teaches an elevated approach to morality and emphasizes public service in government. From 1313 to 1905, Confucian ethics was a major part of the civil service exam in China.

The *Analects* consists of proverbs, anecdotes, and brief dialogues between Confucius and others. Among its many points to ponder are these representative ideas:

- A gentleman considers **justice**, a lesser person considers self-interest (*see* **egoism**). (Confucius redefines the aristocratic term "gentleman" to refer to one who lives virtuously; we do something similar when we describe moral motivation as "noble.")

- You can still be **happy** if you have only coarse grain to eat, water to drink, and your arm for a pillow. Riches and honor without justice are like passing clouds.
- We can learn much from any two random people; we can imitate their good qualities and take their bad qualities as a warning.
- Goodness cannot be out of reach since I attain it when I seek it.
- Rulers should ensure that a state possesses sufficient food, weapons, and trust. Weapons are the least important of these; trust is the most important.
- A gentlemen brings the good out of people; a vulgar man brings the bad out of people.
- Reputation, which comes from appearances, differs from **virtue**.
- Scholars who seek material comforts do not deserve to be called scholars.
- Repay hatred with justice, and kindness with kindness.
- The just sometimes give up their lives to preserve their humanity.
- Demand much from yourself and little from others.
- A gentleman is principled but not rigid.
- Our lives degenerate if we love humanity but not learning.
- A gentleman hates those who dwell on what is hateful in others.

Confucius says almost nothing about the **gods**, the afterlife, or **karma**. He avoids the paradoxical and mystical language found in some other Eastern traditions. His main theme is how to develop one's humanity (or humaneness, or concern for others).

When Confucius was challenged to give the unifying idea behind his teaching, he used a negative form of the **golden rule**: "Do not do to others what you do not wish them to do to you." Since this differs from the positive form that occurs in Christianity ("Do to others what you wish them to do to you"), some have thought that Confucius teaches a negative morality, that he gives us negative duties (not to harm others) but not positive duties (to do good to others). But critics of this idea contend that both Christian and Confucian ethics have a balance of positive and negative duties, and that Confucius sometimes uses his golden rule in a positive way. In his short *The Doctrine of the Mean*, Confucius tells us to serve our fathers as we would expect our sons to serve us, to serve our rulers as we would expect our ministers to serve us, to serve our older brother as we would expect our younger brother to serve us, and to serve our friends as we would expect them to serve us—all positive applications of the golden rule.

Confucius had much in common with **Aristotle** (384–322 BC), who lived in Greece about a century and a half later. Both thinkers had students who put their teacher's ideas into substantial ethical works (the *Analects* and the *Nicomachean Ethics*, respectively) that were the first of their kind in their parts of the world. Both thinkers were enormously influential, and continue to be so today. Both thinkers had devoted followers (Confucians and Aristotelians) and sharp critics (**Buddhists** and **Daoists** in the case of Confucius). Both thinkers teach an elevated approach to morality that stresses morality's social and **political** dimension; there are many parallels in their moral views.

The two differ in their method. Aristotle writes in an analytic, theoretical manner; he is concerned with principles, definitions, alternative views, and arguments in favor of one view over another. In contrast, Confucius writes as a sage, in a practical and less theoretical way; he gives us proverbs and anecdotes, and mostly avoids principles, definitions, alternatives, and arguments.

Mencius (c. 372–289 BC) was the most important disciple of Confucius. Mencius contended, against thinkers of his time, that humans have an innate concern for others that can either grow or wither, depending on social influences and personal effort, but can never totally disappear. So morality grows out of something that is part of our nature.

Classical Confucianism is not a religion but a philosophy of life. However, some forms of Confucianism have added religious elements, including gods, temples, worship, and the veneration of Confucius.

CONSCIENCE. Raises various issues, including what it is, what rational authority it has, whether we morally ought always to follow it, whether we in fact always do follow it, and whether we have a right not to be forced to act against it.

What is conscience? In popular thinking, conscience is that "little voice" inside us that tells us right from wrong. Some skeptical philosophers say they do not hear this voice. Others say they hear it, perhaps faintly at times, but it cannot be trusted because it often just internalizes cultural prejudices like "Treat people of such and such a group badly." Philosophers tend to define "conscience" more abstractly, as the ability to **know right from wrong**.

What rational authority does conscience have? Suppose you think things through in a proper way and conclude that act A is what you morally **ought** to do. Does it then necessarily violate reason if you decide *not* to do A? Some thinkers say no; they argue that the rational thing to do is determined by what promotes our desires or interests, which our moral duties may or may not do. They think morality binds us rationally only as a system of **hypothetical imperatives**: if we have certain goals that moral action promotes, then we ought (rationally) to act morally. Others disagree and argue that it violates reason to act against what we know to be our moral duty. Some look at morality as a system of objective *categorical imperatives* in the manner of **Immanuel Kant**; we are logically **inconsistent** (and thus irrational) if we think we ought to do something and yet do not do it. Others see moral beliefs as just expressing our feelings or desires (*see* **subjectivism, emotivism,** and **prescriptivism**); we are then inconsistent if we act against our moral beliefs since we are acting against our own feelings or desires.

Is it our moral duty always to follow our conscience? Suppose you think things through and conclude that act A is what you morally ought to do. Then are you morally required to do A? Some thinkers answer by distinguishing between your *subjective duty* (which is based on your evaluation of the case, which may be erroneous) and your *objective duty* (which is based on a correct evaluation of the case). If you think it your duty to do A (e.g., commit mass murder), then it could be that your thinking is mistaken and your *objective duty* is not to do A. But even then, they would say, your *subjective duty* is to do A, to follow what you think you ought to do.

Other thinkers give a different answer. They say that we have a duty to avoid inconsistencies between our moral judgments and how we live (*see* **conscientiousness**); we violate this if we combine *believing* that we ought to do A now and with *not acting* to do A now. They say "We ought to follow our conscience" could be taken in two ways:

(1)   We ought to avoid inconsistencies between our moral beliefs and our actions.
(2)   Our conscience is always correct: if we believe we ought to do something, then this really is what we ought to do.

These thinkers say (1) is correct; some add that acting against our moral beliefs is always culpable—but that following our moral beliefs is not culpable unless how we formed these moral beliefs is culpable. (2) is clearly wrong since it entails "If we believe we ought to commit mass murder, then this is really what we ought to do."

Do we always in fact follow our conscience—so if we think we ought to do A then we will in fact do A (if we are able)? **Socrates** thought the answer is yes: we will always do what we know is right, so all bad actions result from ignorance. **Aristotle**, in his discussion of **weakness of will**, disagreed; he thought strong feelings and human weakness can prevent us from doing what we know is right.

Finally, do we have a **right** to follow our own conscience—so it is wrong to force one to act against one's conscience? Many thinkers accept such a right but qualify it for extreme cases; presumably we ought to stop **terrorists** who take it to be their duty to commit mass murder. *See also* AUTONOMY; BUTLER, JOSEPH; DARWIN, CHARLES; FOOT, PHILIPPA; WHY BE MORAL QUESTION.

CONSCIENTIOUSNESS. To be *conscientious*, as we often use the term, is to take one's responsibilities seriously. However, it is also possible to look at *conscientiousness* as a kind of **consistency** between one's moral beliefs and one's life (including one's desires, resolutions, and actions); we violate conscientiousness if our moral beliefs clash with how we live and want others to live. Suppose I hold the pacifist belief that one ought never to kill a human being for any reason. If I am conscientious (consistent), then (a) I will never intentionally kill a human being myself; (b) I will be resolved not to kill for any reason (even to protect my life or the lives of my family); and (c) I will not want others to kill for any reason (even to save my life).

The requirement that we be consistent in this respect leads to a weak form of **Immanuel Kant**'s formula of universal law: "To be consistent in holding a moral principle, you must will people to follow it, even in imagined cases where it would apply to how people are to treat you." Suppose I accept the principle, "All short people ought to be beaten up—just because they are short." If I am consistent, then I must will this as a universal law, which includes desiring that if I were short then I would be beaten up. If I do not desire this, then I am inconsistent in holding my principle and my moral thinking is flawed. *See also* CONSCIENCE; GOLDEN RULE.

CONSEQUENTIALISM/NON-CONSEQUENTIALISM. The two main rival approaches to normative ethics (*see* **ethics: normative**).

Consequentialism is the general view that we **ought** always to do whatever maximizes **good** consequences. Consequentialism denies that any kind of act (such as keeping promises) is right or wrong in itself;

instead, the rightness or wrongness of an act depends on its consequences. Popular kinds of consequentialism include **utilitarianism**, which considers consequences for everyone, and **egoism**, which considers only consequences for the agent. Intermediate views are possible, for example that we ought to consider only our group (our family, city, nation, race, or whatever) or that we ought to consider everyone but ourselves (**altruistic** consequentialism). Another issue is whether to appraise the goodness of consequences in terms of pleasure and pain, or **happiness**, or a variety of goods. Consequentialism is often called **teleological ethics**, although this term is sometimes used more broadly. Prominent consequentialists include the utilitarians **Jeremy Bentham, Richard Brandt, R. M. Hare, James Mill, John Stuart Mill, G. E. Moore, Henry Sidgwick**, and **Peter Singer**, and the egoist **Ayn Rand**.

Non-consequentialism, sometimes called *deontologism*, is the general view that some kinds of action (such as killing the innocent) are wrong in themselves, and not just wrong because of bad consequences. Such kinds of action may be **exceptionlessly** wrong (as **Immanuel Kant** held) or else just have some independent moral weight against them (as **W. D. Ross** held). A major issue is which moral rules to accept and how stringently each is to be applied. Other prominent non-consequentialists include **Elizabeth Anscombe, Joseph Butler, John Finnis, Samuel Pufendorf, John Rawls**, and **Bernard Williams**.

The key issue here is whether consequences alone determine right and wrong, or whether some actions are wrong in themselves independently of consequences. Imagine that your wife is diagnosed as having terminal cancer but does not know about this. She asks you about the diagnosis. Should you tell her the truth, or should you lie? If you were a consequentialist who followed the greatest happiness principle, you would think lying is right if it best promotes happiness. Would your wife be happier if she did not know about the illness? Would she be distressed if she later found out that you lied to her? How would telling her or not telling her affect your happiness and the happiness of others? On this approach, you would not think lying is wrong in itself; instead, you would think lying is right if it maximizes the total happiness of all affected parties. You would look at the issue differently if you were a non-consequentialist. You would then likely think lying is wrong in itself and that your wife has a **right** to know; to lie would be to treat her wrongly, even if it maximized the total happiness. You may hold that lying is always wrong regardless of consequences; or you may hold, more moderately, that the inherent wrongness of lying has to be somehow weighed against considerations about consequences. Many thinkers try to combine the two approaches. For example, *rule utilitarians* sometimes defend strict moral rules, much like non-consequentialist rules, but on the basis of their usefulness to society. And some non-consequentialists recognize and emphasize our duty to bring about good consequences, but limit this duty by others that specify that certain kinds of action are wrong in themselves.

While the consequentialism/non-consequentialism distinction commonly applies to the rightness and wrongness of *actions*, a similar distinction can be applied to **virtue**. We might describe a *virtuous person* as one who habitually acts to maximize good consequences—or as one who habitually acts in a way that is honest, respectful of another's property, and so forth, where these virtues correspond to non-consequentialist duties. *See also* ABORTION AND INFANTICIDE; BENEVOLENCE, DECISION THEORY; DOUBLE EFFECT; END-JUSTIFIES-MEANS; EUTHANASIA; GOLDEN RULE; IMPARTIALITY; INTUITIONISM; LOVE YOUR NEIGHBOR; MATHEMATICS; NATURAL LAW; OUGHT; PUNISHMENT; SCIENCE; SUICIDE; TERRORISM.

CONSISTENCY. To be *consistent* is to have one's beliefs, desires, resolutions, and actions in harmony with each other. Inconsistency is generally seen as a defect or a failing.

Consistency requirements can be expressed conveniently as imperatives. These first two prescribe *consistency among beliefs*:

(1) Do not combine inconsistent beliefs. If A is inconsistent with B, then do not combine *believing A* with *believing B*.

(2) Do not believe something without believing what follows from it. If A logically entails B, then do not combine *believing A* with *not believing B*. (Some would weaken this to apply only to logical entailments of which we are, or should be, aware.)

These tell us to avoid certain inconsistent combinations but do not tell us specifically what to believe. If you violate consistency, perhaps by holding principle A but rejecting B that logically follows from it, then you have to change something: you must reject A or accept B; but consistency alone does not tell you which to do.

The appeal to consistency is important in ethical discussions. When we appeal to moral principles to defend our beliefs, we can be criticized if we do not apply them consistently. So white **racists** who claim that people of lower intelligence ought to be treated poorly can be criticized if they do not also believe that *white* people of lower intelligence ought to be treated poorly.

Here are some further consistency principles:

(3) *Ends-Means Consistency*: Keep your means in harmony with your ends. Do not combine *wanting* to attain end E, *believing* that taking means M is needed to attain this end, and *not acting* to take means M. (This resembles a **hypothetical imperative**.)

(4) *Conscientiousness*: Keep your actions, resolutions, and desires in harmony with your moral beliefs. For example, do not combine *believing* that you ought to do A with *not acting* to do A.

(5) *Impartiality*: Make similar evaluations about similar actions, regardless of the individuals involved. For example, do not combine *believing* that you ought to do A to X with *not believing* that in an imagined reversed situation X ought to do A to you.

(6) *Golden Rule*: Treat others only as you consent to being treated in the same situation. Do not combine *acting* to do A to X with *not being willing* that if the situation were reversed then A would be done to you. (This is like impartiality, except that it deals with the consistency between how we act and how we will that others act toward us, while impartiality deals with consistency of beliefs.)

(7) *Formula of Universal Law*: Act only as you are willing for anyone to act in the same situation—regardless of imagined variations of time or person. Do not combine *acting* to do A with *not accepting* "For some universal property F, F is the complete description in universal terms of my doing A, and, in any actual or hypothetical situation, any act that is F may be done."

(8) *Universalizability*: If it is permissible for you to do something, then it would be permissible for anyone else to do the same thing in the same situation. If act A is permissible, then there is some universal property (or conjunction of such properties) F, such that: act A is F, and in any actual or hypothetical case every act that is F is permissible.

While universalizability is expressed here using "permissible," it also holds for other ethical terms, like "**ought**" or "**good**."

While consistency principles (1) to (7) are formulated using "Do not combine," they also could be formulated using "One *ought* not to combine." While the former is simpler, the latter more clearly brings out the ethical nature of the principles. The broader "One ought to be consistent" principle that such consistency norms assume is subject to unstated qualifications. For the most part, we do seem to have a duty to be consistent. But, assuming that "ought" implies "can," this duty can be nullified when we are unable to be consistent; such inability can come from emotional turmoil or our incapacity to grasp complex inferences. And the obligation to be consistent can be overridden by other factors; if Dr. Evil would destroy the world unless we were inconsistent in some way, then our duty to be consistent would be overridden.

While philosophers generally agree that we *ought* to be consistent (subject to some qualifications), they differ about *why* we ought to be consistent. The consistency norm could be defended from a wide range of perspectives—for example, as a **divine command** (*see* **Biblical ethics**), as a cultural norm (*see* **cultural relativism**), as an expression of our feelings (*see* **emotivism** and **subjectivism**), as a socially useful norm (*see* **utilitarianism**), as a principle that helps us to get along with people and so promotes our own self-interest (*see* **Thomas Hobbes**), or as self-evident (*see* **intuitionism**).

Principles (1) through (8) above are formulated in two ways, the second way using variables like "A" and "B." For example, (1) says:

- "Do not combine inconsistent beliefs."
- "If A is inconsistent with B, then do not combine *believing A* with *believing B*."

The second version is a *formal ethical principle*; it is *formal* in that it is expressed using only variables (for things like persons, propositions, and actions) and abstract logical or quasi-logical notions (including terms like "believing" and "desiring"). *Formal ethics*, which studies such formal ethical principles, is a bridge between **logic** and **ethics** since it can be systematized conveniently in a formal logical system.

Consistency is often included in **rational moral thinking**, along with things like being impartial (which is here seen as a species of consistency) and informed (*see* **information**). *See also* CONSCIENCE; HARE, R. M.; IDEAL OBSERVER THEORY; KANT, IMMANUEL; LEWIS, C. I.; NAGEL, THOMAS; RELATIVISM; SOCRATES.

CONTINENTAL ETHICS. *See* TWENTIETH-CENTURY ETHICS.

CONTRACTARIANISM. *See* SOCIAL CONTRACT.

CORPORATIONS. *See* BUSINESS ETHICS.

CRITICAL THEORY. *See* HABERMAS, JÜRGEN.

CULTURAL RELATIVISM. The view that "X is **good**" means "The majority (of the society in question) approves of X"; more generally, the view that terms like "good," "bad," "right," and "wrong" describe social norms. On this view, moral claims are **relative** to culture: slavery is good in a society that approves of it but bad in one that disapproves of it—it is not good or bad objectively. Morality is a cultural construct; just as societies create different styles of food and clothing, so too they create different moral codes. Societies disagree widely about moral issues (like polygamy and infanticide) and there is no clear way to resolve the differences. Hence there are no objective truths about right or wrong. Cultural relativists view themselves as tolerant; they reject the "we are right and they are wrong" attitude toward other cultures; instead, they think the other side is not "wrong" but just "different."

Cultural relativism is popular among many **anthropologists**, intellectuals, and college students (at least when they first encounter the idea); but philosophers find problems with the view. Imagine that you lived in a society that approved of **racism**. According to cultural relativism, you would have to agree that racism is *good* (since "good" just means "socially approved"). You could not justifiably say "Racism is socially approved but bad" since this is self-contradictory. Cultural relativism denies us the freedom to make moral judgments; it imposes conformity and an uncritical acceptance of social norms, many of which may be based on ignorance.

Some are puzzled about how a society where everyone followed cultural relativism could change its values. Change generally comes when people *disagree* with current norms—as did **Martin Luther King** when he said that segregation was socially accepted but not good—but this is **inconsistent** according to this present view. Another problem is that cultural relativism seems not to allow for moral progress. One cannot say that our social norms improved morally when we abolished slavery; one can say only that our norms changed.

Cultural relativists often see the world as neatly divided into distinct societies. Each society has little or no moral disagreement since the majority view determines what is right or wrong. But the world is not like that. Instead, we see a mixture of overlapping societies and groups; and individuals do not necessarily follow the majority view. This raises the subgroup problem. You are part of a specific nation, state, city, and neighborhood; and you are part of various family, professional, religious, and peer groups. These groups often have conflicting values. On cultural relativism, when you say "Racism is wrong" you mean "My society disapproves of racism." But to which society does this refer? Perhaps most in your national and religious societies disapprove of racism, while most in your professional and family societies approve of it. Cultural relativism could give clear guidance only if we belonged to just one society; but we are all multicultural to some extent.

Cultural relativism does not try to establish common norms between societies. As technology "shrinks" the planet, moral disputes between societies become more important. Nation A approves of equal **rights** for women (or for other races or religions), but nation B disapproves. What is a multinational **business** that works in both societies to do? Or societies A and B have value conflicts that lead to **war**. Cultural relativism provides little help for such problems (*see* **global ethics**).

Cultural relativists often pride themselves on their tolerance. But according to cultural relativism, ridiculing the values of other cultures would be good if it were socially approved. And minority views in our own culture would automatically be wrong.

Those who believe in objective values need not say "We are right and they are wrong." Instead, they might believe that there is a truth to be found in moral matters but that no culture has a monopoly on this truth; to correct our errors and blind spots, we need to learn how other cultures do things and how they react to what we do. According to cultural relativism, however, our society's norms cannot be wrong; so learning about other cultures cannot help us correct our moral errors.

Many say there is less moral difference between cultures than it may appear. Different cultures often accept the same general principles but apply these differently, because of differences in their situations or factual beliefs. If society A uses nursing homes for the elderly while society B includes the elderly in their extended families, both may agree that we ought to provide good care for the elderly.

Many social scientists oppose cultural relativism. The psychologist **Lawrence Kohlberg**, for example, claims that people of all cultures go through roughly the same stages of moral thinking. Cultural relativism is a relatively low stage in which we simply conform to society. At more advanced stages, we reject cultural relativism; we become critical of accepted norms and think for ourselves about moral issues. How to do that is a central issue of moral philosophy. *See also* BENEDICT, RUTH; HUME; DAVID; MOORE, G. E.; NATURALISM.

– D –

DAOIST ETHICS. Daoism (also called Taoism) is a religious and philosophical tradition that for many centuries was the chief rival in China to **Confucianism** and **Buddhism**. Daoists believe in many gods, tend toward the mystical and poetic, emphasize meditation and worship, and have given the West acupuncture, Tai Chi, and Yin-Yang. While the classic Daoist texts *Laozi* (also called *Lao-tzu, Dao De Jing,* or *Tao Te Ching*) and *Zhuangzi* (also called *Chuang-tzu*) date back to about the third or fourth centuries BC, these formulate an older tradition.

Dao (also called Tao, pronounced "DOW") literally means "way" or "road." In Confucianism, Dao means "correct way" and has moral significance. In Daoism, Dao refers instead to the unspeakable primal reality from which everything else comes. Dao is seen not as God but rather as that from which the gods and the universe came. *Laozi* starts by saying that the Dao that can be put into words is not the true Dao; then, in a paradoxical manner typical of Daoism, it goes on to say much about Dao, using the word 82 more times.

Our moral duty is to follow Dao, which is to follow nature. We should interfere with nature as little as possible; so it is wrong to build a dam that blocks a river's natural flow to the sea. In our choices, we follow Dao by living spontaneously and following instinct. We do badly when we follow social convention, or when we rely on theory or rigid rules, as in Confucius's approach. In government, the best ruler is one who is flexible and compassionate, and interferes the least.

Despite this appeal to spontaneity, Daoism teaches standard norms and **virtues**. There are moral rules against **killing**, lying, stealing, and adultery. There are three great virtues: **love** (compassion, kindness); moderation (simplicity in life, which often includes abstaining from meat and alcohol); and modesty (humility). The Daoist version of the **golden rule** states: "Regard your neighbor's gain as your own gain and your neighbor's loss as your own loss."

The Vinegar Tasters painting is a traditional image to explain Daoism. It shows Confucius, Buddha, and Laozi tasting samples from a jar of vinegar. Confucius has a sour expression; he sees the world as out of step with the traditional norms and rules that we ought to live by. Buddha has a bitter face; he sees life as full of suffering and unfulfilled desire. But Laozi has a happy, optimistic smile; he sees nature (Dao) as essentially good, even though beyond our understanding, and he seeks to live in harmony with it.

DARWIN, CHARLES (1809–1882). English evolutionary **biologist.** Darwin thought the moral sense (**conscience**), which had a rightful supremacy over other principles of human action, was the most important difference between man and other **animals.** He was concerned about the place of morality in his evolutionary framework.

Darwin believed that any animal with strong social instincts would develop a moral sense when its intellectual powers became well developed. There are analogues of human morality in other social animals. Wolves work together in packs. Dogs sympathize with another's distress or danger, and have something like a conscience; they can be models of fidelity and obedience. Baboons follow a leader and enjoy being with each other; this promotes their survival. Humans similarly are social animals, living in families or groups. As social animals, we inherit a tendency to help our immediate comrades and obey our tribe's leader; but these social impulses often struggle against hunger, lust, vengeance, and self-preservation. At first our sympathy extends not to all members of our species but just to our tribe and our own kind (*see* **David Hume** and **Lawrence Kohlberg**); so we think little of mistreating women (if we are men) or those of other tribes. But growing intellectual powers bring us increasingly to a higher morality, supported by reason and directed to the welfare of others, where these "others" gradually expand to include all humanity, including its weakest members, and even animals. Our noblest attribute is our disinterested love for all living creatures. Thus we come to a higher morality summed up in the **golden rule**: "Treat others as you want to be treated."

On one of his journeys to collect evidence for evolution, Darwin stopped at a plantation in Brazil. The owner was about to take the women and children from the male slaves, and sell them separately at a public auction in Rio. Darwin was amazed that the cruelty of this never occurred to the man, who otherwise seemed like a good person. He traced the man's blindness to a lack of empathetic **imagination**; those who look coldly at the slave never imagine themselves in the slave's place—they do not imagine what it would be like for *their* wives and children to be taken and sold to another.

Darwin's thinking about morality differs from so-called "Social Darwinism," which holds that groups of humans ought to struggle against each other for supremacy, with strong races and peoples destroying the weak, until only the most fit survive. *See also* EGOISM; EVOLUTIONISM; MORAL AGENT; MORAL PATIENT; NIETZSCHE, FRIEDRICH; RACISM; SOCIOBIOLOGY.

DEATH PENALTY. *See* CAPITAL PUNISHMENT.

DECISION THEORY. A **mathematical** model for making decisions with uncertain outcomes. The model can be **normative** (about how people ought rationally to decide) or *descriptive* (about how people do decide); and it can be about a single agent's choice (which this entry focuses on) or the interacting choices of multiple agents (which is called *game theory* and is exemplified in the **prisoner's dilemma**).

The *expected utility* of an alternative choice is the sum of probability-times-utility of all its possible outcomes. Suppose that a Las Vegas casino offers you a $100 bet; if your coin lands heads then you gain $102, and if it lands tails then you lose your $100. Assuming that that the coin is fair, the two possible outcomes, heads and tails, are both .5 (50 percent) probable. So if you bet, then the expected utility is $1 (which is the average of what you would tend to gain on each bet if you repeated this bet many times); if you do not bet, then the expected gain is $0 (since it is sure that you will win or lose nothing). Here is a chart:

	Bet	Do not bet
Heads Tails	$51 (.5 · $102) −$50 (.5 · −$100)	$0
Expected Utility	$1	$0

Decision theory generally assumes that the rational choice is one that *maximizes expected utility*. So here the rational choice is to bet.

Some see an *ideally rational gambler* as one who acts to maximize expected gain; but this notion is artificial. Such a gambler would bet if the odds were favorable, but not otherwise. Since Las Vegas casinos take their cut, their odds are against the individual gambler; so an ideally rational gambler would not gamble at these places. But people have interests other than money; many find gambling to be fun and are willing to pay for the fun. And some whose only concern is money refuse to gamble even when the odds are in their favor. Their concern may be to have enough money. They may better satisfy this goal by being cautious instead of risking what they have for the sake of gaining more. Few people would endanger their life savings for the 1-in-900 chance of gaining a fortune 1,000 times as great. The extreme "play it safe" strategy is *maximin*, which ranks alternatives by their worst possible outcome and chooses the alternative with the best such outcome. Maximin gamblers only gamble on a "sure thing."

If we view decision theory as an abstract model, its *utility* could be interpreted in various ways: for example, as units of money, pleasure, or preference satisfaction; so the model does not assume a particular view of the **good**. Also, the model is neutral about whose good is to be maximized; it could be the agent's good (**egoism**), everyone's good (**utilitarianism**), or something in between (for example, the good of one's company). But the model typically does assume that probability and utility both can be expressed in numbers.

Decision theory often is used with *subjective probability* and *subjective utility*, which base numbers on the beliefs and preferences of a specific individual. We could in principle determine Anita's subjective probability and utility for any state of affairs M (for example, Michigan beating Ohio State next time) by asking her questions like these:

- If you had to bet either on M or on a coin turning up heads, which would you bet on? (Using answers to such questions, we could determine the *subjective probability* of M for Anita.)
- If you could choose either to have M true or to get $1, which would you choose? (Using answers to such questions, we could determine the *subjective utility* of M for Anita.)

In practice, this idea encounters several problems. First, Anita might give inconsistent answers. Perhaps she says she prefers A to B, B to C, and C to A. Second, she might not be able to answer the questions. Perhaps she cannot decide what amount of money is for her equal in value to Michigan beating Ohio State—or perhaps she cannot say with confidence whether she would bet on "God exists" instead of "The coin will turn up heads." Third, her answers might be "soft." Studies show that we do not have well-defined preference orderings that we can just introspectively "read off" when asked. Instead, we construct a preference ordering on the spot; how we do this is influenced greatly by how questions are worded and arranged. And we may well give a different ordering if we are asked again about our preferences later.

Critics oppose using decision theory's "maximize expected utility" as a guide to life. Some object that the approach is **consequentialist** and thus ignores non-consequentialist values like human **rights**. Others object that the most important values resist being put into numbers; imagine someone trying to use decision theory to pick a marriage partner or design college curricula. Some critics say a better model of rational choice is the *rationalized attitudes* approach that grows out of **ideal observer theory**; this approach tells us to try to be as *rational* as possible (**consistent, informed, impartial, imaginative**, and so forth—*see* **rational moral thinking**) and then see what our attitudes are.

Even critics admit that decision theory can often be a useful tool to help us make choices. Suppose that Anita is planning a flight and has to choose between ticket A and ticket B:

- A costs $250 and allows her to change her return date.
- B costs $200 but has a $125 charge if she changes her return date.

Which ticket is a better deal for her? Intuitively, A is better if a change is very likely, while B is better if a change is very unlikely. But we can be more precise than that. Let x represent the probability of her changing the return. Then:

Expected cost of A	Expected cost of B
= $250	= $200 + ($125 · x)

Some algebra shows that the expected costs are identical if x is 40 percent. Thus A is better if a change is more than 40 percent likely, while B is better if a change is less likely than that. Anita might be able to say, judging from her past history, that the probability of her having to change her return is much less than 40 percent. Then B would minimize her expected cost and thus may well be the better choice for her. Sometimes, however, it might make sense to pick A. Perhaps Anita has $250 but does not have the $325 that option B might cost her; then she would be in great trouble if she picked B but then later had to change the return date. It might then be more sensible for her to follow the "better safe than sorry" principle and pick A. *See also* ARROW, KENNETH; BENTHAM, JEREMY; RAWLS, JOHN.

DEFINITIONS OF MORAL TERMS. "Good," "bad," and "indifferent" are straightforwardly interdefinable: "good" means "not bad or indifferent," "bad" means "not good or indifferent," and "indifferent" means "not good or bad." Similarly, "ought," "permissible," and "wrong" are interdefinable: "A ought to be done" means "Omitting A is wrong (not permissible)"; "A is wrong" means "A is not permissible (ought not to be done)"; and "A is permissible" means "A is not wrong" or "It is not the case that A ought to be omitted."

It is controversial whether "good" is definable in terms of "ought" (perhaps "good" means "what ought to be promoted"), whether "ought" is definable in terms of "good" (perhaps "A ought to be done" means "A is most productive of good"), or whether neither is definable in terms of the other. It also is controversial whether either term is definable in purely descriptive terms. *See also* BRENTANO, FRANZ; ETHICS: METAETHICS; INTUITIONISM; MOORE, G. E.; NATURALISM; ROSS, W. D.; VIRTUE.

DEONTIC LOGIC. *See* LOGIC.

DEONTOLOGICAL ETHICS. The general view that some kinds of action (such as killing the innocent) are wrong in themselves and not just wrong because of bad consequences. *See also* CONSEQUENTIALISM/NON-CONSEQUENTIALISM.

DESCRIPTIVE ETHICS. *See* ANTHROPOLOGY; NORMATIVE/DESCRIPTIVE.

DETERMINISM. *See* FREE WILL AND DETERMINISM.

DEWEY, JOHN (1859–1952). American pragmatist who worked in philosophy, psychology, and education. Although Dewey studied with the American pragmatist C. S. Peirce, he was more influenced by **Georg Wilhelm Friedrich Hegel**. Later, he became less interested in speculative philosophy and more interested in making philosophy relevant to people's lives. He developed the Dewey School in Chicago, a laboratory school for testing ideas about education and psychology. He advocated **academic freedom** and defended his rival Bertrand Russell when Russell was not allowed to teach at the City College of New York.

Dewey was interested in social reform. He saw philosophy's role as identifying new values and ideas and showing how society can achieve them. This is evident in his philosophy of education. He thought the formalistic styles of 19th-century American schools (like rote learning) inhibited student creativity and intelligence. He advocated exposing students to a variety of experiences, believing that this develops creativity, intelligence, and **autonomy**. His thinking resembles **Aristotle**'s idea that we develop our characters through practice and habit. Dewey thought children should learn habits of intelligence by practice, by doing things, rather than by merely learning about ideas.

Dewey's ethics also stresses this active role. Similar to how philosophy should identify new values and ideas and show how society can achieve them, ethical deliberation should help us to identify possible courses of action and choose among them. Although humans naturally have moral values, we must deliberate when those values conflict. Suppose I naturally value both hard work and leisure time. Those values can conflict, as when I feel I should work on this dictionary but also want to watch television. I must deliberate about those values by determining the various courses of actions open to me and their consequences. Dewey believed that I will come to a reasonable decision if I am properly educated and have developed my intelligence adequately. The moral life is an ongoing process. Similar to how philosophy should strive for new values and ideas, we will face conflicts of values throughout our lives and must use ethical deliberation to resolve them.

Although Dewey advocated social reform, he was leery of those who sought to overcome societal problems and injustices once and for all. He thought such efforts are destined to fail. Nevertheless, he was optimistic about our ability to make society better. The key to unlocking that ability is developing our intelligence through an education that instills in us the right habits.

DISABILITY ETHICS. The study of moral issues involving disabilities and people who are disabled.

What does it mean to call a person *disabled*? On the *medical model*, a disabled person is one with a sensory, physical, or mental condition that falls below what is normal for humans and thus necessarily reduces the person's quality of life. The disability may, for example, be sensory (being unable to see or hear), physical (being unable to walk or use one's arms), or mental (having a learning disability or being retarded). Most disability theorists today, however, favor the *social model*, which distinguishes between impairments and disabilities. An *impairment* is a sensory, physical, or mental condition that can be diagnosed by doctors, while a *disability* is not being able to function in certain ways in a given social and physical environment. Persons with the same impairment may function poorly in one society but well in another. For example, the nearsighted may do poorly in a primitive tribe that hunts small game but well in a modern society that provides eyeglasses. Similarly, how people function who cannot use their legs depends, for example, on whether buildings have wheelchair ramps and on whether cars have some means other than foot pedals for accelerating and breaking. To a great extent, whether impairments turn into disabilities depends on the social and physical environment.

Disability-**rights** advocates say that the disabled have often suffered a form of **discrimination** much like **racism** or **sexism**. The disabled have often been devalued, isolated, and treated as second-class citizens. They have been denied educational and employment opportunities to which they are fully qualified. And the physical environment (for example, sidewalks without curb cuts) has been set up without considering their needs. Many countries have passed laws to counter such discrimination. For example, the Americans with Disabilities Act of 1990 (which was somewhat patterned after the Civil Rights Act of 1964) deals with areas like job discrimination and building accessibility. More recently, the United Nations General Assembly adopted a treaty on the rights of disabled people.

The disabled frequently complain about false stereotypes, especially the belief that the disabled have pitiable and miserable lives and would be better off dead. They point to extensive studies that show that the disabled (even quadriplegics and others with severe disabilities) have roughly the same degree of **happiness** as the non-disabled. While measuring happiness is not an exact science, we can look at external signs like rates of suicide or drug addiction (which generally correlate with being very unhappy), and we can ask people to evaluate their lives. The disabled have lower rates of suicide and drug addiction than others; and they report about the same degree of life satisfaction as do other people. They are overwhelmingly glad that their lives were not ended and they tend strongly to oppose views, like those of **Peter Singer**, that try to justify **euthanasia**, **suicide**, **abortion**, and infanticide for the disabled.

Prominent disabled people include Helen Keller (who graduated from Radcliffe College and wrote several books, despite being blind and deaf); Franklin D. Roosevelt (who served as president of the United States from his wheelchair); and Steven Hawking (who is one of the world's greatest scientists, despite being almost completely paralyzed).

See also SOCIAL CONTRACT.

DISCOURSE ETHICS. *See* HABERMAS, JÜRGEN.

DISCRIMINATION. Wrongful difference in how people are treated, usually based on things like race, gender, ethnicity, sexual orientation, religion, disability, or age.

Most of us treat people differently on grounds that raise no ethical issues. A professor gives students different grades depending on test scores; and an employer hires Jack instead of Jill because Jack is more qualified. In these cases, there are morally relevant reasons for differences in treatment. Discrimination becomes an ethical issue when the difference in treatment is arbitrary (has no relevant ethical reason to support it), as it would be if the professor gave grades on the basis of race or the employer hired Jack instead of Jill because Jack is a man.

When we think of discrimination, **racism** and **sexism** often come to mind; but there are many other forms of discrimination. It would be *religious discrimination* to grant tax-exempt status to Christian and Jewish organizations but deny it to similar Muslim and Hindu organizations. It would be *employment discrimination* (*see* **business ethics**) to make decisions about wages and firing based on matters irrelevant to job performance—for example, unrelated **disabilities** or what sports team the employee favors. Many argue that the law discriminates against gays and lesbians; for example, heterosexual couples have the legal **right** to inherit from their partner and receive spousal benefits from employers, while **homosexual** couples have no such right. Others complain against discrimination on the basis of ethnicity, age, or species (*see* **animals** and **Peter Singer**).

Except for libertarians, most ethicists agree in broad terms that discrimination is wrong. Libertarians (*see* **Robert Nozick**) follow **John Locke** in holding that we have the right to life, liberty, and property, and *only* those rights. As long as I do not violate any of those rights, or any contractual agreement to which I have committed myself, I violate no one's rights if I hire or fire because of a person's race, gender, religion, or sexual orientation. Indeed, the government violates my rights if it tells me I cannot hire or fire on such grounds. Despite this ethical stance, most libertarians dislike discrimination and believe that competitive markets work against it in the long run; for my business to prosper, I need to take advantage of people's talents and not hire or fire on the basis of matters irrelevant to job performance.

If discrimination is wrong, then why is it wrong? Ethicists give a wide range of answers to this question. **Utilitarians** argue that discrimination is wrong because it does not maximize the sum-total of good consequences. Suppose that a talented African-American who wants to become a scientist is told that she cannot do this because of her race. She suffers because of this; and the rest of us suffer too, because we cannot gain from what she might contribute to science.

Some critics worry that utilitarianism sees discrimination as not wrong of its very nature but wrong because of empirical contingencies. They may prefer to appeal to **Immanuel Kant**'s principle that we should treat humanity, whether in oneself or another, as an end-in-itself and not only as a means. In effect, this tells us to treat everyone with respect and dignity. Discrimination does not do this. I do not treat you with respect and dignity if I treat you badly for arbitrary reasons.

Some use the **golden rule** against discrimination. Presumably, we would not have others discriminate against us because of our race, gender, religion, sexual orientation, or the like. So, we should not discriminate against others on such grounds. This argument requires us to engage our **imagination** to determine how we believe we should be treated in a certain context. Then, it asks us to use **impartiality** and **consistency** to conclude that we should treat others in a like manner (*see also* **rational moral thinking** and **universalizability**).

Some philosophers appeal to this principle: "It is wrong to treat people differently because of matters beyond their control, such as their skin color." But critics object that racism would still be wrong even if skin color were somehow under our technological control. And it is often right to treat people differently because of matters beyond their control; so a cyclist with a genetic lack of cycling stamina may be rejected for the Tour de France squad.

Others appeal to this principle: "It is wrong to treat people differently because of false stereotypes." But critics point out that this does not cover many cases of discrimination. Suppose that an employer hires Jack instead of Jill because of the belief that *women, but not men, often have to take time off of work because they are pregnant*; many would say that this is discrimination and wrong, even though the underlying italicized belief is true (and not a false stereotype).

Still others see the core problem in discrimination as a negative attitude toward certain groups, who are systematically treated with less concern, sympathy, and compassion. Such attitudes may lead the employer, for example, to be less sympathetic to Jill and to overemphasize her negatives. In extreme cases, such attitudes can lead to *hate crimes* directed at people because of their race, gender, sexual orientation, or the like (for example, the 1998 beating death of Matthew Shepard in Wyoming because he was gay).

Others argue that discrimination is wrong because it reduces groups of people to second-class citizenship; people are given or denied basic rights and opportunities just because they belong to certain groups.

Although their reasons vary, most ethicists reject discrimination and support ways to combat it. This has implications for the **liberalism/communitarianism** debate. Communitarians, who stress the interests of society over the rights of individuals, can more easily restrict the rights of individuals (including the right to decide who is admitted to your school or hired by your company) for the social good. Liberals, who emphasize the rights of individuals, have a more difficult time justifying anti-discrimination laws that restrict individual rights.

There is much controversy about *affirmative action* programs that give preference in hiring and school admissions to some based on race, gender, and the like. The goal is to create greater *diversity* in government, business, and academia by including more people from historically underrepresented groups. Affirmative action comes in two forms: *weak affirmative action* prefers, for example, a black or a woman over a white male when both are equally qualified, while *strong affirmative action* gives such a preference even when the white male is more qualified. Many oppose strong affirmative action as *reverse discrimination*; it treats white males worse because they are white males.

How can affirmative action be defended? Some say it compensates blacks and women for past wrongs done to them (their exclusion from the best jobs and schools) and also compensates for unfair advantages that white males now have (in terms of being better educated, coming from richer families, and dominating the upper levels of business and politics). But critics object that affirmative action most hurts **poorer** white males, while it most helps wealthier minority members who were harmed least by past wrongs. How does it promote **justice** to prefer a black woman who is the daughter of rich Manhattan attorneys over a white male who is the son of poor farmers in rural Oklahoma?

Some defend affirmative action because it promotes equality, which is an important, socially-desirable goal (*see* **egalitarianism**). Affirmative action helps break historical habits of discrimination against blacks and women; by promoting minority role models, it helps youths to expand their horizons and pursue wider possibilities within government, business, and academia. Critics object that affirmative action causes unfair harm to white males, who must achieve higher standards than others to be hired or admitted to schools. Defenders of affirmative action admit this unfair harm to white males, but insist that it is needed, as a temporary measure, to promote important social changes. It is also unfair that some young people die in **war** while others live, but this may be needed if the cause behind the war is just.

Libertarians aside, ethicists generally agree that discrimination is wrong. Their disputes about why it is wrong and how to combat it say much about their differing views on morality and justice. *See also* CONSEQUENTIALISM/NON-CONSEQUENTIALISM; DWORKIN, RONALD; FEMINIST ETHICS; NAGEL, THOMAS; POLITICAL PHILOSOPHY.

DIVINE COMMAND THEORY (also called supernaturalism and theological voluntarism). The view that morality depends on **God**'s will—so ethics is based on religion and God's will creates the moral order. This entry focuses on the form of the theory that takes moral judgments to describe God's will: "X is **good**" means "God desires X."

The word "God" is often defined in ways like "the all-good, all-powerful, all-knowing Creator of the world." But it would be circular to define "God" using "good" and then define "good" using "God"; this would also suggest that there are standards of goodness prior to God's will. So divine command theory would do better to define "God" as simply "the all-powerful, all-knowing Creator of the world."

Proponents point out advantages of divine command theory. The view is popular among ordinary people. It explains morality in a clear way. It gives solid guidelines, unlike the "anything goes" **subjectivism** and **cultural relativism**. It makes morality objective, since human values must conform to a higher law. It can appeal to higher motives (unselfish love and gratitude to God) or lower motives (punishments and rewards); so it answers the **why be moral question**. It can make morality part of our personal relationship with God instead of just abstract truths. While some who base ethics on religion are intolerant and judgmental, Jesus forbade this (Matthew 7:1–5) and said that, as sinners ourselves, we should not "cast the first stone" against others (John 8:7).

How can we know God's will? Suggested sources of this knowledge include the **Bible**, the church, prayer, and reason. Some point out possible pitfalls in using these sources. Biblical passages can lead people in opposite directions (for example, toward militarism or pacifism). The church can have blind spots (as when it supported slavery). Praying for God's guidance and taking our feelings as a sign of his will can lead people to act well; but it can also lead fanatics to think God wants things that in fact are crazy and hateful. Reason, given to us by God to know his will, can be seen as working through moral **intuitions** or through an **ideal-observer** method (where we strive for God-like knowledge and love and then determine what we favor); but this too has its limitations. Perhaps it is best to combine all four sources: the Bible, the church, prayer, and reason. Where the sources speak clearly and in unison, our belief is solid; so it is clear that God wants us to have concern and love for each other. But there are gray areas, like pacifism; here we need to follow our prayer and reason as best we can while we gain insight from the Bible and the church, but being tolerant of those who see God's will differently.

Why should we accept divine command theory? Defenders say that the Bible teaches it (since it uses "good" interchangeably with "what God desires"), that it is a corollary of belief in God (who is the source of everything), and that it gives the only plausible source of objectively binding duties. Critics dispute these reasons. Critics say the Bible does not teach divine command theory but only that we ought to obey God, an idea which is consistent with other views, such as intuitionism, which says what God commands is right in itself and not right just because he commands it. Critics also say God need not be the source of everything; maybe "Hatred is bad," like "x = x," is true in itself and not true because some source makes it true. Finally, critics say there are plausible ways to defend the objectivity of ethics without basing it on God's will (*see* **cognitivism/non-cognitivism**).

Critics also object that divine command theory makes it impossible for atheists to make moral judgments: those who say "Kindness is good but there is no God" contradict themselves since their statement means "God desires kindness but there is no God." Divine command theorists respond in various ways. Some say atheists are contradicting themselves. Atheists first obtained their values from a religious source; they lost their religion but kept the values—even though the values make sense only on a religious basis. Atheists who accept morality are confused; clearheaded atheists like **Jean-Paul Sartre** and **J. L. Mackie** reject morality, saying that everything is permissible if there is no God. Others say atheists are consistent in making moral judgments, since they mean something different by "good" than what believers mean; since the two groups speak a different moral language, there cannot be fruitful discussion between them. Critics dispute these responses.

Socrates, the first major philosopher of ancient Greece, was a religious person who tried to follow the will of God (sometimes he says "gods"). He saw ethics as closely connected with religion. But in the *Euthyphro* dialogue (*see* **Plato**) he rejected divine command theory, largely on the basis of a penetrating question. We can phrase his question as "Is a good thing good because God desires it? Or does God desire it because it is already good?" Socrates and most people would go with the second alternative, which says God desires something because it is already good; but this requires that we recognize a standard of goodness independent of God's will, and thus that we give up divine command theory. Proponents of the theory have to say, seemingly less plausibly, that kindness is good just because God desires it (prior to his desires it is neither good nor bad)—and that hatred would be good if God desired it. This answer seems to make ethics arbitrary. But divine command theorists object that Socrates's answer lowers God by putting an objective right and wrong above him and that it makes religion irrelevant to ethics.

Many religious thinkers reject divine command theory but still connect ethics and religion closely. They say God is supremely good. Calling God "good" does not mean that he fulfills his own desires; instead, it means that his life accords with inherent truths about goodness—for example, that love is good. God created us so that our minds can know the good and our wills can freely choose it; he wants our moral struggles to purify us and lead us toward our ultimate goal of eternal happiness with him. On this religious view, basic moral truths are true in themselves and can be known to believers and atheists alike by our God-given reason. But believers have additional ways to know these moral truths: the Bible, the church, and prayer; these are useful because our reason is often clouded. And believers have additional motives for doing the right thing, including higher motives like gratitude to God and love for his creatures and lower motives like **punishment** and reward; doing the right thing is thus linked to our personal relationship to God. Believers and nonbelievers mostly will come to the same moral beliefs; but there may be some differences. Believers will recognize a duty to worship God while nonbelievers will not. And there may be differences about issues like **euthanasia**, based on differing beliefs about the destiny of our lives. This proposed view links ethics and religion closely but does not base ethics totally on religion. Ethics could exist without religion but would be incomplete.

Divine command theory has many forms. This entry examined a form that defines "X is good" as "God desires X." Some thinkers take "good" as indefinable (in an intuitionist manner) and only define "ought" using God's will. Others take both "good" and "ought" as indefinable and give "We ought to obey God" as the basic self-evident **normative** truth. Others connect *duty* and *being willed by God* in terms of property-identity (*see* **naturalism**). Others analyze "X is good" as "X is like God"; this defines "good" in terms of God's nature but not his will. Defenders of some form of divine command theory include Robert Adams, John Hare, Sharon Kaye, C. S. Lewis, George Mavrodes, Richard Mouw, William of Ockham, **Samuel Pufendorf**, Philip Quinn, and Edward Wierenga. *See also* AQUINAS, THOMAS; AUGUSTINE; BEAUVOIR, SIMONE DE; MEDIEVAL ETHICS; MORAL EDUCATION; MORAL THEOLOGY; NATURAL LAW.

DOMAIN OF MORALITY. *See* MORAL AGENT; MORAL PATIENT.

DOUBLE EFFECT. The principle that under certain conditions it is permissible to do something that has a morally **good** intended effect and a morally bad unintended side effect.

Suppose you are offered a contract to build a big bridge. Judging from similar projects in the past, you see that this project would surely cause the death of one or more innocent persons. You believe it is **exceptionlessly** wrong to **kill** an innocent person. So is it then wrong to build the bridge, since this will kill an innocent person?

The principle of double effect says building the bridge may be permissible, even if it has the unintended side affect of killing an innocent person. It is permissible to do an act (building the bridge) that has a good effect (the bridge is built) and a gravely bad effect (killing innocent human beings), provided that:

(1)   The act is in itself either good or indifferent;
(2)   the good effect is intended and the bad effect is not intended (so if you could bring about the good effect without bringing about the bad then you would);
(3)   the bad effect is not the means to produce the good effect (instead, the bad effect is just an unintended byproduct of an act aimed to bring about the good effect); and
(4)   there is a proportionate reason for permitting the bad effect (so the good effect outweighs the bad effect and there is no way to

produce the good without producing more bad).

Condition (4) roughly comes to the condition that act **utilitarianism** would approve of the act. If act utilitarianism forbids the act, then double effect does too; but if act utilitarianism permits the act, then double effect may or may not permit the act.

Suppose your country is engaged in **war** and you are bombing the enemy. Assume that killing innocent civilians is intrinsically wrong and your bombing will kill innocent civilians. Is your bombing morally permissible? Double effect says it can be, so long as conditions (1) through (4) apply. Crucial here are (2) and (3): you do not intend to kill innocent civilians (your target is military and if you could hit it without killing innocent civilians then you would) and killing innocent civilians is not a means to the good end (but is instead an unintended side effect). Strictly forbidden would be a **terrorist** approach that intends to kill innocent civilians or that uses the killing of innocent civilians to bring about a good effect (perhaps by demoralizing the enemy in order to end the war more quickly).

Double effect has also been applied to cases like these (by those who believe that **euthanasia, abortion**, and **suicide** are wrong):

- Prescribing pain medication which in fact will shorten the patient's life can be permissible; directly killing the patient is not.
- Performing a hysterectomy on a pregnant woman with uterine cancer can be permissible even if the unborn child will die; directly killing the fetus by crushing its head is not.
- Throwing yourself on a live grenade to protect others can be permissible, even if you know you will die, if you see your death as an unintended side effect of shielding others from the grenade; it is wrong to jump on the grenade in order to kill yourself.

Some cases are controversial, for example whether double effect would have justified the Allied bombing of Dresden or the American use of atomic bombs against Hiroshima and Nagasaki in World War II.

The principle of double effect was formulated by **Thomas Aquinas** and is an important part of the **natural law** approach to ethics. Many legal systems and rule utilitarians accept it. But the principle has had critics. Act utilitarians like **Peter Singer** reject it, saying that only condition (4) is needed; we should do what has the best total consequences, even if this involves directly killing innocent people (*see* **end-justifies-**

means). Others see problems with the principle's wording but may accept the general idea. *See also* ANSCOMBE, ELIZABETH; CONSEQUENTIALISM/NON-CONSEQUENTIALISM.

DUTY. *See* OUGHT.

DWORKIN, RONALD (1931–). American legal and **political** philosopher known for defending **liberalism** and critiquing *legal positivism* (which holds that legal validity has no connection with morality). Dworkin was a Rhodes Scholar at Oxford and graduated from Harvard Law School before clerking for the famous U.S. Federal Court Judge, Learned Hand. He held many appointments in law and philosophy in the U.S. and England, and he followed his teacher H. L. A. Hart as Chair of Jurisprudence at Oxford.

In *Taking Rights Seriously* (1977), Dworkin argues against Hart's view that judges can use social usefulness to decide problematic cases where the law does not determine which side should win. Dworkin regards this view as not sufficiently respecting **rights**. He holds that one side or the other of such cases has a legal right on its side and that such rights override considerations of social utility. Rights safeguard the freedom of the individual, since they set boundaries that the state cannot cross to promote social utility. This *rights thesis* helped Dworkin become an important defender of liberalism at a time when many began to blame it for various injustices in the world. Like **John Rawls**, Dworkin argues that the key to overcoming injustices is for society to become more committed to liberalism.

Dworkin's rights thesis, which he applies to law, has also been applied to morality. Many argue that **utilitarianism** is flawed because it permits rights to be violated on grounds of social utility; but the rights thesis claims that rights "trump" utility calculations. Some try to defend a more sophisticated utilitarianism that recognizes the rights thesis.

In *Law's Empire* (1986), Dworkin argues that the role of legal philosophy is to justify law and legal restrictions; in the spirit of liberalism, he sees any restriction on the freedom of individuals as requiring justification. Legitimate laws treat citizens equally (*see* **egalitarianism**), by applying rules and principles that allow us all to have an equal right to the resources necessary to live our conceptions of the **good** life. As we make choices about how to obtain or use resources, inequalities will result. These inequalities are justified, however, because they reflect our various values about the good life.

Dworkin sees equal treatment as grounding our individual freedoms. The state must remain neutral on the good life and cannot promote a certain conception by restricting our liberty to pursue the lives we choose. He has applied this approach to free speech, affirmative action (*see* **discrimination**), **abortion**, physician-assisted **suicide** (*see* **bioethics**), **homosexuality**, and **pornography**.

Many challenge Dworkin's ideas. Some legal philosophers, such as Joseph Raz, defend legal positivism against Dworkin's objections. Some **feminist** philosophers, such as Catharine MacKinnon, object to his position on pornography. Others, such as **John Finnis**, use **natural law** theory to criticize his liberal notion of equality. Dworkin's ideas, defended or attacked by many, have been very influential. *See also* LOCKE, JOHN; MARX, KARL; MILL, JOHN STUART; NOZICK, ROBERT; ROUSSEAU, JEAN-JACQUES.

– E –

EGALITARIANISM. The belief in human equality, especially equality in social, political, and moral **rights**. A range of ethical and **political** views share the basic idea that all humans have equal moral worth or status, but they draw different conclusions. For example, some argue for equal wealth for all, while others argue for equal opportunity to create wealth for oneself (even if this results in unequal wealth). Some extend equal moral status to the unborn (*see* **abortion and infanticide**), to **animals**, or to all living things (*see* **environmental ethics**).

Ancient Greek philosophers tended not to support egalitarianism. **Plato** advocated a hierarchical society in which power rests in the hands of philosopher-kings. **Aristotle** also approved of a hierarchical society, but one that gives more power to the middle class.

Egalitarian theories became popular in the **modern** era. **Thomas Hobbes** used the **social contract** to show how the state arises from popular consent; however, he advocated a sovereign with absolute power, which he thought was needed to avoid the horrendous conditions of the state of nature. **John Locke** and **Jean-Jacques Rousseau** argued instead that the social contract supports equality and democracy (representative democracy for Locke, and direct democracy for Rousseau). **Immanuel Kant** later advocated an egalitarian ethical theory; he argued that we achieve rational **autonomy** by following rules that we prescribe for everyone, and thus for how we are to treat others as well as for how they are to treat us. His *formula of universal law* states: "Act only on a maxim that you can will to be a universal law."

In the **nineteenth century**, **Jeremy Bentham** and **John Stuart Mill** advocated the **utilitarian** view that we ought to do whatever maximizes the sum of the **goodness** of **consequences** for everyone. In determining this, the interests of everyone count equally; no one's interests are to count less because of the person's race, gender, or religion. Mill also advocated extending the vote to everyone except those who do not pay taxes or cannot read, write, and do simple math. Although this excludes many people, one must remember that at that time neither women nor African-Americans had a legal right to vote in the U.S. Moreover, Mill advocated a representative democracy that would help ensure that the interests of minorities would be respected.

While utilitarians seek to maximize the total good, they argue that this is more likely to be achieved by spreading wealth more equally. The reason for this is the *diminishing marginal utility* of money; as we get richer, each extra dollar makes less difference to how well we live. So it would likely bring about more total good if A and B both had $5000 than if A had $9900 and B had $100.

About the time Mill wrote, **Karl Marx** developed his communist theory. He argued that capitalism exploits and alienates the proletariat workforce. Eventually the proletariat will revolt, seize factories and other means of production, and bring about the classless, communist state—which will ensure economic and social equality for all.

In the **twentieth century**, **John Rawls** advocated equal human rights and a modified ideal of economic equality; he saw social and economic inequalities as justified only when they somehow (e.g., by encouraging some to become doctors) make the least advantaged better off than they would be without the inequalities. In contrast, **Robert Nozick** argued that the best a society can do is produce equality of opportunity; each person should have the same rights to acquire and trade goods. **Ronald Dworkin** held a somewhat similar view: we need laws that let us all have an equal right to the resources needed to live our version of the good life. Although Nozick and Dworkin disagreed about what rights people should have, they agreed that some people can justly gain greater wealth and status than others; distributions of goods along the lines of Marx or Rawls can be achieved only by violating the rights of free individuals.

What is the root idea of egalitarianism? Some suggest *we ought to treat everyone the same.* But others say this is absurd—since we would then have to treat children and adults the same (*see* **paternalism**) and we would have to let men use women's rest rooms. Others suggest *we ought to count everyone's interests equally when we decide what we ought to do.* But others argue that we ought to count the interests of some more than others (e.g., the interests of our daughter more than the interests of a complete stranger, *see* **W. D. Ross**). Still others suggest *everyone is entitled to the same basic rights.* But there are disputes about what rights we have (e.g., the right to conduct business freely versus the right to a minimal level of wealth). Still others suggest **impartiality** (which can mean different things) or *we ought to treat others only as we are willing to be treated in their situation* (the **golden rule**, which would give form but not content to egalitarianism).

While most philosophers today advocate some form of equality, there continues to be much debate about what form this should take.

EGOISM. The view that we **ought** always to do whatever maximizes **good** consequences for ourselves. This is sometimes called *ethical egoism* to distinguish it from *psychological egoism*, which says people by nature are motivated only by self-interest. Ethical egoism differs from **utilitarianism**, another **consequentialist** view, by not having us consider everyone's good, but just our own. Egoism can prescribe that we promote the good of others, but only when this promotes our own good.

Critics say egoism could justify gross immorality. Imagine other people following this view toward us. Egoism entails that others ought to harm us greatly (even paralyze us for life) if that would even slightly maximize their own interests. This goes against strong moral **intuitions** and would be difficult to accept or desire.

Critics also say egoism is self-defeating. The "egoism paradox" is that we likely will fail to promote self-interest if we focus on it. If we follow egoism, others likely will despise us and exclude us from mutually beneficial enterprises; and we likely will end up despising ourselves. We promote our own interests better if we respect the good of others in the same way that we respect our own good.

A major role of morality, critics say, is to help settle problems that arise when the self-interests of individuals clash. Egoism would provide no help; instead, a society of egoists would live in a moral chaos that promotes no one's interests. And if a morality necessarily involves an **impartial** concern for the good of others, then it is doubtful that egoism even qualifies as a morality.

Another problem is how we are to give advice to others. Should we tell them what is in *our* interest to say, or should we tell them what is in *their* interest to hear? Egoism would seem to support the former, which would nullify the point of giving advice.

In response to such criticisms, some egoists say that morality is for fools and that smart egoists can maximize their interests by breaking moral rules. Most egoists, however, try to show that egoism, if correctly understood, harmonizes with traditional moral practices. They say we promote our interests better by keeping egoism in the background and following moral rules and motivations that respect the good of others; an enlightened egoism forms the ultimate justification for this way of life but not the immediate guide for daily actions.

Following **Thomas Hobbes**, we might imagine a society of egoists. Irrational egoists would lie, steal, and kill when that was to their immediate advantage; this would make life miserable for everyone and promote no one's interests. Rational egoists would set up rules to make life better for themselves. There would be rules against lying, stealing, and **killing**—and in favor of cooperation and concern for others. Hobbes suggests that egoists would set up an absolute monarch to **punish** offenders; **Richard Brandt** instead suggests social and psychological sanctions. On Brandt's approach, anti-social behavior would bring both external sanctions (alienation from others, social disapproval, legal penalties) and internal sanctions (guilt, anxiety, loss of self-respect); and people who follow the moral rules would be praised and made to feel good about themselves. These ensure that it is in our interest to follow the moral rules. In short, it is in everyone's interest to bring about an atmosphere in which anti-social behavior is in no one's interest—and such an atmosphere by and large exists.

Many egoists think this defense of moral rules works fairly well. While a few anti-social actions may promote self-interest, generally a policy of following moral rules, instead of assessing individual actions in terms of self-interest, will be in our interest (*see* **why be moral question**). Some tighten the harmony between moral rules and self-interest further by appealing to religious beliefs about **karma** and reincarnation (*see* **Buddhist Ethics** and **Hindu Ethics**), or about divine rewards and punishments. Others identify our ultimate good not with pleasure but with personal relationships that presuppose mutual concern, or with a **virtuous** life that includes being just toward others (*see* **Aristotle**), or with a heavenly knowledge of God that we prepare for by living morally (*see* **Thomas Aquinas**); on these views, living a moral life would more obviously promote our own good.

Some egoists, such as **Ayn Rand**, taking a different tack, argue that we are all better off if each of us does what is in our own interest. This seems to take utilitarianism as more basic and to justify egoism as a corollary; it also faces an objection in the **prisoner's dilemma**.

Some defend ethical egoism by appealing to psychological egoism. If by nature we cannot be motivated by anything other than self-interest, then any view that says we *ought* to be so motivated is impractical and violates **Immanuel Kant**'s idea that "ought" implies "can."

Against psychological egoism, **Joseph Butler** claimed that what motivates us is not just self-interest but also duty; concern for friends, relatives, and even strangers; and impulses like hunger, sex, and revenge. But egoists say that here our ultimate motivation is self-interest. Hobbes argued that we help the poor just so we can feel better about ourselves; heroes who cover live grenades with their bodies to protect others act either instinctively (which avoids issues about motivation) or out of a self-interested motivation (perhaps to avoid a life of guilt). Critics say such explanations are far-fetched and cannot cover all cases. They also say this strategy, which explains away any possible empirical objection, removes psychological egoism from being a genuine empirical claim; the mark of an empirical claim is that it is falsifiable, in that some possible sense experiences could show it to be false.

Some argue for psychological egoism on the basis of a theory of voluntary action. Each of our voluntary actions is something that we want to do, and thus something that we do to satisfy our desires, and thus something that we do to promote our interests. Critics contend that this argument is based on confusion. When we do what we want to do (for example, help another), our motivation is not just to satisfy our desires (since it may instead be to help another). And acting to promote our other-regarding desires is not acting to promote our interests.

The debate over psychological egoism is much like the debate over psychological hedonism, which is examined in the entry on good.

Other forms of egoism are possible. *Rational egoism* holds that rational individuals will do whatever maximizes their own interests; in contrast, **Humeans** argue that rational individuals will do whatever best satisfies their desires (some of which may be altruistic) and Kantians argue that rationality requires being impartial and **consistent** (*see* **rational moral thinking**). *Limited ethical egoism* says our main but not only duty is to promote our own interests. *Limited psychological egoism* says our main but not only motivation is self-interest. Quite apart from these various theories are character traits like selfishness, self-centeredness, and egotism.

How self-interest relates to morality is a complex topic; it has been debated since the **ancient** era, when **Plato** argued that being just promotes our own good. *See also* BIOLOGY; DARWIN, CHARLES; DECISION THEORY; FALLACIES ABOUT ETHICS; FREE RIDER; GILLIGAN, CAROL; KOHLBERG, LAWRENCE; NIETSZCHE, FRIEDRICH; PARFIT, DEREK; PSYCHOLOGY; ROUSSEAU, JEAN-JACQUES; SIDGWICK, HENRY; SOCIOBIOLOGY.

EMOTIVISM (sometimes called expressivism). The view that moral judgments express feelings instead of truth claims. "X is **good**" is equivalent to an exclamation like "Hurrah for X!" and hence cannot be true or false. So there cannot be moral truths or moral knowledge.

Emotivism differs in a subtle way from **subjectivism**, which holds that "X is good" describes and asserts truths about feelings. In contrast, emotivism says "X is good" expresses feelings but does not assert truths about them. Compare these examples:

Just express feelings (emotivism):	*Truths about feelings (subjectivism):*
"Brrr!"	"I feel cold."
"Ha, ha!"	"I find that funny."
"Hurrah for X!"	"I like X."

While "Brrr!" is not true or false, "I feel cold" is true if the speaker feels cold and false if the speaker does not. Emotivists believe that moral judgments are like "Brrr!" (which just expresses feelings) and not like "I feel cold" (which is a truth claim about feelings). This distinction lets emotivism avoid some objections that plague subjectivism. Suppose Hitler, who likes the killing of Jews, says "The killing of Jews is good"; subjectivists must say Hitler's statement is true (since it just means that he likes the killing of Jews), which seems strange to many people. Emotivists say Hitler's statement is an exclamation ("Hurrah for the killing of Jews!"), and thus is not true or false.

While moral judgments express feelings, they also serve to influence others. If I say to a child "It is *good* to pick up our toys," I am trying to get her to feel positively about picking up her toys and to act accordingly. Sometimes we use moral judgments to influence ourselves. When the alarm rings, I might say "It is good to get up now," which means

"Hurrah for getting up now!"; here part of me is a cheerleader, trying to influence the other part.

We can reason about moral issues if we assume a system of norms; we then can appeal to empirical facts to show that, given these norms and these empirical facts, a particular moral conclusion follows. Such reasoning can be useful within a group that shares common norms. But we cannot reason about *basic* moral principles. If you argue with a Nazi, you likely will disagree on basic moral principles about how people are to be treated. **Intuitionists** see this as a difference in moral intuitions while emotivists see it as a difference in feelings; but neither view can progress further by reasoning. Following emotivism, we can go further by appealing to emotions; to convince Nazis, we have to make them *feel* differently about people of other races.

A. J. Ayer based emotivism on **logical positivism**, which holds that any genuine truth claim has to be either analytic (true by language conventions, like "All bachelors are single") or testable by sense experience (like "There is snow outside"). Any statement that fails this test is nonsensical; it says nothing that can be true or false. For example, "There is a **God**," being neither analytic nor empirically testable, has to be nonsensical. Ayer applied the same reasoning to moral judgments like "**Racism** is wrong." He was sure that moral judgments are not analytic. And he thought **G. E. Moore** refuted **naturalism**; so moral judgments cannot be empirical. It follows that moral judgments are nonsensical; they say nothing that can be true or false. Moral judgments have only emotive meaning.

Logical positivism, however, led to so many problems that even supporters like Ayer abandoned it. For one thing, the view is self-refuting. The claim that *every genuine truth claim is analytic or empirically testable* is itself neither analytic nor empirically testable; so, by its own standard, it has to be nonsensical.

Recent emotivists argue that their view is better than other approaches because it is simpler and explains more of the facts. Emotivism can easily explain why "good" (being emotional) cannot be defined using (emotionally neutral) descriptive terms, why we cannot prove (emotional) moral conclusions from just descriptive facts, why we cannot resolve basic moral differences (which are emotional) intellectually, why we differ so much in our moral beliefs (because our emotions differ), and why we are motivated by moral beliefs (which are emotional). Emotivism appeals to something simple—positive and negative feelings—and avoids ideas that are difficult to defend, like the existence of

God or self-evident ethical truths. And translating moral judgments into "boo" and "hurrah" seems to bring out their meaning.

Critics object that emotivism does not explain morality adequately; by denying moral knowledge and moral truth, emotivism goes against common sense. And does the implicit premise that views are *better* if they are simpler and explain more really mean "Hurrah for views that are simpler and explain more!"? **Science** itself seems to need value judgments like "We *ought* normally to believe our sense experience" and "Views are *better* if they are simpler and explain more." Are these simply expressions of feeling and objectively no more true than alternatives like "A view is *better* if it accords with my horoscope"?

Critics also object that moral judgments are not always emotional. We all have some moral beliefs that are emotional for us and others that are unemotional. Since moral judgments may be very unemotional, especially when we deal with issues where we have little personal involvement, it is implausible to equate them all with exclamations—like "Boo!" and "Hurrah!"—that express emotion as their main function.

Another problem is that "good" and "bad" do not always translate plausibly into exclamations. Consider these examples:

(1)   Do what is good.
(2)   Hurrah for good people!
(3)   Either it is good to go or it is bad to go.
(4)   This is neutral (neither good nor bad).

Here is what we get if we replace "good" and "bad" with exclamations:

(1a)   Do what is hurrah!
(2a)   Hurrah for hurrah! people!
(3a)   Either hurrah for going! or boo on going!
(4a)   Neither hurrah for this! nor boo on this!

If we use exclamations in the normal way, none of these translations make sense. So some sentences using "good" and "bad" seem to have no plausible "hurrah" and "boo" equivalents. Subjectivists have no problem here, since they would translate sentence 1 into "Do what I like" or "Do what I would say 'Hurrah!' to"; but this makes "X is good" into a truth claim about feelings—and emotivists reject this.

Many are disturbed by emotivism's claim that disputes about basic moral principles cannot appeal to reason but only to emotion. They fear that this model of moral thinking would lead to propaganda wars in which each side, unable to resort to reason, simply tries to manipulate the feelings of the other side (as some political speeches do).

Emotivists like Charles Stevenson, Simon Blackburn, and Allan Gibbard try to respond to such objections. They especially try to show that emotivism would not destroy morality and the moral life. Blackburn's *quasi-realism* claims that emotivists, while they deny the existence of moral facts, can think and talk about morality in much the same way as everyone else. Emotivists can say "It is *true* that act A ought to be done" if they only intend this as a longer way to say (or agree with) "Act A ought to be done" or if they are referring to the truth of the factual claims (perhaps that act A would maximize human happiness) to which they would appeal in defending their moral judgment. Emotivists can speak of "moral knowledge" if by this they mean "strong moral convictions." And emotivists can distinguish "propaganda" from "good reasons" for ethical judgments; these terms express our negative and positive feelings about the type of reasoning used. But critics object that such approaches do not capture the nuances of our moral convictions and language.

Some *moderate emotivists*, like **William Frankena**, try to bring more rationality to emotivism. While still seeing moral judgments as emotional exclamations and not truth claims, they insist that feelings can be rationally appraised to some degree; for example, rational moral feelings must be **consistent**, **impartial**, and based on correct **information**. On these grounds, we could argue that the Nazi's principles are irrational. This approach works much like **ideal observer theory**; we would determine our moral principles by following our feelings—but we would first develop feelings that are **rational**. *See also* BRENTANO, FRANZ; COGNITIVISM/NON-COGNITIVISM; EPISTEMOLOGY; HARE, R. M.; HUME, DAVID; KNOWING RIGHT FROM WRONG; MACKIE, J. L.; MORAL REALISM.

EMPATHY. *See* IMAGINATION.

EMPIRICISM. *See* EPISTEMOLOGY; KNOWING RIGHT FROM WRONG; LOGICAL POSITIVISM.

END-IN-ITSELF, FORMULA OF. *See* KANT, IMMANUEL.

END-JUSTIFIES-MEANS. Does the end justify the means? Is it permissible to do evil so that good will result? Some think these questions point to an important divide between two approaches to normative ethics (*see* **ethics: normative**). Others object that the questions are unclear and produce more heat than light.

Some **consequentialists** say that *the end justifies the means* and that means are justified only by their results. So then is it permissible to lie or cheat to bring about a good result? Most consequentialists would say "usually not"—since lying and cheating usually bring bad results that outweigh the intended good results. Only in rare cases do such actions bring about a balance of good results; but then, consequentialists argue, such actions are right.

Some *non-consequentialists* insist that *the end does not justify the means*. They say it is wrong to do evil to bring about good; for example, it is wrong to cheat during an election so that a superior candidate gets elected. But is such cheating, then, *always* wrong?

Most moral philosophers, instead of embracing or attacking the slogan that *the end justifies the means*, prefer to discuss more directly some clearer issues that this slogan suggests, such as:

- If means M maximizes good consequences, is M thereby right regardless of the kind of act that it is? (*See* **utilitarianism**.)
- Are some means M always wrong, even if we need to do them to avoid disastrous consequences? (*See* **exceptionless duties**.)
- If means M1 and means M2 bring about the same total consequences, is it indifferent which we pick? (*See* **W. D. Ross**.)
- Under what conditions may we promote a good end by a means M that has some bad results? (*See* **double effect**.)

See also AQUINAS, THOMAS; ARISTOTLE; BENTHAM, JEREMY; HYPOTHETICAL/CATEGORICAL IMPERATIVES; KANT, IMMANUEL; MILL, JOHN STUART; SINGER, PETER.

ENVIRONMENTAL ETHICS. The study of moral issues involving the environment. For example, do we have a duty to protect the environment? Do we have duties about plants, nonhuman **animals**, endangered species, rivers, mountains, population growth, natural resources, and global warming? If we have such duties, do they depend totally on our responsibilities toward existing or future humans? Or do we have independent responsibilities toward the natural world itself, whose value goes beyond how it contributes to human life?

Environmental ethics as an academic discipline dates back to Aldo Leopold's *A Sand County Almanac* (1949). Leopold's *land ethic* states: "A thing is right when it tends to preserve the integrity, stability, and beauty of the biotic community. It is wrong when it tends otherwise." Leopold extended the things that deserve moral consideration (**moral patients**) beyond humans to include other things of the natural world, such as lakes, rivers, plants, and animals.

Several events of the 1960s combined to promote Leopold's ideas. Rachel Carson's *Silent Spring* (1963) warned about harm caused by pesticides, while Paul Ehrlich's *The Population Bomb* (1968) discussed the strain of an increasing human population on natural resources. The Cuyahoga River caught on fire, and Lake Erie, which it empties into, was declared "dead," both victims of pollution. There was much debate over the Glen Canyon Dam which created the massive Lake Powell out of a desert. Such events led many to think more about the environment.

Many thinkers seek to preserve the natural world solely for the sake of humans. Their *anthropocentric view* sees humans and their interests as central and attach only *instrumental value* to the environment. A part of the natural world, such as Lake Erie, has value only to the extent that it benefits humans; so people promoted the restoration of the lake for the sake of benefits like recreation, safe water, and edible fish.

Some thinkers argue for the more radical *biocentric view* that the natural world is of value in itself, in addition to what it contributes to human life. Richard Routley (now Sylvan) argues that it is "human chauvinism" to deny *intrinsic value* to the natural world; he links this with the biases and prejudices we have for our own religion, race, or gender (*see* **racism** and **sexism**). His "last man" argument has us imagine that, due to some tragic event, there is one person left on Earth who could arrange for the destruction of the natural world after he dies. We would see this action as wrong; but we can justify this belief only by attaching intrinsic value to the natural world.

Arne Næss distinguishes "shallow ecology" from "deep ecology." The former preserves the natural world for the sake of humans, and often for the sake of humans in developed countries. The latter recognizes the intrinsic value of the natural world and values it independently of its human benefits. Næss also defends "biospheric **egalitarianism**," which contends that the interests of all living beings count equally; so human interests do not necessarily override nonhuman interests. Næss urges us to see ourselves as part of an ecological community and to see how our interests interconnect with others in this wider community. Just as communitarians accuse **liberals** of ignoring their place in the larger human community, Næss accuses his opponents of ignoring humanity's place in the larger ecological community.

Françoise D'Eaubonne and Karen Warren connect deep ecology to **feminist ethics**. Extending some of Routley's ideas (which compare environmental biases to racial and sexist biases), they argue that the same male approach to life that oppresses women also oppresses the environment. In both areas, we need to abandon the male approach.

Many are critical of Næss's views. **Peter Singer** and others claim that rivers, trees, and the like do not have "interests" in any relevant sense since they cannot feel pleasure or pain, or be happy or sad. Since only sentient beings can have interests, our approach to ecology should stress the intrinsic importance of human and nonhuman animals. Others object that deep ecology is too radical to be effective politically; John Passmore suggests that we instead appeal to the Judeo-Christian notion of humans as stewards of the natural world.

There also is the question of whether we have duties to *future generations* of humans. If we have such duties, then we ought not to leave future generations without natural resources or with air and water that is so polluted that it harms their health. Especially important is *global warming*, which is the warming of the Earth's atmosphere from greenhouse gases such as carbon dioxide. Over the last several decades, with more factories and cars, our greenhouse gas emissions have increased greatly. Scientists warn of climatic changes that are beginning to take place and may produce future catastrophes, including massive flooding (as the polar icecaps melt), droughts that deplete the food supply and bring starvation, and stronger hurricanes. Such changes would harm future generations more than they harm us today.

Some philosophers argue that we do not have duties to future generations because we cannot have duties to what does not yet exist. But critics say this violates firm moral intuitions, such as that we ought not to bring children into the world that we are unwilling to care for; such duties exist even though future children do not yet exist. Others contend that we do not have duties to future generations because we cannot be sure what they will want and need; perhaps they will not appreciate beautiful scenery and will see the Grand Canyon as an ugly hole that should be filled and turned into a sports arena. But critics say it is highly likely that future generations will need clean water to drink, clean air to breathe, and other natural resources; so we ought not to leave future generations without such things. Such critics often argue that it is sheer bias to promote our current interests at the expense of future generations, and that this is much like a bias that ignores the interests of those of a different religion, race, or gender.

As humans advance, we likely will address new environmental issues. Many environmental problems are **global** in scope and require international cooperation. *See also* BUSINESS ETHICS; SCIENCE.

EPICURUS. *See* ANCIENT ETHICS.

EPISTEMOLOGY. Theory of knowledge. In ethics, a major issue is how we can **know right from wrong** and whether there is anything objective to know. Disputes here mirror disputes about other alleged objects of knowledge, like material things, **mathematical truths, scientific laws**, other minds, and **God**. So in ethics, as in other areas, we have *rationalists* (who base knowledge on pure thinking), *empiricists* (who base knowledge on sense experience), and *skeptics* (who deny that we have knowledge); we have *foundationalists* (who appeal to basic knowledge, like self-evident truths) and *coherentists* (who appeal to how our beliefs fit together, as in reflective-equilibrium or rational-attitudes approaches); we have *reductionists* (who reduce ethics to something else) and *non-reductionists* (who think ethics is irreducible); and we have *realists* (who believe in objective moral facts—*see* **moral realism** and **cognitivism/non-cognitivism**) and *anti-realists* (who reject such facts).

Another issue is whether epistemology is **normative** or descriptive. Epistemology often is seen as *normative*, as about how we **ought** to think and believe (e.g., why we *ought* to believe in astronomy but not astrology). Some define key epistemic terms ethically: so the *probability* of a belief is the degree it is *worth* being believed on intellectual grounds, and an *evident* belief is one that we *ought* to believe on this basis. There also are epistemic **virtues**, like being **consistent** and open-minded. Epistemology assumes that, as rational beings, we have two **prima facie duties**: to believe truths and avoid believing falsehoods (*see* **ethics of belief**). Epistemology proposes *normative epistemic principles* that are much like ethical principles (*see* **ethics: normative**):

- Other things being equal, we *ought* to prefer the simplest theory that adequately explains the data.
- If I believe that I see that a material object has a certain property

(e.g., that this pencil is yellow), then it is *evident* to me that it has that property (i.e., I *ought* to believe this) unless I have specific reason to doubt my senses in this particular case.

Scientific method is based on such principles; so empirical science is indirectly based on normative principles. We can ask about these principles the same questions that we ask about ethical principles: How can we *know* normative epistemic principles? Are they self-evident (as in **intuitionism**)? Are they somehow based on sense experience (as in **naturalism**)? Do they perhaps express feelings or imperatives about how to live instead of truths about independent normative facts (**emotivism** and **prescriptivism**)?

This normative view brings epistemology close to ethics: both use similar concepts and raise similar problems. This has disturbed thinkers who see empirical science as the realm of rationality and ethics as the realm of murky feelings. So Willard Quine has proposed that epistemology be naturalized. Epistemology ought to be cleansed from any normative function and made into a part of empirical science, so that it just *describes* how current scientists reason and arrive at knowledge. Critics object that *naturalized epistemology* is sociology, not philosophy. Sociology can describe how astronomy and astrology arrive at beliefs, but it leaves open which method gives beliefs that are *better* grounded and more *worthy* of acceptance. Critics also argue that this sociological approach avoids the most important epistemological issue: How *ought* we to form our beliefs? *See also* METAPHYSICS; PHILOSOPHY AND ETHICS.

ERROR THEORY. *See* MACKIE, J. L.

ETHICS (also called moral philosophy). The **philosophical** investigation of questions about morality. Ethics commonly divides into three areas: *metaethics* (the nature and methodology of moral judgments), *normative ethics* (general principles about how we **ought** to live), and *applied ethics* (specific moral issues). This dictionary adds three additional areas: the *history of ethics*, *interdisciplinary issues*, and *miscellaneous topics*. Each of these six areas has a general entry that starts with "ethics:" and points to more specific entries (together they point to *all* the substantive entries in this dictionary):

- **ethics: metaethics** is about the nature and methodology of moral judgments.

- **ethics: normative** considers general principles about how we ought to live.
- **ethics: applied** is about specific moral issues such as lying or abortion, or moral questions in areas like business or medicine.
- **ethics: history** is about historical periods and figures.
- **ethics: interdisciplinary** relates ethics to science, world religions, and other parts of philosophy.
- **ethics: miscellaneous** is about areas that do not fit neatly into the other five categories.

While this is a useful way to divide the subject matter of this dictionary, sometimes the boundary between areas is unclear and a particular entry could be situated in more than one area.

ETHICS: APPLIED (also called practical ethics). The study of specific moral issues such as lying or abortion, or moral questions in areas like business or medicine. Applied ethics examines issues like: Is abortion right or wrong? Is it ever permissible to lie? What roles should doctors play in their patients' end-of-life decisions and actions? What are the main **rights** of employees? Do corporations have social responsibilities? Do nonhuman animals have rights?

Applied ethics differs from *metaethics*, which studies the nature and methodology of moral judgments, and *normative ethics*, which seeks to specify general principles about how we ought to live (*see* **ethics: metaethics** and **ethics: normative**). This dictionary has many entries on applied ethics:

- The most developed branches are **bioethics** and **business ethics**. Other branches deal with **animals, computer ethics, disability ethics, environmental ethics, ethics of belief, global ethics, moral education, professional ethics,** and **sexual ethics.**
- Other ethical issues include **abortion and infanticide, academic freedom, capital punishment, civil disobedience, discrimination, euthanasia, forgiveness, homosexuality, human rights, killing, paternalism, pornography, poverty, privacy, property, punishment, racism,** rational discussion (*see* **charity, principle of**), **sexism, socialism, stem-cell research, suicide, terrorism,** and **war.**
- Figures whose main focus is practical ethics include **Hannah**

Arendt, Kenneth Arrow, Simone de Beauvoir, Carol Gilligan, Martin Luther King, Lawrence Kohlberg, Peter Singer, Simone Weil, and Mary Wollstonecraft. Most other ethicists at times deal with concrete, practical issues.

These covers only a sample of the growing field of applied ethics.

ETHICS: HISTORY. The entries in this dictionary about the historical periods and figures of Western philosophical ethics are:

- Ancient ethics, including **Aristotle, Plato,** and **Socrates.**
- Medieval ethics, including **Thomas Aquinas** and **Augustine.**
- Modern ethics, including **Joseph Butler, Thomas Hobbes, David Hume, Immanuel Kant, John Locke, Samuel Pufendorf, Thomas Reid, Jean-Jacques Rousseau, Adam Smith,** and **Mary Wollstonecraft.**
- Nineteenth-century ethics, including **Jeremy Bentham, Franz Brentano, Charles Darwin, Georg Wilhelm Friedrich Hegel, Karl Marx, James Mill, John Stuart Mill, Friedrich Nietzsche,** and **Henry Sidgwick.**
- Twentieth-century ethics, including **Elizabeth Anscombe, Hannah Arendt, Kenneth Arrow, A. J. Ayer, Simone de Beauvoir, Ruth Benedict, Richard Brandt, Martin Buber, John Dewey, Ronald Dworkin, John Finnis, Philippa Foot, William Frankena, Carol Gilligan, Jürgen Habermas, R. M. Hare, Gilbert Harman, Martin Luther King, Lawrence Kohlberg, C. I. Lewis,** logical positivism, **Alasdair MacIntyre, J. L. Mackie, G. E. Moore, Thomas Nagel, Robert Nozick, Darek Parfit, Ayn Rand, John Rawls, Paul Ricoeur, W. D. Ross, Jean-Paul Sartre, Peter Singer, Simone Weil,** and **Bernard Williams.**

See **political philosophy** for a short history of political philosophy in the West. There also are religious and non-Western ethical traditions (*see* **ethics: interdisciplinary**). *See also* the chronology.

ETHICS: INTERDISCIPLINARY. Many entries in this dictionary relate ethics to other disciplines, including **science** (**anthropology, biology, mathematics, psychology,** and **sociobiology**), world religions (**Biblical ethics, Buddhist ethics, Confucius, Daoist ethics, God, Hindu**

ethics, **Islamic ethics, Jewish ethics,** and **moral theology**), and other areas of **philosophy (aesthetics, epistemology, logic,** and **metaphysics**). Applied ethics (*see* **ethics: applied**) is often interdisciplinary.

ETHICS: METAETHICS. The study of the nature and methodology of moral judgments. Metaethics examines questions like: What do "**good**" and "**ought**" mean? Are there moral truths and moral facts? How can we know or rationally defend beliefs about right and wrong?

Metaethics differs from *normative ethics*, which seeks to specify general principles about how we ought to live, and *applied ethics*, which studies specific moral issues (*see* **ethics: normative** and **ethics: applied**). Metaethics is sometimes called *second-order ethics*, to distinguish it from normative and applied ethics, which are considered *first-order ethics*. The entry on **knowing right from wrong** sketches the main alternatives about metaethics.

A metaethical view often has two parts. One part is about the nature of moral judgments; this often includes a definition of "good" or "ought." The other part is about methodology; this tells how to select moral principles. For example, **cultural relativism** takes "good" to mean "socially approved"; it tells us to select our moral principles by following what our society approves of. While cultural relativism bases morality on social conventions, other metaethical views may base it on personal feelings (**subjectivism** and **emotivism**), what we would feel if we were fully rational (**ideal observer theory**), the course of **evolution**, God's will (**divine command theory**), self-evident truths (**intuitionism**), or what we can consistently will (**prescriptivism**).

Several other entries are included under **rational moral thinking: consistency, imagination, impartiality,** and **information.** The entry on **ought** brings together issues like whether "ought" is rationally authoritative, whether it is inherently motivating, whether it implies "can," and how to distinguish moral from non-moral oughts. There are further entries on **cognitivism/non-cognitivism, definitions of moral terms, global ethics, moral realism, natural law, naturalism, relativism, self-evident truths,** supervenience, and **universalizability.**

' Metaethics sometimes is taken more broadly to include questions about ethics not covered by normative or applied ethics, for example how **free will and determinism** connect with ethics and whether there is a distinctly **feminine** approach to morality. These topics are included under **ethics: miscellaneous** in this dictionary.

ETHICS: MISCELLANEOUS. This covers entries that do not fit neatly into the other five major categories (**ethics: applied, ethics: history, ethics: interdisciplinary, ethics: metaethics,** and **ethics: normative**). Miscellaneous entries include **autonomy/heteronomy, conscience, decision theory, fallacies about ethics, feminist ethics, free will and determinism, happiness, hypothetical/categorical imperatives, normative/descriptive, ought, prisoner's dilemma, responsibility, weakness of will,** and **why be moral question.**

ETHICS: NORMATIVE. The study of general principles about how we **ought** to live. Normative ethics seeks to formulate and defend answers to questions such as: What are the basic principles of right and wrong? What things are ultimately good or worthwhile in life? What would a just society be like? What makes someone a good person? What are the main virtues and vices? What are the basic human **rights**?

Normative ethics differs from *metaethics,* which studies the nature and methodology of moral judgments, and *applied ethics,* which studies specific moral issues (*see* **ethics: metaethics** and **ethics: applied**). A good introduction to normative ethics is the entry on **consequentialism/non-consequentialism**; other good starters are the entries on **good, utilitarianism,** and **egoism.** There are further entries on **altruism, benevolence, conscientiousness, consistency, double effect, egalitarianism, end-justifies-means, exceptionless duties, free rider, golden rule, justice, liberalism/communitarianism, love your neighbor, moral agent, moral patient, political philosophy, praiseworthy, prima facie duty, social contract, supererogatory,** and **virtue.**

ETHICS OF BELIEF. The study of moral responsibilities about beliefs. William Clifford (1845–1879), in his essay "The Ethics of Belief," defended this **exceptionless** principle: "It is wrong always, everywhere, and for anyone, to believe anything upon insufficient evidence." He wrote of a ship owner who, without proper investigation, talked himself into believing that his ship was trustworthy; the ship sank, killing all the passengers. Even if the ship had not sunk, the owner still would have been irresponsible and blameworthy. Believing on weak evidence is always harmful, since it ruins our intellectual character and this will have bad consequences later.

William James (1842–1910) criticized Clifford's principle, which he took to mean "It is wrong to accept what is not proved." James objected that the view is inconsistent in two ways. First, the view is itself not proved; so it would be wrong on its own standard to accept it. Second, Clifford's principle is inconsistent with our practice; in daily life we all, including Clifford, have beliefs based on hunches rather than proof, and such beliefs do not have such dire consequences as Clifford claims. We follow our hunches about political candidates, moral issues, whom to marry, and which **scientific** hypothesis is most promising; it would paralyze us if we always had to wait for proof on such matters. In personal relations, we believe good things about others until these are proved otherwise. In disaster situations, we believe without proof that we will survive, and this belief may be the force that brings about our survival and thus makes itself true; forbidding such beliefs would be absurd.

James also claims that Clifford's principle is unbalanced. James thinks truth seekers have two duties: to believe truths and to avoid believing falsehoods. Clifford's principle puts all the weight on the second, on avoiding error; but this would make us lose many truths. We ought, instead, to steer between the vices of being too gullible and being too skeptical. James thought that where proofs exist they ought to be accepted; but on important issues that we cannot decide on intellectual grounds, we often must, and rightfully may, follow our feelings.

ETIQUETTE. *See* OUGHT.

EUTHANASIA (mercy killing). Killing or otherwise bringing about the death of another animate being for that being's good, usually to end its suffering. It is customary to euthanize nonhuman **animals**, such as family pets that have become so ill they cannot eat or are in constant pain; few ethicists object to this. Euthanizing humans is more controversial and is much debated in **bioethics**.

Two distinctions are important to the debate. First, euthanasia can be *voluntary* (in accord with the person's competently expressed desires), *involuntary* (against the person's competently expressed desires), or *nonvoluntary* (the person is unable to express competent desires either way because, for example, the person is a child, mentally disabled, senile, or in a coma). Ethicists agree that involuntary euthanasia is unjustified, since ending the life of competent persons against their will violates their **autonomy** and **right** to self-determination. The other two kinds of euthanasia are more controversial.

Second, euthanasia can be *active* (where steps are taken to kill the person, for example by poison or lethal injection) or *passive* (lifesaving treatment is withheld, for example the respirator is turned off or an emergency operation is not performed, thereby allowing the illness to take one's life). Most ethicists approve of passive euthanasia in appropriate circumstances; active euthanasia is more controversial. Many non-**consequentialists**, especially those who hold that the direct killing of an innocent human being is seriously wrong (the *sanctity of human life* view), see the active/passive distinction as crucial. This seems to be the position of hospice organizations, who seek to relieve pain and anxiety but not to hasten or postpone dying. On the other hand, **Peter Singer** and other consequentialists evaluate actions in terms of consequences; they see the active/passive distinction as less important since both have the same main result (the person's death).

In ordinary usage, "euthanasia" often means "active euthanasia"; ethicists use "euthanasia" more broadly, to include the passive form.

Let us consider active nonvoluntary euthanasia. Peter Singer and a few others argue that it is morally permissible to kill severely **disabled** infants (*see* **abortion and infanticide**). Singer defends this on **utilitarian** grounds; the consequences of letting such infants live are worse (on them, on their families, and on their caretakers) than are the consequences of ending their lives. Others say that such killing is wrong because it violates the sanctity of human life or fails to treat persons as ends-in-themselves (*see* **Immanuel Kant**).

Sometimes a previously competent person can no longer express a desire on the matter. Suppose Lance crashes his bicycle and is so severely injured that his healthcare providers contemplate whether his life should continue. Suppose further that he left no "living will" instructions about what to do in such cases. Then who is the right person to make decisions about his healthcare? Is it permissible for that person to choose some form of active or passive euthanasia? If so, then should one choose as Lance would have chosen or as one thinks is best? Some argue that the former better respects Lance's autonomy, while others say we cannot be sure about what Lance would have chosen.

Now let us consider passive voluntary euthanasia. Most ethicists accept this in cases where the treatment withheld is extraordinary. Suppose Kristin suffers from a disease that, at some point, will render her unable to breathe on her own. She explicitly directs her healthcare providers not to place her on a respirator when that time comes. Most agree that the respirator is extraordinary treatment and that it is morally permissible to honor her wishes. If, however, she asks healthcare providers not to connect her to a feeding tube when she no longer can eat, the case is more controversial. Some believe it is morally permissible to withhold the feeding tube because doing so merely allows Kristin's illness to run its course. Others argue that food and water are ordinary treatments that healthcare providers must provide.

There is much debate about active voluntary euthanasia, especially *physician-assisted suicide*. The latter is where a physician sets up a mechanism to end a patient's life which the patient then can trigger. Many oppose such active euthanasia as violating the sanctity of human life; religious arguments often are made against **suicide**. Others argue that permitting euthanasia in voluntary cases would inevitably lead to permitting it in nonvoluntary and even involuntary cases (*slippery-slope argument*). Others argue that a miracle cure always is possible, so we should not actively (or perhaps even passively) euthanize people. Still others argue that we should not trust the wishes of those who say they want to be killed since such people often change their minds and may be too ill to think competently.

Proponents of active euthanasia reject these concerns. They reject or qualify the sanctity-of-life view. They counter the slippery-slope argument by claiming that there is a clear and morally relevant difference between voluntary euthanasia and euthanasia of other sorts. They also argue that miracle cures are not real possibilities. With respect to the competence of those who claim they desire to be killed, they respond in two ways. First, often those who express such desires are clearly competent; many express their desires before they reach extreme pain and confusion. Second, it may be advisable to have a "cooling off" period between the time one expresses the desire to be euthanized and the time it is carried out, to make sure that the desire is stable. Finally, in favor of active euthanasia, they argue that respecting the decisions of those who wish to be put to death is necessary in order to respect their autonomy and human dignity.

Debates over euthanasia will continue. Medical advances likely will complicate these issues further and raise new issues. *See also* ARENDT, HANNAH; DOUBLE EFFECT.

EUTHYPHRO PROBLEM. *See* DIVINE COMMAND THEORY; NATURAL LAW; PLATO.

EVOLUTIONISM. The view that "X is **good**" means "X accords with evolution" or "X is more evolved." As a form of ethical **naturalism**, evolutionism defines moral terms using empirical concepts and thus tries to make ethics part of empirical **science**.

Social Darwinism, which was popular in the late 19th century, saw evolution in terms of the survival of the fittest, whereby the strong survive and overcome the weak. It saw similar struggles in human life: individuals, businesses, social classes, and nations all struggle for supremacy. The **poor** and the weak are unfit to survive; helping them violates the evolutionary process and thus is wrong. Social Darwinism meshed with Western capitalism, imperialism, and **racism**.

Many evolutionists saw the main trend of evolution differently. Some saw it as moving toward greater consciousness; therefore, they concluded, it is right to promote this. Others saw evolution as moving toward a higher morality in which our sympathies extend to all humanity, including the weak and the poor; so, they concluded, it is right to follow this. **Marxists** saw evolution as moving toward the classless, communist society; so, they concluded, it is right to support this.

Critics accuse evolutionism of committing the *naturalistic fallacy* (*see* **G. E. Moore**). It is wrong, they say, to identify the evaluative term "good" with the descriptive term "more evolved." If something is *more evolved*, it is a further question whether it is *good*. Suppose that evolution moves us toward more misery (as some believe); would it follow that promoting misery was good? Depending on what the path of evolution is, it could be either good or bad to support it. *See also* BIOLOGY; DARWIN, CHARLES; SOCIOBIOLOGY.

EXCEPTIONLESS DUTIES. Duties that hold always, in all cases—for example, that one ought never to **kill** an innocent human being. The belief in exceptionless duties is called *absolutism*.

Immanuel Kant accepted several exceptionless duties, as do some rule **utilitarians** and **natural law** thinkers. Many *classical utilitarians* accept just one exceptionless duty, to always do whatever maximizes the balance of pleasure over pain. **W. D. Ross** and many others accept only **prima facie duties** that can be overridden by other duties.

There are several arguments against exceptionless duties. First, some claim that any ethical system with more than one exceptionless duty will lead to contradictions. Suppose we accept "Always obey your parents" and "Never break promises." Cases arise where your parents tell you to break a promise; then the first norm tells you "Break the promise" while the second tells you "Do not break the promise."

Absolutists respond that not all groups of exceptionless duties conflict. Suppose we accept these three negative duties: "Never kill an innocent person," "Never take heroin for recreational purposes," and

"Never commit adultery." These will not conflict. So, exceptionless norms can be consistent if they are formulated carefully.

A second argument is that exceptionless duties should be rejected because they lead to inhumane results in unusual cases. "Stealing is always wrong," for example, would forbid us to steal a loaf of bread from a wealthy store when this is needed to keep our family from starving; but surely it would be permissible to steal in this case.

Some absolutists hold to their guns and say that stealing the bread would be wrong. Others avoid exceptionless norms that have inhumane results but embrace those that forbid inhumane actions. They point out that Socrates and Jesus were innocent and yet, for utilitarian reasons, were put to death; "Never kill an innocent person" would stop such inhumane actions.

Some opponents of absolutism think "Never kill an innocent person" has inhumane results since it forbids **euthanasia**. But perhaps euthanasia is wrong. Or perhaps it is right, and we just need to qualify the principle about killing to read something like "Never kill an innocent person who is not suffering from an incurable and painful disease." One still can claim that this longer principle, since it has "never," is *exceptionless*. Or can one? Some object that a long principle with many qualifications is not *exceptionless* in any meaningful sense.

A third argument is that we can refute any exceptionless norm with hypothetical disaster cases, where Dr. Evil will torture everyone and destroy the world unless we violate the norm. Surely, they say, we should kill an innocent child if this is needed to prevent such a disaster.

Absolutists respond in various ways. Some insist that we should not kill the innocent even to stop Dr. Evil. Others qualify their principle to avoid the problem, moving to something like "Never kill an innocent person when this is not needed to prevent disaster." Still others, while admitting that killing the innocent is justified in some hypothetical cases, insist that in real life we do not know enough to recognize such cases. In real life, for example, we cannot trust Dr. Evil to do what he says he will do; perhaps he will bring disaster even if we kill the innocent. So they say, in the spirit of rule utilitarianism, that we will make better decisions if we follow the practical rule *never* to kill the innocent; following this rule strictly will prevent tragic mistakes.

Absolutists sometimes argue that we should take a norm more strictly, or even exceptionlessly, if doing so would tend to prevent great evils or foolish choices. Here "great evils" covers things like the killing of an innocent person, the bringing about of a drug addiction, or the ruining of a happy marriage. When such things are at stake, and when following a looser rule is apt to lead to bad choices, it makes sense to follow a strict rule like: "Never kill the innocent," "Never take dangerous drugs for recreational reasons," or "Never risk a happy marriage by committing adultery." Absolutists say that many problems in the world come from people who, since they take moral rules too loosely, easily can be tempted into doing very harmful things.

Critics can accept the importance of taking some norms very strictly; but they object to norms with "never." And they point to the difficulty of formulating norms to which creative people cannot find possible exceptions. For example, consider "Never burn a child in gasoline just for fun." Could not this be right if we invented a gasoline that burned at harmlessly low temperatures? And what would happen to our killing norms if we found out a way to kill and then instantly bring back to life? *See also* CONSEQUENTIALISM/NON-CONSEQUENTIALISM; DOUBLE EFFECT; END-JUSTIFIES-MEANS; ETHICS OF BELIEF; FINNIS, JOHN; OUGHT; RIGHTS.

EXPLOITATION. *See* MARX, KARL.

EXPRESSIVISM. *See* EMOTIVISM.

EXTERNALISM. *See* OUGHT.

– F –

FALLACIES ABOUT ETHICS. A fallacy is a common error of reasoning, especially one apt to mislead. Ethical fallacies include these:

- Confusing **egoism** (we ought to promote our own good) with **utilitarianism** (we ought to promote everyone's good) or **hedonism** (the good is pleasure, which leaves open whose good we ought to promote).
- Confusing the **golden rule** (treat others as you want to be treated) with the law of retaliation (treat others as they treat you) or the empirical generalization that people treat you as you treat them.
- Thinking that those who reject objective ethical truths must be selfish or evil—or that those who accept objective ethical truths must be dogmatic and intolerant.

- Speaking of "the Enlightenment view of ethics" as if there were only one such view; in fact, Enlightenment thinkers like **Thomas Hobbes, David Hume**, and **Immanuel Kant** differed greatly.
- Thinking that there are only two basic options in ethics: the one you favor and some outlandish alternative. This is related to the "straw man" fallacy that distorts the views of an opponent.
- Concluding that there are no solutions to be found when ethical problems prove difficult to resolve.

FAMINE RELIEF. *See* POVERTY.

FEELINGS. *See* ARISTOTLE; AYER, A. J.; BRENTANO, FRANZ; EMOTIVISM; ETHICS OF BELIEF; FEMINIST ETHICS; GILLIGAN, CAROL; HUME, DAVID; IDEAL OBSERVER THEORY; KNOWING RIGHT FROM WRONG; MACKIE, J. L.; PLATO; SMITH, ADAM; SUBJECTIVISM; WHY BE MORAL QUESTION.

FEMINIST ETHICS. Ethics that emphasizes gender and womanhood. Not all who do feminist ethics are women; **John Stuart Mill** wrote one of the classics in the field, *The Subjection of Women*. And not all ethics done by women is *feminist*; many women ethicists explore areas where gender is less important. Since feminist ethicists disagree much, feminist ethics is best characterized not by giving common doctrines but by giving representative issues, as we will do here.

(1) What is **sexism** and why is it wrong? Early feminists worked for the **right** of women to vote, which was gained in the United States in 1920. Then interest turned to areas like job discrimination, equal pay for equal work, maternity leave and day care, discrimination in athletics, and sexual harassment. Today there is much concern with subtle sexism, where issues are less clear. As this entry was being drafted, for example, there was public debate over whether men and women tennis champions at Wimbledon ought to receive equal prize money. Defenders of the current unequal practice say that men play more sets (a match being the best 3 of 5 sets with men, but the best 2 of 3 with women) and bring in more revenue (because of larger audiences). Others say both groups should be treated equally. Which side is correct? (Historical note: they decided in favor of equal prize money.)

(2) What issues ought ethics to deal with? Many think ethicists have emphasized areas of greater interest to men. Many feminist ethicists treat issues of special interest to women, like gender discrimination,

gender roles, bodily ideals, feminist **political** activism, nurturing relationships, bringing up children, marriage, lesbianism, prostitution, and **abortion**. It turns out that many men are interested in these areas too.

(3) Do men and women differ in ways important for ethics? Some think men tend more to value things (objects) and to be competitive, violent, and rational; women, by contrast, tend more to value personal relationships and to be nurturing, self-sacrificing, and emotional. These are tendencies: a specific man may be more emotional and a specific woman more rational. Are these alleged gender differences just popular stereotypes, or are they real? If they are real, do they come from social conditioning, or from **biology**? Many favor social conditioning. Little boys are taught to win and little girls are taught to look pretty and be helpful; so husbands sacrifice personal relationships in order to win at business, and wives serve their families so much that they forget about being good to themselves. If these gender differences are from social conditioning, should we try to raise the next generation in a more balanced way in terms of traditional male and female qualities? Some object that this idea would fail, because, they argue, gender differences are biologically based; they point to how violent little boys are in their early stages, even before we teach them to be violent.

(4) Is there a distinctively female way to think about ethics? After **Lawrence Kohlberg** developed his stages of moral thinking based on interviews with males, his colleague **Carol Gilligan** objected that his stages applied mainly to males; she thought women tend to think differently. Men tend to think of morality in terms of **justice**, principles, rights, and duties; women tend to think in terms of caring for others, feelings, personal relationships, and responsibilities. Some feminists see as masculine the **utilitarian** approach, which stresses calculation and a type of **impartiality** that considers equally the welfare of one's child and of a stranger; a feminine ethics sees responsibilities as growing out of relationships, such as mother-child or friend-friend. Many thinkers, however, question whether ethical thinking is gendered. Some think there is one correct ethics for all; in formulating it we need to incorporate the experience of both males and females. Others say there are many approaches to ethics, but these do not divide neatly into male and female views. Many women appeal to justice and rights (especially women arguing for gender equality), and many women are utilitarians. Many men (like **David Hume**) base ethics on positive feelings toward others, and many men (like **W. D. Ross**) criticize utilitarianism for neglecting the moral relevance of relationships. Some say we can find men

and women on both sides of all major issues in ethics (*see* the chronology). *See also* ANSCOMBE, ELIZABETH; ARENDT, HANNAH; BEAUVOIR, SIMONE DE; BENEDICT, RUTH; ENVIRONMENTAL ETHICS; FOOT, PHILIPPA; PORNOGRAPHY; RAND, AYN; SEXUAL ETHICS; WEIL, SIMONE; WOLLSTONECRAFT, MARY.

FINNIS, JOHN (1940–). Australian philosopher who works in ethics, law, and legal philosophy. His *Natural Law and Natural Rights* (1980) restates the **natural law** ethics of **Thomas Aquinas** in contemporary **intuitionist** terms. Finnis argues that we can uncover the basic **goods** of human life by rational reflection, after which their goodness becomes self-evident. These basic goods include seven items: life/health, knowledge, play, aesthetic experience, sociability, practical reasonableness/autonomy, and religion. We cannot say that one of these goods is more important than another; each of the goods can, from a certain perspective, seem like the most important thing in life. Since these goods cannot be measured on a common scale and totaled, the **consequentialist** norm to maximize total value is meaningless. Instead, we are free to choose which basic goods we want to emphasize in our lives; we might, for example, choose research (which emphasizes knowledge) or medicine (which emphasizes health). Choosing directly against a basic good, however, is always wrong; this leads to **exceptionless** norms (for example, against murder, which contravenes the basic good of life). Thus Finnis arrives at a non-consequentialist ethics.

FIRST PRINCIPLES. Truths that are known but that require no further proof or justification. *See* INTUITIONISM.

FOOT, PHILIPPA (1920–). English philosopher who stimulated interest in **naturalism, virtue,** and **Aristotle.** Foot objected when **emotivists** and **prescriptivists** claimed that moral beliefs were a matter not of truths but of feelings or decisions. She counters that evaluative terms like "rude" have descriptive content; not just anything can be said to be "rude." Similarly, not just any directive, for example "Clap three times before you go to bed," can be a moral principle. Moral principles have to relate to human well-being and needs, which are not arbitrary; so there are constraints on what can count as "**good**" or "moral." Foot's *Natural Goodness* (2001) argues further that "good" refers to what fulfills a biological life form. A tree has good roots if these enable it to fulfill what it is to be a tree. Similarly, to be a good human is to fulfill what it is to be a human, which is to be rational in practical affairs. Foot's Aristotelian approach sees values as a kind of fact.

Foot was good at raising issues. She once asked whether we necessarily have reason, in terms of promoting what we want, for being moral. She thought the answer was no; at least in some cases, a person might have no reason to be moral. In **Kantian** terms, she looked at moral beliefs as **hypothetical imperatives** (which rationally bind us only if we have certain desires) and not as categorical imperatives (which rationally bind us regardless of our desires); she saw categorical imperatives as unintelligible pretense. Not everyone agreed with her on this (*see* **why be moral question**).

Foot proposed the "trolley problem." You are on a rapid-transit train that is out of control and is heading down track-A, where it would kill five people that Dr. Evil tied to the track. If you press a button, the train will instead go down track-B, where it would kill one person that Dr. Evil tied to the track. Should you press the button? Plain act **utilitarians** say yes without hesitation. But many fear that to press the button is to murder one person yourself, which is wrong, whereas not to press it is just to let Dr. Evil murder five people; so they think you should not press the button. *See also* DOUBLE EFFECT; OUGHT.

FORGIVENESS. I forgive you if I give up angry feelings of resentment toward you for how you treated me wrongly. Forgiveness often comes after the other person admits error or seriously resolves to change.

We can view forgiveness as a **virtue** midway between two vices (*see* **Aristotle**). One extreme vice is *moral passivity*, which is to have too little resentment toward those who treat us wrongly. Imagine a wife who is regularly beaten by her husband but does nothing, suffering in a passive way, forgiving excessively, and avoiding angry feelings. Moral passivity harms both victims (who suffer) and oppressors (who need to be confronted about their wrongdoing).

The other extreme vice is *vengefulness*, which is to have too much resentment toward those who treat us wrongly. If we are vengeful, then we bear grudges and want to get even, returning evil for evil. Vengefulness harms both the vengeful person (whose inner life is tormented with anger) and those who suffer retaliation. Vengefulness can destroy personal relationships and harm the community; it also can lead to unending feuds between groups who consider themselves enemies.

Between the vices of moral passivity and vengefulness, there is the virtue of *proper forgiveness*, which is to have the right degree of resentment but be ready to give up this up when appropriate (especially when the other person admits error and seriously resolves to change). How exactly to define "proper forgiveness" is a matter of controversy. For example, are there unforgivable crimes? Ought we to forgive Adolph Hitler for his atrocities? Can we forgive only wrongs done to us personally (or perhaps to those close to us)? Does forgiving my daughter's killer entail that I want the killer not to be punished?

Forgiveness often has a religious dimension. **Christians** stress purity of heart; they pray the Lord's Prayer, where they ask God to forgive them as they forgive others. **Jews** stress the community dimension of forgiveness and the duty to forgive one who sincerely apologizes. **Buddhists** stress the inner torment that we suffer if we do not forgive others. *See also* CAPITAL PUNISHMENT; PUNISHMENT.

FORMAL ETHICS. *See* CONSISTENCY.

FRANKENA, WILLIAM (1908–1994). American philosopher who taught at the University of Michigan and contributed to various areas of moral philosophy. Early on, he published an article criticizing attacks on the so-called "naturalistic fallacy"; he then was a **naturalist** about "**good**" and an **intuitionist** about "**ought**." In his mature thought, as expressed in his classic *Ethics* (1963) textbook, he adopted moderate **emotivism**. "Good" and "ought" express our feelings and attitudes. These terms can be used in moral and non-moral (aesthetic, prudential, etc.) ways; what distinguishes moral evaluations is that they rest, at least in part, on the good or harm done to other sentient beings besides oneself. Frankena argues that we would all agree on our moral beliefs if we were ideally rational (*see* **relativism**); this leads to a kind of "moral truth," defined in terms of an ideal agreement between rational inquirers, much like **ideal observer theory**. He asks "**Why be moral?**" and takes this to ask "Would we choose the moral way of life if we were rational in the sense of being factually **informed, consistent**, and clearheaded?" He argues that most (or perhaps all) would choose to be moral under such conditions, assuming that most (or perhaps all) have desires that are not purely **egoistic**. Even though acting morally is not always in our self-interest (since it may demand sacrifices), still it may be that we would choose it if we were rational in this sense.

In normative ethics (*see* **ethics: normative**), he accepts a principle of beneficence (*see* **benevolence**) with four parts (where earlier parts take precedence, other things equal, over later parts):

- One ought not to inflict evil or harm (what is bad).
- One ought to prevent evil or harm.
- One ought to remove evil.
- One ought to do or promote good.

He adds a **justice** principle about treating people equally and a pluralistic list of what things are good in themselves. All other moral norms can be derived from these, sometimes in a rule-**utilitarian** manner. *See also* VIRTUE.

FREE RIDER. One who benefits from a social practice while working against it or at least not contributing to it. Suppose that in Niceville, where you live, almost everyone follows the practice of respecting each others' property; this benefits everyone, since there is almost no crime and people need not worry about buying door locks or security systems. But you, who benefit from this practice, take advantage of it by stealing; you are then a "free rider." Here are some other examples:

- You benefit from the general practice in Niceville of telling the truth and keeping promises; but you lie and break promises whenever this is to your advantage.
- You fish in Lake Niceville, where the accepted practice, in order not to deplete the supply of fish, is to take at most only four fish per year; you take fifty fish per year.

John Rawls argues that free riding is wrong because we have an obligation to do our part under the rules of a reasonably just practice from which we have voluntarily accepted benefits or opportunities.

How to respond to free riders is an important problem for most societies and institutions; most turn to **punishment** to discourage free riding. *See also* EGOISM; HOBBES, THOMAS; JUSTICE; POLITICAL PHILOSOPHY; PRISONER'S DILEMMA.

FREE WILL AND DETERMINISM. *Determinism* is the view that for any event, given the conditions preceding it, the event had to occur. So given previous conditions that directly affect the weather (such as water temperatures and wind patterns), as well as other conditions that may or may not relate clearly to the weather, it was impossible for Hurricane Katrina not to have occurred in precisely the way that it did.

This view has important implications for ethics since choices and actions also would be events determined by previous conditions. I selected a gray shirt from my closet this morning. According to determinism, I could not have chosen otherwise given the conditions that preceded my choice. These conditions include both my genetic makeup and various socialization factors (family, friends, schools, churches, etc.) to which I have been subject. Or suppose, to take an example of moral relevance, that I caused an accident by driving my car while drunk. Authorities and the general public would blame me morally for the accident, especially if it resulted in injuries or deaths. If determinism is true, however, it is not apparent how this blame can be justified. After all, I could not have done other than I did given the previous conditions. How can I be blamed for an act that I had to perform?

Many philosophers, such as **Immanuel Kant**, believe that if determinism is true I am not morally **responsible** for my act. They think freedom is necessary for moral responsibility; we are not morally responsible for our actions unless we can choose and act otherwise. *Free will* is the capacity to choose one way or another in some contexts. Although I cannot choose to be taller (genetics have determined my height), I could have chosen a black shirt rather than a gray one. And, in the fictional example, I could have chosen not to drive while drunk. Even if genetics predispose me to abuse alcohol and society pushes me toward drunk driving, I still could have chosen not to get drunk and then drive my car. Likewise, no matter how I was abused as a child, I can choose not to continue the cycle of violence by abusing my children. It is this ability to choose otherwise that justifies the **punishment** and moral blame that we receive when we act wrongly.

Determinists respond in various ways. Some *hard determinists* agree that free will is needed for justified moral responsibility; they conclude that our concept of moral responsibility should be abandoned. Others argue that the point is moot since we are determined to assign moral responsibility just as we are determined to act as we do. Still others adopt *compatibilism* or *soft determinism*, as formulated by **David Hume**; this says determinism is compatible with the freedom needed for justified moral responsibility. For compatibilists, the only freedom we need is the ability to have done otherwise if we had different beliefs and desires. If I had different beliefs and desires, then I could have kept from driving while drunk. This does not mean that I actually could have had different beliefs and desires, but, rather, merely the hypothetical idea that I could have acted differently had my beliefs and desires been different. For compatibilists, moral responsibility requires that one is the cause of the act. I am responsible for drunk driving because *I* became drunk and *I* drove the car; blame and punishment make sense here since they can influence my motivation and thus make it less likely that I will act similarly in the future. But if I am forced physically to do something, then I am not morally responsible; blame and punishment here make no sense, since they cannot influence how I will act in similar cases in the future. Proponents of the *indeterminist* or *libertarian* view of free will find this unsatisfying, however, because we still cannot choose otherwise given previous conditions; accordingly, they reject determinism to preserve free will.

There are other debates about determinism. **Socrates** and **Aristotle** disagreed about whether we are determined to act in the way we think is best (*see* **weakness of will**). Boethius and other **medievals** disagreed about whether **God**'s foreknowledge of how we will act would thereby determine our choice. **Thomas Hobbes** and **Jean-Jacques Rousseau** disagreed about whether we are **psychologically** determined to do what we believe to be in our best interests (*see* **egoism**).

With the emergence of quantum physics, which seems to posit random events in the universe, the general thesis of determinism has come under attack; but there are controversies about this and how it applies to free will. Some defend a "randomizer in the brain" model of free will, whereby some of our actions, like events of quantum physics, are ultimately unpredictable; others object to this because it leaves no room for *personal agency*, the idea that *I* decide what to do (as opposed to physical events in my brain deciding this).

The determinism/free-will debate continues today. Although some philosophers choose indeterministic free will and some adopt hard determinism, still others hold some form of compatibilism. *See also* AUGUSTINE; BIOLOGY; SARTRE, JEAN-PAUL.

FUTURE GENERATIONS. *See* ENVIRONMENTAL ETHICS.

– G –

GAME THEORY. *See* DECISION THEORY; PRISONER'S DILEMMA.

GANDHI, MAHATMA. *See* HINDU ETHICS.

GILLIGAN, CAROL (1936–). American **psychologist** and **feminist ethicist**. Her Harvard colleague **Lawrence Kohlberg** developed a view about six stages of moral thinking, based on interviews with males; he found that females tended to be at a lower level of moral thinking than males. Gilligan objected that Kohlberg's stages apply mainly to males; she thought women tend to think differently.

Gilligan's *In a Different Voice* (1982) claims that there are two mature ways to think about morality: **justice** and caring. Men tend to think of morality in terms of justice, principles, **rights**, and duties; women tend to appeal to caring, feelings, personal relationships, and responsibilities. Gilligan proposes that these three stages of moral thinking represent the process more common in females:

(1) *Pre-conventional*: one is self-centered and **egoist**; the only concern is one's own needs.
(2) *Conventional*: one is self-sacrificing; the needs of others are of greater concern than one's own needs.
(3) *Post-conventional*: one adopts the mature ethics of caring, which puts in balance the needs of oneself and of others.

Nel Noddings and others developed this care perspective further.

Gilligan, while influential in feminist circles, has faced criticism. Christina Sommers contends that Gilligan's view is poorly evidenced (resting on small samples and anecdotes) and is divisive and harmful to both sexes. And some lesbians object that Gillian's view is based too much on motherhood. But others defend Gilligan.

Kohlberg claims that extensive empirical research continues to show that females go through the same stages of moral thinking as males; for example, little girls also have a "what makes Mommy and Daddy proud of me" stage 3 and then move toward a "all my friends are doing it" stage 4. But Kohlberg now recognizes that care and the tension between care for oneself and care for others have a special importance for many females. He modified his scoring system to account for this, and now males and females score equally well on developmental stages.

Some object that a care ethics, if it includes concern for strangers (as in the **Biblical** Good Samaritan story), sounds much like ideas developed by males, such as sympathy for others and natural **virtues** based on these (**David Hume**), treating others as ends-in-themselves (**Immanuel Kant**), doing **good** to others (**W. D. Ross** and **utilitarians**), and **love your neighbor** and the **golden rule** (all world religions).

GLOBAL ETHICS. The study of moral issues that are global or international in character. These range from broad issues, such as whether it is possible to have a consensus across the globe about core values, to more specific issues about **war** and **terrorism**, the **environment** (including global warming), international **business**, **just** trade policies, human **rights**, **poverty** and hunger, world government, and regulating the Internet (*see* **computer ethics**). While global ethics is in its infancy, it is becoming more important as globalization increases.

Globalization began on a large scale in 1492, when Christopher Columbus discovered America. Some say "discovered" here reveals a Western bias: what really happened was the first well-documented visit of a European to the Americas. Europe proceeded to colonize much of the world. Some saw this as the bringing of a rich European culture and religion to backward tribes; the Spanish Jesuit Francisco Suárez saw it as the violation of the **natural** rights of sovereign peoples. Most of the colonies became self-governing only after World War II; India, for example, became independent of Britain only in 1947. Since then, globalization has intensified. Advances in transportation, communication, and the Internet have "shrunk" the planet; these forces and the rise in immigration and multinational companies have brought people of diverse backgrounds in contact with each other. The globe is now covered with items of popular Western culture: movies, music, business suits, blue jeans, Coca Cola, McDonald's, and so forth; and Eastern religions have made an impact on the West. The mixing of peoples and cultures has raised new problems, most of which cannot be solved without intercultural understanding and cooperation.

Is it possible to have a consensus across the globe about core values? Many are skeptical about this. They say Western ethics is incompatible with Eastern ethics (which is more mystical and believes in things like jihad, reincarnation, nirvana, karma, and Dao). They point to the terrorist attacks of 11 September 2001 as a sign of how the two sides will never understand each other. Some Westerners say the rest of the world needs to be more like the West in terms of values and development. But some Easterners disdain the Western obsession with material things and **sex**, and its neglect of family and community values; and they point to how Western "development" ruins the environment and contributes disproportionally to global warming.

Others complain that speaking of "Western ethics" and "Eastern ethics" as unified systems is an oversimplification. Western ethics is a sea of disagreement, as is Eastern ethics. China (which differs much from India, Africa, and the Arab countries) traditionally had three competing schools: **Confucianism**, **Buddhism**, and **Daoism**. Of these, Confucianism is perhaps the closest to Western values and Daoism the most alien; the latter starts by saying that the Dao that can be put into words is not the true Dao. But there are analogues of this mystical Dao tradition in the West; Ludwig Wittgenstein, an influential 20th-century philosopher, claimed that ethics was above language and cannot be put into words. Some say many of the views of the East can be found in the West, and vice versa, but not in the same proportion.

Still others, including Mahatma Gandhi (**Hindu**) and the Dalai Lama (Buddhist), contend that the core moral ideals of all religions and peoples are the same. Almost all the religions and secular cultures of the world teach the **golden rule** and concern for the well-being of others. These groups do not always follow their ideals; and all have sub-groups that de-emphasize these core teachings. Many claim, however, that the best hope for world peace and harmony is for people to follow these core teachings of their own individual traditions.

Two documents give evidence for the harmony of core moral beliefs across the globe. In 1948, the United Nations by a 48–0 vote approved a strong **human rights declaration**; while eight countries abstained, most of these (like South Africa and the Soviet countries) would support the declaration today. In 1993, the Parliament of the World's Religions, at the urging of the Catholic theologian Hans Küng, adopted a global ethics declaration about common values of the world religions. Both documents came from a broad discussion between the traditions, which tried to learn from each other and uncover common values.

Psychology and **biology** also give hope for a widely shared global ethics. **Lawrence Kohlberg** claims that research shows that people from all cultures progress through the same stages of moral thinking, leading eventually to a high justice perspective. **Sociobiology** claims that humans evolved an innate tendency toward **benevolence**.

William Sullivan and Will Kymlicka's *The Globalization of Ethics* (2007) is optimistic about attempts to set minimal global standards for the treatment of persons and cooperation across cultures. Kymlicka argues for a two-level approach to global ethics, where the various ethical traditions agree to (1) certain minimal ethical standards and (2) free discussion about other issues and disagreements. *See also* ANIMALS; ANTHROPOLOGY; CULTURAL RELATIVISM; KNOWING RIGHT FROM WRONG; ISLAMIC ETHICS; POLITICAL PHILOSOPHY; RATIONAL MORAL THINKING; RAWLS, JOHN; RELATIVISM.

GLOBAL WARMING. *See* ENVIRONMENTAL ETHICS.

GOD. Raises many issues about morality, including these four:

(1) Is God the source of morality? **Divine command** theorists think morality comes from God's will; without God there is no right or wrong. Some atheists (like **Jean-Paul Sartre, Simone de Beauvoir,** and **J. L. Mackie**) say, in partial agreement, that objective morality can exist only if there is a God; they add that, since there is no God, there is no objective morality. Many believers (like **Augustine, Thomas Aquinas,** and other **natural law** thinkers) believe morality is part of God's plan and governance; but God's moral law reflects his intelligence and reason, not his arbitrary will. Many believers and nonbelievers go further and base ethics on rational or emotional grounds independent of religious beliefs (*see* **knowing right from wrong**).

(2) Do God's **punishments** and rewards provide the reason or motivation for **why we should be moral**? While some believers think this, other believers see this motive as **egoistic** and inferior; they say it is better to be moved by gratitude and love toward God and his creatures. Some see religious motives as supplementing but not replacing nonreligious motives; nonreligious motives can be higher (like our desire to do what is right or to help others) or lower (like our desire to conform to social expectations or to promote our own interest). Others appeal only to these nonreligious motives to be moral.

(3) Is there a strong moral argument for the existence of God? Some argue from an objective moral law to God as its source:

> There is an objective moral law.
> If there is an objective moral law, then the moral law has a source.
> If the moral law has a source, then there is a God. (Other possible sources, like society or the individual, are claimed not to work.)
> ∴ There is a God.

Some dispute these premises. **Subjectivists, emotivists,** and **cultural relativists** deny objective moral norms. **Intuitionists** affirm such norms but deny that they have a source; basic moral truths, like **mathematical** axioms, are seen as necessarily true in themselves and not true because someone made them true. **Ideal observer** theorists and others say objective norms have a source in idealized human reason.

Immanuel Kant had his own moral argument for God's existence:

> People ought to be **happy** in proportion to their **virtue**.
> What ought to be is possible.
> Necessarily, if people are happy in proportion to their virtue, then virtuous people will be rewarded either in the present life or in an afterlife.
> It is not possible that virtuous people are rewarded (sufficiently) in the present life.
> ∴ It is possible that virtuous people are rewarded in an afterlife.
> If it is possible that virtuous people are rewarded in an afterlife, then there is a God.
> ∴ There is a God.

Here the most disputed premise is the second one (called "Kant's law" —*see* **ought**). While many agree that *actions* that ought to be done are thus possible to do (since we cannot have a duty to do the impossible), many dispute that the same works for *ideals* that "ought to be." There could be such ideals that cannot ever be actualized.

(4) Is there a strong moral argument *against* the existence of God? Many propose that, given the suffering in the world, there cannot be a God who is both all good and all powerful:

> If God does not want to prevent evil, then he is not all good.
> If God is not able to prevent evil, then he is not all powerful.
> Either God does not want to prevent evil or he is not able.
> ∴ Either God is not all powerful or he is not all good.

Here the most disputed premise is the first one. Many believers claim that God is all good but has reasons for not wanting to prevent evil; perhaps God could prevent evil only at the cost of taking away our **free will** (and thus our capacity for doing evil) or by destroying the significance of human action (which requires that we struggle against evil).

There are other issues that cannot be dealt with here, such as our duties toward God, whether God is free to do evil, and how to understand God's moral properties (like goodness). *See also* BIBLICAL ETHICS; BUBER, MARTIN; BUTLER, JOSEPH; ETHICS: INTERDISCIPLINARY; LOCKE, JOHN; LOVE YOUR NEIGHBOR; MEDIEVAL ETHICS; MORAL THEOLOGY; PLATO; PUFENDORF, SAMUEL; SIDGWICK, HENRY; WEIL, SIMONE.

GOLDEN RULE. "Treat others as you want to be treated." With some variation in wording, this same principle occurs in a wide range of different religions and cultures. **Confucius,** Rabbi Hillel, and Jesus all used the rule to summarize their teachings. **Buddhism, Daoism, Hinduism, Islam,** and Zoroastrianism also support the rule, as do secular thinkers from diverse cultures; many give the rule a central status in moral thinking. The golden rule is close to being a **global** principle—a norm common to all peoples of all times.

The golden rule is important for people of our own culture. For example, professionals often use the rule to explain their responsibilities toward others. So a thoughtful nurse might say, "I try to treat my patients as I would want to be treated in their place." Many in education, **business,** or government say similar things.

President John Kennedy in 1963 appealed to the golden rule in an anti-segregation speech at the time of the first black enrollment at the University of Alabama (*see* **racism**). He asked whites to consider what it would be like to be treated as second-class citizens because of skin color. Whites were to imagine themselves being black and being told that they could not vote, go to the best public schools, eat at most public restaurants, or sit in the front of the bus. Would whites be content to be treated that way? He was sure that they would not—and yet this is how they treated others. He said the "heart of the question is . . . whether we are going to treat our fellow Americans as we want to be treated."

Many philosophers reject or ignore the golden rule, largely because it leads to absurdities if taken literally: "If you want X to do something to you, then do this same thing to X." Many absurdities follow using cases where you are in *different circumstances* from X; for example:

(1)   To a son (with good hearing) speaking to an older father (who is hard of hearing): If you want your father not to speak loudly to you, then do not speak loudly to him.

(2)   To a parent: If you want your daughter not to punish you, then do not punish her.

The literal rule implausibly says "If you want others to treat you in a given way in your present situation, then this is how you are to treat them—even if their situation is very different." In (1), a better way to apply the golden rule is to imagine yourself in the place of your father (who is hard of hearing), and to ask how you desire that you would be treated in this situation; you likely would desire that if you were in that situation then people speak loudly to you. In (2), if the punishment is sensible and in the daughter's interests, a parent should be able to say "I desire that if I were in the place of my daughter then I be punished."

Harry Gensler has proposed this way to formulate the golden rule to avoid the absurd implications:

Golden rule:	*This combination is forbidden:*
Treat others only as you consent to being treated in the same situation.	• I do something to another. • I am unwilling that this be done to me in the same situation.

This formulation has a "do not combine" form (forbidding a combination) and has you imagine an exactly reversed situation. To apply the rule, you imagine yourself in the exact place of the other person on the receiving end of the action. If you act in a given way toward another and yet are unwilling that you be treated that way in the same circumstances, then you violate the rule.

On this view, the golden rule is a **consistency** principle. It does not replace regular moral norms. It is not an infallible guide on which actions are right or wrong. It only prescribes consistency—that we not have our actions (toward another) be out of harmony with our desires (toward a reversed situation action). Applying the golden rule adequately requires knowledge (*see* **information**) and **imagination**. We need to *know* what effect our actions have on the lives of others. And we need to be able to *imagine* ourselves, vividly and accurately, in the other person's place on the receiving end of the action.

It is possible to satisfy golden-rule consistency and still act wrongly, especially if we have flawed desires about how we are to be treated. Suppose that the owner of a coal mine pays his workers a miserly $1 a day. He wrongly believes one can live well on $1 a day, and so desires that he would be paid that much in his workers' place. He treats his workers as he wants to be treated. His error is not inconsistency but ignorance. We need to correct his view of the facts; only then can the golden rule criticize how he pays his workers.

Imagine a Nazi fanatic who tortures Jews but satisfies golden-rule consistency; he hates Jews so much that he desires that if he were Jewish then he would be tortured too. The Nazi has flawed desires which come from his hatred of Jews. We might try to get him to understand the source of this hatred (which may come from social conditioning, false beliefs, stereotypes, and so forth) and expand his knowledge and personal experience of Jews in an open way. Presumably his hatred of Jews would diminish or disappear if he did this, which would allow golden-rule reasoning to work in the normal way.

The golden rule follows from two other consistency norms, namely, that we ought to be **conscientious** and **impartial**. Suppose you want to steal Detra's bicycle. And suppose you are *conscientious* (keep your actions and desires in harmony with your moral beliefs) and *impartial* (make similar evaluations about similar actions). Then you will not steal her bicycle unless you also are willing that your bicycle be stolen in the same situation. This chart shows the steps in the derivation:

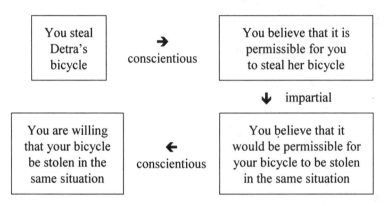

So if we are conscientious and impartial, then we will follow the golden rule: we will not do something to another unless we are willing that it be done to us in the same situation.

People have defended the golden rule from various perspectives—for example, as a **divine command** (*see* **Biblical ethics**), as a **cultural** norm, as expressing **benevolent** feelings (*see* **emotivism** and **subjectivism**), as having good social consequences (*see* **utilitarianism**), as helping us to get along with people and so promoting our self-interest (*see* **Thomas Hobbes** and **Karma**), as based on the meaning of moral terms (*see* **R. M. Hare**), or as a consistency demand of pure reason (*see* **Immanuel Kant**, whose *formula of universal law* was somewhat similar). *See also* ABORTION AND INFANTICIDE; AESTHETICS; ANTHROPOLOGY; ARENDT, HANNAH; AUGUSTINE; BENEVO-

LENCE; DARWIN, CHARLES; ETHICS OF BELIEF; FALLACIES
ABOUT ETHICS; KNOWING RIGHT FROM WRONG; KOHL-
BERG, LAWRENCE; LOVE YOUR NEIGHBOR; MORAL EDU-
CATION; NAGEL, THOMAS; RACISM; RATIONAL MORAL
THINKING; RELATIVISM; RICOEUR, PAUL; SOCIOBIOLOGY;
UNIVERSALIZABILITY.

GOOD. What is worth being sought, either as an end or as a means. Views
about the good relate to what in life is desirable or valuable, how to describe the good life, what constitutes our interests or well-being or welfare or utility, and what is bad (and thus to be avoided).

Hedonism holds that pleasure is the good; a quite different view is
that there are several ultimate goods, like **virtue**, knowledge, pleasure,
life, and freedom. Most views about how we **ought** to live depend in
part on some view about the good; compare these three views:

- **Egoism**: We ought always to do whatever maximizes good consequences for ourselves.
- **Utilitarianism**: We ought always to do whatever maximizes
  good consequences for everyone.
- **W. D. Ross**: Other things being equal, we ought to do good to
  others, return good to those who have done good to us, avoid
  doing bad to others, make up for bad that we have done to others
  in the past, and so forth. (Ross also includes duties, like promise-
  keeping, that do not mention good or bad.)

Applying any of these approaches requires some view about the good.

Hedonism holds that all pleasure is *intrinsically good* (good in itself,
abstracting from further consequences), all pain is *intrinsically bad*, and
nothing else is intrinsically good or bad. Other things can be *extrinsi-
cally good* (good as a means, instrumentally good, good because of further consequences); painful things, like visits to the dentist, can be ex-
trinsically good if they lead to future pleasure or prevent future pain.
According to *quantitative hedonism*, comparative judgments about value depend entirely on the *amount* of pleasure or pain; if we compare
two ways of life, the intrinsically better one is the one with the greater
balance of pleasure over pain.

Hedonists include under "pleasure" not just physical pleasures (like
those that come from eating and drinking) but also any kind of contentment or satisfaction. Higher pleasures (from friendship, knowledge,

achievements, virtue, art, and so forth) often are more satisfying and enduring than physical ones; but an experience that is devoid of pleasure, even if it involves friendship or knowledge, has no intrinsic value. Hedonists often use "**happiness**" as synonymous with "pleasure."

The view that pleasure is the good is sometimes called *ethical hedonism* to distinguish it from *psychological hedonism*, which says that we in fact, because of our psychological makeup, are motivated only by pleasure and pain. Hedonists sometimes base the ethical view on the psychological view. They argue that pleasure must be the good since it is the only thing that we can desire for its own sake; other views about the good are impractical since we cannot be motivated by anything other than pleasure and pain.

Against psychological hedonism, critics say that we sometimes desire other things for their own sake, for example, knowledge. We get pleasure when we gain knowledge, because we get pleasure when our desires are satisfied; but we do not desire knowledge just because we think it will give us pleasure. The debate over psychological hedonism is much like the debate over psychological egoism, which is addressed in the entry on egoism.

Critics of *ethical* hedonism say that some pleasures (for example, sadistic pleasures) are intrinsically bad. Suppose your husband is upset over losing his job; it would be intrinsically bad if you felt pleasure over his distress and intrinsically good if you felt distress over his distress. The last part shows that some pains are intrinsically good.

Another objection compares two lives equal in pleasure. In the first life, your pleasure is mindless and comes from a pleasure machine that stimulates your brain. In the second, you have slightly less pleasure but it comes from a normal exercise of your higher powers. Most people would prefer the second life, even though it has slightly less pleasure. This objection concedes to hedonism that it makes sense to compare amounts of pleasure. In practice, we can do this only roughly; to see this, ask yourself what amount of pleasure you are experiencing right now. Adding up amounts of pleasure seems like a dubious enterprise.

Critics also object that we can harm others in ways other than diminishing their pleasure or increasing their pain. Suppose you have slaves whom you drug so that they enjoy being slaves; you harm them because you take away their freedom—which is of value in itself. Or suppose you painlessly kill someone who wants to live but has more pain than pleasure; you harm the person because you violate the person's life and **autonomy**—which are of value in themselves.

Not all hedonists are convinced by these objections. Those who are convinced may want to move to a *pluralistic approach to values*. This view gives a list of things that are good in themselves, like virtue, knowledge, pleasure, life, and freedom. Having knowledge or virtue would be good in itself even if it did not include any pleasure; but having knowledge or virtue with pleasure would be even better.

Pluralism faces several challenges. First, what exactly goes into the list of things that are good in themselves? Pluralists produce somewhat different lists. Should we include, for example, the appreciation of beauty as an independent item, or does pleasure adequately provide for this? Does the appreciation of beauty have value even when it is not pleasant? These are difficult questions.

William Frankena tried to avoid this problem by giving a long list without caring about duplicate or non-basic items. His goods include life, consciousness, and activity; health and strength; pleasures and satisfactions of all or certain kinds; happiness, beatitude, contentment, etc.; truth; knowledge and true opinions of various kinds, understanding, wisdom; beauty, harmony, proportion in objects contemplated; aesthetic experience; morally good dispositions or virtues; mutual affection, love, friendship, cooperation; **just** distribution of goods and evils; harmony and proportion in one's own life; power and experiences of achievement; self-expression; freedom; peace and security; adventure and novelty; good reputation, honor, esteem, etc.

A second problem is that most items need qualification. For example, pleasure is not always intrinsically good (think of sadistic pleasures) and neither is knowledge (think of knowing trivial facts, like the number of tiles in your bathroom floor, or a serial killer's knowing many ways to kill slowly and painfully). It is difficult to make precise claims about what things are intrinsically good.

Third, are the various goods *commensurable*? Can we evaluate their worth on a common scale, so that this much knowledge and that much virtue and this much pleasure add up to a total of X units of value? *Ideal utilitarians* think this can be done, at least in a rough way. Non-**consequentialists** often deny this and claim that in most cases we cannot say that one life is objectively of greater total worth than another; the moral life involves choosing some mix of valuable features (emphasizing some over others) but not aiming for the life that has the greatest total value (a notion that makes no sense).

Intermediate between ordinary hedonism and pluralism is the *qualitative hedonism* of **John Stuart Mill**. Mill held that, while only pleasures are intrinsically good, higher pleasures (like those of poetry) count more than lower pleasures (like those of the mindless push-pin game). While he thought knowledge has no intrinsic value if it does not involve pleasure, he denied that intrinsic value depends just on the amount of pleasure and pain involved; higher pleasures are intrinsically more valuable than lower pleasures, even if the amount of pleasure is the same in both cases.

Some thinkers prefer a *preference account of value*, which defines intrinsic goodness in terms of desires. This approach seeks to combine the breadth of the pluralistic approach with the systematic unity of the hedonistic approach. Since people can have desires that are inconsistent or misinformed (so a child might desire to eat the whole box of candy, not knowing that this will lead to an upset stomach), the good should not be defined using *actual* desires. It would be better to say that something is in your interests (or would be good for you) if it would satisfy what you would desire for yourself if you were rational (**informed, consistent**, vividly aware of consequences, and so forth).

This preference view faces two problems. First, it would make it difficult to maintain that **animals**, especially lower animals, have interests. While it makes sense to speak of the frog's pleasure and pain, it is more questionable to speak of what the frog would desire if it were rational. A second problem is that preferences are "soft." Studies show that we do not have well-defined preference orderings that we can just introspectively "read off" when asked. Instead, we construct a preference ordering on the spot; how we do this is greatly influenced by how questions are asked and arranged. And we may well give a different ordering if we are asked again about our preferences later.

Aristotle begins his ethics by asking about *the good*, which he says "has rightly been declared to be that at which all things aim." He says our ultimate good is called "eudaimonia" or "happiness," although people differ on what this is. Superficial people identify the good with pleasure or honor; but Aristotle identifies it with virtue, or the excellent exercise of our rational powers (thinking and willing). Sometimes he identified our highest good with contemplation, which involves knowing (which is our highest faculty) the highest objects (necessary truths). **Thomas Aquinas** later Christianized this view by saying that our highest good is to know **God** (the highest object) in the afterlife; but since we prepare for this by living a moral life, ordinary intrinsic goods (like virtue) get recognized as lower parts of the hierarchy of goods.

Further questions about the good include:

- What character traits are morally good or **praiseworthy**?
- Can we make interpersonal comparisons of value—for example, that some element of *my* life is of greater or lesser worth than some element of *your* life?
- Is the value of a life over time just the sum of the values of the parts? T. D. J. Chappell argues that the answer is no, and that we have to account for the "narrative structure" of the life; going from rags to riches is more valuable than going from riches to rags, even if the values of the parts total in the same way.
- Can the state of an animal be inherently good or bad? Is it a bad thing if an animal is in pain? (*See* **moral patient**.)
- Can a state of affairs that is not directly about an experience—like the mere existence of a plant, waterfall, or canyon—be in itself good or bad? (*See* **environmental ethics**.)
- Can actions like keeping promises, showing gratitude, or treating others justly have intrinsic worth? Would this break down the distinction between consequentialism and non-consequentialism?
- Finally, there are metaethical questions (*see* **ethics: metaethics**): What does "good" mean? Is "good" to be analyzed in terms of personal feelings, social approval, or God's desires? Are there objective truths about what is good? Or is "X is good" a pure expression of feeling, like "Hurrah for X!"? What is the best way to justify beliefs about what is good? Should we follow our **intuitions**, or what we desire, or what is **rational** to desire? Or should we follow another method?

See also BENEVOLENCE; BENTHAM, JEREMY; BRENTANO, FRANZ; DECISION THEORY; FINNIS, JOHN; KNOWING RIGHT FROM WRONG; MOORE, G. E.; NATURALISM; PLATO; RAWLS, JOHN; SCIENCE; WHY BE MORAL QUESTION.

GREATEST HAPPINESS PRINCIPLE. *See* MILL, JOHN STUART.

– H –

HABERMAS, JÜRGEN (1929–). German philosopher in the critical theory and pragmatism traditions. He is well known in Germany for his commentaries on social issues. He started in the 1950s by challenging Martin Heidegger's apparent praise of Nazism. When Heidegger did not respond, Habermas concluded that German philosophy had failed when it was needed most; intellectuals needed to stand up to Nazis. Habermas's writings cover social and **political** theory, epistemology, philosophy of language, philosophy of religion, and **aesthetics**. Most important in ethics are his theory of rationality and his discourse ethics.

Habermas claims that non-**cognitivist** views that reject ethical truth impair social progress since they deny that oppression is objectively wrong. Social cooperation requires that we recognize the intersubjective validity of ethical duties. This is done best by adopting the perspective of all others and accepting as valid only those claims that all affected parties can accept. His *discourse ethics* holds: Only those norms can claim to be valid that meet (or could meet) with the approval of all affected parties in their capacity as participants in practical discourse.

Habermas tries to achieve **impartiality** by bringing all affected parties into a *dialogical* discourse. He thinks this is closer to "real-life argumentation" than *monological* views that imagine a solitary individual thinking through moral issues. He thus criticizes forms of **universalization** like those of **Immanuel Kant**, who says we should act only on a maxim we can will **consistently** to become a law for all, and **John Rawls**, who selects moral norms by imagining what would be chosen by rational agents who do not know their place in society. Such views ignore the role of the communicative process. Instead of reasoning through ethical conflicts by themselves, the parties need to communicate with each other in order to move from conflict to consensus.

Some object that Habermas's discourse ethics could subject the individual's interests to a tyranny of the majority (*see* **John Stuart Mill**). Habermas rejects this worry. He argues that the **rights** of individuals are well served by his communicative process since it allows individuals to explain how their interests are affected by proposed actions. In addition, he requires that *all* affected parties agree (or be able to agree) to a proposed norm; thus every person has the power to veto a norm. On the other hand, some object that his "all must be able to agree" requirement is impractical and overly idealized; in real life, almost no norms except very vague ones get universal agreement. *See also* ARENDT, HANNAH; HARE, R. M.; LIBERALISM/COMMUNITARIANISM; RATIONAL MORAL THINKING.

HAPPINESS. What is happiness? Is it **virtue**, pleasure, or a union with **God**? Or is it an overall satisfaction with one's life?

Several thinkers connect happiness with virtue. For **Aristotle**, happiness is the final goal of our actions, the **good** life that we all seek. But what is this happiness, this good life? Aristotle argues that it is not a life of pleasure or honor; instead it comes from personal development, where we exercise rationality in thought and action in an excellent way, a way that accords with virtue. He adds that happiness requires external goods as well, such as wealth, friends, children, and beauty. The **ancient** Stoics rejected that addition; they contended that happiness comes from virtue and that we should be stoically indifferent to external goods. **Confucius** similarly argued that we can still be happy if we have only coarse grain to eat, water to drink, and our arm for a pillow. **Joseph Butler** saw a natural order in our motivations, as did **Plato**, whereby the higher (conscience and **benevolence**) should rule the lower (self-love and particular impulses); we are happy if we follow this order, which is part of God's plan and our human nature.

Several thinkers define happiness as pleasure and the absence of pain. The ancient Cyrenians saw bodily pleasure as the good. Epicurus instead advocated a simple life, where we pursue social and mental pleasures (like friendship and study) and try to avoid pain. **Jeremy Bentham** and **John Stuart Mill** supported the "greatest happiness principle," that we ought to do what maximizes the balance of pleasure over pain for all those affected by our actions; Mill saw mental pleasures as higher and more valuable parts of happiness than lower pleasures, thus bringing him closer to Aristotle.

Immanuel Kant attempted a synthesis between the virtue and pleasure approaches. Happiness is the satisfaction of all our desires, many of which have to do with pleasures and pains. But this is not the complete good since we can imagine an evil person being happy. The complete good is happiness combined with virtue (*good will*, which makes us worthy of happiness).

Several thinkers connect happiness with religious or mystical ideas. **Buddha** saw happiness in nirvana, a release from pain which in this life brings peace and later brings the freedom from being reincarnated into another life; virtue and meditation can lead to enlightenment and nirvana. Plotinus, at the end of the ancient Greek era, saw happiness as attainable through a withdrawal from matter and a mystical grasp of the Good. **Augustine** saw happiness as consisting in the love of God; God made us for himself and our hearts are restless until we find him. **Thomas Aquinas** saw happiness as having two levels, which combine Aristotle with Augustine. Natural happiness comes from a proper use of our rational facilities (intellect and will); this brings us a degree of fulfillment. Supernatural happiness is the contemplation of God, the beatific vision, in the afterlife; this will bring us ultimate fulfillment.

Some contemporary thinkers see happiness as an *overall satisfaction with one's life*. This makes our happiness depend on both life and attitude. Virtue, pleasure, and a sense of purpose can contribute to life and thus to happiness; but they do not guarantee happiness. We could have all these things and still find ourselves dissatisfied with our lives, and thus unhappy. We also need the proper attitude, so we can find satisfaction in the life we have. *See also* DISABILITY ETHICS.

HARE, R. M. (1919–2002). The British philosopher Richard Mervyn Hare was one of the most important moral thinkers of the last fifty years. The three phases of his thought correspond to three key books.

The Language of Morals (1952) claims that moral judgments are a kind of prescription or imperative, a view called **prescriptivism**. Compare these two sentences:

The door is open.	Close the door.
(indicative)	(imperative)

The indicative tries to state a fact about the world and is true or false; to accept it is to have a belief. The imperative does not state a fact and is not true or false; instead, it tells what to do—it expresses our will or desire that someone close the door. Moral judgments are like the imperative. They do not state facts and are not true or false; instead, they express our will or desire about how we and others are to live.

Imperatives need not be emotional. Many products of human reason are expressed in imperatives: a cookbook with recipes, a system of laws, the rules for chess, and the instructions for using a car. Imperatives have logical properties; they can be logically inconsistent with or logically entail other imperatives, as in this imperative argument:

Take all these boxes to the station.
This is one of these boxes.
∴ Take this to the station.

By contrast, exclamations (like "Hurrah for X!") are primitive grunts.

Despite **emotivism**, moral judgments in ordinary speech are closer to imperatives than to exclamations. In discussing ethics, we often shift between imperatives ("Do not kill") and **ought** judgments ("You ought not to kill"); the two seem similar. It would be strange to equate this with the exclamation "Boo!"

Moral judgments about concrete actions presume general principles. We justify a moral judgment by referring to moral principles and facts. In the end, which moral principles we accept are a matter of decision.

Freedom and Reason (1963) begins with the claim that a moral theory should show us how moral thinking can be both free and rational. We are free to form our own moral beliefs, since these express our desires and are not provable from facts alone. On the other hand, moral thinking ought to involve our reason to the limits, so not just anything goes. Hare's earlier views had been criticized as deficient about rationality. If moral principles are just a matter of decision, we may decide on a Nazi principle like "We ought to put Jews in concentration camps." Hare previously had no strong way to criticize such principles; now he does. His new answer depends on two features of moral language from his earlier book: **universalizability** and prescriptivity.

Since evaluative judgments are *universalizable*, they logically commit us to making similar evaluations about similar cases. Suppose I say "I ought to put X in a concentration camp because he is Jewish." Then I have to hold that in an identically reversed situation, where I imagine myself in X's exact place and hence being Jewish, *I* ought to be put in a concentration camp. Since evaluative judgments are *prescriptive*, they must express our will. So then I have to *desire* that if I were in the reversed situation then I would be put in a concentration camp. If I cannot desire this, then I cannot consistently hold my original belief: "I ought to put X in a concentration camp because he is Jewish." A moral principle has to be willed as universal law (*see* **Immanuel Kant**), even for imagined cases where I am on the receiving end of the action.

Thus a form of the **golden rule** emerges as a **consistency** condition: if I think I ought to do A to X, but do not desire that A be done to me in an imagined reversed situation, then I am inconsistent. **Rational moral thinking** involves understanding the *facts* (especially about how our actions affect others—*see* **information**), **imagining** ourselves in a vivid and accurate way in the other person's place, and determining if we can hold our moral beliefs consistently (which involves the golden rule). Such rational moral thinking would lead almost everyone to reject Nazi principles.

Nazis can evade Hare's reasoning if they avoid making moral judgments (like "I ought to do this") about their actions, if they make such judgments but not in a way that is universalizable or prescriptive, if they are ignorant of the facts, or if they cannot put themselves in the place of their victims. Or some *Nazi fanatics* may actually desire that they would be put in concentration camps if they were Jewish; Hare at that time thought that we could not say much about such fanatics.

Perhaps such fanatics could be criticized using **Richard Brandt**'s *cognitive therapy*. A Nazi fanatic would have to hate being Jewish in an intense and disinterested way. We might try to get the Nazi to understand the source of this hatred (which may come from social conditioning, false beliefs, stereotypes, and so forth) and expand his knowledge and personal experience of Jews in an open way. Presumably his hatred of Jews would diminish or disappear if he did this; but then his **racial** hatred can be rationally criticized.

Moral Thinking (1981) argues that the golden-rule method leads to a preference **utilitarianism**: we ought to maximize as far as possible the satisfaction of everyone's desires. Hare believes that we will be preference utilitarians if we are rational in our moral thinking.

Hare admits that preference utilitarianism clashes with our moral **intuitions**. Most people feel it would be wrong to torture a Jew even if this would maximize the total satisfaction of everyone's desires in a Nazi society. Hare tries to blunt this criticism by appealing to a two-level view of moral reasoning.

Hare thinks humans sometimes resemble archangels (**ideal observers** with great powers of thought and no human weaknesses) and sometimes resemble proles (with many weaknesses and little time or ability to think things through). The *critical level* of moral thinking tries to think things through rationally, as would an archangel; it rests on critical thinking instead of moral intuitions, and it follows preference utilitarianism. One task of critical thinking is to arrive at rules that would be built into the intuitions of proles and humans; these rules would likely resemble conventional morality and include such items as "Do not torture others." The *intuitive level* of moral thinking follows intuitions instead of thinking things through; we would follow these intuitions when, as is usually the case, we lack the time or energy to think through a moral issue in a full-blown critical way. So moral intuitions do have a legitimate place in our moral thinking, but not at the more ultimate critical level. It is illegitimate to use moral intuitions at the critical level, for example against preference utilitarianism.

Critics are skeptical about Hare's justification of preference utilitarianism from universal prescriptivism. And some say there is a standard golden-rule consistency argument *against* preference utilitarianism. If we hold "I ought to torture Jew X if this maximizes the satisfaction of everyone's desires," then we have to desire that we would be tortured in an imagined reversed situation; but we are not likely to desire this. This argument appeals to consistency, not moral intuitions.

Hare has done much work in applied ethics (*see* **ethics: applied**). For example, he argues, against his student **Peter Singer** (who accepts Hare's moral framework but applies it more radically), that moral thinking leads not to strict vegetarianism but rather to the "demi-vegetarian" policy of eating little meat and selecting it carefully. Hare argues that this is at least as healthy as strict vegetarianism, better for world hunger (since some hilly or arid land is suitable for grazing but not farming), and in the interest of farm **animals** who are raised in a happy manner (since otherwise they would not exist). If meat is labeled as to its source, demi-veg buying habits can discourage cruel factory-farming practices and thus bring about much **good** for animals.

Hare has been the center of many controversies for his rejection of **naturalism**, his acceptance of a non-**cognitive** approach, his golden-rule reasoning, and his utilitarianism. Because of the subtlety of his approach, his views are often misinterpreted. *See also* FOOT, PHILIPPA; MORAL REALISM; WEAKNESS OF WILL.

HARMAN, GILBERT (1938–). American philosopher who contributed to epistemology, philosophy of mind, and ethics. His **relativistic** *The Nature of Morality* (1977) provides an influential attack on **moral realism**. Harman notes that we use "observe" in both **science** and ethics. So scientist Sara, seeing a vapor trail in a cloud chamber, says "I observe that a photon went by"; and moral philosopher Meg, seeing hoodlums burn a cat in gasoline, says "I observe that that act is wrong." Sara and Meg take their experiences to confirm a belief about an external fact. Sara is right in doing this, but Meg is wrong. To explain Sara's observation, we have to consider the fact that a photon did go by. To explain Meg's observation, however, we only have to consider her psychological makeup; any assumption about moral facts (that the act is wrong) is irrelevant to why Meg made her observation. The best explanation of our experiences involves positing scientific facts but not moral facts. So it is reasonable to believe in scientific facts but not moral facts.

Moral realists respond in various ways. Nicholas Sturgeon claims that moral facts sometimes are part of the best explanation of our experiences; for example, the wrongness of slavery helps explain why the Civil War occurred. Or perhaps the best explanation of Meg's observation is the fact that cat-burning is clearly wrong plus the fact that Meg has a normal knowledge of right and wrong. Others dispute a principle that Harman assumes: "It is reasonable to posit a given fact only if positing this fact is part of the best explanation of our experiences." This seems to be self-refuting and inadequate for mathematical knowledge, since neither it nor "2+2=4" seems to be part of the best explanation of our experiences. Others object that philosophy needs to look for the best explanation of our commonsense view of the world (which posits facts about material objects, other minds, mathematical truths, and moral truths) and not just the best explanation of our sense experiences. *See also* KNOWING RIGHT FROM WRONG; LOGICAL POSITIVISM; MACKIE, J. L.

HEDONISM. *See* GOOD.

HEGEL, GEORG WILHELM FRIEDRICH (1770–1831). German idealist philosopher known for his thesis/antithesis/synthesis analysis of how ideas progress. He attended a Protestant seminary and became interested in the connection between theology and philosophy. Despite teachers who found his philosophical abilities lacking, he became one of the most famous of the German philosophers.

Like **Aristotle**, Hegel emphasizes the social nature of humans; only in a civil society under a state can one achieve one's true potential. Ethics itself is meaningful only in a social context. While Hegel holds that only mind (often translated "spirit") is real, he seems to accept material objects (like chairs, rocks, and human bodies) and to mean that only minds can exercise true freedom. A rock is limited to being what it is; but mind is free and not limited in this way. Persons develop their potentials in complex ways; but this requires society. Alone or even in a family, we cannot build pyramids, cure diseases, or achieve military victory; but humans in society can do such things. Using Hegel's dialectic, we have thesis (possible achievements), antithesis (limitations on the individual's ability to bring these about), and synthesis (humans in society overcoming these limitations).

The social role of philosophy is to free the mind. Without philosophy, we act without being conscious of what we do. Think of filmmakers who churn out the same style movie over and over again, without thinking about how to be more original and creative. Philosophy helps us to become more reflective and to grow in what we do.

Hegel is a hero of communitarians, who emphasize the community instead of the individual (*see* **liberalism/communitarianism**). Liberals think society should be set up to promote the **rights** and interests of individuals. Hegel rejects this view and thinks we find our true freedom in society. This freedom is not merely the absence of constraints on our behavior, as liberals emphasize. Instead real freedom or **autonomy** accepts social constraints as enabling us to achieve our true potential. We should use our **free will** to bring about a society where our interests are in line with those of others; those who do not do this freely can be forced to do so by society (this is like **Jean-Jacques Rousseau**'s idea that we can be "forced to be free" by society's general will). Liberals like **John Stuart Mill** see Hegel's "freedom" as a tyranny whereby the majority oppresses the rights and interests of individuals.

Hegel sees history as progressing toward higher consciousness and freedom. Forms of society that initially provide progress later become constraints that still later will be overcome. Eventually history will lead to a society where community interest coincides with self-interest; society will care for its members, who will find much of their **happiness** in the group. There is debate over what kind of state such ideas support. **Karl Marx** thought Hegel was too conservative. For Marx, new means of production can provide progress but eventually become constraints. So capitalism produces great wealth but increasingly becomes a way to exploit and alienate workers. Following Hegel's notion that such constraints must be overcome, Marx thinks workers eventually will seize the means of production and bring about the stateless, classless, communist society with ultimate freedom. *See also* DEWEY, JOHN; NINETEENTH-CENTURY ETHICS; POLITICAL PHILOSOPHY.

HETERONOMY. *See* AUTONOMY/HETERONOMY.

HINDU ETHICS. Hinduism, the traditional **religion** of India, started before recorded history and has no recognized founder. It rests on religious writings, the Veda, which include the *Bhagavad Gita* and *Upanishads*. While Hinduism often is seen as accepting many gods, many Hindus take these to represent one supreme **God**; but some Hindus are atheists. Sikhism, Theosophy, and Hare Krishna are offshoots of Hinduism. Hindus tend to be tolerant of doctrinal differences, believing that ultimate reality is beyond our ability to put into words.

Three beliefs provide a context for Hindu ethics. First, there is a divine cosmic order about how people ought to live; people ought to be truthful and chaste, for example, and ought not to injure others or steal or be overly attached to material things. Those who violate this order bring harm and chaos into their lives and the lives of others. Second, there is a belief in reincarnation and karma, that the soul after death returns to live in another human or **animal** body, a higher or lower one depending on the moral character of one's life, and so the good or evil that we do to others comes back to us (*see also* **Buddhist ethics**). Third, in some mystical way we are all identical to our neighbor and to God (who is within us); so if I harm my neighbor then I harm myself. These three beliefs ensure that it is in one's self-interest to be moral (*see* **egoism** and **why be moral question**). These beliefs also provide a context for the Hindu version of the **golden rule**: do nothing to others which if done to you would cause you pain.

Hinduism recognizes four basic **goods**. The three worldly goods are pleasure, wealth, and moral righteousness. These promote the supreme good, spiritual liberation (salvation), which is communion with God.

Traditional Hinduism supports a caste system. The Veda describe the world as having been created from the dismembered god Purusha. The Brahmins were made from Purusha's head, and so serve as leaders, intellectuals, and priests; they are to abstain from meat and alcohol. The Kshatriyas came from Purusha's arms, and so serve as warriors. The Vaisyas came from Purusha's thighs, and so work in farming, ranching, and business. The Sudras were made from Purusha's feet, and so are devoid of intelligence but suited for physical labor. Even lower, and outside the caste system, are the untouchables, so called because touching them contaminates a member of the upper castes. Society works best if each group follows its proper function (as in **Plato**). Which caste one is born into is determined by how one lived in a previous life; those who live well move up in caste when they are reincarnated, while those who live badly move down. Although the caste system was outlawed by the Indian government in 1949, it remains a force in Indian life.

Mahatma Gandhi (1869–1948) opposed the British colonial rule of India and the harsh treatment of the untouchables (whom he called "the children of God"). While a firm Hindu all his life, Gandhi was much influenced by other religions; besides being a Hindu, he also claimed to be **Christian, Islamic, Buddhist,** and **Jewish** (*see* **global ethics**). He preached nonviolent resistance to British rule; his approach included a commitment to truth, faith, vegetarianism, simplicity of life, universal **justice** and **love**, and understanding between people of all faiths, races, and castes. He emphasized that if we act immorally then we cannot claim to have God on our side. He is sometimes called "the father of

India" for his role in bringing about India's independence; he was also influential in South Africa, where he worked for several years against apartheid, and in the United States, where he provided the model for **Martin Luther King**'s nonviolent resistance.

HISTORY OF ETHICS. *See* ETHICS: HISTORY.

HOBBES, THOMAS (1588–1679). English philosopher who began the **modern** movement away from the other-worldly focus that dominated **medieval ethics**. He employed the **scientific** method and the methodology of Euclid's geometrical proofs to develop a theory of ethics that starts with assumptions about humans and the world and draws logical conclusions about how we should live (*see* **normative/descriptive**). He tried to justify government authority without appealing to arbitrary claims of birthright and divine right.

Hobbes wrote of the *state of nature*, which is the pre-societal condition in which we would live if we had no common rules or authority to govern us; while this is more a hypothetical idea than an actual historical state, some savage and lawless groups may approximate to it. Imagine life in this lawless condition. People would lie, cheat, or steal whenever it was in their interest. Agriculture would be impossible because people would steal crops; most forms of social cooperation could not exist. We all would fight for scarce resources and live in fear of attack; since we are relatively equal in physical strength and mental capacity, no individuals could effectively protect themselves from others. In this state of nature, we would enjoy absolute freedom; but our lives would be "solitary, poor, nasty, brutish, and short."

Hobbes saw humans by nature as both **egoistic** and rational. As egoists, we are motivated only by our own **good** (where "good" is what satisfies our desires), which requires security and survival. As rational, we are willing to do what is needed to promote our own good. Since we want to live long and well and since we cannot do that in the state of nature, we choose to leave it by making a **social contract**. We all agree to give up our natural freedom to harm others so long as others give this up too; we are content to have as much liberty toward others as we would allow them to have toward us. This leads to something like the **golden rule**: "Whatsoever you require that others should do to you, do that to them." To enforce the new social order, we agree to obey a sovereign with absolute power. Only such a sovereign can enforce rules that check our self-interest and let us cooperate in mutually beneficial ways; without the sovereign, we would return to the state of nature.

The social contract accomplishes three things for Hobbes. First, it provides a non-arbitrary justification for governmental authority: the consent of the governed. Second, it provides a standard for judging the morality of our acts: the will of the sovereign. Finally, it provides an answer to the **why be moral question**, which philosophers had long struggled with: we are motivated to act morally out of self-interest, to avoid the wrath of the sovereign.

Philosophers have objected to Hobbes in many ways. **Jean-Jacques Rousseau**, **David Hume**, and **Joseph Butler** argued that people are more altruistic and less egoistic than Hobbes claimed; if so, then the state of nature might not be as terrible as Hobbes suggests and we might not need an absolute sovereign to protect us from it. Hobbesians respond by asking for proof of altruistic acts. Suppose we give the example of soldiers jumping on grenades to save others; is not this a clear proof of altruism? Hobbesians think not. Perhaps the soldiers act out of instinct instead of altruistic motivation. Or perhaps they are motivated by some self-interest, such as a desire to be remembered as a hero or a fear of living with guilt after their comrades are killed.

John Locke and Rousseau were troubled that an absolute sovereign might be corrupted by power and mistreat the subjects; this could be worse than the state of nature itself. Hobbesians respond that most sovereigns, being self-interested, will want to be remembered as good sovereigns. And even the most brutal tyrant is better than the war-of-all-against-all state of nature. In defense of this idea, some might point to the chaos and brutality in Iraq after the era of Saddam Hussein, which was worse for the Iraqis than was Hussein's reign.

Others object that morality ought to restrain even the sovereign's actions and thus does not depend on the sovereign's will; they add that fear of **punishment** is not the sole or best reason to act morally. Hobbesians counter by asking for the source of this morality and the motivation to abide by it. If these are based on **God**, then they will ask for proof that God exists. If these are based on some ethical theory, then they will raise objections.to that theory.

Hobbes raises many further issues and has had a lasting impact on contemporary ethicists and **political** philosophers. *See also* BRANDT, RICHARD; FREE RIDER; NATURAL LAW; PRISONER'S DILEMMA; PUFENDORF, SAMUEL; RAWLS, JOHN.

HOMOSEXUALITY. Sexual attraction to those of the same sex. This differs from *homosexual relations* (same-sex genital activity), since one can occur without the other. This entry considers whether homosexuality is natural, whether it is a mental illness, whether homosexual relations are morally wrong, and what rights homosexuals should have.

Is homosexuality **natural**? It seems to occur in every culture and era; so it is "natural" in the sense of being part of the usual course of events. But attitudes vary widely. Some cultures abhor homosexuals, see homosexuality as an abomination, and punish homosexual relations by death; other cultures esteem homosexuals as special and approve of homosexual relations. Some cultures expect a grown man to have sexual relations both with women and with adolescent boys; others condemn and punish sex between adults and minors.

Are homosexual relations natural **biologically**? Many say no, since sex organs are intended (by **God** or **evolution** or both) for reproduction; homosexual relations are unnatural and perverted and hence wrong. Many object that it need not be wrong for organs to be used for something other than their primary purpose. If the biological purpose of feet is to enable us to walk, run, and jump, then it need not be wrong to use them to kick a football or brake a car. Similarly, if the biological purpose of sex organs is reproduction, then it need not be wrong to use them to promote pleasure or strengthen human relationships. Some **sociobiologists** give another answer. They say that homosexuality exists because human survival chances improve by having individuals who can help support families without being rivals at reproduction. This suggests that homosexuals and heterosexuals are complementary, just as males and females are complementary.

Is homosexuality a mental illness? Many have thought that it is, and that it arises from some defect in genetics or upbringing. Until 1973, the American Psychiatric Association officially regarded homosexuality as a mental illness. Now most **psychologists** see it as a minority condition but not a mental illness; they argue that homosexuality (unlike schizophrenia, bipolar disorder, anorexia, dementia, and autism) does not *in itself* (apart from social oppression) disrupt one's general ability to think, feel, relate to others, or cope with life's demands. They further argue that, while the causes of homosexuality are unclear, one's basic sexual orientation is decided in childhood, before about age seven, and cannot be changed later. Today there is much debate about whether the real disorder is homosexuality or homophobia.

Are homosexual relations morally wrong? What we say about this depends on our basic approach to **sexual ethics**. *Conservatives* hold that sexual relations are morally proper only if they occur between husband and wife in a form of sexual intercourse that is open to the procreation of children. So they see homosexual relations as morally wrong; but they need not hate or punish sexually active homosexuals, since they might have a "hate the sin but love the sinner" attitude.

Liberals reject special moral norms for sexual conduct and instead evaluate sexual conduct only by the ordinary moral norms, such as not to harm oneself or others, not to treat others only as a means to getting what one wants (*see* **Immanuel Kant**), to promote good consequences, to keep promises, and to respect **autonomy**. So liberals would approve of consensual homosexual relations, so long as these do not harm others or violate other ordinary moral norms. Some liberals think that casual (uncommitted) sex is morally wrong, since it harms people by trivializing sex for them, so it serves more for immediate gratification than for building a deeper life-bond. Such liberals would approve of *committed*, but not casual, homosexual relations.

Moderates see liberal sexual attitudes as having bad social consequences, especially on children and families; they want to keep those conservative norms, and only those, that are needed to have a well-functioning society in which children are well nurtured. The issue then becomes, "Does insuring that children are well nurtured require a moral prohibition against homosexual relations?" Some, including **John Finnis**, argue for a yes answer on the grounds that homosexual relations attack the integrity of marriage and the family. Others disagree and say that, while strict moral rules about *heterosexual* sex may be needed to safeguard families and children, committed homosexual sex does not attack families and children in any obvious way.

What **rights** ought homosexuals to have? While **discrimination** against homosexuals is subsiding, it still is strong in many places; homosexual relations were illegal in many parts of the U.S. until 2003 and still are punishable by death in several countries. However, many today say that homosexuals should have the same rights as everyone else. For example, homosexuals should have the right to think and act for themselves (autonomy), to follow their **conscience**, to express their views (freedom of speech and the press), and to have recourse to a fair trial before being **punished**; and they ought not to be insulted, brutalized, or **discriminated** against regarding educational or employment opportunities (*see* **business ethics**). Some want to prevent homosexuals from adopting children or becoming grade-school teachers on the grounds that they are bad influences on small children; but critics point to studies showing that homosexuals make just as good parents and teachers as do heterosexuals.

Should homosexuals be allowed to marry each other? Some homosexuals desire to marry in order to have certain legal rights, such as the right to inherit from their partners and receive spousal benefits from employers. Critics object that this distorts the usual meaning of "marriage" (which is between a man and a woman) and attacks family values that are essential to bringing up the next generation of children. Still others favor having "civil unions" that are somewhat patterned after marriages and convey the same legal rights but are not called "marriages." *See also* FEMINIST ETHICS; SEXISM.

HUMAN RIGHTS DECLARATION. The *Universal Declaration of Human Rights* approved in 1948 by the United Nations General Assembly by a 48–0 vote, with South Africa, Saudi Arabia, and six Soviet nations abstaining. The document has a preamble and thirty short articles. It begins by stating that "recognition of the inherent dignity and of the equal and inalienable **rights** of all members of the human family is the foundation of freedom, **justice**, and peace in the world" and that "disregard and contempt for human rights have resulted in barbarous acts which have outraged the **conscience** of mankind." It later addressed the "dignity and worth of the human person" and "the equal rights of men and women."

Article 1 states: "All human beings are born free and equal in dignity and rights. They are endowed with reason and conscience and should act towards one another in a spirit of brotherhood." Human rights apply to those of every **race**, color, **sex**, language, religion, nation, and political perspective (article 2). Everyone has the right to life, liberty, and security of person (article 3). No one shall be held in slavery (article 4). Men and women have the right to marry and found a family without racial, national, or religious limitation (article 16). Everyone has the right to own property (article 17). Everyone has the right to freedom of thought, conscience, and religion; this includes the right to change one's religion and to exercise it freely (article 18). The will of the people, based on free and universal elections, is the basis of government (article 21). Everyone has the right to join trade unions and to receive equal pay for equal work (article 23). Everyone has the right to a standard of living adequate for health and well-being, including food, clothing, housing, and medical care (article 25). Everyone has the right to education, and it should be free at the elementary stage (article 26). Everyone has duties to the community, in which alone the free and full development of personality is possible (article 29).

Despite wide **global** support, the declaration has had critics. Some libertarians (*see* **Robert Nozick**) object to *positive liberties*, like the right to education and healthcare, which they say can be achieved only by taxes that violate property rights. Some **anthropologists** object that the document absolutizes Western values that cannot be shown to be superior to conflicting values of other cultures. And some **Islamic** thinkers object to provisions that violate traditional Islamic law. *See also* POLITICAL PHILOSOPHY.

HUME, DAVID (1711–1776). Scottish philosopher who argued that our moral judgments are based on feelings (which he often calls "senti-ments" or "passions"). Our judgment that an act or character trait is vir-tuous (or vicious) comes from our feeling of approval (or disapproval) about it. This **subjectivist** theory places Hume at odds with **Immanuel Kant**, who argued that reason is the source of moral judgments. For Hume, reason plays the secondary role of enabling us to be **informed** about that on which our feelings pass judgment. Reason has this sec-ondary role because it is unable, apart from emotions, to move us to act. All it can do is provide our feelings with an understanding of the act or trait in question. Since moral judgments can move us to act and only feelings can do this, feelings are the source of moral judgments. This is the basis of *Hume's law* that we cannot derive an "**ought**" (what we should do; *see* **normative/descriptive**) from an "is" (our under-standing of how things are) and of his claim that "Reason is and ought only to be the slave of the passions, and can never pretend to any other office than to serve and obey them."

For Hume, our natural sympathy for others explains natural **virtues**, such as generosity, charity, and **benevolence**, that produce **good** for people. Our sympathy approves of such acts even if we do not know those who benefit; we have sympathy even for strangers, though our sympathy is stronger for those close to us.

The story is more complicated for *artificial virtues*, such as obeying the government, keeping promises, and acting **justly**. Not every in-stance of such virtues produces good; instead, the good comes from the entire system associated with the virtue. For example, acquitting the accused in a criminal trial on a technicality may not produce a good that engages our feelings; instead, our sympathy for the crime's victim may move us to have feelings against the acquittal. But we may see the good produced by requiring the state to follow rules of evidence in criminal cases and prove its case, and this good engages our feelings.

Hume criticized **social contract** theorists such as **Thomas Hobbes** and **John Locke**. While Hobbes saw only **egoism** in human behavior, Hume saw a degree of benevolence and natural sympathy for others; this led him to reject Hobbes's view that we need an absolute sovereign to keep us from lapsing into the state of nature. He also rejected the centerpiece of social contract theory: that our obligation to obey the government comes from our promise to do so. Hume argued that our obligation to keep our promises and our obligation to obey the government both have the same source: our common interest. Promises and governments both benefit us by allowing forms of cooperation that would not be possible otherwise. Finally, Hume rejected Locke's notion that one implicitly consents to the government by doing something as simple as staying within its borders. He argued that consent is binding only if one has a real choice; but necessity compels the **poor** and many others to stay within the state's borders.

Many critics argue that Hume's theory lapses into **relativism**. Since moral judgments are based on feelings that vary greatly from person to person, Hume's theory leads to moral judgments that vary greatly between persons. This is undesirable since we need substantial agreement about right and wrong in order to live together harmoniously and productively. Some Humeans respond that Hume insisted that moral terms like "vicious" (as opposed to personal terms like "my enemy") demand the *general point of view*. This is an **impartial** viewpoint that we adopt when thinking morally. In judging Earl's act as *vicious*, Harry must move beyond personal biases and adopt a position common with others who lack such biases. Insofar as we adopt the general point of view and use reason to get an adequate understanding of Earl's act, our judgments about it will tend to agree. Such agreement is not surprising to one who accepts **Darwinian** theory, since our species' survival would have been hurt if we had vast moral differences (*see* **sociobiology**).

Others object to Hume's answer to the **why be moral question**. At least since **Plato**, philosophers have tried to explain the motivation for people to act morally. Those with an other-worldly focus, like **Thomas Aquinas**, appeal to **God**; the reason for one to be moral is to find salvation in the afterlife. Since Hume takes a worldly approach, he cannot make such an appeal; instead, he appeals to our feelings. Most of us cannot feel good about ourselves unless we act morally. Since we want to feel good, this is our motivation to act morally.

Many interpret Hume as a proto-**utilitarian** since he claimed that we have feelings of approval for utility. Others think that interpretation is misleading since Hume thought utility is one of many things about which we have feelings of approval.

Although Hume is often dismissed as a skeptic who offers little to advance philosophy and ethics, he has received much attention in recent decades. While some contemporary Humean theories are skeptical (*see* **A. J. Ayer** and **J. L. Mackie**), others use Hume's ideas on being informed and impartial to bring **rationality** to moral thinking (*see* **ideal observer theory** and **William Frankena**). *See also* BUTLER, JOSEPH; FEMINIST ETHICS; FREE WILL AND DETERMINISM; INTUITIONISM; LOGIC; MODERN ETHICS; MOORE, G. E.; REID, THOMAS; ROUSSEAU, JEAN-JACQUES; SMITH, ADAM.

HYPOTHETICAL/CATEGORICAL IMPERATIVES. A *hypothetical imperative* is one that prescribes the means necessary to achieve a given end: "If you want to relieve your headache, then you **ought** to take aspirin." By contrast, a *categorical imperative* is one that commands us unconditionally: "You ought to treat others **justly**." *See also* CONSCIENCE; CONSISTENCY; END-JUSTIFIES-MEANS; KANT, IMMANUEL; MACKIE, J. L.

– I –

IDEAL OBSERVER THEORY. The view that "X is **good**" means "We would desire or favor X if we were ideally rational," where being *rational* might be spelled out as being **consistent, informed, impartial, imaginative**, and so forth. This view is often explained using the idea of an imaginary *ideal observer* of supreme rationality. To call something "good" means that we would desire or favor it if we were such persons. We will never be such ideal observers since we always have some ignorance and bias; but the idea is useful since it gives a vivid picture of wisdom and a way to understand the meaning and methodology of moral judgments.

On this view, we would select our moral beliefs by determining what we desire or favor after we first try to become as rational (or wise) as we can. The latter involves being consistent, being informed on the facts, being impartially concerned with everyone's good, using our imagination to put ourselves in the place of the various parties affected by the action, and so forth. If we do this and come to favor something, then we are justified in thinking that this thing is good and that others who try to be rational about the issue will also favor it.

Ideal observer theory recognizes that our feelings can clash with our evaluative judgments, as in "I like smoking but it is bad" (*see* **weakness of will**). "Like" is about our actual feelings while "bad" is about how we would feel if we were rational; here our pro-smoking impulses conflict with a rational appraisal, which would include knowing about and taking account of smoking's harmful consequences.

To see how the view works in practice, suppose you are elected to Congress. On what basis would you evaluate a proposed law as good, and thus as worthy of your vote? **Cultural relativism** tells you to go with what the majority favors; but the majority can be ignorant or swayed by propaganda and lies. **Subjectivism** tells you to follow your feelings; but your feelings can be ignorant or biased. Ideal observer theory tells you to form your values in a way that is factually informed, impartially concerned for everyone, and so forth.

Ideal observer theory sees some value systems as more rational than others. Nazi values can be criticized if they come from factual errors (about racial superiority or about what benefits Aryans), ignorance (about the suffering Nazis cause to Jews, about how diverse groups in other societies have learned to live in harmony, or about how the Nazi hatred of Jews comes from lies or false stereotypes), or a lack of impartial concern for everyone (especially Jews).

Defenders of ideal observer theory argue that it has several advantages over views like cultural relativism and subjectivism. It adds a rational element while also recognizing the role of feelings. It provides a stronger argument against **racism**. It gives a firmer basis for **moral education** since it shows us how to develop wise and responsible feelings. And it accords well with how we form our moral beliefs when we try to be as rational and wise as possible.

Critics, however, point out problems. First, different forms of the view give different lists of features required for **rational moral thinking**. What should we include on the list? And how should we decide what goes on it? Since the view is a definition of "good," would the list of rational requirements be determined by the conventional meaning of "good" as used in our (perhaps partially unenlightened) society?

Second, the elements of moral rationality need to be explained more clearly. We need to see in detail how the consistency, information, and impartiality requirements work in practice. Does impartiality require that we have an equal concern for everyone, regardless of whether the person is our child or a complete stranger? Would this be a good thing? If impartiality does not require this, what does it require?

Third, there is the challenge of metaethical **relativism**: would ideal observers disagree on some moral issues? If they would, then should we take "X is good" to mean "Most ideal observers would favor X"— or perhaps "I would favor X if I were an ideal observer"?

Fourth, there is the challenge of **moral realism**: Is something good because ideal observers would favor it? Or would ideal observers favor it because it is already good? Ideal observer theory has to accept the former alternative, but is this plausible? (This is similar to the Euthyphro problem—*see* **divine command theory**, **natural law**, and **Plato**.)

Fifth, there is the challenge of divine command theory: Why not take **God** as the ideal observer and explain "good" as what God favors? This avoids the problem of what qualities to put into an "ideal observer" (since a perfect God would have the right qualities) and what to do if ideal observers disagree (since God cannot disagree with himself).

Thinkers who have accepted some form of ideal observer theory include **Richard Brandt**, Thomas Carson, Roderick Firth, F. C. Sharp, and **Adam Smith**. Some thinkers reject the view's definition of "good" but accept something like its approach to moral rationality, that the proper way to arrive at or justify ethical beliefs is to ask which beliefs we would favor if we were rational in our moral thinking. Variations on this latter idea are found in thinkers like Kurt Baier, **William Frankena**, **R. M. Hare** (whose "archangels" are ideal observers), Harry Gensler, **Immanuel Kant**, **John Rawls**, and many others. *See also* HUME, DAVID; KNOWING RIGHT FROM WRONG.

IMAGINATION. To be *imaginative*, in an important sense, is to have a vivid and accurate awareness of the situation of another (or of our own situation at another point in time) and an appreciation of what it would be like to be in that situation. Being imaginative (or *empathetic*) is often included in the features of **rational moral thinking**, along with being **consistent**, **informed**, and **impartial**.

Being imaginative differs from just knowing facts. In dealing with the **poor**, besides knowing facts about them, we also need to appreciate and envision what these facts mean to their lives. Movies, literature, and personal experience can help us to visualize another's life.

Imagining another's perspective is a common human experience. A child pretends to be a mother or a soldier. A chess player asks, "If I were in my opponent's place, how would I respond to this move?" A writer dialogues with an imagined reader who misunderstands and raises objections. A teacher asks, "How would I respond to this assignment if I were a student?" The ability to take another's perspective—and to vividly and accurately imagine ourselves in the place of another on the receiving end of the action—is crucial for applying the **golden rule**.

We also need to appreciate future consequences of our actions on ourselves. Knowing that drugs have harmful effects differs from being able to imagine these effects in a vivid and accurate way. An essay on drug addiction might give us the facts, while a story or movie about drug addicts might help us empathize with the addicts' lives. Other things being equal, I am less rational in evaluating an action that will impact my future if I cannot accurately visualize the future effects of this action on myself. *See also* KNOWING RIGHT FROM WRONG.

IMPARTIALITY. To be *impartial* is to be neutral, fair, and objective, to in some sense treat everyone equally and favor no one over another. Since this is vague, philosophers have proposed two clearer senses of the term, here called "weak impartiality" and "strong impartiality."

To be impartial in the *weak* sense is to make similar evaluations about similar actions, regardless of the individuals involved. If we are impartial in this sense, then we will evaluate an act based on what the act is like, not on who plays what role in the situation. If we judge that an act is right (or wrong) for one person to do, then we will judge that the same act would be right (or wrong) for anyone else to do in the same situation. To be impartial in the weak sense is to have one's evaluations be consistent with the **universalizability** principle.

To be impartial in the *strong* sense is to give everyone's interests equal weight when we decide how we ought to act. If we are impartial in this sense, then we will not give X's interests greater weight because of how X is related to us. If X's pain is equal to Y's pain, then both get the same consideration.

To see how the two senses of "impartial" differ, consider the Smiths and their daughter Julia. The Smiths give greater weight to Julia's interests than they do to the interests of strangers, and they do this just because Julia is their daughter. If Julia and a stranger are both hurt equally, and no one else can help, they will first help Julia and then help the stranger. The Smiths think this is how parents ought to treat their children; they make this same judgment regardless of the individuals involved. Here the Smiths satisfy *weak impartiality*: they make similar evaluations about similar actions. But they violate *strong impartiality*: they do not give everyone's interests equal weight.

Here is another example. **W. D. Ross** thought many duties depend on how we relate to other people. We have special duties to X if we made a promise to X, harmed X, were helped by X, or if X is our spouse, child, or friend. Each such relationship leads to special duties, whereby we ought to give special consideration to X's interests. While this violates strong impartiality, Ross would respond that strong impartiality is a bad idea because it denies our special duties toward specific individuals. Strong impartiality is really act **utilitarianism** in disguise; both see relationships as morally irrelevant and hold that our only duty is to maximize the sum-total of good consequences.

It is important not to confuse *weak impartiality* (which is less controversial) with *strong impartiality* (act utilitarianism). It is a fallacy to argue that, since morality requires that we evaluate similar cases similarly, it must also require that we weigh all interests equally. And it is a fallacy to argue that, since weighing all interests equally is a bad idea, evaluating similar cases similarly must also be a bad idea.

Impartiality, in the weak sense generally used in this dictionary, is often included in **rational moral thinking**, along with things like being **informed** and **consistent**. *See also* ARENDT, HANNAH; BIBLICAL ETHICS; EGALITARIANISM; EGOISM; EMOTIVISM; FEMINIST ETHICS; FRANKENA, WILLIAM; GOLDEN RULE; HARE, R. M.; HUME, DAVID; IDEAL OBSERVER THEORY; KANT, IMMANUEL; KNOWING RIGHT FROM WRONG; MORAL EDUCATION; NAGEL, THOMAS; RACISM; RAWLS, JOHN; ROUSSEAU, JEAN-JACQUES; SEXISM; SIDGWICK, HENRY; SMITH, ADAM.

INFANTICIDE. *See* ABORTION AND INFANTICIDE.

INFORMATION. To be *informed* is to have factual knowledge. Being informed is one of the most obvious features of **rational moral thinking**. Other things being equal, moral judgments based on knowledge are more rational than those based on error or ignorance.

We need different sorts of knowledge to make rational moral judgments. First, we need to know the situation: circumstances, alternatives, consequences, and so on. To the extent that we are misinformed or ignorant, our thinking is flawed. An exception is that it may be desirable to eliminate information that may bias or cause cognitive overload.

Second, we need to know alternative moral views, including arguments for and against them. Our thinking is less rational if we are unaware of alternative views. If we are concerned with how to deal with a problem area (such as how to care for the elderly), it is especially important to learn how other cultures deal with the problem since we may be able to learn from them.

Finally, we need self-knowledge. By understanding our biases, we can to some extent neutralize them; so we need to know how our feelings and moral beliefs originated. For example, some people are hostile toward a group because they were taught this when they were young. Their attitudes might change if they understood the source of their hostility and broadened their experience; attitudes that exist because of ignorance are less rational.

We can never know *all* the facts. We often must act quickly and have little time to research an issue; many choices involve guesswork about the facts. But we can act out of greater or lesser knowledge; other things being equal, a more informed judgment is a more rational one.

Becoming clear on the facts often can resolve ethical disagreements. The **emotivist** Charles Stevenson once claimed that this was the *only* rational tool for resolving ethical disagreements. Later he accepted **universalizability** as a second such rational tool. *See also* HUME, DAVID; KNOWING RIGHT FROM WRONG.

INFORMED CONSENT. *See* BIOETHICS.

INTEREST. *See* GOOD.

INTERNALISM. *See* OUGHT.

INTRINSIC GOODNESS. *See* GOOD.

INTUITIONISM. The view that "**good**" (or sometimes "intrinsically good" or "**ought**") is indefinable, that there are objective moral truths, and that some moral truths are either self-evident to a mature mind or known by moral intuition.

Intuitionists hold that "good" is a simple, indefinable, non-empirical notion—and is not to be confused with descriptive ideas like "socially approved," "what I like," or "what God desires." Suppose someone claims that "good" means "socially approved." Intuitionists would ask "Are socially approved things necessarily good?"; the answer is "no," which refutes the definition. Other definitions of "good" can be criticized in a similar way. Likewise, if you claim that "good" means "XYZ" (some descriptive phrase), intuitionists object that it is consistent to say that some XYZ things are not good—or that some good things are not XYZ—which refutes the definition.

A corollary of indefinability is **Hume**'s law: we cannot deduce an "ought" from an "is": we cannot prove moral conclusions solely from purely descriptive, non-**normative** premises. Such inferences would be possible only if we could define terms like "good" using descriptive language—which is impossible. According to Hume's law, we cannot give facts about society (or **evolution**, or **God**, or desires, or whatever) and then from these alone logically deduce a moral conclusion; one could always consistently accept the facts and yet reject the moral conclusion. But then neither **science** nor **religion** can establish the basic principles of morality.

Intuitionism is sometimes called *non-naturalism*, both because it rejects **naturalism** (the view that "good" is definable using ideas from sense experience) and because it regards "good" as non-empirical. Intuitionists sometimes define "good" using other evaluative terms, as perhaps "what ought to be pursued"; but they deny that it can be defined using purely descriptive language. Some intuitionists see "good" (or "intrinsically good") as indefinable, some see "ought" as indefinable, and some see both as indefinable. Of course, "good," "bad," and "indifferent" are interdefinable (*see* **definitions of moral terms**); but the real issue is whether these can be defined in non-evaluative terms, which intuitionists deny.

As a form of **moral realism**, intuitionism claims that some moral truths are objective in the sense that they do not depend on human thinking or feeling. For example, "Hatred is wrong" is true in itself and not true just because of how humans think or feel; hatred would still be wrong even if everyone approved of it. Mature common sense believes in the objective wrongness of hatred—and so, intuitionists argue, we should accept this so long as it is not disproved.

Many intuitionists hold that basic moral truths are self-evident: they are known but require no further proof or justification. When we deliberate about moral issues, we must appeal eventually to moral principles that we cannot justify further; we accept or reject these principles depending on how they fit our intuitions. The test of basic moral principles is not their initial plausibility but whether a careful examination uncovers implications that clash with our intuitions.

Many intuitionists believe that **mathematics** and morality both depend on self-evident axioms. We are not born with these axioms in our minds; instead, we arrive at the axioms as we grow in reflection and intellectual maturity. While we can make mistakes about the axioms, we can correct such mistakes with further reflection. A beginner may think "$-(x \cdot y) = (-x \cdot -y)$" is self-evident but later see that this gives a wrong result (namely "$-4 = +4$") if we substitute "2" for "x" and "y"; so we can correct one intuition by appealing to further intuitions. Since both mathematics and morality depend on unproven first principles, there is no reason to trust our minds in one area but not the other.

Many intuitionists say that in morality only *general* principles are self-evident; we must add empirical facts to draw conclusions about concrete cases. Others say that what is self-evident is concrete judgments like "It is wrong to lie in this particular case." Others say that the best evidence for a moral principle is that it fits our moral intuitions as a whole after we try to achieve a *reflective equilibrium* between general principles and concrete judgments. Still others see moral intuition as less like grasping a truth and more like an experience of "seeing," "perceiving," or "feeling" goodness or badness in certain situations.

While intuitionism has been popular among philosophers since **Plato**, the view received its clearest formulation in the early-20th-century British thinkers, **G. E. Moore** and **W. D. Ross**; other prominent intuitionists of that era include C. D. Broad, E. F. Carritt, A. C. Ewing, and H. A. Prichard. Later thinkers, however, raised strong objections to intuitionism and the view has lost much of its popularity—even though philosophers still tend to appeal to moral intuitions when they discuss concrete moral issues.

Some thinkers are skeptical about self-evident principles in general, seeing arithmetic as being about conventions or constructions instead of an independent reality. Even apart from such skepticism, it is less plausible to accept self-evident principles in ethics than in arithmetic. Purportedly self-evident mathematical principles (like "$x+y = y+x$") are precise and largely accepted by mathematicians; ethical principles often are vague and widely disputed.

Intuitionists and other reflective, mature thinkers disagree widely about basic ethical principles. Some accept one overarching rule about duty. Of these, some prefer a **utilitarian** rule like Moore's, that we ought to do whatever maximizes good consequences for everyone. Others take **egoism** to be self-evident, that we ought to do whatever maximizes good consequences for ourselves. **Henry Sidgwick** perplexingly took both utilitarianism and egoism to be self-evident. Some instead take a set of rules about duty to be self-evident. Some favor **exceptionless** rules—for example, that killing a human fetus is always wrong or always permissible; Ross takes as self-evident only weaker principles that hold other things being equal. There are many disputes about these principles, and some take as self-evident only concrete judgments of duty, not general principles. Because of such disagreements, appealing to intuitive or self-evident truths in ethics is far weaker than a similar appeal in mathematics.

Critics contend that moral intuitions come largely from social conditioning; the norms we are taught as children become our "moral intuitions" later on. Moral intuitions can vary greatly across cultures; some cultures see infanticide (or slavery) as "self-evidently right" while others see it as "self-evidently wrong." Intuitions that clash so much cannot be a reliable guide to objective moral truths. And the appeal to moral intuitions can lead to an early stalemate in moral disputes since opposing sides may have radically different intuitions.

Some thinkers accept the irreducibility and objectivity of values but reject intuitionism's approach to how we know these values. Instead of basing moral knowledge on intuitions, they appeal to an **ideal observer** or *rationalized attitudes* model (*see* **knowing right from wrong**). We strive toward moral knowledge by taking our current attitudes (which we largely inherit from society) and trying to become more **rational** (more **consistent, informed, impartial, imaginative,** and so forth). This model perhaps could explain better the diversity of moral beliefs without giving up the claim that genuine moral knowledge is possible.

The term "intuitionism" sometimes is used in a different way, to indicate an approach to normative ethics (*see* **ethics: normative**) that recognizes a plurality of basic moral principles that have to be weighed against each other when they conflict. Ross's system of *prima facie* duties is an "intuitionism" in this sense; while he defended it on the basis of moral intuitions and self-evident truths, it could be defended also on the basis of **emotivism**, naturalism, or **divine command theory.** *See also* ABORTION AND INFANTICIDE; BRENTANO, FRANZ; BUTLER, JOSEPH; CULTURAL RELATIVISM; HARE, R. M.; KOHLBERG, LAWRENCE; MACKIE, J. L.; MORAL EDUCATION; RAWLS, JOHN; REID, THOMAS; RELATIVISM; TWENTIETH-CENTURY ETHICS; WILLIAMS, BERNARD.

ISLAMIC ETHICS. Muhammad (570–632), the founder of Islam, was born in Mecca in what is now Saudi Arabia. After being raised as an orphan by his uncle, he worked in trade between Arabia and Syria; in his travels, he learned much about **Jewish, Christian,** and local polytheistic religions. In Mecca in 610, the Angel Gabriel purportedly began revealing the Quran to him and missioned him to convert his people from immorality and paganism. In 622, he traveled north to Medina to escape persecution; after setbacks, his influence grew, partly through military conquest, and Arabia became Muslim.

Islam believes in one supreme **God**. It holds that God revealed himself through the Jewish prophets (such as Abraham, Moses, and David), through Jesus (who was a prophet but not God), and through Muhammad (the last and greatest prophet). At the end of the world, people will be judged for their actions; sinners and unbelievers will be punished in Hell while the good will be rewarded in Heaven.

Muslim ethics is based on the Hadith, which gives Muhammad's sayings, and more especially the Quran. There are rules against killing, adultery, stealing, lying, and disrespecting parents. The Muslim form of the **golden rule** says "True believers will desire for others what they desire for themselves." We are to assist anyone in need, whether Muslim or non-Muslim, and pardon anyone who injures us. There is much emphasis on purity of intention. In waging **war,** which is permitted only for self-defense or to protect oppressed Muslims, we must use as little force as possible, treat prisoners humanely, not show anger, and not injure innocent civilians.

Islam has special religious duties, called the Five Pillars: (1) to proclaim "There is no god but Allah, and Muhammad is his prophet"; (2) to pray five times a day facing Mecca; (3) to donate to charity for the **poor**; (4) to fast during Ramadan, the month when Muhammad first received the Quran; and (5) to make a pilgrimage, if possible, to Mecca. There also are duties to abstain from alcohol, pork, and gambling.

Muslim ethics has been influenced by **ancient** Greek philosophy, particularly **Aristotle** and his **virtue ethics.** Arab countries were the center of philosophical thought in early **medieval** times; here Christian Arabs translated into Arabic works of Aristotle that were as yet unknown in the West, and Muslim philosophers like Avicenna and Averroës developed their own philosophies. Muslim thinkers disputed whether wrong things are wrong because God forbids them (as held by **divine command theory**) or whether they are wrong in themselves. The former view was more in line with Muslim thinking and came to predominate; indeed "Islam" means "submission to God's will," which suggests that moral distinctions come from God's will. Another influence on Muslim ethics was the mystical Sufi tradition, which emphasizes the centrality of **love** in the nature of God and the human response to God.

Today there is much turmoil about values in the Muslim world. Should Islam try to adapt better to the modern world and its Western values? Many conservative Muslims say no. They see the West as godless and decadent. They want to preserve the union of church and state that exists in many Muslim countries, whereby the state enforces Islamic law and forbids (sometimes under the penalty of death) giving up Islam. On these grounds, Saudi Arabia in 1948 abstained from voting in favor of the United Nations **Human Rights Declaration**, which, among other things, claims that everyone has the **right** to be free in the choice and exercise of religion.

Most conservative Muslims are peaceful. But a few Muslim extremists resort to **terrorism**, as in the attacks on the U.S. of 11 September 2001 in which several thousand people died. It would be wrong to conclude from this that *all* Muslims are terrorists—just as it would be wrong to conclude from Protestant and Catholic terrorism in northern Ireland that *all* Christians are terrorists. It also would be wrong for the West to ignore criticisms that even moderate Muslims make against the West: for example, that the West sides too much with Israel against the Palestinians; that it often ignores Muslim sensibilities, as exhibited by how it acts in the holy land of Saudi Arabia; or that it tends to be obsessed with material things, **sex**, and individual freedoms.

There are liberal Muslims who, although often critical of the West, want to adapt better to the modern world. They believe in freely elected government and individual rights, including the right to choose and exercise one's religion and the rights of women (*see* **sexism**). Most Muslims who emigrate to the West enjoy these rights and regret that women and people of other faiths do not enjoy similar rights in many Muslim countries. These liberal Muslims think democracy and human rights are in line with the essential message of Islam. And they tend to emphasize how Islam is similar to other religions (instead of how it differs), how different faiths need to understand each other (instead of resorting to stereotypes), and how various religions can learn from each other.

– J –

JESUS OF NAZARETH (c. 4 BC–27 AD). *See* BIBLICAL ETHICS.

JEWISH ETHICS. The Jewish religion, with its belief in one supreme God and its high moral ideals, has had a vast influence on the world; both **Christianity** and **Islam** build on Judaism. The Jewish Bible, the most important source for Jewish ethics, is dealt with in the entry on **Biblical ethics**. This entry deals with further items.

Much Jewish ethical reflection has taken the form of commentaries on the Bible, especially on the Torah (or "Law"), which includes the first five books of the Bible. The rabbis at first gave mostly oral commentary. According to a traditional story, the Rabbi Hillel (c. 15 BC–50 AD) was asked by a Gentile to summarize the Torah while the Gentile stood on one foot. Hillel responded using the **golden rule**: "What is hateful to you, do not do to your neighbor. That is the whole Torah. The rest is commentary. Go and learn."

After the Romans in 70 AD crushed a Jewish revolt and destroyed the Temple, many Jews scattered to distant lands. To support and unify these Jews, much of the rabbinic Biblical commentary was put into written form in the Talmud. The Talmud gives detailed regulations about things like diet, the Sabbath, marriage, and criminal law. It also includes stories, proverbs, and sermons; it often presents conflicting views from different rabbis. The Talmud assumes that humans are free to choose between good and evil, that the individual and society suffer when we choose evil, and that the Jewish Law is a great gift from God. Talmudic scholars traditionally were honored highly in Jewish society. Today Jews vary greatly in their attitudes toward the Talmud, with Orthodox Jews respecting it the most.

Jewish philosophers have often contributed their own ethical commentaries on the Bible, using resources from a given philosophical perspective. Philo of Alexandria (c. 20 BC–50 AD) used **Plato**, Moses Maimonides (1135–1204) used **Aristotle**, Hermann Cohen (1842–1918) used **Kant**, and Emmanuel Levinas (1906–1995) used continental philosophy.

Two events of the 20th century have occasioned much ethical reflection on the part of Jews. First, there was the Holocaust (1941–1945), in which the Nazis killed six million Jews. Jewish thinkers like **Hannah Arendt** (1906–1975) tried to understand what went wrong here, partly to help ensure that such **racist** atrocities will not happen again. Second, there was the Zionist movement that led to the creation of the state of Israel in 1948. **Martin Buber** (1878–1965), a German leader of the Zionist movement who later taught in Jerusalem, hoped for a state in Palestine that would **justly** represent and respect both Jews and Palestinians. His voice did not win out and there remains much tension in the Middle East; how Israelis are to live in peace with their **Islamic** residents and neighbors continues to be a major problem.

JUSTICE. Many ethicists, following **John Rawls**, take justice to be about the **rights**, duties, benefits, and burdens of fair social cooperation. Rawls sees justice as the first virtue of social institutions; unjust laws and institutions, regardless of their other virtues, must be changed.

Some take "just" more broadly, to be interchangeable with "morally proper." In **Plato**'s *Republic*, a *just person* is a moral person—one who lives in harmony with the **virtues**, and thus one whose soul is guided by reason. Similarly, a *just society* is one guided by those who possess reason. For most thinkers today, in contrast, justice is only part of morality; so some duties (like fulfilling our contracts) are duties of justice, while other duties (like giving to charity) are not duties of justice.

Some thinkers, especially *legal positivists* (*see* **Ronald Dworkin**), take "just" in a narrow way to apply only to what is "legal" in a given society. They think moral justifications for law are misguided. Thrasymachus, in Plato's *Republic*, holds that justice is what serves the interest of the stronger; so justice is nothing more than rules laid down by those in power. In the **modern** era, **Thomas Hobbes** holds that justice is whatever the sovereign deems it to be; the sovereign himself can do no injustice since his will determines what is just.

Many reject this narrow view of justice and argue that legal systems can be criticized on moral grounds. The **natural law** tradition sees human law as legitimate only if it accords with an objective moral law, which is either based on **God**'s rational will (as in **Thomas Aquinas**) or developed in a more secular way (as in **Samuel Pufendorf**). **John Locke** discusses the right to life, liberty, and property that government must respect and promote. **Immanuel Kant** argues that human laws should treat people as ends-in-themselves. **Utilitarians**, such as **Jeremy Bentham** and **John Stuart Mill**, hold that human laws should be arranged to maximize human **happiness**. Broader moral perspectives like these give ways of examining specific spheres of justice, such as retributive or distributive justice.

Retributive (criminal) justice is about **punishment**. **Aristotle** holds that punishment is justified to the extent that it rehabilitates the criminal and moves his character toward virtue. Utilitarians argue that punishment is justified to the extent that is useful to promote social happiness; they stress deterrence (discouraging crime) but also include rehabilitation. Still others follow Kant and argue that punishment is justified as retribution; it "balances the scales" by giving criminals what they deserve and will upon themselves by their actions. There is much debate about **capital punishment**.

Racial and *gender justice* concern the treatment of those of different races and genders (*see* **racism** and **sexism**). Not long ago, for example, many places had laws denying people the right to vote on the basis of skin color or the nature of their genitals. Many thinkers criticized these laws as unfair since they treated people differently on arbitrary grounds that had nothing to do with their ability to vote responsibly. These thinkers accept some restrictions on voting, for example an age restriction (although we might quibble about whether 18 is the right age to begin voting); but such restrictions must be based on what is required for responsible voting.

Distributive (economic) justice, which deals with the distribution of wealth and other goods, is a large and much disputed area. Is it just to have great disparities in the wealth of citizens? Should society's goods be distributed equally or according to some other scheme? Should markets be regulated or allowed to function on their own?

David Hume highlights two facts that provide the background for distributive justice. First, resources are relatively scarce. For example, food is not so naturally plentiful that we can easily have all we need; but the earth's resources do permit us, with human cooperation, to have enough food. Rules of justice evolved so we could cooperate to satisfy our needs; without such cooperation, our lives would be miserable (as emphasized by Hobbes). Second, human **benevolence** is limited. If we had complete benevolence toward all, we would perhaps not need rules of justice. And if we had no benevolence, then perhaps rules of justice would not be workable. So rules of justice are designed to help people of limited resources and benevolence to cooperate in satisfying their needs. This harmonizes with **social contract** thinking, even though Hume is not part of that tradition.

So how ought wealth to be distributed? Suppose we are dividing up a pie. If there are no relevant differences between individuals, it seems fair to give everyone an equal slice (*see* **egalitarianism**); this recognizes the equal dignity of each person. But things get complicated if there *are* relevant differences. Suppose you love pie while I like it just a little; should you get more pie on the grounds that this would maximize the sum-total of **happiness**? While many utilitarians would say yes, they would also say that we usually can promote the sum-total of happiness better by spreading out wealth more equally. Or suppose you made the pie and would continue to make pies for everyone if you were allowed to have a larger piece; then it might be just to let you have a larger piece since this inequality in the long run promotes everyone's interests. This suggests the *difference principle* of Rawls, which allows benefits and burdens to be distributed unequally if this makes everyone better off. Or suppose you bought the pie for yourself and do not want to share; then it might be just for you to eat the whole pie yourself— and if others want pie they can work for it and buy their own. This suggests the *libertarian* view of **Robert Nozick**, who holds that what people have justly acquired in a free market belongs to them and cannot justly be taken away (for example, by a graduated income tax) to achieve a more equal distribution. So a large discrepancy between rich and **poor** could be just, so long as it came about through just acquisitions. For many thinkers, the real challenge of distributive justice is to put together a coherent view that somehow recognizes and harmonizes the conflicting intuitions that we have on this subject.

Procedural justice is about making and implementing decisions in a way that is fair and **impartial** toward everyone. Utilitarians suggest that we achieve this by counting equally the happiness of each person, regardless of race, gender, or religion; we are to aim for the greatest sum-total of everyone's happiness. Rawls objects that violating the rights of some, perhaps a minority group, may sometimes maximize the total happiness; he proposes an alternative "justice as fairness" model in which a *just procedure* is one that we would accept if we were fully rational but did not know our place in the situation (including our race, gender, or religion). Libertarians, however, fear that such procedures may violate the rights of individuals; with Locke, they argue for a procedural justice that respects our natural right to life, liberty, and property. But communitarians (*see* **liberalism/communitarianism**), in turn, protest what they see as an overemphasis on individual rights that ends up harming the community. Many from these various groups, however, would agree that those affected by decisions should somehow have a say in how these decisions are made (*see* **political philosophy**).

Those working on justice today continue to raise new issues and concerns. Some **feminists**, such as **Carol Gilligan**, see the stress on justice and rights, rather than on caring, as overly male (*see also* **Lawrence Kohlberg**). Others say that we need to be more concerned with *international justice*, and especially the great gap between rich and poor nations, which in part results from how rich nations set the terms of economic interchange (*see* **business ethics** and **global ethics**).

– K –

KANT, IMMANUEL (1724–1804). Influential German philosopher who held that morality is based on reason. We know what is right not by relying on moral intuitions or facts about the world, but by seeing what we can will **consistently**. To test a moral maxim, we ask whether we can will consistently that everyone follow it (and thus also act that way toward us); we must reject the maxim if we cannot will this.

Kant's monumental *Critique of Pure Reason* (1781 and 1787) saw the mind as active, imposing a rational order on the raw data of sense experience. For example, we do not derive our notions of space and time from sense experience; instead, we impose these structures on our sensations. Morality works the same way; moral rationality imposes its own abstract, formal laws on our actions. Morality ultimately rests not on sense experience or feelings, but on reason.

Kant's brief *Groundwork of the Metaphysic of Morals* (1785) tried to formulate the basic principle behind ethics and defend morality against those who reduce it to self-interest, feelings, or empirical fact. It claims that basic ethical principles cannot be empirical ideas from sense experience; since ethics gives necessary truths that hold for any rational being, these cannot be based on facts about humans but must come from pure reason. So the basis of morality is *a priori*—evident through reason alone and not based on sense experience. We need an a priori ethics because empirical motives, like self-interest, can lead us to violate our duty. Such motives lessen our moral worth; the highest motive is to do our duty not from ulterior motives, but just because it is the right thing to do. Only a **good** will is good without qualification, or always good; other goods can be bad if used for the wrong purpose (e.g., intelligence is bad if used by a serial killer to trap his victims). A good will is good in itself, not just for what it produces. A grocer who gives correct change from a sense of fairness, and not from fear of getting caught, has a good will.

The goal of reason is not to produce **happiness** (since it is a poor means to this end) but to produce a will that is good in itself. Happiness, the satisfaction of all our desires, is too indeterminate to be a workable guide. Good will is not the sole and complete good, but it is the condition of our worthiness to be happy. The highest and complete good is happiness combined with good will.

Rationality has its own objective laws about how to act. Purely rational beings would have a "holy will" and would follow these laws of necessity, as part of their nature; since we are partly rational and partly sensuous, we experience these laws as constraints—as imperatives that we **ought** to follow but do not always succeed in following. These rational laws of action, which are valid for every rational being as such, are called "imperatives" and are of two sorts: hypothetical and categorical. *Hypothetical imperatives* prescribe the means necessary to achieve a given end: "If you want to fulfill end E, then you ought to do A" (for example, "If you want to relieve your headache, then you ought to take aspirin"). An ethics based on hypothetical imperatives is *heteronomous*—since it involves following the laws of another, namely the laws of our sensuous nature and its desires.

In contrast, *categorical imperatives* command us unconditionally: "You ought to do A" (for example, "You ought to treat others **justly**"). Morality is about categorical imperatives, which are objective truths that command us regardless of our ends and thus rationally commit us to acting accordingly. The basic categorical imperative is that we act consistently on principle—that we act on principles that we can will consistently for everyone. An ethics based on categorical imperatives is **autonomous** since we follow our own laws; we follow, not momentary impulses, but rules that we prescribe for everyone, and thus for how we are to act toward others as well as how others are to act toward us. The supreme moral principle is the *formula of universal law*: "Act only on a maxim that you can will to be a universal law."

Kant thought his formula led to two kinds of duty. *Perfect duties* are **exceptionless**; for example, we *ought never* to commit **suicide** or make a promise that we do not intend to keep. Perfect duties are based on maxims that could not exist as a universal law. While I might want to make a promise that I do not intent to keep, this could not become a general practice since this would destroy the institution of promises. In making an insincere promise, I both will to use the system and will what destroys it. I thus act wrongly; I make an exception for myself, acting in a way that could not be a law of nature and that I could not will to be universally followed.

Imperfect duties are looser and give us more leeway in how we are to fulfill them; so while we ought to develop our talents and help others who are in need, we can to a great extent choose which talents to develop and which people to help. Imperfect duties are based on what could exist as a law of nature but which we could not will to be a law of nature; while it could become a general practice that no one helps others who are in need, we could not will this because cases could arise in which we much need the help of others. In addition, we cannot always help others (since we have finite resources) but we can always refrain from making insincere promises.

We can express the same supreme moral principle more loosely in several other ways, including the *law-of-nature formula*, "Act as if the maxim of your action would become a universal law of nature," and the *end-in-itself formula*, "Treat humanity, whether yourself or another, as an end-in-itself and not only as a means." The latter can be put roughly as "Use things but respect people"; we act wrongly when we use people as mere things, as mere tools to promote our own desires.

Kant connected morality and **free will** closely. To be free is to follow our own legislation, to act on maxims that we will to be universal laws. So to be free is to be moral; freedom and morality are ultimately the same mystery. We cannot explain free will; we only can assume it and refute objections against it. To see ourselves as free, we must see ourselves as part of two worlds: a sensible world subject to deterministic laws and a higher rational world in which we are free. Acting morally has supreme worth because it lets us participate in a higher order of existence; this is the basis of our dignity as an end-in-itself.

Kant argued that practical reason requires three beliefs that theoretical reason cannot prove: freedom, immortality, and **God**. All three are based on the principle that "ought" implies "can" (what we *ought to do* we thereby *can do*), a principle often called "Kant's law." We know that we are free by knowing that we have duties that we violate. In these cases, we ought to have acted otherwise, and so we could have acted otherwise, and thus we are free. The other two are based on the idea that the highest good, complete happiness combined with complete good will, *ought to be*, and therefore is possible. But since this highest good is not possible in the present life, we must assume the conditions that would make it possible in an afterlife, including the existence of a powerful, moral God who rewards goodness. Note that reward is not the proper motive for right action; rather it is required if the highest good is to be possible.

Kant has had both critics and admirers. Critics often charge that he is too much of an absolutist, that he takes too little account of emotions and empirical knowledge, that he is obscure and too metaphysical, and that it is unclear how to apply his formulas to actual moral issues.

On this last point, suppose I am tempted to make a promise that I do not intend to keep. I say, "I promise to pay you back tomorrow if you lend me $5 for a hot fudge sundae," but I do not intend to pay you back. Can I will my maxim to be a universal law? One problem is that my maxim can be expressed in varying degrees of specificity: (a) to make a promise that I do not intend to keep when this is convenient, (b) to make a promise that I do not intend to keep about paying back $5 for a hot fudge sundae, or (c) to make a promise that I do not intend to keep on a hot Tuesday evening in July about paying back $5 for a hot fudge sundae. Perhaps I could will (b) or (c) to be a universal law, but not (a); then what am I to do? Such examples show that it is not clear how to apply Kant's principle.

Despite such problems, Kant has had many admirers. These admirers, while they generally admit problems in Kant's theory, think he had great insights that need to be worked out in a better way. So Kant's writings have provoked much original thinking about ethics. Kant's admirers include **Hannah Arendt**, Steven Darwall, Alan Donagan, Alan Gewirth, **Jürgen Habermas**, **R. M. Hare**, Barbara Herman, Thomas Hill, **C. I. Lewis**, **Lawrence Kohlberg**, Christine Korsgaard, Onora O'Neill, **John Rawls, Jean-Paul Sartre**, and Marcus Singer—plus others who defend **universalizability**, **impartiality**, and consistency—plus some rule **utilitarians**.

Kant and his contemporary **David Hume** are often seen as opposites: Kant based ethics on reason while Hume based it on feelings. But their support of impartiality is an important similarity. Both thinkers have had a large influence on **twentieth-century ethics**. *See also* BUTLER, JOSEPH; CONSCIENCE; CONSEQUENTIALISM/NON-CONSEQUENTIALISM; EGOISM; EUTHANASIA; IDEAL OBSERVER THEORY; KNOWING RIGHT FROM WRONG; LIBERALISM/COMMUNITARIANISM; LOVE YOUR NEIGHBOR; MACINTYRE, ALASDAIR; MACKIE, J. L.; MORAL AGENT; MORAL PATIENT; MODERN ETHICS; NATURAL LAW; PLATO; POVERTY; PUNISHMENT; ROUSSEAU, JEAN-JACQUES; ROSS, W. D.; WHY BE MORAL QUESTION; WILLIAMS, BERNARD.

KARMA. The belief that the good or evil that we do to others will come back upon us, now or in a future life. *See* BUDDHIST ETHICS; GOLDEN RULE; HINDU ETHICS; WHY BE MORAL QUESTION.

KILLING. Causing the death of a living being. Most people see nothing intrinsically wrong in killing bacteria, plants, or trees for legitimate human purposes (such as producing food or lumber); but such killing can be wrong indirectly if it harms humans or the **environment**, for example by using harmful pesticides or destroying a rainforest. **Peter Singer** argues that it is not seriously wrong to kill lower **animals** (like spiders or worms) if this is done painlessly, but that it is seriously wrong to kill higher nonhuman animals (like pigs or dogs) who have self-awareness and strong desires about their future. This questions our killing of higher animals for food, clothing, and **biomedical** research.

All believe that killing humans is wrong unless justified by some overriding reason. Except for pacifists, who hold that killing is never justified, most believe that self-defense can provide such a reason. So most believe that we do nothing wrong if we kill someone if that is the only way to prevent that person from killing us or another innocent person. Likewise, it is generally considered permissible to kill an enemy soldier in a just **war**; however, there is debate about what constitutes a just war and justified methods of warfare.

Some defend **capital punishment** on the grounds that it deters crime or gives criminals what they deserve; others argue that such deterrence is ineffective and that "giving criminals what they deserve" is wrongful revenge. Others oppose capital punishment as violating the **sanctity of human life** or as being unfairly applied toward minorities.

Some defend **euthanasia** on the grounds that it respects the desires and **autonomy** of those who want to end their lives while they endure painful illnesses. Others oppose euthanasia as violating the sanctity of human life or as following the desires of a patient who may not be rational. Further issues about killing involve areas like **abortion**, dueling, gladiatorial games, genocide, **stem-cell research**, **suicide**, and **terrorism**. *See also* EXCEPTIONLESS DUTIES; DOUBLE EFFECT; FOOT, PHILLIPA; FORGIVENESS; MEDIEVAL ETHICS; NAGEL, THOMAS; UTILITARIANISM; WILLIAMS, BERNARD.

KING, MARTIN LUTHER (1929–1968). Baptist minister who led the struggle against **racial** segregation in the U.S. In 1963 he was jailed in Birmingham, Alabama, for an illegal civil rights march. His fellow clergy called him a lawbreaker and an extremist. While in jail, King wrote a letter defending his policy of nonviolent **civil disobedience**, which was inspired by Mahatma Gandhi (*see* **Hindu ethics**); his letter appealed to the conscience of the American people. Eight weeks later, a comprehensive civil rights law was proposed by President John Kennedy, who unfortunately would be assassinated in a few months (as King would be five years later). The law was passed by Congress in 1964, under the leadership of a southerner, President Lyndon Johnson.

Was King a lawbreaker? King responds that laws can be **just** or unjust. The segregation laws he protested were unjust, since they violated a higher **natural moral law** about how people ought to be treated. Segregation laws degraded and damaged human personality, were imposed on one group but not another, and were created by a process that blacks could not participate in. King broke these laws—openly, lovingly, and with willingness to accept the penalty—as a symbolic protest, to dramatize the issue so the door could open to free discussion and change. He says such actions show the highest respect for law.

Was King an extremist? He responds that blacks, almost a hundred years after being freed from slavery, still did not have basic freedoms guaranteed to other Americans; blacks were insulted and brutalized, kept **poor** and ignorant, and were denied the right to use many public facilities and to vote. He saw nonviolent civil disobedience as a policy of moderation, midway between advocating violence and doing nothing, as a policy that can bring change without bloodshed.

KNOWING RIGHT FROM WRONG. How do we know right from wrong? Is there anything to know? Philosophers have explored these questions from a wide range of perspectives.

If we know some general moral principles, we can use ordinary reasoning to gain more specific moral knowledge. Suppose we know that *lying is always wrong*; then we can, if we know that act A is an act of lying, conclude that act A is wrong. Or suppose we know that *one ought always to do what maximizes the total balance of pleasure over pain*; then we can, if we know that act A maximizes this total balance, conclude that act A **ought** to be done. There are complications with **prima facie** principles like "Other things being equal, one ought not to lie"; applying these requires a further moral premise that no further moral considerations override a presumptive duty to do or not to do A.

The biggest problem is how we can know general moral principles in the first place. Many philosophers think there are only two ways of knowing. Some things, like "2+2=4" and logical principles, we know *a priori*, in a *rational* way, from pure thought; *rationalist* moral philosophers, starting with **Plato**, think our knowledge of right and wrong works like this. In contrast, some things, like "There is snow outside," we know *a posteriori*, in an *empirical* way, from sense experience; *empiricist* moral philosophers, beginning with **Aristotle**, think our knowledge of right and wrong is empirical.

The classic *rationalist* approach is **intuitionism**, which holds that basic moral truths are either self-evident to a mature mind or else known by moral intuition. Many intuitionists think **mathematics** and morality both depend on self-evident axioms; while we are not born with these axioms, they come to us as we grow in intellectual maturity. Many intuitionists hold that in morality only *general* principles are self-evident; we must add empirical facts to draw moral conclusions about concrete cases. Others hold that what is self-evident are concrete judgments like "This particular lie is wrong." Others hold that the best evidence for a moral principle is that it fits our moral intuitions as a whole after we try to achieve a *reflective equilibrium* between general principles and concrete judgments. Still others see moral intuition as less like grasping a truth and more like an experience of "seeing," "perceiving," or "feeling" goodness or badness in certain situations.

Immanuel Kant presented another form of rationalism. He thought we know what is right, not by relying on moral intuitions or facts about the world, but by seeing what we can will **consistently**. To test a moral maxim, we ask whether we can will consistently that everyone follow it (and thus also act that way toward us); we must reject the maxim if we cannot will this. What is self-evident in ethics is that our moral beliefs are to be submitted to this universal-will test, that we are to act only on a maxim that we can will to be a universal law.

The classic *empiricist* approach is **naturalism**, which analyzes moral terms like "**good**" and "ought" in empirical terms. Naturalists might claim, for example, that "good" means:

- "socially approved" (**cultural relativism**),
- "what I like" (**subjectivism**),
- "what we would desire if we were ideally rational" (**ideal observer theory**),
- "what accords with evolution" (**evolutionism**), or
- "either pleasant or else productive of the balance of pleasure over pain" (a naturalistic form of classical **utilitarianism**).

Such views see moral judgments as ordinary empirical judgments and let us deduce an "ought" from an "is" (against **Hume**'s law).

Some views do not fit neatly into this rational/empirical divide, which assumes that we have genuine moral knowledge and that it is either rational or empirical. For example, **divine command theory** explains "good" in terms of **God**'s will. On this view, we would determine what is good by determining what God desires, perhaps by appealing to the **Bible**, the church, prayer, or reason.

There also are *skeptics* who deny the possibility of knowledge, either in general or in some specific area. **J. L. Mackie**'s *error theory* is a skepticism about ethics. Mackie held that moral judgments are intended to make a claim about an objective realm of values; but there are no objective values, no moral facts, and no moral knowledge. **Emotivism** is another form of skepticism; it holds that, since moral judgments express feelings instead of truth claims, there cannot be moral truths or moral knowledge. So the question of how we can *know* right from wrong is misguided. We can reason about moral issues if we assume a system of norms; we then can appeal to empirical facts to show that, given these norms and these empirical facts, such and such a moral conclusion follows. But we cannot reason about *basic* moral principles.

Moderate emotivists dispute some of the extreme emotivist claims. While these thinkers see moral judgments as emotional, they insist that emotions can be rationally appraised to some degree; rational feelings and moral judgments are perhaps those that are consistent, **informed**, **impartial**, **imaginative**, and so forth. Some, like **William Frankena**, argue that our moral beliefs would all agree if we were ideally rational; this leads to a kind of "moral truth"—which is defined not in terms of correspondence to independent facts but in terms of what ideally rational inquirers would agree upon.

R. M. Hare's **prescriptivism** combines ideas from rationalism, empiricism, and skepticism. It claims that moral judgments are a kind of prescription or imperative; so they do not state facts and are not true or false. But moral judgments are subject to a certain logical framework, which includes **universalizability**, prescriptivity, and a form of the **golden rule**. To make moral judgments in a rational way involves understanding the *facts* (especially about how our actions affect others), *imagining* ourselves in a vivid and accurate way in the place of the other person, and determining if we can hold our moral beliefs *consistently* (which involves the golden rule).

Many thinkers today endorse a *rationalized attitudes* or *rational choice* approach to knowing right from wrong, somewhat along the lines of prescriptivism or moderate emotivism. On this approach, to determine our basic moral principles we try to be as *rational* as possible (consistent, informed, impartial, imaginative, and so forth) and then see what our attitudes are about how we want people to live. People who share this general approach often disagree on issues such as:

- the underlying basis of moral thinking (which might, for example, be seen in intuitionist, ideal observer, divine command, moderate emotivist, or prescriptivist terms);
- whether this "rational attitudes" procedure gives us genuine knowledge of independently existing moral facts, or perhaps something weaker (like knowledge of a constructed morality, justified beliefs, or reasonable attitudes);
- whether, or to what extent, ideally rational moral thinkers would agree (*see* **relativism**); and
- the exact list of the features of **rational moral thinking**, how we are to arrive at this list, and whether this list has some objective justification (as perhaps based on self-evident truths) or just some pragmatic justification (as perhaps things we agree to out of self-interest or **benevolent** feelings).

The "rational attitudes" approach would work out somewhat similarly in practice, despite disagreements on such issues. *See also* EPISTEMOLOGY; ETHICS: METAETHICS; GLOBAL ETHICS; MORAL EDUCATION; NAGEL, THOMAS.

KOHLBERG, LAWRENCE (1927–1987). American psychologist who was a major figure in moral **psychology**. Being unhappy with the **relativism** of many social **scientists**, he sought psychological support for a more objective approach to morality. He built on Jean Piaget (who saw moral development as going from heteronomous conformity and constraint to **autonomous** rationality and cooperation) and **John Dewey** (who saw education as stimulating thinking and problem-solving).

On the basis of extensive empirical studies, Kohlberg claims that, regardless of our culture, we all develop in our moral thinking through a series of six stages divided into three levels:

Pre-conventional Level (Self-seeking)
(1) **Punishment**/*obedience*: "**good**" is what is commanded and re-

warded; "bad" is what is forbidden and punished. (We all start off thinking of morality this way.)

(2) *Self-interest*: "good" is what brings you what you want; "bad" is what frustrates your self-interest. (Children, seeing that obedience does not necessarily promote their self-interest, become more **egoistic** and manipulative.)

Conventional Level

(3) *Parental approval*: "good" is what makes Mommy and Daddy proud of you; "bad" is what brings their disapproval. (Children come to see their self-worth, and thus their self-interest, in terms of gaining parental admiration; external punishments and rewards become less important.)

(4) *Group approval or law-and-order*: "good" is what one's group approves of; "bad" is what it disapproves of. (Teenagers start looking to their peer group instead of parents for support and values; later "good" and "bad" are defined by the attitudes of the larger society. This **cultural relativism** stage is sometimes followed by an intermediate stage of confusion and skepticism.)

Post-conventional Level (Rationality and Autonomy)

(5) **Social contract** *or* **utilitarian**: moral rules are criticized on the basis of whether they promote the good of society. (So now rules are not just conventional but may be rationally defended.)

(6) *Principled* **conscience**: moral beliefs are evaluated using principles about **justice, consistency**, and concern for the equal dignity of every person. (Ideas from **Immanuel Kant, R. M. Hare**, and **John Rawls** are used to explain this stage. Kohlberg often mentions the formula "Act only as you would be willing that everyone should act in the same situation" and illustrates it by the image of *moral musical chairs*, where we **imagine** people switching roles in the situation; a *reversible action* is one that is satisfactory to us even if we are on the receiving end of the action.)

Kohlberg claims that, while we do most of our moral thinking at one stage, we sometimes use the stage above or below. Later stages on the list are "higher" in that they appear later in time, are preferred by those who understand both stages, and are philosophically more adequate. Kohlberg rejects the idea that children are just passive sponges who internalize values they are taught. While children do absorb values, they also are little philosophers struggling for more adequate ways to understand and reason about values.

The **golden rule** covers all the stages, but with increasing clarity and purer motivation at the higher stages. We treat others as we want to be treated because this helps us escape punishment (stage 1), encourages others to treat us better (stage 2), wins the approval of Mommy and Daddy (stage 3), is socially approved (stage 4), is a socially useful practice (stage 5), or treats others with dignity and respect (stage 6). The way to teach children the golden rule is by appealing to a stage that they can understand, not to one that is too high for them to grasp.

Kohlberg began his research by asking a group of 72 young boys about moral dilemmas. The Heinz case, for example, is about whether it would be right to steal overpriced medicine that your wife needs. The reasons the boys gave for their answers were scored as fitting one stage or another. The original subjects were interviewed again every three or four years to keep track of their progress. Similar studies were later done with other groups throughout the **globe**. The same stages were seen in every culture, although some groups made less progress through the stages. Those who progressed to higher stages tended to be more advanced in logical thinking and to have more social experience of the sort that promotes empathetic role-playing (imagination).

Kohlberg contrasts three approaches to **moral education**, which rest on different ideas about moral philosophy and moral psychology:

- *Commonsense approach*: Adults just know what is right and wrong (**intuitionism**) and can teach moral truths to children by words, example, **praise**/blame, and reward/punishment. (Kohlberg objects that this teaches children the values of their elders but not the ability to think for themselves about morality.)
- *Relativistic-emotional approach*: Moral rules are the arbitrary standards of our culture (cultural relativism) instead of independent truths. Children internalize these standards, and adults need to help children adjust to these standards.
- *Cognitive-developmental approach*: Morality is based on principles of justice and human welfare valid for every culture. Children develop through stages of moral thinking as they grow up. Adults need to help children grow in moral rationality by helping them advance to higher stages of moral thinking.

Kohlberg supports the last approach. Adults can help children to progress in their moral thinking by helping them grow in logical skills, expand their social experience (and thus their ability to empathize), and discuss moral dilemmas (in which the teacher clarifies the responses of the students and helps them to understand the moral reasoning in the stage just above where they are). Since those at higher stages tend more to act on their moral beliefs, promoting growth in moral thinking also promotes increased moral action.

Kohlberg's ideas, while very influential, have faced criticism. Some think his stage sequence makes matters neater than they actually are. Others, especially utilitarians (whom he places in stage 5), are skeptical about stage 6, which Kohlberg admits is rarely achieved and thus based on less empirical evidence than the other stages. Others argue that, while Kohlberg has done good work on people's thinking about justice, there are other areas of morality that need investigation too. **Carol Gilligan**, a Harvard colleague of Kohlberg, objected that Kohlberg's stages, which were originally developed from interviews with boys, apply mainly to males; she thought women tend to think differently (*see* **feminist ethics**). Kohlberg and his followers have used criticisms to refine their theory. *See also* ANTHROPOLOGY.

– L –

LAW. *See* ABORTION AND INFANTICIDE; ANIMALS; AQUINAS, THOMAS; AUTONOMY/HETERONOMY; BENTHAM, JEREMY; BIBLICAL ETHICS; BIOETHICS; BUSINESS ETHICS; CAPITAL PUNISHMENT; CIVIL DISOBEDIENCE; COMPUTER ETHICS; DOUBLE EFFECT; DWORKIN, RONALD; ISLAMIC ETHICS; JUSTICE; KANT, IMMANUEL; KING, MARTIN LUTHER; LOCKE, JOHN; MARX, KARL; MILL, JOHN STUART; NATURAL LAW; PATERNALISM; POLITICAL PHILOSOPHY; PORNOGRAPHY; PRIVACY; PUFENDORF, SAMUEL; PUNISHMENT; RAWLS, JOHN; ROSS, W. D.; ROUSSEAU, JEAN-JACQUES; STEM-CELL RESEARCH.

LEWIS, C. I. (1883–1964). Clarence Irving Lewis was an American philosopher at Harvard who contributed to logic, epistemology, and ethics. He wrote the first history of logic in English and was the father of modern modal logic. He was a bridge between pragmatism and the new American analytic tradition that he helped construct; his students included Willard Van Orman Quine, Nelson Goodman, Roderick Chisholm, and **William Frankena**. He spent his last decades on ethics. He defends moral truths, which he thinks are presupposed by intelligent action. His *An Analysis of Knowledge and Valuation* (1947) argues that both scientific inquiry and morality are goal oriented and that human goals provide a **naturalistic**, empirical basis for judgments about what is **good**; this accords with the pragmatist tradition of William James, **John Dewey**, and Ralph Perry. His *The Ground and Nature of the Right* (1955) is more **Kantian**; its principles of right action are *pragmatic a priori* imperatives that a rational being cannot reject. Those who argue for skepticism are caught in a pragmatic contradiction since their arguments assume epistemic, logical, and ethical norms. The basic rational imperative is "Be **consistent** in thought and action." This involves the idea that no way of thinking or acting is valid for anyone unless it would be valid for everyone else in the same circumstances. Lewis formulates his supreme categorical imperative in several ways, including: "Act toward others as if the effects of your actions were to be realized with the poignancy of the immediate—hence, in your own person" and "Act as if you were to live out in sequence your life and the lives of those affected by your actions."

LIBERALISM/COMMUNITARIANISM. The competing positions in an important debate in **political philosophy**. Very roughly, liberalism emphasizes the **rights** of the individual while communitarianism emphasizes the interests and values of the community.

Although the current debate arose after **John Rawls**'s *A Theory of Justice* (1971), its roots are much deeper. Rawls developed ideas from classical liberal philosophers such as **John Locke, Immanuel Kant**, and **John Stuart Mill**. Using instead thinkers such as **Aristotle, Jean-Jacques Rousseau**, and **Georg Wilhelm Friedrich Hegel**, contemporary philosophers such as **Alasdair MacIntyre**, Michael Sandel, Charles Taylor, and Michael Walzer criticized Rawls in ways labeled "communitarian" (though some of these thinkers do not like the term).

Liberalism holds that individuals have rights and liberties and that the state exists to promote these. People should be free to live as they wish as long as they respect the equal rights of others; so I cannot shoot a gun at you since that violates your rights. Locke's **social contract** theory was perhaps the first systematic formulation of liberalism. Locke argued that government obtains its legitimate authority from the consent of the governed and that its authority is limited to enforcing rights that all individuals possess. Governments overstep their bounds if they act in a **paternalistic** manner to force competent adults to live in certain ways (for example, not to smoke) for their own good; instead, the state should interfere with our freedom only when this is needed to prevent people from harming others.

"Liberalism" covers a wide range of views that share the general ideas sketched above. At one end of the spectrum are libertarians, such as **Robert Nozick**, who argue for a minimal state that exists only to enforce our right to life, liberty, and property—and not to bring about a certain distribution of societal goods. At the other end are thinkers like Rawls, who argue that people have the right to fairness in the distribution of society's wealth; Rawls thinks the state ought to combat disparities in wealth that are not ultimately in everyone's interests.

"Communitarianism" also covers a wide range of views; but all reject the liberal primacy of the individual and instead give primacy to the community. Communitarians think liberals are wrong in seeing individuals as existing prior to society, as the product of their own natures and choices, while society comes from individuals coming together to cooperate. Instead, individuals are products of their communities. Who you are comes mostly from what your community formed you to be through institutions like schools, churches, unions, and clubs. So we ought to reject the liberal view that sees the state's role in the protection of individual rights and liberties and ignores its social responsibility to promote the good of society. The liberal agenda of merely promoting the rights of individuals would lead government to ignore important problems such as **poverty, racism,** and the political apathy of youth. People who have received so much from the community have a duty to that community and to contribute to solving its problems. Emphasizing the liberal idea that people are to look after themselves will impede the moral progress of society.

Liberals worry that, without the protections for individuals afforded by liberal states, communities could enslave the individual. Communities can trample on personal **autonomy** (as in Nazi Germany) if they are not held in check. Communitarians respond that individuals are not to sit back and accept whatever those in power do. Instead, they should bring their ideas about what is right and wrong to their communities in order to promote moral progress. *See also* DWORKIN, RONALD.

LIBERTARIANISM. For *metaphysical libertarianism, see* **free will and determinism**. For *political libertarianism, see* **Robert Nozick**.

LOCKE, JOHN (1632–1704). English empiricist philosopher who sought to justify representative government. His family were Puritans, and his father fought with parliamentarians against King Charles I. He became involved in politics when he assisted his friend the Earl of Shaftesbury in writing the constitution of the Carolina colony; when Shaftesbury was later tried for treason, Locke feared for his own life and fled to Holland. There he was declared a traitor in connection with Monmouth's failed rebellion against King James II. He returned to England after his friend William of Orange assumed the throne. Later, Locke's writings greatly influenced the American Declaration of Independence (1776) and Constitution (1789).

Locke's major contribution to ethics is his **social contract** theory presented in *Two Treatises of Government* (1690). Like **Thomas Hobbes** before him, he justified government on the basis of a social contract; but, while Hobbes argued for an absolute monarchy, Locke argued for a representative government. This difference stems from their views on the state of nature. Both see the state of nature as a presocietal condition in which we would live if we had no common rules or authority to govern us. Hobbes believes that in the state of nature we would act out of **egoism** without any sense of right and wrong; since we would fight for scarce resources and live in fear of attack, our lives would be "solitary, poor, nasty, brutish, and short." The only way to avoid this is for all to agree to be subject to an absolute sovereign. Locke does not see the state of nature as quite so grim. In the state of nature, we would have a **natural moral law**, laid down by **God** and discoverable through reason, that precludes us from violating the **rights** of others to "life, health, liberty, or possessions." Thus the state of nature would not be so miserable. But there would be problems, such as how to **punish** those who violate the natural moral law; so we would agree to set up a representative government to enforce it. If the government fails in its charge, we are justified in removing it.

Many argue that Locke has paid too high a philosophical cost in his conception of the state of nature. Since he appeals to God to support a natural moral law, he needs a sound argument for the existence of God, something Hobbes did not need since he did not appeal to God. Many philosophers believe Locke has no such argument available to him.

Locke's *Two Treatises* also is known for its labor-mixing theory of property. It begins with the commonsense notion that what I produce with my own efforts belongs to me. Although my body belongs to God, I am the earthly owner of my body. If I mix my labor (which I own) with something that is not owned, the result becomes mine. So, if I mix my labor with unappropriated land by plowing it and planting seeds, the crop it produces is mine. Locke places two limitations on how much property one can accumulate in this fashion:

(1) one cannot take so much that it will spoil in one's possession, and
(2) one must leave enough and as good behind for others.

At first glance, these so-called "Lockean provisos" are somewhat puzzling since it is clear that Locke seeks to support capitalism. The first proviso seems inconsistent with the property-accumulation aspect of capitalism because one could not collect even the fruit of one apple tree and use it all before it spoils. As Locke explains, however, money overcomes this problem since it allows one to sell the apples and accumulate money that does not spoil.

Critics object that the second proviso precludes any appropriation of land. If Sara appropriates the last plot of available land, she does not leave enough and as good behind for Phil. So Sara's appropriation is illegitimate. But then those who appropriated land before her also did so illegitimately since they did not leave enough and as good behind for her. So no appropriation of land is just. Locke explains, however, that Sara's and others' appropriations are legitimate because cultivated land produces far more than uncultivated land. When Sara and others use the land, they leave enough and as good behind for others in the form of the useful products of the land.

While libertarians such as **Robert Nozick** accept the labor-mixing account of property, **Jean-Jacques Rousseau** and **Karl Marx** see it as justifying the unjust holdings of the wealthy and as keeping the exploited **poor** from rising above their conditions. *See also* BUSINESS ETHICS; HUME, DAVID; LIBERALISM/COMMUNITARIANISM; MODERN ETHICS; POLITICAL PHILOSOPHY; PUFENDORF, SAMUEL; RAND, AYN; SMITH, ADAM.

LOGIC. The study of deductive reasoning. Taken broadly, logic also includes topics like inductive and other kinds of reasoning (like analogical, pro-con, and inference to the best explanation), informal fallacies, how to clarify meaning, issues about concepts central to thinking (like truth, meaning, and reference), and various related philosophical issues (like the analytic/synthetic distinction, the existence of abstract objects, and how to justify basic logical principles). Many such ideas arise when we theorize about ethics. This entry focuses on five special connections between logic and ethics.

(1) What logical laws cover key ethical terms? *Axiological logic* studies arguments whose validity depends on "**good**," "**bad**," and "better." One approach builds on quantificational logic and takes the relation "a is better than (preferable to) b" ("Pab") as basic, where a and b are states of affairs; an example is "That I experience pleasure is better than that I experience pain." The "better than" relation is assumed to be asymmetrical (if a is better than b, then b is not better than a) and transitive (if a is better than b, and b is better than c, then a is better than c). Then "a is good" is defined as "a is better than not-a" and "a is bad" as "not-a is better than a."

Deontic logic studies arguments whose validity depends on "**ought**," "permissible," and "wrong." Often "OA" is used for "It ought to be that A" and "RA" for "It is all permissible (all right) that A." These two notions are interdefinable; for example, OA = ~R~A (It ought to be that A = It is not permissible that not-A). The logical rules for "O" and "R" are somewhat like the rules for "□" ("It is necessary that") and "◇" ("It is possible that") in modal logic.

Imperative logic studies arguments with imperatives, like "Do this." **Prescriptivists** like **R. M. Hare** claim that imperatives have logical properties; they can be logically inconsistent with or logically entail other imperatives, as in this imperative argument (where Bx = *x is one of these boxes* and Tuxy = *you take x to y*):

Take all these boxes to the station.	$(x)(Bx \supset T\underline{u}xs)$
This is one of these boxes.	Bt
∴ Take this to the station.	∴ T\underline{u}ts

The formulas on the right symbolize the argument in an expanded quantificational logic that underlines the agent in imperative formulas. One problem here is that "valid argument" is usually defined in terms of the impossibility of having premises true and conclusion false; since imperatives are not true or false, imperative logic must develop a broader definition of "valid argument."

(2) What **consistency** principles apply to ethical beliefs? If we combine propositional and quantificational logic, deontic and imperative logic, **universalizability**, and a few more things, we can construct a *formal ethics* that includes consistency principles about **conscientiousness**, **impartiality**, the formula of universal law, and the **golden rule**.

(3) *Metaethics* (*see* **ethics: metaethics**) raises a key logical issue: Can we deduce an "ought" from an "is"? (**Hume**'s law is that we cannot.) Can we take strictly factual, non-evaluative premises (perhaps about what produces pleasure or what is socially accepted or what the creator commands) and, without assuming any further premises about what is "good" or "ought to be done," validly deduce conclusions about what is "good" or "ought to be done"? **Naturalistic** views and **divine command theory** say yes, while **intuitionism, emotivism,** and **prescriptivism** say no.

(4) Normative ethics (*see* **ethics: normative**) raises the question of how logic can apply ethical principles to concrete cases. **Exceptionless** principles apply in a simple deductive manner, as in: "All actions that are F are wrong; this action is F; therefore this action is wrong"; here F stands for a type of action, like *intentionally killing an innocent human being*, or a property about consequences, like *not maximizing the balance of pleasure over pain for sentient beings*. **Prima facie** principles use a more complex form of reasoning, perhaps like: "Any action that is F is wrong unless there is an overriding consideration; this action is F; there is no overriding consideration; therefore this action is wrong."

(5) Logic can contribute much to the *ethics of thinking and rational discussion*. When we reason, whether alone or in a public forum, we ought to reason clearly and correctly and avoid fallacies (such as inconsistencies or distorting another's views). *See also* CHARITY, PRINCIPLE OF; DECISION THEORY; FALLACIES ABOUT ETHICS; PHILOSOPHY AND ETHICS; RACISM.

LOGICAL POSITIVISM. A philosophical movement that was strong in the first half of the 20th century. It started with the *Vienna Circle*, a group of Austrian **scientists** and philosophers who met in the 1920s to develop a scientific approach to philosophy; they were skeptical of traditional philosophy and saw science as our main source of knowledge. They saw **logic** and **mathematics** as *analytic*, or true by virtue of language conventions. Their central doctrine was the *verifiability criterion of meaning*, which held that the meaning of a non-analytic statement is determined by what conceivable observable tests would settle whether the statement is true. Any genuine truth claim has to be either analytic or empirically testable; whatever fails this criterion, like metaphysics and theology, is nonsensical. **A. J. Ayer** and most other positivists argued that moral judgments like "**Racism** is wrong," being neither analytic nor empirically testable, were nonsensical; so most positivists became **emotivists**, holding that moral judgments express not truth claims but only emotion. A notable exception was the positivist Moritz Schlick, whose **naturalistic** approach saw ethical judgments as empirical truth claims.

The Nazis opposed logical positivism and forced most positivists to leave Germany and Austria. While most positivists had little interest in politics, their emphasis on clear thinking was seen as a threat.

Logical positivism by now has been almost universally abandoned since (1) the view is self-refuting (its central doctrine is neither analytic nor empirically testable, and so is nonsensical on its own terms), (2) the difference between what is or is not empirically testable proved impossible to draw in a clear way, and (3) many things that positivists declared nonsensical did not seem to be nonsensical at all.

LOVE YOUR NEIGHBOR. "Love your neighbor as yourself" is the central norm of **Biblical ethics** about how to treat others. **John Stuart Mill** saw the love norm as another way to express **utilitarianism**, that we ought to do what has the best total consequences for everyone. Non-**consequentialists** object to this totaling; they sometimes see the love norm as another way to state separate **benevolence** and *non-malefi-cence* duties ("Do good to others" and "Do not harm others"—*see* **W. D. Ross**), the latter binding more strongly, or perhaps as stating **Immanuel Kant**'s end-in-itself principle ("Treat humanity, whether yourself or another, as an end-in-itself and not only as a means"). Still others see the love norm as telling us to act from a motivation of concern for others for their own sake; this motivation is compatible with many views about normative ethics (*see* **ethics: normative**).

In the Bible, both the love norm and the **golden rule** are said to summarize our Biblical duties about how we are to live. How do these two norms relate? Some think the two are equivalent, just different ways to say the same thing. Others say the two norms are different but complementary: loving others (caring about them for their own sake) is the highest motive for following the golden rule (which we also might follow for lower motives like self-interest), while the golden rule gives a workable way to operationalize the somewhat vague idea of "loving your neighbor." To love your neighbor in the golden-rule way:

(1)   know your neighbor as well as you can (*see* **information**);
(2)   **imagine** yourself in the place of your neighbor, as vividly and accurately as you can; and

(3)   act toward your neighbor only in ways in which you are willing to be treated in the same situation.

If you love your children in this way, for example, you will make a great effort to know and understand them (including their needs and desires), you will put yourself in their place and try to imagine what their lives are like for them, and you will treat them only in ways that you are willing to be treated yourself by a parent in the same situation.

While the love norm is often associated with Christianity, it occurred earlier in the **Jewish** Bible (Leviticus 19:18). The love norm, or a similar idea, can be found in a wide range of different religions and cultures, including **Confucianism, Buddhism, Daoism, Islam, Hinduism**, and many indigenous religions. Sometimes words are used like "caring," "compassion," "respect for living things," "the brotherhood of humanity," "concern for others," "altruism," "acting humanely," "seeing others as if they were yourself," or "kindness." The Dalai Lama summarized this by saying that every religion emphasizes human improvement, love, respect for others, and sharing other people's suffering. Many nonreligious people have this same orientation.

– M –

MACINTYRE, ALASDAIR (1929–). Scottish philosopher and proponent of **virtue** ethics. He has taught at several universities in Britain and the U.S. and has published widely in ethics, history of philosophy, philosophy of religion, and **political philosophy**.

MacIntyre criticizes **modern ethics** and its emphasis on individual actions. Classical ethicists such as **Thomas Hobbes, Immanuel Kant**, and **John Stuart Mill** tried to give a **normative** principle to separate right acts from wrong acts. MacIntyre prefers instead the approach of **ancient** and **medieval ethics**, in particular that of **Aristotle** and **Thomas Aquinas**, that emphasizes virtue and personal character. One problem with the virtue approach is that different thinkers propose different lists of virtues. MacIntyre analyzes differences in the virtues of Homer, Aristotle, the **Bible**, Jane Austen, and Benjamin Franklin. He argues that, despite differences, there is a core, shared conception among these differing accounts of the virtues.

For MacIntyre, a *practice* is a social activity in which humans cooperate in order to achieve certain **good**s. Agriculture, sciences, and sports all count as practices. In each, we cooperate in socially recognized ways to achieve ends such as food, knowledge, and entertainment. Virtues are habits or dispositions that we develop in connection with such practices. Certain traits are necessary to achieve excellence in a practice and thus to obtain the goods that are internal to that practice. To obtain the goods internal to baseball, I must develop the traits needed for excellence in baseball: an understanding of its rules and strategies, physical fitness, habitual ways of responding to game situations, and so on. Those traits are the virtues associated with baseball.

MacIntyre thus emphasizes the historical values and traditions of a community instead of individual **rights**. He criticizes **John Rawls** and defends communitarianism (*see* **liberalism/communitarianism**).

Critics question whether MacIntyre's account of virtues provides a satisfactory guide for human conduct. Some human practices (like Nazism) may be evil. We need to understand more clearly what practices we should accept and what goods should be internal to particular practices. Nevertheless, MacIntyre has been influential in the rebirth of virtue ethics in contemporary philosophy.

MACKIE, J. L. (1917–1981). John Leslie Mackie was an Australian philosopher who was skeptical about ethics. Mackie was not a conventional **subjectivist** or **emotivist**. According to Mackie, "X is **good**" is not intended to describe or express our feelings; so it is not equivalent in meaning to "I like X" or "Hurrah for X!" Instead, moral judgments are intended to make claims about an objective realm of values—claims that are objectively prescriptive. **Intuitionism** and **Immanuel Kant**'s *categorical imperatives* capture well what ethical judgments attempt to do, namely express objective truths that rationally commit us to acting accordingly. But the problem, according to Mackie's *error theory*, is that there is no such objective realm of values, no moral facts. So moral judgments, taken literally, are all false; they only succeed in expressing feelings. Error theory makes morality fraudulent.

Mackie admits that, since the moral concepts of ordinary people and most Western philosophers are concepts of objective value, there is a presumption that there are objective values. To attack this presumption, he gives two arguments against the objectivity of values. His *argument from* **relativity** has us consider the variations in moral codes between different societies, historical periods, and social classes. Mackie claims that these variations are more easily explained by the hypothesis that they reflect ways of life than by the hypothesis that they express perceptions of objective values. If we did directly perceive moral truths, as we perceive colors or perhaps **mathematical** axioms, then surely there would be a larger conformity in moral beliefs than what we see when we study **anthropology**.

Mackie's argument here seems oriented against a *perception* or *intuition* model of moral knowledge. Perhaps we could do better with a *rationalized attitudes* model, where we strive toward moral knowledge by taking our current attitudes (which reflect a way of life that we inherit from our society) and trying to become more **rational** (more **consistent, informed, impartial, imaginative**, and so forth). This model perhaps could explain the diversity of moral beliefs without giving up the claim that genuine moral knowledge is possible.

Mackie's *argument from queerness* points out that objective values, if they existed, would be entities or qualities or relations of a very strange sort, utterly different from anything else in the universe. And our knowledge of them would require a special faculty of moral perception or intuition, utterly different from our ordinary ways of knowing everything else. So **moral realism** consists of weird, strange, and peculiar ideas—and so is better avoided.

Critics complain that what seems "weird" to someone is highly subjective and variable. If we take knowledge of material objects as the norm all knowledge must conform to, then our knowledge of mathematics will seem weird and unintelligible. But if we take knowledge of mathematics as the norm, then our knowledge of material objects will seem weird. Mackie admits that most thinkers in the history of philosophy accepted objective values; perhaps such values seem more weird to Mackie than to them because Mackie takes **science** and mathematics as the norm to which all knowledge must conform. But why do this? And do not even science and mathematics have weird ideas—like *charmed quarks* and *transfinite numbers*? Some say any area of life—not just ethics—will lead to weird issues and ideas if we push it far enough.

Others object that error theory is wrong since not all moral judgments can be false. As a matter of logic, if "Act A is wrong" is false, then "Act A is not wrong" has to be true—so at least one of the two has to be true. Perhaps the theory should say that, since there are no objective values, everything is permissible. *See also* AESTHETICS; COGNITIVISM/NON-COGNITIVISM; DIVINE COMMAND THEORY; GOD; HUME, DAVID; KNOWING RIGHT FROM WRONG.

MARX, KARL (1818–1883). German revolutionary communist, economist, and activist philosopher. He wrote, "Philosophers have only
interpreted the world, the point is to change it." He did change it, since
for much of the 20th century his teachings guided the Soviet Union
(1922–1991) and many other Marxist countries.

Marx completed a dissertation in philosophy, but his association
with radical groups kept him from securing an academic position. He
became editor of a liberal newspaper, but it was suppressed by the
government. Marx fled to Paris where Friedrich Engels, the son of a
factory owner, became his friend and provided him with financial support. Together they wrote the *Communist Manifesto* (1848), which
states principles and calls for action.

Georg Wilhelm Friedrich Hegel taught that societies progress by
free actions through stages toward an ideal. Hegel's ideal is a state
where our interests coincide with those of others and where we accept
social restraints that help us to achieve our ultimate **autonomy** and potential. Marx adopted this scheme but changed it considerably. Marx's
historical materialism sees history in terms of class struggle and economic determinism. The end result, the ideal society, will of necessity
be a stateless, classless, communist society of ultimate freedom.

For Marx, each stage of society is marked by a means of production
and the class struggles it produces. In feudal times, the lords owned the
land, which was the means of production, and the serfs made the land
productive through their work. While the two groups were at odds, the
lords kept power through laws and customs that protected their land
ownership. In capitalist times, the bourgeoisie (capitalists) own the
means of production (land, factories, shops, and the like), while the
proletariat (workers) make them operational. Again, the bourgeoisie
keep their power by controlling the laws and customs.

Private property is a key element in capitalism. **John Locke** thought
protecting private property was an essential role of the state, and **Adam
Smith** argued that a free market based on private property produces the
best society. Contemporary libertarian thinkers such as **Robert Nozick**
and **Ayn Rand** support these notions. Marx rejects them and follows
Jean-Jacques Rousseau's idea that private property promotes a kind
of slavery; it makes the **poor** depend on wealthy property owners and
widens the gap between rich and poor. Marx's vision of the bourgeoisie
and the proletariat develops this picture further.

Marx argues that capitalism oppresses workers in three ways.
(1) Capitalism alienates workers from their work. Owners direct the

work based on what will bring them the most profit. Workers have little say in how the work is done, and little attention is given to their health, needs, and desires. In addition, workers see only a small part of the production process. They do not see a pair of shoes or a car produced from beginning to end; instead, they spend their shifts installing the same bolts over and over again as part of a larger assembly line.

(2) Capitalism exploits workers. Since they lack alternatives, they must work long hours for little pay. The bourgeoisie make huge profits by taking for themselves what Marx terms the *surplus value* of a product: the difference between its selling price and the costs (raw material, labor, and overhead) needed to produce it. Marx argues that workers create this surplus value and rightfully own it; owners exploit workers by taking it from them. Defenders of capitalism argue instead that the owners produce and own this value, since they, at financial risk to themselves, set up the mechanisms to develop the product.

(3) Capitalism tends toward crises of overproduction that hurt workers. When more is produced than can be consumed, which inevitably happens, recessions follow and production is cut. Workers are laid off and suffer, especially since, unlike owners, they have not been able to accumulate enough wealth to guard against such eventualities.

Marx believes that these deplorable conditions will bring workers together and develop their class consciousness. When they unite, they will revolt and seize control of the means of production, by violence if necessary. This will usher in a new stage of society, the **socialist** dictatorship of the proletariat. The bourgeoisie will be forced to accept this. Class distinctions will fall away, as will the need for the state. At last, the ideal society will be born: pure communism.

Despite all this, Marx admired some of capitalism's accomplishments, particularly its production efficiency and how it moved many people into the cities where they could more easily develop a class consciousness. Both factors were necessary steps toward the ideal society and the proletarian revolution.

The failure of the U.S.S.R. and other communist states leads to objections. If communism is so ideal, why did it fail in so many places and why do other societies not try it? If it produces freedom, why did people under communist regimes complain about their lack of freedom? Contemporary Marxists respond in two ways. First, they argue that Marx would not have approved of how the communist revolution occurred in Russia, which went directly from feudalism to communism; the intermediate capitalist stage was needed to build up the means of production and allow the proletariat to develop a class consciousness. Also, Marx would not have approved of a strong, centralized state; he saw the state as fading away. Second, Marxists argue that Marx underestimated the flexibility of capitalist societies in dealing with the problems of workers, which led to programs like social security and unemployment compensation in the U.S. and universal healthcare in Canada. Contemporary Marxists argue that such concessions have slowed the movement toward the proletariat revolution, but have not ended it.

Many object to Marx's historical materialism; though they see history as marked by class struggles, critics reject the idea that society is destined to progress in certain preordained ways. And many **liberals**, such as **John Stuart Mill**, focus on the **rights** of the individual; they argue that Marxist ideas like the classless society can only be achieved by infringing on the rights of individuals, by keeping them from exploring their own ideas and moving in their own direction. Nozick claims that a socialist society would have to forbid free capitalist acts between consenting adults, lest these produce inequalities. But such tyranny would not produce ultimate freedom.

Despite such objections, Marx has an important legacy. Better than anyone before him, he saw the bad effects of unchecked capitalism. For many, Marx's story is a cautionary tale about the negative impacts of an economic system that, by many significant measures, is extremely effective. *See also* POLITICAL PHILOSOPHY.

MATHEMATICS. Has provided at least three different models for ethical thinking. **Plato** thought ethics was much like geometry; just as a *perfect circle* is an ideal form that the mind can grasp apart from sense experience, so too *perfect* **goodness** and *perfect* **justice** are ideal forms that the mind can grasp apart from sense experience. Much later, **W. D. Ross** and other **intuitionists** would compare our grasp of first principles in arithmetic and in ethics; in both cases, the mature mind can come to grasp self-evident principles that neither have nor require any further proof. So this first model is a **rationalist** one.

A second model recognizes that the foundations of mathematics are as controversial as the foundations of ethics. Just as some ethicists are skeptical of non-empirical but objective ethical properties, so too some mathematicians are skeptical of the non-empirical, abstract entities that seem to be part of mathematics. Some propose that mathematics is not about external, objective, abstract truths that we can discover. Instead, mathematics is based perhaps on human **psychology** and how we think, on human conventions and constructions, on empirical results about counting, on a game with meaningless symbols, or on ideas in **God**'s mind; the disagreements here somewhat parallel disagreements about ethics (*see* **ethics: metaethics**). People who disagree about the foundations of mathematics may still agree significantly on practical matters about mathematics, like how much they should be charged at the supermarket. This leads to a second model for ethics, an *overlapping consensus* model (a term from **John Rawls**). People who disagree radically about the foundations of ethics may still be able to agree on many issues about ethics, but for their own individual reasons. Some who argue for a *rationalized attitudes* approach to **knowing right from wrong** argue on this basis, claiming that the requirement that moral thinking be **informed, consistent, impartial**, and so forth can be based on a wide range of views about the foundations of ethics.

A third mathematical model for ethical thinking is **decision theory**, which deals with making decisions with uncertain outcomes, usually with the aim of maximizing the probable utility (**good** consequences). **Consequentialists** (including **utilitarians** and **egoists**) can use decision theory to make more precise their calculations about what we ought to do. An important subdiscipline is *game theory*, which provides a mathematical model of the interacting choices of multiple agents and is exemplified in the **prisoner's dilemma**; game theory has clarified the limits of egoism and the need for social cooperation.

MEDICAL ETHICS. *See* BIOETHICS.

MEDIEVAL ETHICS (including the Patristic era). Even though scholars date the beginning of the Middle Ages much later, it is convenient here to begin with the rise of Christianity and end before the Renaissance and Protestant Reformation; so this entry covers the first 14 centuries AD. Ethics in this period had a strong religious orientation; this distinguishes it from the earlier **ancient ethics** of **Socrates**, **Plato**, and **Aristotle** and the later **modern ethics** of **Thomas Hobbes**, **David Hume**, and **Immanuel Kant**.

At the beginning of the Christian era, the dominant philosophy was Plato and various Platonisms. The **Jewish** Philo of Alexandria (c. 15 BC–45 AD) and the Neoplatonic Plotinus (c. 205–270) both built on Plato's metaphysical and mystical elements. Many Platonic themes fit well with Christianity: a higher reality beyond the senses, the immortality of a spiritual soul, divine providence, and objective moral values.

The Stoics also were influential; Roman Stoics thinkers include the orator Cicero (106–43 BC), the statesman Seneca (c. 4 BC–65 AD), the ex-slave Epictetus (c. 55–135), and the emperor Marcus Aurelius (121–180). They provided further ideas that fit with Christianity: a **natural moral law** based on reason, an engagement in the affairs of the world, an inner happiness resistant to outer circumstances, the rational order of the universe, the importance of discipline and **virtue**, the duty to be **just** and considerate toward everyone, and the **golden rule**. Aristotle was then less important since his main works were not available in the West until centuries later.

The initial task for Christian thinkers was how to combine the best elements from these philosophies with Christian faith and the **Bible**. One of the first to attempt this was Aristides the Philosopher (early second century), an Athenian who defended Christianity to the Roman Emperor; Aristides argued for belief in **God** as the world's designer and mover, claimed that Christianity was religiously and morally superior to polytheism, and protested religious persecution. His work echoed St. Paul's speech at Athens (Acts of the Apostles 17:22–34).

Irenaeus (c. 120–200) argued for **free will**, which he saw as presupposed by moral praise and blame; Boethius (c. 470–524) later argued for the compatibility of human freedom and divine foreknowledge. Irenaeus also proposed an approach to the problem of evil; God created the first humans weak and imperfect, and intended life to be a significant, free struggle against evil in which we gradually grow toward moral and spiritual maturity and eternal happiness. Irenaeus's view contrasts with the Augustinian view, which saw evil as coming from the sin of the first humans, Adam and Eve, who were created perfect.

Augustine (354–430) had a great influence on subsequent Christian thought. Even today, many are moved by his philosophical struggles and conversion to Christianity; they find insightful his works on theology (including Biblical commentaries) and philosophy (which aimed at a synthesis between Platonism and Christianity). He summarized his ethics as: "Love, and do as you will"; central here are love of God, in which our ultimate **happiness** consists, and **benevolence** toward others. Later Christian philosophers in the Platonic tradition include Pseudo-Dionysius (c. 500) and Bonaventure (1217–1274). In general, this Platonic influence tended to accentuate the other-worldly strains in Christianity and to devalue the material and bodily aspects of life.

Peter Abelard (1079–1142) approached ethics with an emphasis on our inner motivation. If Al and Bob do the same externally right act, but Al acts out of loving concern and Bob acts selfishly, then Al's act is good (**praiseworthy** and meritorious) but Bob's act is bad (blameworthy and sinful). Sin has nothing to do with our external act but everything to do with our intention to do what goes against God's will.

Three factors helped bring in the "golden age" of Christian philosophy in the 13th century. First, there was the rise of **Islamic** philosophers such as Avicenna (980–1037) and Averroës (1126–1198) and Jewish philosophers like Moses Maimonides (1138–1204). Christian philosophers learned much from them and built on their ideas. Second, many of Aristotle's writings, which had been lost for centuries, suddenly came into Christian Europe. While some thought the Aristotelian texts were dangerous to faith, others embraced them with enthusiasm. Soon Aristotelianism replaced Platonism as the dominant perspective of Christian philosophers. Third, there was the rise of the medieval universities, which moved philosophy toward greater technical rigor.

Thomas Aquinas (1224–1274) was the most important medieval philosopher. His central theme was the harmony between human reason (especially as explained by Aristotle) and Christian faith (based on the Bible and church Tradition). His thinking about morality divides into two parts. His *moral philosophy* mostly follows Aristotle; its norms, called "natural (moral) laws," are knowable from natural reason and do not require Christian revelation (which Aristotle lacked). His **moral theology** requires Christian revelation; it adds further norms, called "divine (revealed) laws," and gives a larger religious context for viewing reason's natural laws. Aquinas's special genius was his ability to combine ideas from previous thinkers into a coherent synthesis.

John Duns Scotus (1266–1308) emphasized the will over the intellect; he claimed, with Platonic Christian thinkers but against Aquinas, that our final end is not *knowing* God, but rather *loving* him, which was seen as a matter of will.

William of Ockham (c. 1285–1349) was the most influential philosopher of the 14th century. He was skeptical of metaphysics and of basing belief in God on reason; he advocated believing in God on the basis of faith alone. His ethics rested on God's will; **good** is what God wills, and God could have set up the moral norms in the opposite way from how he did (so that stealing and hatred, for example, were good). Ockham was one of the few important Christian philosophers to clearly endorse **divine command theory**. One implication of this view is that the problem of evil dissolves; since what God wills is necessarily good, God's will would be good even if it created a world with uninterrupted pain and hatred. Many later Protestant thinkers accepted Ockham's approach to ethics, which tended to place morality on the turf of theologians rather than philosophers. Most Catholic thinkers followed Aquinas's Aristotelian view, which based ethics on right reason.

Soon the Renaissance and Enlightenment were to give philosophy a secular direction, but two issues that Christian thinkers raised remained in the forefront: benevolence and free will. Christians also taught the **sanctity of human life**; they rejected the ancient Roman practices of **abortion**, infanticide, **suicide**, and **killing** in gladiatorial games. **Peter Singer** thinks the Christian influence here was mostly negative; he supports looser rules about killing humans and rejects the special moral status of membership in our species.

MERCY KILLING. *See* EUTHANASIA.

METAETHICS. *See* ETHICS: METAETHICS.

METAPHYSICS. The study of the nature of reality. Views about metaphysics strongly influence ethical theories.

Consider the issue of materialism: Is physical matter (as is studied in physics and chemistry) the only reality? Non-materialists say no; they believe in a higher reality above matter and tend to connect it to ethics. **Plato** believed in the Forms and based ethics on the Form of the Good. The **ancient** Stoics accepted a non-material cosmic order as the basis of morality's **natural laws**. Plotinus saw our **good** in the soul's ascent from matter to a mystical union with the One. **Medieval** thinkers like **Augustine** and **Thomas Aquinas** saw our highest good in a mystical union with **God**. A group of later **intuitionist** thinkers (including **Joseph Butler, Thomas Reid, Henry Sidgwick, G. E. Moore**, and **W. D. Ross**) saw ethics as about moral facts that are objective but not reducible to the material or the empirical (*see* **moral realism**).

Materially minded thinkers, including many who are not strict materialists, reject such ideas; they try to construct an ethics on premises that do not appeal to anything non-material. Epicurus saw pleasure as the good. **Thomas Hobbes** took morality to be a social construct for mutual benefit. **David Hume** based morality on our **benevolent** feelings, while **John Stuart Mill** based it on our desires. **A. J. Ayer** thought ethical judgments express feelings, while **J. L. Mackie** thought they express falsehoods about some nonexistent realm of moral facts. Some recent thinkers accept objective moral facts but see these as empirical facts about the natural world (*see* **naturalism**).

Other metaphysical issues that are often thought to have a bearing on ethics include **free will**, the afterlife, the existence of God, and the existence of a self that persists through time (*see* **Derek Parfit**). **Immanuel Kant** was somewhat unusual in that he based metaphysics on ethics; because we see ourselves as moral beings, we must believe in God, freedom, and immorality and we must see ourselves as citizens of a higher world beyond the material.

Some ethicists, such as **John Rawls**, try to build ethics on a metaphysically neutral framework that can be accepted by people with various metaphysical or religious views, but perhaps for different reasons. *See also* EPISTEMOLOGY; KNOWING RIGHT FROM WRONG; PHILOSOPHY AND ETHICS.

MILL, JAMES (1773–1836). Scottish-born British philosopher who, with his friend **Jeremy Bentham**, was among the leaders of the British **utilitarian** movement. Confident that utilitarianism promotes moral, **political**, and economic progress, he applied this view to social and political issues. He influenced and supervised the education of his son, **John Stuart Mill**, who became the most influential utilitarian thinker.

MILL, JOHN STUART (1806–1873). English **utilitarian** philosopher who greatly influenced liberal thought (*see* **liberalism/communitarianism**). His father, **James Mill**, and his father's friend, **Jeremy Bentham**, were leaders of the British utilitarian movement; John Stuart Mill later emerged as the most important philosopher in that movement. In addition to his work on ethical theory, he also defended the **rights** of women and minorities (*see* **sexism** and **racism**). He brought his ideas to practice by working for the East India Company and by serving as a Member of Parliament.

Mill's *Utilitarianism* (1861) argued for the *greatest happiness principle*, which holds that when one is faced with multiple possible courses of action one should choose the act that produces the greatest balance of **happiness** over unhappiness. The happiness at issue is the sum of the happiness of all who are affected by one's possible acts. If you must choose between keeping your promise to pick up a friend at the airport or helping an injured motorist on the highway, presumably more happiness would be produced by helping the injured motorist; here the gain in happiness to the motorist and the motorist's family and friends would outweigh the loss of happiness for you and your friend.

Mill defines happiness as pleasure and the absence of pain, but he does not think all pleasures are of equal value. The lower pleasures, the bodily pleasures that nonhuman **animals** also experience, are not worth as much as the higher pleasures, those that involve our intellect; we know this because those who have experienced both prefer the higher pleasures. Mill argues that we would not agree to become pigs, even if we knew that we would be very happy pigs with no pig pains. We would choose to remain human even though it brings many human pains. This shows that the higher pleasures greatly outweigh the lower; when choosing between lower pleasures with no pains and higher pleasures with pains, we would choose the latter.

Mill wants to produce a theory that is **egalitarian** by counting equally the happiness of all persons regardless of sex, race, or religion; but many believe that Mill's views on pleasures defeat this goal. By counting the higher pleasures more, Mill gives preference to the interests of the elite members of society since they have more opportunity to experience the higher pleasures. Mill likely would respond that his approach benefits society by providing people with the incentive to seek more education so that they can experience the higher pleasures.

Some critics object that utilitarianism is godless. Mill argues that it is sensible to see **God** as wanting us to be happy and thus as approving of what maximizes happiness. God, according to Mill, is a utilitarian.

Many object that utilitarianism is impractical since there is seldom time to perform utilitarian calculations before we act. Mill responds by advocating *secondary principles* to guide us as to how to maximize happiness so that we do not always have to do a direct utilitarian calculation. The experience of the human species shows us what kinds of acts tend to produce happiness, and gives us secondary principles such as "Do not murder" and "Do not steal." We generally should follow these secondary principles; we should turn to a utilitarian calculation only when the secondary principles conflict, as in the airport/motorist example above (where "Keep your promises" conflicts with "Help others in need"). There is much dispute today over whether Mill is better seen as an *act* or as a *rule utilitarian*.

The secondary principles illuminate another feature of Mill's ethics. Mill rejected **intuitionism**, the view that bases ethics on moral truths that are self-evident or known by moral intuition. He saw secondary principles as neither self-evident nor based on intuition. Instead, we know such principles from experience. Human experience teaches us that to maximize happiness we need to refrain from murdering, stealing, and the like. In this way, Mill bases his ethics, like the rest of his philosophy (including his view of **mathematics**), on empiricism.

Many object to Mill's attempt to prove the greatest happiness principle. Mill argued, first, that only happiness is intrinsically desirable because only happiness is desired for its own sake. He argued further that then the happiness of all should be our end. Critics like **Henry Sidgwick** and **G. E. Moore** criticize the idea that we can prove what is desirable by premises about what is desired; they say that this is fallacious (since we might desire bad things) and violates **Hume**'s law that we cannot derive **normative** claims (such as "x is desirable") from purely descriptive claims (like "x is desired). Others counter that, although Mill's argument does not give a strict proof, we must somehow base what is good on facts about human **psychology**, for example that we seek pleasure and avoid pain. Other critics contend that we desire not just happiness but also things like artistic achievements. Still others say that Mill's argument, even if it showed that only happiness is intrinsically desirable, does little to show that we should desire the happiness of all instead of just our own happiness (**egoism**).

Mill's greatest happiness principle is the basis for his ideas in other works. In *On Liberty* (1859), Mill argues that society should not interfere with the acts of an individual unless these harm someone else. Mill believes that a society that follows such a rule will be happier than one that does not (*see* **paternalism**); such a society will allow individuals to explore new ideas in ways that promote moral, political, and economic progress. In *Considerations on Representative Government* (1861), Mill argues that a representative government, though one that is considerably different than those in Great Britain and the United States, would produce a happier society than would a direct democracy or an ideal despot. Such government promotes the rights of individuals better, thereby promoting moral, **political**, and economic progress.

MODERN ETHICS (Renaissance and Enlightenment). The Renaissance was a time of turmoil, with the Protestant Reformation, the colonization of the New World, the rise of modern **science**, and increasing secularization. It was an apt time to rethink ethics. Many were eager for a new, secular, non-**medieval** approach that did not use other-worldly ideas (like **God**'s will, eternal salvation, or how to love God) but instead gave practical advice on how to live together in this world. Niccolò Machiavelli (1469–1527) gave a new, amoral approach; he suggested that rulers, while appearing to be ethical, use or not use ethical means depending on what furthers their interests. Many saw this as too radical and feared that all would suffer if society became amoral.

Thomas Hobbes (1588–1679) tried to justify ethics in a secular way using only ideas that can be based on science. He saw humans as **egoistic** and amoral· by nature. He had us imagine a *state of nature* where people are not restrained by external rules. He argued that chaos would result since people would kill, steal, and otherwise hurt others to get what they needed. So rational egoists in a state of nature would, out of self-interest, agree in a **social contract** to treat each other in a civil way; they would set up an absolute monarch to **punish** them if they broke the rules. This shows why morality exists. Morality is a construct to promote cooperation between humans, who are inherently egoistic; the motive to act morally is fear of punishment.

Hobbes set the agenda for much subsequent ethical debate. Many argued that humans by nature are more moral and less egoistic than Hobbes described. And many contended that ethics is based on reason (self-evident principles known through **intuition**) or feelings (especially feelings of **benevolence** toward others), which are part of our nature.

The "reason" approach saw moral laws as independent, objective truths that the mind grasps in a direct intuitive way, as the mind grasps **mathematical** axioms. Against Hobbes, rationalists contended that it is part of human nature to grasp objective moral norms and that these are not a human invention. Many ethicists of this period shared this view, including Francisco Suárez (1548–1617), Hugo Grotius (1583–1645), Henry More (1614–1687), Ralph Cudworth (1617–1688), **Samuel Pufendorf** (1632–1694), **John Locke** (1632–1704), Samuel Clark (1675–1729), **Joseph Butler** (1692–1752), **Thomas Reid** (1710–1796), Richard Price (1723–1791), and **Mary Wollstonecraft** (1759–1797).

Many rationalist ethicists wrote of natural **rights**, in the **natural law** tradition. Suárez opposed Spanish colonization as violating the natural rights of sovereign peoples. Locke inspired the American Declaration of Independence (1776), which speaks of the self-evident right to life, liberty, and the pursuit of happiness. Wollstonecraft defended the natural rights of men *and women* (*see* **sexism**).

Rationalists rejected the Hobbesian view that humans are ultimately motivated only by self-interest. Butler instead proposed that our ultimate motives include specific impulses, like hunger, anger, and greed; self-interest; benevolent feelings; and **conscience** (our intuitive grasp of right and wrong). Many rationalists sought principles to move us from a concern for ourselves to a concern for others. So More proposed as self-evident the idea that if it is **good** for X to be happy, then it must be doubly good for X and Y to be happy. Clark proposed as self-evident the idea (later called **universalizability**) that what is right or wrong for someone to do to me must thereby be right or wrong for me in a like case to do to that person.

Some rationalists appealed to the idea of a social contract, but as a means to protect natural rights that we already have (or ought to have) as humans, not as a means to create these rights. They argued that people would agree to set up a democracy, not an absolute monarchy.

The minority Enlightenment view was that ethics is based on feelings, especially benevolent feelings, not on reason. This "moral sense" school included the Earl of Shaftesbury (1671–1713), Francis Hutcheson (1694–1746), **Jean-Jacques Rousseau** (1712–1778), **Adam Smith** (1723–1790), and especially **David Hume** (1711–1776). Shaftesbury argued that we get greater personal satisfaction by following other-regarding feelings than by being selfish. Rousseau thought humans have an innate repugnance to see others suffer. Smith saw moral judgments as expressing not just feelings but *sympathetic feelings*, a view that later developed into **ideal observer theory**.

David Hume argued that moral beliefs can move us to act and so must be based on feelings, since only feelings can move us to act. We must understand an action before we can evaluate it; but our evaluation is based on how we feel. External facts by themselves cannot give us a moral belief; we cannot deduce an "ought" from an "is" (an idea later called "Hume's law"). We have both benevolent and selfish feelings, and moral beliefs express benevolent feelings. Moral terms like "vicious" (as opposed to personal terms like "my enemy") assume a general or **impartial** view. We largely will agree on our moral beliefs if we use reason to understand the facts and then see how we feel from the standpoint of impartial benevolence.

Immanuel Kant (1724–1804), in contrast, based ethics on reason. Basing ethics on self-interest debases our dignity as moral beings; the purest motive is to do our duty just because it is the right thing. Moral laws, since they must hold of necessity for every rational being, cannot rest on feelings, contingent facts about human nature, or even moral intuitions (as proposed by earlier rationalist thinkers), as all of these can fluctuate. Instead, moral laws are laws we would choose to live by if we choose rationally, and hence **consistently**. To test a moral maxim, we ask whether we can consistently will that everyone follow it (and thus act that way toward us); we reject the maxim if we cannot will this. The basic moral imperative is "Act only on a maxim that you can will to be a universal law." A looser but more intuitive formulation goes "Treat humanity, whether yourself or another, as an end-in-itself and not only as a means"; we act wrongly when we use people as mere things, as mere tools to promote our own desires.

Enlightenment ethicists began examining **utilitarianism**, which became a major ethical theory in the **nineteenth century**. Hutcheson proposed that we do whatever promotes "the greatest happiness for the greatest number," and he based this idea on our benevolent feelings. William Paley (1743–1805), in contrast, based utilitarianism on **divine command theory** plus the belief that God desires our happiness.

MOORE, G. E. (1873–1958). George Edward Moore was a British philosopher who greatly influenced **twentieth-century ethics**. With Bertrand Russell and Ludwig Wittgenstein, he founded the analytic philosophy approach that has dominated in Britain and the U.S. Moore was renowned for his commitment to common sense, his opposition to reductionism and support of realism (*see* **moral realism**), and his careful and analytic approach to philosophy. His 1903 *Principia Ethica* focused on what "**good**" means and on how we can know that something is good. These metaethical questions (*see* **ethics: metaethics**) became the central issues in ethical theory. Whether or not they agreed with him, later thinkers took seriously his questions and arguments.

Moore saw ethics as the general inquiry into what is good. To do ethics correctly, we must distinguish two questions:

(1)   What is good in itself (intrinsically good)?
(2)   What actions ought we to perform?

Our answers to (1) are "intuitions"—in the sense that we can know them to be true but cannot prove them (*see* **intuitionism**); the best we can do is to keep in mind clearly what question we are trying to answer, namely what would be of value if it existed, even if it were the only thing that ever existed. Moore's general answer to (1) is that many sorts of things are intrinsically good, including pleasure (usually), knowledge, personal affections, and the existence or experience of beauty. By his *principle of organic unities*, the value of a whole need not equal the sum of the value of the parts; for example, the pleasure we get from a thing of beauty is greater than the value of the pleasure itself plus the value that the beauty would have if it were not experienced.

The general answer to (2) is that we ought to do whatever action will bring about the best consequences. What we ought to do in the concrete situation depends on empirical judgments about consequences plus an intuitive appraisal of the intrinsic goodness of these consequences. So Moore advocated a **utilitarianism**, but an "ideal" kind where more than just pleasure is good in itself.

Moore at first claimed that "right action" just meant "action with the best consequences"; so it is true by definition that the right action is the one with the best consequences. After criticisms by **W. D. Ross**, he gave up the idea that this is true by definition, but not that it is true.

Moore thought that many mistakes about ethics come from confusing "good" with empirical properties, like pleasure or desire. Moore claimed that "good" is a simple, unique, non-empirical notion. "Good" cannot be defined since it is not a complex that can be analyzed into simpler notions; instead, it is one of the simple notions on which any analysis ultimately rests. We can specify those things to which "good" applies as an adjective. We can make true statements like "Pleasure is good." Saying "Pleasure is good" joins two distinct concepts ("pleasure" and "good"). The two terms are not synonymous. "Pleasure is good" does not mean "Pleasure is pleasure."

Naturalism defines "good" to be a natural (empirical) property, like pleasure or desire. Moore argues that this confuses **normative** with descriptive notions and commits the *naturalistic fallacy*. Suppose someone defines "good" to mean "desired." This does not capture what we mean by "good" since we can significantly ask, "Are things that are desired always good?" This is an *open question* and does not just mean "Are things that are desired always desired?" So "good" and "desired" are distinct concepts. The same open-question argument works if we substitute any other descriptive property (even a metaphysical one like "desired by the creator"). So "good" is not identical to any descriptive property. Since "good" is indefinable, we cannot prove moral conclusions solely from non-moral premises (or, as **Hume**'s law puts it, we cannot deduce an "ought" from an "is"); we could deduce moral conclusions from purely descriptive premises only if we could define terms like "good" using descriptive language—which is impossible.

Moore's attack on naturalism, while anticipated by **Henry Sidgwick** and others, formed the opening chapter of 20th-century ethics. Many later thinkers, including **emotivists** and **prescriptivists**, accepted his attack on naturalism but tried to avoid his self-evident ethical truths.

MORAL AGENT. A being that is morally **responsible** for its actions and has obligations to other beings. Adult humans are the most obvious examples of moral agents. Parents have obligations to their children to provide them with food, clothing, and shelter, and each of us has obligations not to cause undue harm to others. Very young children are not moral agents since they have not yet developed the rational **autonomy** needed for them to be responsible for their actions and have obligations. Mere things have no moral agency; a hurricane is not responsible for its actions and has no duties.

Some argue that moral agency is an "all or nothing" matter. At some point, one matures enough to be a moral agent; before then, one lacks moral agency. Others see moral agency as a continuum. While competent adults have full moral agency and infants have no moral agency, those in between have varying degrees of moral agency, depending on their maturity and competency.

Can institutions such as corporations and universities be moral agents? Some say no. Institutions are merely abstract entities constituted by individuals; abstract entities cannot be held responsible for their actions, but individuals can. Others claim that such institutions can be moral agents since they have decision structures that constitute a kind of rational autonomy; institutions can make decisions, act, have obligations, be held responsible for their actions, and be **punished**.

Moral agency raises other issues. Does moral agency require **free will**? Do the severely mentally retarded have moral agency? Do some nonhuman **animals** (perhaps primates and dolphins) have some degree of moral agency? Could **computers** have moral agency (as some have claimed)? *See also* BUSINESS ETHICS; MORAL PATIENT.

MORAL DILEMMAS. *See* OUGHT.

MORAL EDUCATION. The teaching of morality, especially to children. How we ought to do this is much disputed. Our views about the nature of ethics and ethical reasoning influence what we think about this.

For **cultural relativists**, "good" means "socially approved"; moral judgments describe the norms of our culture. If we accepted this idea, we would bring up our children to conform their moral beliefs to the norms of their society; so we would teach that this is correct reasoning: "My society approves of such and such (e.g., treating people of other races badly), so this must be good."

Subjectivism and **emotivism** see ethical beliefs as describing or expressing emotion. On these views, we would bring up our children to follow their feelings, to go by their likes and dislikes. If our child said "I like hurting Rachel—this is good" then we could not say that the child was mistaken; but we might explain that we feel differently and try to change the child's feelings.

Divine command theory bases ethics on religion and **God's** will. If we accepted this view, we would see moral education as part of religious education; in teaching children about the **Bible**, church teaching, and praying to God for guidance, we would at the same time be teaching them morality. We likely would think moral education would not work without religion.

Intuitionism bases ethics on principles that are self-evident or known by moral intuition. If we accepted intuitionism, we would see adults as instinctively knowing the basic moral truths. We would teach these to children by example, verbal instruction, praise and blame, and reward and **punishment**. We would also teach children not to be swayed so easily by their feelings and by group pressures. Eventually, the children would become mature enough to recognize in their own hearts and minds the truth of the principles that we taught them.

Critics say the intuitionism approach is incomplete because it can teach ideas like **racism**. Parental example can teach that Jews are to be hated; and we can praise our children when they follow our example and punish them when they act otherwise. If such moral training succeeds, our children will end up internalizing racist values; it will seem "self-evident" to them that Jews ought to be hated. So besides teaching specific *moral content* (by words, example, and so forth), we also need to teach *moral rationality*. We need to teach children to think for themselves in a rational way about values and to criticize inherited moral intuitions. The next view suggests tools for doing this.

Many ethicists support a *rationalized attitudes* approach to **knowing right from wrong**. On this approach, we would try to form our attitudes in as **rational** a way as possible, where this involves elements like **information, conscientiousness, impartiality, imagination,** and the **golden rule**. We can teach such things to children by personal example and by encouraging the corresponding skills and attitudes. Here are five key "commandments of rational moral thinking" that grow out of this general approach.

(1) *Make informed decisions.* To teach this by example, follow it yourself, especially in actions that affect your children; get to know them well before making decisions about them. To teach children the

corresponding skills and attitudes, talk with them about their decisions and get them to raise questions like "What are my alternatives?" "What effect would this action have on myself and on others?" and "What are the pros and cons here?" Encourage them to obtain and reflect on the information needed to make their own decisions.

(2) *Live in harmony with your moral beliefs.* First follow it yourself; do not teach your children by your example to say, "Yes, it is wrong, but I do not care." To teach children the corresponding skills and attitudes, encourage them to take their moral beliefs seriously and follow them conscientiously; stress the importance of doing the right thing.

(3) *Make similar evaluations about similar actions.* First follow it yourself; apply the same standards to everyone and give reasons for differences in treatment. Respond carefully when asked things like, "Mom, why can Jimmy do this but not me?" Do not answer, "Just shut up and do what I say!" Challenge children to think through their moral issues and to propose principles or reasons (applicable to everyone alike) why actions are right or wrong. Encourage them to apply the same principles to themselves that they apply to others.

(4) *Put yourself in the other person's place.* Do this yourself, especially in your dealings with your children. Listen sympathetically to them and try to imagine what their lives are like; this teaches by example how important it is to understand another person's perspective. Encourage children to listen to others, to share ideas with them, and to reflect on what an action would look like from another person's perspective. Encourage them to ask questions like, "What would it feel like if I were Suzy and this happened to me?" And have them read stories or watch movies that portray people's lives in a realistic way.

(5) *Treat others as you want to be treated.* Follow the golden rule yourself, especially in dealing with your children. Reflect on how your actions affect them, imagine yourself in their place, and treat them only as you are willing to be treated in the same situation. Do not be seen treating them or others in mean or thoughtless ways—in ways that you do not want to be treated yourself. Encourage children to follow the golden rule. Challenge them, when they do something rude or vicious, by asking, "How would you like it if we did that to you?" Help them to think through moral issues using the golden rule.

While this *rationalized attitudes* approach does not require a religious perspective, it easily can be integrated with religious beliefs and attitudes. Then our attempt to grow wiser in our moral thinking would be seen as an attempt to draw closer to God's supreme wisdom. *See*

also GILLIGAN, CAROL; HARE, R. M.; KOHLBERG, LAW-
RENCE; PSYCHOLOGY.

MORAL EPISTEMOLOGY. *See* EPISTEMOLOGY; KNOWING
RIGHT FROM WRONG.

MORAL LUCK. The idea that random, unintended factors can be relevant for moral **praise** or blame. *See* NAGEL, THOMAS; RESPONSI-
BILITY; WILLIAMS, BERNARD.

MORAL PATIENT. A being that is the beneficiary of a **moral agent**'s
obligation. "Moral patient" is the converse of "moral agent": if X has a
duty toward Y, then X is a moral agent and Y is a moral patient. A
moral patient, alternatively, is a being whose **good** and harm **ought** morally to be considered for its own sake; such a being is said to have
moral standing and to belong to the *moral community*.

Humans are clear examples of moral patients since we all benefit
from the obligations of others. As a car passes me as I ride my bicycle,
I benefit from the car driver's obligation not to run me off the road.
Children benefit from their parents' obligations to provide them with
food, clothing, and shelter. At the end of our lives, we benefit from the
obligation of family and healthcare providers to treat us with dignity.

There is much dispute about which beings are moral patients. A
white **racist** might include all and only white people; then the welfare
of just white people would be considered in making moral decisions.
Others might include only members of their group, however this is
viewed. Others might include all and only humans, perhaps including
infants and the unborn, or perhaps not (*see* **abortion and infanticide**).
Immanuel Kant regarded all and only moral agents as moral patients;
what earns us moral consideration is our ability to make **autonomous**
moral judgments. Many **social contract** theorists agree, but for different reasons; since moral rules are based on an agreement between moral agents concerned to promote their own welfare, these moral rules ultimately will be concerned only with the good and harm done to these
agents. **Utilitarians** like **Peter Singer** think we ought to consider the
interests of any being capable of suffering, including **animals**; the animal's pain is to be given the same weight as an equal pain of a human.
Some consider the interests of any living thing (including plants), or
any part of the **environment** (like species and canyons), or the environment as a whole. Finally, there is dispute about future generations;

while many think we are responsible for the world we leave them, others think we have obligations only to beings that exist now. *See also* DARWIN, CHARLES.

MORAL PHILOSOPHY. *See* ETHICS.

MORAL REALISM. Roughly, the view that moral beliefs are robustly true or false and that there are objective moral truths that we can know and discover but do not depend on human attitudes or conventions. Sometimes "moral realism" is said to be the belief in *moral facts*. Some use "moral realism" in slightly different senses. The realism/anti-realism distinction differs in subtle ways from the older **cognitivism/non-cognitivism** distinction.

The recent debate about moral realism began with **J. L. Mackie**'s *Ethics: Inventing Right and Wrong* (1977). Mackie admits that moral language, as commonly used, is intended to assert independent moral facts; so he thinks **Kantians** and **intuitionists** are right about the *meaning* of moral terms. For various reasons, however, he thinks there are no moral facts; so Kantians and intuitionists are wrong about the **metaphysics** of morality. Thus he arrives at an *error theory*: all moral judgments literally are false. That same year, **Gilbert Harman**'s *The Nature of Morality* attacked moral facts on the grounds that we need not assume them to explain people's experiences and moral beliefs. There followed much debate about moral realism and the existence of moral facts. Some accept moral facts, others reject them, and still others argue that moral facts exist in a manner of speaking.

Cornell realists like Nicholas Sturgeon and David Brink posit moral facts that are identical to empirical facts; this is a sort of **naturalism**, even though it does not claim that "**good**" is **definable** or has the same meaning as some other empirical predicate. They use this analogy: just as water is identical to H_2O, even though "water" and "H_2O" have different meanings, so also goodness is identical to some empirical property or complex of properties, even though "good" is not identical in meaning to empirical terms ascribing this property or complex of properties. Critics find Cornell realism puzzling. They point out that we have different empirical criteria for "water" (roughly, the common clear liquid found in lakes and rivers) and "H_2O" (roughly, a chemical compound that decomposes into two parts hydrogen and one part oxygen), and we find by experience that the two terms refer to the same thing. Let us suppose that "good" is *identical* to "honest and altruistic" and that the latter is empirical. How do we know that "good" is identical with "honest and altruistic"? Do we know this empirically (as with the water case)? Consider **egoists** like **Ayn Rand** who think altruism is not good. Is the difference between egoists and others empirical, so we could set up an empirical test to see which one of us is right (as we could set up an empirical test to see whether water is "H_2O" or "CO_2")? If not, then the water analogy fails.

Moral realists tend to be *motivational externalists* (*see* **ought**): it is empirically contingent (not conceptually necessary) that we care about doing what is good. We could imagine an amoralist who believes that something is good but has no attraction toward it.

David Wiggins and John McDowell propose another realist view. They argue for moral facts, of a sort, that correspond with our moral sensibilities; for them, what counts as a "fact" is a function of our language and how it works, in a way reminiscent of the latter thinking of Ludwig Wittgenstein about language.

A less realist approach is the Kantian constructivism of **John Rawls**'s *Political Liberalism* (1993), which accepts moral facts as a human construct. We arrive at moral beliefs by searching for what fits our moral intuitions as a whole after we try to achieve a *reflective equilibrium* between general principles and concrete judgments—but we do not claim that the beliefs at which we arrive correspond to preexisting truths about morality or that people of other cultures are wrong if their intuitions lead them in a contrary direction.

Richard Brandt's *A Theory of the Good and the Right* (1979) contends that moral concepts are confused and need replacement rather than analysis. He proposes an empirical definition of "rational desire" that would replace "good" and not presuppose any preexisting moral facts. If we use "good" in the new sense, then there are facts about what is good, namely **psychological** facts about what we would favor under ideally rational conditions.

Emotivists hold that "X is good" is like "Hurrah for X!" and expresses feelings; the emotivist **A. J. Ayer** denied that there were moral truths or moral facts. But some recent emotivists, including Simon Blackburn and Allan Gibbard, support *quasi-realism*, which involves believing anti-realism but speaking like realists. They hold that, while there literally are no moral truths or moral facts, speaking of these is harmless and even useful. Emotivists can say "It is *true* that act A ought to be done" if they only intend this as a longer way to say (or agree with) "Act A ought to be done" or if they are referring only to the truth of the factual claims (perhaps that act A would maximize human happiness) to which they would appeal in defending their moral judgment. Emotivists can speak of "moral knowledge" if by this they mean "strong moral convictions."

R. M. Hare, whose **prescriptivism** should put him in the anti-realist camp, argues that the existence of moral facts does not matter. What matters is that we have some rational way to argue about ethics. Like the moderate emotivist **William Frankena**, he believes that there is such a method and that we would all agree on our moral beliefs if we ideally followed this method.

Other thinkers defend a moral realism of one of the more traditional sorts: intuitionist, **natural law**, **ideal observer**, **divine command**, or Kantian (if indeed these last three are seen as moral realisms).

MORAL THEOLOGY. The theological investigation of questions about morality. Moral theology appeals both to the data of religious faith (like the **Bible** or church teaching) and to philosophical argumentation (which does not use premises based on religious faith). In contrast, **ethics** (moral philosophy) appeals only to philosophical argumentation, not to religious faith. While some moral theologians hold that morality is based on religion (*see* **divine command theory** and **natural law**), many instead see morality as based on human reason but as brought to a higher level by religious revelation and experience.

While moral theology overlaps somewhat with moral philosophy, the emphasis is often different. Moral theology emphasizes things such as **loving your neighbor**; sin (blameworthy wrongdoing seen as an offense against **God**), conversion, and **forgiveness**; the duties of the faith community; preaching, exhortation, and prayer; the **moral education** of youth; religious and moral heroes, like Jesus, Muhammad, or the saints; Biblical passages, including those about prophets, parables, and proverbs; **virtues** to be promoted, including family values, social responsibilities, and a concern for others; and the role in moral thinking of prayer, church authority, and the scriptures.

Christian moral theology is sometimes called *Christian ethics* (*see* **Thomas Aquinas**, **Augustine**, and **Medieval ethics**). **Buddhist ethics**, **Daoist ethics**, **Hindu ethics**, **Islamic ethics**, and **Jewish ethics** are types of moral theology.

MORAL WORTH. *See* PRAISEWORTHY.

MORALITY, DEFINITION OF. *See* OUGHT.

MUSLIM ETHICS. *See* ISLAMIC ETHICS.

– N –

NAGEL, THOMAS (1937–). American Professor of Philosophy and Law at New York University who argues that ethical claims are objective. Nagel was born in what is now Serbia and did his Ph.D. under **John Rawls** at Harvard. He is known for work in ethics, **political philosophy**, and philosophy of mind. In 1981, he defended affirmative action (*see* **discrimination**) before a U.S. congressional subcommittee.

Nagel builds his view of the human person on the subjective/objective distinction. He rejects materialist views that equate the mind with the physical workings of the brain; he argues that such views do not account for our subjective experiences. In perhaps his most well-known article, "What Is It Like to Be a Bat?" (*Philosophical Review* 1974), he argues that, just as a complete neurological understanding of the bat's brain would not convey what it is like to be a bat, a complete neurological understanding of the human brain would not convey what it is like to be a human. In neither case would the subjective experiences be conveyed. For Nagel, the fundamental problem in philosophy of mind is to reconcile our subjective experiences with objective reality.

Nagel extends this problem to ethics. We must develop an ethical theory that accounts for subjective experiences without lapsing into **subjectivism** or **relativism** (*see* **knowing right from wrong**). His solution, presented in *The Possibility of Altruism* (1970) and developed further in later works, argues for **impartiality**. Suppose that I recognize that slavery would harm me, and I give that as a reason against slavery. Then I must recognize that "Slavery hurts others" is also a reason against slavery (*see* **consistency** and **universalizability**); so I must attach objective disvalue to slavery. So when I make ethical judgments I must consider not only my own interests but also the interests of others. In this way, we account for subjective experience (that such and such actions would benefit or harm us) but avoid skeptical conclusions about ethics (since we attach objective value to these benefits and harms in other people too).

Nagel also addresses *moral luck*, which deals with the subjective side. Most of us intuitively think people are **responsible** only for what is under their control. We think it would be unfair to blame a school bus driver for the deaths of children under his care if the deaths were due to a boulder rolling down a hill and crashing into the bus. Yet there seem to be cases where our moral responsibility is influenced by matters of luck that are beyond our control. Consider two gunmen in separate incidents, both intending to **kill** an innocent person. The first fires a shot that merely wounds his target; due to mechanical problems beyond his control, his shot is slightly off target. The second fires a shot that kills his target. If we apprehended the two, we would punish the second more harshly than the first. This seems counterintuitive since the difference in the cases is something beyond their control (a matter of luck). Nagel sees this as a paradox; he believes that we are responsible only for what is under our control and he also believes that subjective luck outside our control influences our responsibility.

Nagel has contributed to our understanding of **privacy**. He argues that there are personal matters that are rightfully private for the individual. These matters should not be subject to public surveillance and control; the individual is justified in concealing them from the public. *See also* CULTURAL RELATIVISM; PRAISEWORTHY; RATIONAL MORAL THINKING; WILLIAMS, BERNARD.

NATURAL LAW. An ethical tradition that sees basic moral principles (called *natural laws*) as objective, based on nature instead of convention, and knowable to everyone through natural human reason. Such natural moral laws are distinct from *positive laws*, which come from human legislation, and *supernatural laws*, which require divine revelation. **Thomas Aquinas** (1224–1274) is the central figure in the tradition. While the boundaries of the tradition are unclear, many see it as starting with **Aristotle** (384–322 BC), whose *Rhetoric* considered a natural justice that is binding on everyone, and the **ancient** Stoics, who spoke of our duty to live in accord with nature. Other figures include **Augustine**; various **medievals**; Francisco Suárez (1548–1617), a Spanish Jesuit who opposed Spanish colonization as violating the natural **rights** of sovereign peoples; Hugo Grotius (1583–1645), who addressed natural rights and international law; **Samuel Pufendorf** (1632–1694), who developed a system of duties to **God**, oneself, and others; **Joseph Butler** (1692–1752), who criticized **Thomas Hobbes**; and the 20th-century thinkers **Elizabeth Anscombe**, **John Finnis**, Peter Geach, Anthony Kenny, Jacques Maritain, and **Alasdair MacIntyre**.

Natural law thinkers tend to be diverse and disagree significantly, but they also tend to share several key beliefs. First, they tend to think our knowledge of **good** and right is somehow built into us and based on human inclinations (desires) and reason. A simple approach would say that "good" means "object of desire" (*see* **naturalism**). It may be objected that what we desire is not always good; we can, for example, desire to eat the whole pie (which would make us sick) or to promote our wealth through dishonesty. The response is that, even in these cases, we desire something that is good (the pie's taste or our wealth); our error is to prefer a lesser good to a greater good. But then how do we determine the greater good? Many answers are possible, consistent with the natural law tradition; the greater good, for example, might be:

- what better promotes the ultimate goods (here goods are seen as forming a hierarchy, as in Aristotle, with the most ultimate perhaps being happiness);
- what we would desire more if we were more rational, including having a more vivid awareness of the effects of actions on ourselves and others (**ideal observer theory**);
- what is self-evidently more valuable (**intuitionism**); or
- what God favors more (**divine command theory**).

To clarify how to recognize the greater good, natural law theorists can rely on views much like the standard metaethical alternatives (*see* **ethics: metaethics**).

Aquinas gives "Do good and avoid evil" as the central ethical norm. This is not intended in a **utilitarian** way, to say that our duty is always to do whatever maximizes the total balance of good over bad consequences. John Finnis and others hold that there are several basic goods—like knowledge, companionship, aesthetic experience, life, and health—and that they cannot be measured on a common scale and totaled; so the imperative to maximize the *total* balance of good over bad consequences is meaningless. Instead, we must choose which basic goods we want to emphasize in our own lives; we might, for example, choose research (which emphasizes knowledge) or medicine (which emphasizes health). Some natural law theorists argue that we may never choose *directly* against any of the basic goods; for example, we may never directly **kill** an innocent human being (which chooses directly against life). While this approach leads to **exceptionless duties**, these can be moderated by the principle of **double effect**.

Natural law theorists generally hold that the universe is purposeful, that humans are here for a reason, and that responsible living requires that we live in accord with this. On Aristotle's approach, our purpose is to develop what makes us unique, our rationality; we do this by developing **virtues**, which are good habits that develop our thinking and acting and thus promote our flourishing and happiness. Aquinas accepted this; but he added, based on revelation, that we also have a supernatural purpose or destiny, namely eternal **happiness** with God; we prepare for this both by Aristotle's natural virtues and by living lives of faith, hope, and love (supernatural virtues). Of course, not all natural law theorists want to bring in this supernatural element; and even Aquinas admitted that this element goes beyond natural human reason and thus beyond natural law as such.

Some natural law theorists argue from the inherent natural purpose of specific kinds of action. For example, some hold that the inherent natural purpose of speech is to communicate truth; so, they conclude, direct lying always is wrong. More notoriously, Pope Paul VI's *Humanae Vitae* (1967) argued that the inherent natural purpose of intercourse is to procreate life; he concluded that the use of the birth control pill and other forms of artificial birth control (but not the rhythm method) are wrong. While Elizabeth Anscombe defended the Pope's reasoning, many thinkers of a natural law slant (including most of the committee that the pope had established to advise him) disagreed with it. Some such thinkers argue that it is fallacious to draw moral conclusions from claims about what is **biologically** "natural."

Aquinas situated natural law in a wider theory of law. He defined law in general as an ordinance of reason for the common good, made by one who has care of the community, and promulgated. He distinguished four main types of law. *Eternal law* is a wide category and includes the physical laws, moral laws, and revealed religious laws through which God governs the universe. *Natural law* (*moral law*) is the part of the eternal law that applies to free human choices and can be known by our natural reason. *Human law* is the civil law created by human societies to apply the natural law to their particular circumstances. *Divine law* is the law revealed through the **Bible**, to supplement and reinforce the natural law and to guide us to our supernatural end of eternal happiness with God.

Many natural law theorists see moral laws as God's commands; but some in the natural law tradition, like Grotius, try not to make their views about morality depend on beliefs about God. Those who see moral laws as God's commands must face **Plato**'s *Euthyphro* question:

"Is cruelty wrong just because God forbids it (so if he did not forbid it then it would not be wrong)? Or does God forbid cruelty because it is already wrong (of its very nature)?" Many natural law theorists would say that cruelty's wrongness depends on God's intellect, not on his will. If God creates beings of this specific nature, such that they are capable of inflicting cruelty on each other, then God's intellect sees that for such beings it would be wrong in itself to be cruel; here God's intellect sees that cruelty is wrong—it is not his sheer will that makes it wrong. Some object that if cruelty for humans would be wrong in itself then it makes no sense to say that this wrongness is based on God's intellect. Others of a more voluntarist slant, like William of Ockham, think it simpler to say that cruelty is wrong just because God forbids it.

Some use "natural law" language but are far from the natural law tradition. For example, **Thomas Hobbes** called a "law of nature" any rule of rational self-interest. He saw humans as inherently self-interested. He thought the only effective way to promote the survival of such beings was by agreed-upon social rules enforced by an absolute monarch; outside such social agreements, there is no right and wrong. Despite his use of the term "law of nature," Hobbes is rejecting the natural-law tradition; this tradition holds that humans by nature are not entirely self-interested, that we have some sense of right and wrong built into us, that basic right and wrong do not depend on self-interest or social agreements, and that agreements that command what is wrong are not genuine laws at all.

David Hume objected that, since the word "natural" can have so many senses, it is unphilosophical to base morality on what is natural. "Natural" may refer what is "typical"—as opposed to what is "unusual." Or "natural" may be opposed to "artificial" or "miraculous." In none of these senses is the natural always better than its opposite. While Hume's point is well taken, it is less a refutation of the natural law tradition than a reminder that it should make it clear what it means when it uses "natural" in a given context.

Immanuel Kant objected to basing morality on the nature of humans on the grounds that the basic rules of morality (like "Treat others as ends-in-themselves and not just as means to your own ends") must hold for all rational beings as such, not just for humans. But natural law theorists could argue that, while basic moral rules for humans depend on our nature *as rational beings*, other derived rules depend on our nature as beings that need food, shelter, and companionship. *See also* BEAUVOIR, SIMONE DE; GLOBAL ETHICS; LOCKE, JOHN;

SARTRE, JEAN-PAUL.

NATURALISM. The view that moral terms like "**good**" or "**ought**" are definable using ideas from sense experience. Naturalists might claim that "good" means "socially approved" (**cultural relativism**), "what I like" (**subjectivism**), "what we would desire if we were ideally rational" (**ideal observer theory**), "in accord with evolution" (**evolutionism**), or "either pleasant or otherwise productive of the balance of pleasure over pain." *Analyzing naturalists* examine the actual meaning of "good" as used by ordinary people. In contrast, *reforming naturalists* such as Ralph Perry and **Richard Brandt** see our ordinary usage as confused and propose a new and clearer meaning for "good"; they claim that this new meaning more effectively satisfies the purposes for which we use the word "good." Views opposing naturalism include **intuitionism**, **divine command theory**, **emotivism**, and **prescriptivism**.

Naturalism in a second sense is the claim that goodness is identical with some empirical property or complex of properties; such a naturalism need not claim that "good" is definable or has the same meaning as some other empirical predicate. In a parallel way, water is sometimes claimed to be identical to H_2O, even though "water" and "H_2O" have different meanings. (*See* **moral realism**.)

In many areas of philosophy, "naturalistic" theories are those that keep to what can be understood by empirical, **scientific** methods and thus exclude appealing to **God** or non-empirical moral properties. Emotivism and prescriptivism are *naturalistic* in this third sense. *See also* KNOWING RIGHT FROM WRONG; MOORE, G. E.

NATURALISTIC FALLACY. *See* MOORE, G. E.; NATURALISM.

NIETZSCHE, FRIEDRICH (1844–1900). German philosopher who scathingly criticized the ideals of his day. Although his father was a Lutheran minister, he often attacked Christianity. Nietzsche suffered from poor health all his life and insanity at the end.

The *will to power* is Nietzsche's central idea and was inspired by **Charles Darwin**'s theory of **evolution**. Like other animals, humans have evolved with the hunger for power as our basic motivation (but *see* **sociobiology**); unless this motive is held in check by external forces, it leads us to exert our own strength, often to the point of apparent cruelty. Nietzsche believes that the ideals of his day, especially Christianity, quash this natural trait, violate our nature, lead to conformism, and bring us to resent the powerful. So we do not exert our power, even though this is our nature.

Nietzsche sees traditional ethics as *slave morality*: a conformist morality of the weak and fearful lower classes that emphasizes self-denial, compassion, and concern for others; it represses our natural hunger for power and leads us to resent the powerful. In contrast, the noble and brave accept *master morality*: the morality of the powerful who see themselves as questioning traditional values, creating their own values, and promoting their own power. Master morality brings the highest products of human intelligence and thus advances our species. The ideal of master morality is the noble "superman" (*Übermensch*) who accepts his true nature and exerts his own power.

Nietzsche has had much influence, especially among continental thinkers. Many see his greatest contribution in his criticism of **nineteenth-century** ideas and traditional ethical theories. Many worry, however, that he leaves us without an objective ethics; he seems to give us a **subjectivism** where right and wrong just express what one likes, or a kind of **relativism** where morality exists only in relation to an individual. But some see him as proposing objective norms.

NINETEENTH-CENTURY ETHICS. Much of the ethical thinking in this period examined either **utilitarianism** or historical processes.

Jeremy Bentham (1748–1832), the father of utilitarianism, proposed that we ought always to do what maximizes the total balance of pleasure over pain for those affected by our action. Pleasures of equal amounts count the same, regardless of recipient (whether aristocrat, slave, or **animal**) or source (whether sublime poetry or the mindless pushpin game). He and **James Mill** (1773–1836) used utilitarianism to promote social change. The latter's son, **John Stuart Mill** (1806–1873), refined the view by specifying that higher (intellectual) pleasures are more valuable than lower (bodily) ones, even if the amounts are the same. He based ethics on desires. We know that only pleasure is **good** for its own sake because we observe that only pleasure is desired for its own sake; but those who have experienced higher and lower pleasures prefer the higher. **Henry Sidgwick** (1838–1900) based utilitarianism on **intuitionism**. Against Mill, he thought that showing that people desired something would not show that it was good, since people might desire bad things. Instead, he took utilitarianism to be self-evident. He also saw as self-evident "Everyone's good is equally important" and "Rational beings ought to aim at the general good."

Other thinkers connected ethics with historical processes. **Georg Wilhelm Friedrich Hegel** (1770–1831) saw history as progressing toward higher forms of consciousness and freedom. History will lead to a society where community interest coincides with self-interest; society will care for its members, who in turn will find much of their **happiness** in the group. **Karl Marx** (1818–1883) added that history will lead through class struggles to a classless, communist society (*see* **socialism**). While conventional ethics is a tool of the wealthy to control the **poor**, a genuine ethics would end class divisions and the miseries of workers. *Social Darwinists* like Herbert Spencer (1820–1903), however, saw the historical process as mirroring capitalism. **Evolution** is a dog-eat-dog struggle where the strong survive and overcome the weak. Human life rightly follows this same pattern, whereby stronger individuals, corporations, classes, and nations dominate weaker ones. Along similar lines, **Friedrich Nietzsche** (1844–1900) thought evolution built into us the *will to power* and domination. Thus an ethics of **benevolence**, as in Christianity or utilitarianism, violates our nature and leads to frustration. **Charles Darwin** (1809–1882), on the contrary, saw humans as social animals, like wolves, with an inbred tendency to help each other. This natural sympathy, which at first was applied mainly to one's clan or tribe, was extended more widely as human rationality progressed, eventually covering all humanity, including its weakest members, and even animals. Leslie Stephen (1832–1904) tried to establish a somewhat utilitarian ethics on natural facts about evolution.

Also in the 19th century, Arthur Schopenhauer (1788–1860), who was influenced by **Buddhism** and **Hinduism**, saw suffering as pervading all of life. The moral imperative is to sympathize with all who suffer and to reduce suffering, which can in part be done by minimizing desire. Since the distinction between persons is an illusion, in some deep sense all persons are one; so we should have the same concern for others that we have for ourselves. William Whewell (1794–1866) based ethics on commonsense intuitions, but said we first need to make these intuitions consistent (*see* **John Rawls**). He defended norms about benevolence, **justice**, truth, purity, and order. He was John Stuart Mill's main opponent, in both ethics and philosophy of **science**. Ralph Waldo Emerson (1803–1882) saw self-reliant introspection as an access to eternal moral truths; his transcendentalism attracted individuals who promoted abolitionism, women's suffrage, and experiments in communal living. **Franz Brentano** (1838–1917) proposed a synthesis of the "reason" and "feelings" approaches of **modern ethics**: while there are irreducible, objective moral truths, these are known to us by our feelings, by our positive or negative emotions, which are correct or incorrect in a basic unanalyzable way. Francis Herbert Bradley (1846–1924) was an Hegelian foe of Mill; his "My Station and Its Duties" saw duties in light of specific social roles instead of in general terms that would apply to everyone. *See also* TWENTIETH-CENTURY ETHICS.

NON-CONSEQUENTIALISM. The general view that some kinds of action (such as killing the innocent) are wrong in themselves, and not wrong just because of bad consequences. *See also* CONSEQUEN-TIALISM/NON-CONSEQUENTIALISM.

NON-NATURALISM. *See* INTUITIONISM.

NORMATIVE ETHICS. *See* ETHICS: NORMATIVE.

NORMATIVE/DESCRIPTIVE. *Normative* claims state how things **ought** to be, not how they are; "You ought not to kill" is *normative* in that it tells what one ought to do. *Descriptive* claims state how things are, not how they ought to be; "Foot binding was practiced and accepted in China" is descriptive in that it states how things were but not whether the Chinese should have promoted the practice. Similarly, *normative ethics* (*see* **ethics: normative**) states how things ought to be, while *descriptive ethics* (*see* **anthropology**) describes the moral beliefs of humans. *See also* ETHICS: METAETHICS; HUME, DAVID.

NOZICK, ROBERT (1938–2002). American libertarian **political philosopher**. He abandoned his previous leftist political ideas after reading capitalist and libertarian thinkers such as F. A. Hayek and **Ayn Rand**. His Harvard colleague **John Rawls** defended a **liberal** conception of distributive **justice** in his *A Theory of Justice* (1971); Nozick's *Anarchy, State, and Utopia* (1974) was a libertarian response.

Nozick's libertarianism, rooted in the ideas of **John Locke**, argues for a minimal state, the authority of which is limited to enforcing individuals' **rights** to life, liberty, and property. This is the standard libertarian position: government should comprise only a police force to protect us from each other, a military to protect us from foreign threats, and a court system to settle disputes. When government attempts to do more, it inevitably violates the rights of individuals. Suppose government wishes to eradicate **poverty** by taxing those who make over

$200,000 per year and giving the funds to the poor. Libertarians see nothing wrong with trying to eradicate poverty but argue that such government actions deprive citizens of their rightful property (assuming that they acquired their wealth justly) and thus violate their rights. The libertarian alternative to such tax schemes is **Adam Smith**'s *invisible hand* theory: if government does not interfere with the marketplace and allows us all to pursue freely our interests, competition will allocate societal resources in the most efficient way possible, allow the economy to grow, and thus benefit everyone, including the poor.

Some argue that government should bring about some patterned distribution of goods, such as a distribution of wealth that is equal or that satisfies Rawls's *difference principle*. Nozick opposes this; he argues that an existing distribution of goods is just if the members of society acquired their goods in a just manner. His *entitlement theory* contains three principles about how to obtain goods in a just way:

(1)   *just acquisition*: acquiring goods that no one else owns;
(2)   *just transfer*: obtaining goods justly from others; and
(3)   *just rectification*: obtaining goods in a way that rectifies previous unjust acquisitions and transfers.

If I grow crops on land that no one owns, by (1) I justly acquire the land. (Here Nozick uses Locke's *labor-mixing theory of property*.) If I sell you the land for $5000, then by (2) you now justly hold the land and, assuming you justly held the money, I now justly hold the money. If, instead, I steal your money, I do not justly hold it and (3) lets authorities return it to you forcibly. If all the holdings in society result from acquisitions and transfers that satisfy the three principles, the distribution of goods is just, even if some have much more than others.

Nozick uses an example about a professional basketball player. Suppose LeBron James (Nozick uses Wilt Chamberlain) lives in a society with an equal distribution of goods. When James signs his contract, the Cleveland Cavaliers agree to charge $10 extra per ticket and give this to him. The team makes public this surcharge and 1,000,000 adoring fans voluntarily buy tickets that contribute $10 each to James. Now James has $10,000,000 more than anyone else. Nozick argues that this is just. James acquired his additional wealth through just transfers. He did not steal the $10 from each fan, nor were the fans forced to purchase tickets. If fans had objected to the surcharge, they could have refused to purchase tickets. Since there is no basis to say the outcome is unjust, society can return to an equal distribution of goods only by taking money from James and redistributing it, thereby violating the property rights of James and his fans. In short, a **socialist** society would have to forbid free capitalist acts between consenting adults.

Although some accept Nozick's theory, many think that whether a distribution of goods is just depends on more than merely how it came about. Rawls argues, using his difference principle, that it is a matter of whether everyone is made better off by the existing distribution than they would be with an equal distribution. **Karl Marx** argues that it is a matter of the differences in social power that the distribution produces. Whether or not they agree with the entitlement theory, however, most philosophers credit Nozick and Rawls for reviving interest among philosophers in questions of distributive justice. *See also* BUSINESS ETHICS; PUFENDORF, SAMUEL; ROUSSEAU, JEAN-JACQUES.

– O –

OBLIGATION. *See* OUGHT.

ORIGINAL POSITION. *See* RAWLS, JOHN.

OUGHT. Duty or obligation. The main branches of **ethics** deal with central issues about "ought":

- *Metaethics*: What does "ought" mean, are there truths about how we ought to live, can we deduce an "ought" from an "is," and how can we know or defend beliefs about how we ought to live? (*See* **ethics: metaethics** and **normative/descriptive**.)
- *Normative ethics* and *applied ethics*: What are the general and specific principles about how we ought to live? (*See* **ethics: normative** and **ethics: applied**.)

Deontic **logic** deals with the logical rules governing "ought" and the interdefinability of "ought," "permissible," and "wrong" (*see* **definitions of moral terms**). This entry focuses on 10 further issues about "ought" that are not sufficiently treated elsewhere.

(1) Is there a difference between "ought," "duty," "obligation," and "the right thing to do"? Many thinkers claim that these terms are interchangeable, but that one may seem more appropriate in a given context.

For example, "duty" more naturally goes with roles and "obligation" with promises; so it sounds better to say "parental duties" but "contractual obligations." But it makes sense to say "parental obligations" and "contractual duties."

Some people distinguish these terms more radically. Suppose someone says "I don't want any *oughts*; I just want to think about *the right thing to do*." This person likely thinks of *oughts* as imposed by others and *the right thing to do* as determined by our own thinking (*see* **autonomy/heteronomy**); but this is not standard usage.

(2) How does "ought" differ from "**good**"? While both can be used somewhat interchangeably, philosophers tend to relate "ought" to how to act and "good" to what ends are worthwhile; how these connect is controversial (*see* **consequentialism/non-consequentialism**).

(3) Does "ought" imply "can"? **Kant**'s law says that if we *ought* to do something then we *can* do it; we cannot have a duty to do the impossible. This law fails for some weaker **prima facie** or descriptive senses of "ought"; if company policy requires impossible things, then it could happen that we "ought" (according to company policy) to do impossible things. But it is difficult to believe that we could have an all-things-considered moral obligation to do the impossible (such as swimming to save a drowning person if one cannot swim).

Some critics point out that we say things like "I really ought to do A, but unfortunately I cannot do it." But perhaps this "ought" is only prima facie and is overridden by my inability to do the act; then it would be more correct to say "If I could do A, then it would be the case that I ought to do A; but unfortunately I cannot do it."

(4) Can one at the same time have all-things-considered duties both *to do A* and *not to do A*? Some thinkers, wanting to defend **exceptionless duties** that can conflict, think such *irresolvable moral dilemmas* are possible. Others say such cases are impossible, since the inability to fulfill both duties would nullify at least one of them.

(5) Is "ought" inherently motivational? *Motivational internalists* like **David Hume** think it is a **logical** truth that when we have an all-things-considered evaluative belief that we ought to do A then we must have at least some motivation to do A; they argue that this eliminates views that make morality depend on external facts instead of individual feelings or desires. *Motivational externalists* deny that "ought" is inherently motivational; they say we can imagine amoralists who make genuine moral judgments but have no motivation to follow them.

(6) Does an ought judgment entail the corresponding imperative?

Hare's law (the prescriptivity principle) claims that it does, and that "You ought to do it, but do not do it" is logically inconsistent. This law fails for some weaker prima facie or descriptive senses of "ought"; there is no inconsistency in "You ought (according to company policy) to do it; but do not do it." The law seems to hold for the all-things-considered, evaluative sense of "ought"; this seems inconsistent: "All things considered, you ought to do it; but do not do it." Some philosophers, however, especially those who see "ought" as describing an empirical fact about the world, reject Hare's law.

Does Hare's law entail internalism? Arguably it does not, since we can imagine an *inconsistent amoralist* who has moral beliefs but does not accept the imperatives for action that these moral beliefs entail. But Hare's law entails a weaker form of internalism: that it is a logical truth that *if we are consistent* and hold "I ought to do A" as an all-things-considered evaluative belief, then we are motivated to follow it.

(7) Is "ought" rationally authoritative? Suppose your considered view is that act A is what you morally ought to do. Does it then necessarily violate reason if you decide *not* to do A? **Philippa Foot** and others say no; they argue that the rational thing to do is determined by what promotes our desires or interests, which our moral duty may or may not do. They think morality binds us rationally only as **hypothetical imperatives**: if we have certain goals that moral action promotes, then we ought (rationally) to act morally. Others disagree and argue that it violates reason to act against what we take to be our moral duty. Some look at morality as a system of *categorical imperatives* in the manner of Immanuel Kant; we are logically inconsistent (and thus irrational) if we think we ought to do something and yet do not do it. **Emotivists** and **subjectivists** see moral beliefs as expressing our feelings or desires; we are then inconsistent if we act against our moral beliefs since we are acting against our own feelings or desires.

(8) Is following duty the highest motive? Kant thinks it is; doing what is right because it is right, and not because of inclination, is for him the essence of a good will. Critics object that it is better to act out of positive feelings; we would be insulted if our friends helped us "out of duty" rather than because they like us. Kant would answer that such feelings are unstable and that we ought to treat others properly even if we have no warm feelings toward them; acting from a principle of duty thus is superior. Some combine both views; they say that the highest motive is to act both from warm feelings and from the idea that our act is the right thing to do. (*See* **praiseworthy**.)

(9) Are there objective and subjective senses of "ought"? Suppose that someone secretly put poison pills in the aspirin jar. The doctor, having no way of knowing this but knowing that her patient needed aspirin, gave the patient the pills. The patient died. Ought the doctor to have given the patient the pills? Here the usual approach is to distinguish two senses of "ought," one *objective* (based on the total facts of the case) and one *subjective* (based on the agent's limited data). The doctor objectively ought not to have given the pills—because in fact they were poison; but she subjectively ought to have given the pills—because her data indicated that was the right thing to do. Some criticize this proposed solution.

(10) What distinguishes "morally ought" from other senses of "ought"? Sometimes we use "ought" to express rules of etiquette, like how one *ought* to dress for a formal upper-class American wedding. We also use "ought" to express legal regulations, **aesthetic** norms, prudential rules, rules of a club, rules of a game, how to bake a cake, and so forth. What makes "morally ought" different?

Some say "morally ought" means "ought all-things-considered"; while other kinds of "ought" are prima facie based on considering just part of the facts (such as facts about aesthetics, self-interest, or etiquette), a *moral ought* takes account of the whole picture and so is more authoritative. But critics (like Philippa Foot and **William Frankena**) insist that there must be some restriction on content since otherwise "All things considered, everyone ought to put on their right shoe first" could be a moral judgment. They propose that *moral judgments*, by definition, must consider the interests of other people, and that this distinguishes morality from other areas that use "ought." Others object that evaluative judgments about other areas, like law or etiquette, typically also consider the interests of others. Still others argue that there is no clear way to distinguish moral from non-moral oughts, but this does not matter; ethicists should be more concerned with what we ought all-things-considered to do than with what distinguishes morality from other areas. *See also* CONSCIENCE; RIGHTS; VIRTUES.

– P –

PARFIT, DEREK (1942–). English philosopher who works in ethics and philosophy of mind. His *Reasons and Persons* (1984) explores how views on personal identity affect ethics. Most people begin their ethical thinking with this assumption:

> The choices I make, now and in the future, are important because in many ways they will affect *myself, now and throughout the rest of my life*, as likewise they will affect other people.

The italicized words assume that there is a "self" that persists through time. Parfit thinks this is wrong; he argues for the **Humean/Buddhist** view that what we misleadingly call the "self" is merely a collection of experiences. This blurs the distinction between "my" and "your" pleasures since neither belongs to a *self* that persists over time. It also undermines *self*-interest (*see* **egoism**) and may encourage an impersonal concern for good results wherever they occur. Parfit's views here have been criticized by Roderick Chisholm and Richard Swinburne, who defend the belief in a self that literally persists through time. Parfit's book also raises other issues, including duties toward future generations (see **environmental ethics**), which is a problem for utilitarians and others.

The set of experiences associated with the name "Parfit" has been working on another book, *Climbing the Mountain*, which is widely discussed even though as yet (as this entry is written) unpublished. This book will defend a **Kantian** ethics and make provocative claims about the **golden rule**, **consequentialism**, and **social contract** theory.

PATERNALISM. Controlling another person for that person's own good. Parents who do not let a child ride a bicycle without a protective helmet act paternalistically. Here the child is not yet competent to make decisions about safety and risks; such cases, where the person controlled is not fully competent (a child, mentally disabled, senile, etc.), are known as *weak paternalism* and are less controversial. More controversial is *strong paternalism*, which involves controlling competent adults. A law that requires adults to wear bicycle helmets is strong paternalism; it controls adults to protect them from harm.

John Stuart Mill, libertarians (*see* **Robert Nozick**), and others reject strong paternalism. They argue that controlling competent adults to prevent them from harming themselves is unjustified because it violates their **autonomy**; controlling competent adults is justified only when necessary to keep them from harming others. Other philosophers argue that some strong paternalism is justified because society must care for those adults who, say, are injured by not wearing bicycle helmets. Also, they argue, individuals have obligations to the community besides not harming others; paternalism often is needed to ensure that individuals can fulfill those obligations. *See also* BIOETHICS; LIBERALISM/ COMMUNITARIANISM; ROUSSEAU, JEAN-JACQUES.

PHILOSOPHY AND ETHICS. Philosophy can be defined as *reasoning about the ultimate questions of life.* **Ethics** (moral philosophy) reasons about ultimate questions that deal with values and how we are to live. Ethics has been a central part of philosophy since **Socrates**.

Philosophy's sub-disciplines interconnect and overlap. Here are some key issues about ethics from three such sub-disciplines:

- **Logic**: How does moral reasoning work? Can we deduce moral principles from descriptive facts alone? Can we **define** moral terms like "**good**" or "**ought**" using just descriptive concepts, perhaps empirical or religious ones? How can we become clear on what moral terms mean? Are there **consistency** principles that are useful for moral thinking?
- **Epistemology**: Regarding how we **know right from wrong**, should we be *rationalists* (basing knowledge on pure reason), *empiricists* (basing knowledge on sense experience), or *skeptics* (denying knowledge)? Should we be *foundationalists* (appealing to basic knowledge, like self-evident truths) or *coherentists* (appealing to how our beliefs fit together)?
- **Metaphysics**: As we approach ethics, should we be *materialists* (rejecting any reality that is not physical) or *non-materialists* (and thus open to things like non-empirical moral facts and properties)? Should we be ***moral realists*** (believing in objective moral facts) or *anti-realists* (rejecting such facts)? Should we be *reductionists* (reducing ethics to something else) or *non-reductionists* (rejecting such reductions)? Should we assume **free will**, the afterlife, the existence of **God**, and the existence of a self that persists through time?

Ethics connects in a similar way with areas outside philosophy. *See also* AESTHETICS; ETHICS: INTERDISCIPLINARY.

PLATO (c. 428–347 BC). Ancient Greek philosopher who was a student of **Socrates**. Plato used Socrates as the main character in many of his dialogues and often further developed his ideas. Plato founded an

Academy where **Aristotle** later studied. Like most ancient Greek philosophers, Plato sought to understand the **good** life.

Although Plato's philosophy encompasses other areas (especially metaphysics and epistemology), ethics underlies his system. His theory of Forms places the Form of the Good at the top of the hierarchy of Forms. The Forms constitute a realm of ideas beyond the physical world. Since the physical world changes and we perceive it through our senses, knowledge of it is uncertain and transitory. The Forms, on the other hand, are constant and we understand them through the mind; so knowledge of them is certain and eternal, like our knowledge of geometry. Each Form is the perfect instance of a category of things in the physical world; physical things are imperfect copies of Forms. No physical circle is a perfect instance of the Form of Circle, no art work is a perfect instance of the Form of Beauty, and no tree is a perfect instance of the Form of Tree; perfection is found only in the realm of the Forms themselves. To say that a thing (person, act, character trait, life) is good is to say that it approaches the perfect goodness found in the Form of the Good. Ultimately, Plato is concerned with how our lives in this world can approach the Form of the Good.

As is illustrated in the *Apology*, Plato was committed to following the truth wherever it led. He described how his mentor, Socrates, held firm to this ideal even in the face of his own death sentence for "corrupting the youth of Athens." Socrates had pushed the youth to search for truth rather than merely accept commonly held views.

In the *Euthyphro*, Plato examines the difficulty of identifying objective standards in ethics. Socrates questions a young man, Euthyphro, who intends to report his father for killing a slave. Euthyphro defends his decision by saying it is a pious (good) act; he explains that piety is what the gods love. Socrates challenges Euthyphro's view and any view that bases morality on **God**'s will (*see* **divine command theory**): Is a thing good because the gods love it or do the gods love it because it is good? If one answers the former, then one renders the gods' love arbitrary; they have no reason to love one thing rather than another. If one answers the latter, then the gods' love is not arbitrary but we must continue our search for the standard of goodness.

Plato explores **justice** in the *Republic*. Socrates responds to the accounts of justice provided by other characters. Cephalus suggests that justice is speaking the truth and paying one's debts. Socrates objects that it is not always just to return a borrowed weapon to an insane friend or to speak the truth to that friend. Cephalus then claims that justice is giving good to friends and evil to enemies. Socrates objects that a just man never does harm. Thrasymachus then argues that justice is what is in the interest of the stronger; this is evident in the fact that rulers makes laws to their own advantage. Socrates objects that rulers seek not what benefits themselves, but rather what benefits their subjects, just as a ship's captain seeks what benefits the sailors, not the captain. Thrasymachus rejects Socrates's analogy by arguing that shepherds fatten their sheep for their own advantage, not the sheep's.

Plato sees justice as the proper relationship between the three parts of the soul. The soul has thought and reason, appetites and impulses, and spirit and will. *Wisdom* is excellence in thought and reason, *temperance* is control of appetites and impulses, and *courage* is control of spirit and will. *Justice* is the correct ordering of the parts of the soul, whereby thought and reason guide the other parts. And so we have the four cardinal **virtues**: wisdom, temperance, courage, and justice.

The *Republic* follows this same scheme in laying out the **political** structures for the just society. The population should be divided into three classes. The ruling class contains those for whom thought and reason dominate; their wisdom can devise the best plans for society. The laborers are those for whom appetites and impulses dominate; they are called upon to exhibit temperance as they follow the plans of the rulers. The army and police are those for whom spirit and will dominate; they are called upon to exhibit courage as they enforce the plans of the rulers. Although many later thinkers speak fondly of the philosopher-kings that form the ruling class, others object to the rigid power scheme in Plato's society and its inability to promote reform over time.

The *Republic* also examines the **why be moral question**. Glaucon argues that the unjust person lives better than the just person; he argues that people would act unjustly if they could do so without being punished (this is the point of his story about the ring of Gyges which renders the wearer invisible). The best life is to act as we wish without fear of **punishment**; the just life is a compromise that we accept to prevent us from falling into the worst life, where we suffer from the whims of others without being able to respond. Socrates responds that justice does not merely have instrumental value, as Glaucon argues, but also is an intrinsic part of the health and good of one's soul. Virtue and wisdom allow us to perform our functions properly. Thus, one who understands justice will want to act justly. Injustice comes from ignorance; the unjust person either does not understand justice or else does not know that the act in question is an act of injustice.

In the *Philebus*, Plato addresses the role of pleasure in the good life. While rejecting hedonism, the view that pleasure is the good, he does not exclude pleasure from the good life; the best life will have pleasures, but these will have a lower place than thought and knowledge. When the soul is properly ordered, the rational part rules the appetitive part (physical needs and pleasures) and the spirited part (emotions and will); so the rational part has a special role in promoting the harmony of the soul and the good life.

Plato has been a hero and inspiration to later thinkers such as **Immanuel Kant** and the **intuitionists**, who want to place the foundations of ethics in pure reason, as opposed to sense experience. *See also* AUGUSTINE; EGOISM; KNOWING RIGHT FROM WRONG; MATHEMATICS; MEDIEVAL ETHICS.

PLOTINUS. *See* ANCIENT ETHICS.

POLITICAL PHILOSOPHY. The study of what government and social institutions ought to be like. Political philosophers examine questions such as: How can government be justified, if indeed it can? What is human nature like and what does this say about the proper role of government? What kind of state best promotes **justice** and human welfare? Should the state control manufacturing and business? Should government emphasize the **rights** of individuals or the interests of the community? Should there be censorship and an imposed state religion, or should individuals have freedom of speech and religion?

Political philosophy relates closely to political science and to **ethics**. Political philosophy tends to be **normative** (studying what the state ought to be like), while political science tends to be descriptive (studying how actual governments function); but there is some overlap in practice and much of what is called political science is actually political philosophy. There also is overlap between political philosophy and general ethical theories, since both deal with areas such as justice, rights, property, and human nature.

This entry gives a broad sketch of the history of political philosophy in the West. It ends by mentioning some current issues, most of which are examined in separate entries.

Ancient philosophers were concerned with the best life for humans, which is affected by the state. At the time of **Socrates**, ancient Greece was undergoing dramatic shifts: from monarchy to democracy and from an agricultural to a commercial economy. Sophists discussed political and social issues, but often with a rhetoric aimed more to persuade than to seek the truth. Socrates, in contrast, developed a rational, dialogical method of inquiry, which involves clarifications, arguments, objections, and responses. His example teaches something that is equally valid today, that we should as far as possible deal with social and political questions by **rational** inquiry and debate, instead of by rhetoric and **fallacies** (such as distorting a view that we reject).

Plato's *Republic* was the first systematic treatment of political philosophy in the West. Plato first asks what justice is. He rejects various accounts, including the "might makes right" idea that justice is what serves the interests of the stronger party. His view is that justice, at least for the individual, is the correct ordering of the three parts of the soul, whereby thought and reason guide the two other parts: appetites and impulses, and spirit and will.

Plato then asks how society (the Greek city-state) ought to be arranged. His answer divides the populace into three classes, which mirror the three parts of the soul. The ruling class contains those for whom thought and reason dominate (philosopher-kings); their wisdom can devise the best plans for society. The laborers are those for whom appetites and impulses dominate; they are called upon to exhibit temperance as they follow the plans of the rulers. The army and police are those for whom spirit and will dominate; they are called upon to exhibit courage as they enforce the plans of the rulers. Justice for the state is for each group to perform its proper role; this will ensure social cooperation and harmony. Later thinkers object to Plato's rigid class and power structure, though many are drawn, in varying degrees of seriousness, to his notion of philosopher-kings.

Plato distinguishes various forms of government: aristocracy (rule by a wise few, which he favors), oligarchy (rule by a corrupt few), monarchy (rule by a wise one), tyranny (rule by a corrupt one), democracy (rule by the many, which he thinks would be rule by a foolish mob), and anarchy (no rule, which he does not take seriously). Today many favor representative democracy (which aims at rule by a wise few who are elected by the many).

Aristotle sees humans as "political animals" who need society to help them pursue the **good** life, which consists in rational activity that accords with **virtue**. The ideal society, the one that best promotes the good life, is one structured by classes, as with Plato. Aristotle divides the populace into citizens and those who, by nature, are inferior to citizens: slaves and barbarians (non-Greeks). There are three classes of citizens: the aristocrats; the middle class comprising farmers, merchants, and craftsmen; and the class of laborers and peasants. While Plato thinks the classes would fit together harmoniously to promote the good of all, Aristotle thinks this is unrealistic and sees conflict of interests as inevitable. The role of politics is to identify and resolve these conflicts, which can be done only through a system of laws.

Augustine was the most important transitional thinker between the ancient and **medieval** eras. He thinks the ideal society is the "City of God," which can be achieved only in the afterlife. The role of the state is to give order and stability in an inherently evil world. Only the church has the authority to install government.

Thomas Aquinas, the great **medieval** thinker, thinks the good life has two levels: the natural good life, as described by Aristotle, and the supernatural good life, which is heavenly **happiness** (contemplation of **God**, the beatific vision, in the afterlife). Society should be set up to help us achieve the good life in both its levels. To be binding, human law has to harmonize with the **natural moral law** that we know by natural human reason; an unjust law is not really a law at all.

As the **modern** era began, Niccolò Machiavelli proposed an amoral approach: that rulers, while appearing to be ethical, use or not use ethical means depending on what furthers their interests. Some think he was satirizing existing politics instead of proposing a new ideal.

The **social contract** theorists began a debate about the source of the state's legitimacy and how the state should be structured. **Thomas Hobbes** thinks humans by nature are amoral **egoists**. If we imagine a "state of nature" prior to government and society (either as an actual condition of the past or as part of a thought experiment), we see that people would rob and hurt each other to promote their individual interests; their lives would be "solitary, poor, nasty, brutish, and short." So amoral egoists in a state of nature would give up their freedom and equality in order to subject themselves to a civil structure that would protect their interests; thus the source of the state's legitimate authority is the consent of the governed. Hobbes advocates absolute monarchy as the best way to keep people in check and **punish** offenders.

John Locke and **Jean-Jacques Rousseau**, while accepting this social contract idea, see human nature more optimistically and reject absolute monarchy. Locke thinks people in a state of nature would recognize the natural right to life, liberty, and possessions; to protect these rights and avoid the "inconveniences" of the state of nature, we would agree to set up a representative democracy. Rousseau believes that people are naturally good but can be shaped by the kind of society they live in; he advocates direct democracy.

Some object to the social contract view on the grounds that, with rare exceptions such as immigrants seeking citizenship, people do not actually consent to governments; instead, they merely follow the government under which they are born. Locke answers that we all, in the act of living under a state's laws and enjoying its benefits, give *tacit consent* to the government. **David Hume** counters that such consent is legitimate only if it depends on a genuine choice. Leaving one's country is not a live option for a **poor** person who knows no other language. Hume also argues that the obligation to obey one's country cannot be based on the obligation to keep one's promises since both obligations rest on a similar basis: social usefulness. So we gain nothing by appealing to a social contract (a promise) in order to justify the obligation to obey one's country.

Locke provided an influential account of property. He argues that what no one owns becomes our possession if we mix our labor with it; so unclaimed land becomes ours if we clear it and grow crops on it. A major purpose of government is to protect our natural right to property. Locke's labor-mixing theory supported the growing capitalism of his time. Rousseau, however, argues that private property and capitalism are sources of great evil; they lead us to envy and depend on those who have more than we do and to seek wealth by oppressing the poor.

Nineteenth-century thinkers focused on how government institutions should be arranged. **John Stuart Mill** argues that the state should allow us to do as we wish, provided that we do not harm others. The state can outlaw drunk driving since this puts at risk the lives of others. But it should not outlaw rock climbing on the grounds that this is dangerous to one who engages in it; such a **paternalistic** law would violate the **autonomy** of competent adults, who have a right to decide for themselves what is good for them. He similarly argues for freedom of speech and religion. If a deviant opinion is true, we gain by learning about it; if it is false, we gain by coming to understand better the truth of the mainstream view. So society benefits by permitting deviant opinions (*see* **academic freedom**). While Mill supported representative government, he insists that the rights of individuals be safeguarded so the majority does not tyrannize the minority by forcing conformity.

Georg Wilhelm Friedrich Hegel put greater emphasis on the community than on individual rights. History will lead to a society where community interest coincides with self-interest; society will care for its members, who in turn will find much of their happiness in the group.

Karl Marx argued that capitalism exploits and alienates the workforce (proletariat). Eventually the proletariat will rise up and seize the means of production, ushering in a classless, communist state. New social and economic relationships will end class divisions and the miseries of workers. Marx had a vast influence on the 20th century, as one-third of the planet came to live in states that claimed to be patterned after his ideas. He also influenced in a lesser way **socialist** parties and practices such as socialized medicine.

Anarchism, while not a mainstream view, has had its defenders, including two 19th-century thinkers: Pierre-Joseph Proudhon, also known for his socialist slogan "Property is theft," and Mikhail Aleksandrovich Bakunin, who quarreled with Marx about whether the state should fade away quickly or (Marx's view) only after socialism was achieved. Anarchists think government is unnatural, violates our freedom, and brings many evils; they hope for a decentralized society with small communities and no centralized government, a society based on cooperation instead of coercion. Opponents of anarchism contend that eliminating all governmental structures would lead to chaos; we at least need laws against stealing and a police force to arrest those who steal. Some with anarchist tendencies, such as libertarians, favor a minimal state. Indeed how strong the state should be is a major issue; options range from complete anarchism (the "state of nature") to highly centralized, totalitarian states that control almost everything.

After a period of relative dormancy, political philosophy took center stage with the 1971 publication of **John Rawls's** *A Theory of Justice*. Rawls used social-contract notions to defend liberal democratic ideas, including aggressive views about human rights and the distribution of wealth. **Robert Nozick** published an opposing libertarian view. Then communitarians, such as **Alasdair MacIntyre**, criticized both as overemphasizing individual rights (*see* **liberalism/communitarianism**). Since then, there has been much discussion of justice, political philosophy, and rights (*see* **Ronald Dworkin**).

In the continental tradition, **Hannah Arendt** and **Jürgen Habermas** both analyzed totalitarianism, especially its Nazi form, and defended liberal democratic perspectives. Currently the **Islamic** tradition is debating whether Islamic states should be traditional theocracies (ruled by religious leaders) or something closer to Western democracies (with freely elected governments, equal rights for women, and the right to choose and exercise one's religion).

Views on political philosophy often influence other moral views. Consider **egalitarianism**. Plato and Hobbes provide for little equality since power rests either in Plato's philosopher-kings or in Hobbes's sovereign. Aristotle provides for more equality in that he puts more power in the hands of the middle class. Locke, Rousseau, and Mill all advocate equality of individuals through the forms of democracy they advocate, but they differ in what this equality entails. Marx's classless, communist society is meant to provide for ultimate equality, though some argue that it actually produces the opposite.

Many moral issues have a political dimension; this is true of **abortion, animal rights, bioethics, business ethics, capital punishment, computer ethics, disability ethics, discrimination, environmental ethics, euthanasia, global ethics, homosexuality, killing, moral education, pornography, poverty, racism, sexism, suicide, terrorism,** and **war**. Consider the issue of abortion. Let us suppose that abortion is wrong; ought it then to be against the law? How we answer depends in part on our view of the proper function of the state. Do we favor a minimal state that as far as possible does not interfere with our lives? Do we favor a state that strongly protects human rights, including those of the unborn? Or do we take a more pragmatic approach and ask whether a law would significantly lower the number of abortions? Political philosophy raises difficult questions. *See also* BUBER, MARTIN; CIVIL DISOBEDIENCE; CONFUCIUS; HINDU ETHICS; HUMAN RIGHTS DECLARATION; NAGEL, THOMAS.

PORNOGRAPHY. Movies, pictures, songs, writings, or other materials that are both sexually explicit and intended and likely to be sexually arousing. The main philosophical issues treated here are how to define pornography, whether it is wrong, and whether it ought to be illegal.

What is pornography? The somewhat standard definition in the previous paragraph is vague. In some cultures or groups, female ankles or bare male chests are "sexually explicit"; in others, bare female breasts or complete nudity are normal. We can clarify matters by appealing to local community standards, especially if the community is homogeneous. The "sexually arousing" phrase is meant to distinguish materials in an adult video store from non-pornographic explicit materials, like the Venus de Milo statue or pictures in an anatomy textbook. Some add a "lacking in redeeming artistic or social values" clause. Some say that they cannot define "pornography" but they know it when they see it.

Is pornography wrong? Some say yes because it is degrading or has harmful effects on attitudes (by depersonalizing **sexuality**, threatening family values, encouraging us to treat women as mindless sex objects, and promoting sex crimes). Others say no; porn is harmless. Still others hold a more nuanced view; while most porn is harmless, some kinds are harmful and wrong, such as porn that shows sexual relations with children or encourages the physical or mental abuse of women (including things like rape or mutilation). Many **feminists** oppose any pornography that encourages the mistreatment of women (*see* **sexism**).

Ought pornography to be illegal? Some say yes; the state needs to protect people from something so harmful. Others say no; anti-porn laws violate our **autonomy** and our **right** to free expression, and are excessively **paternalistic**—especially since there is no proof that porn harms non-participants. Still others hold a more nuanced view; while most porn should be legal, some kinds clearly are harmful and should not be allowed, such as porn that is accessible to children (for example, on broadcast television), is forced on people against their will (for example, pornographic spam e-mails), shows sexual relations with children, or encourages the physical or mental abuse of women. The legalization question quickly moves into issues about **political philosophy** and the proper role of the state.

POVERTY. Not having the food, shelter, healthcare, and wealth needed for a minimally decent life. Many people around the world live in poverty, while others live in comfort or luxury. What duty do individuals and society have to help the poor?

The **utilitarian** thinker **Peter Singer** argues that those who live in comfort are obligated to contribute to famine relief. He proposes that if it is within our power to prevent something bad from happening without sacrificing anything of comparable moral importance, we ought to do so. If we see a child drowning and can save the child's life, then we are obligated to do so even if this involves ruining our nice suit (which is trivial compared to the value of a life). Famine brings similar conclusions. If we can save a starving person's life by giving up some luxury, then we ought to do so since the luxury is trivial compared to the value of a life. So we act wrongly if we buy fancy clothing, a newer car, or a larger house—things we do not really need—instead of using the money to alleviate the suffering and death caused by famine. Singer's view requires that we donate to the point where further sacrifice would lower our quality of life to that of the famine victims; critics see this as too demanding. And his view does not let us contribute more to those who are closer to us; this clashes with the common belief that we have stronger obligations to our family and loved ones than to strangers.

Onora O'Neill gives a less demanding approach based on **Immanuel Kant**'s principle that one should treat humanity, whether oneself or another, as an end-in-itself and not only as a means. She argues that we treat famine victims as a mere means if we use their ignorance or needs to entice them to sell land or other resources at giveaway prices or to accept things not in their interests (such as military bases on their land). Such actions are based on deception or coercion, and thus do not treat famine victims as ends-in-themselves. She further argues that we treat famine victims as ends-in-themselves if we help them to pursue their own ends as **autonomous** agents; we can do this by helping to relieve their famine, which blocks their ability to act. So we have a **benevolence** duty to help famine victims, and a strong duty because of their desperate condition; a given sum of money will contribute more to their autonomy than to the autonomy of someone who is better off. But there remains the problem of how to rank and decide among the various benevolence duties that clamor for our attention; we have benevolence duties to ourselves, family, friends, employees, and others—and it is unclear how we should channel our limited resources.

Besides the issue of famine relief, there is a larger question: Do we all have a **right** to at least a minimal share of society's goods, in terms of food, shelter, healthcare, wealth, and so forth? Those who say yes believe that society ought to ensure that we all have such things.

Libertarians (*see* **Robert Nozick**) deny that we have such a right. They follow **John Locke** in holding that we have the right to life, liberty, and property, but no other rights. No matter how much wealth we have, if we earned it **justly** then it is ours and ours alone; the government violates our rights and acts wrongly if it takes what we own against our will (for example, by a progressive income tax) in order to give it to others. We have no duty to share our wealth with the poor. While this may sound harsh, many libertarians are distressed about poverty and make voluntary contributions to help the poor; they regard this as **supererogatory**, as going beyond the demands of duty. Many libertarians also believe, following **Adam Smith**, that poverty will be alleviated or eliminated over time if the market is allowed to operate freely, without interference from government.

On the other side, **Karl Marx** and other radical **socialists** favor an **egalitarian** distribution of wealth over supposed property rights. Marx thought the poor should seize factories in order to bring about a fairer sharing of goods; other socialists believe in a more peaceful and orderly redistribution of goods. Some **political philosophers** point out that those who suffer from great poverty cannot enjoy the benefits of equal liberty; for example, they cannot have an influence on the political process that compares with the influence of the wealthy. So genuine liberty cannot exist unless all share fairly in the goods of society.

Between these extremes is the view of **John Rawls**. Rawls proposes that we determine principles of justice for society by asking what principles we would choose if we were free, pursued our self-interest, and knew the relevant facts about humans and the world, but did not know our specific situation, such as whether we are wealthy or poor. He argues that, in this **impartial** position, we would choose the *difference principle* for the distribution of wealth: Social and economic inequalities are to be arranged so that they are both (a) to the greatest benefit of the least advantaged, and (b) attached to offices and positions open to all. Disparities in wealth are justified only if they make everyone better off than an equal distribution (perhaps by providing monetary incentives for some to become doctors or inventors, which would benefit everyone). Society is justified in redistributing wealth that violates the difference principle, perhaps by imposing a progressive income tax.

These last three views—libertarian **capitalism**, socialism, and Rawlsian **liberalism**—give different ideals of society and how it should deal with poverty. Today many countries combine all three approaches. The poor benefit from private contributions (libertarianism); from government regulations and services, such as a minimum wage, unemployment compensation, free public education, and free medical care for the poor or the elderly (socialism); and from graduated income and inheritance taxes that are set up to provide some redistribution of wealth but without destroying personal incentive (liberalism).

Today there are many debates about details. Some utilitarians, for example, favor spreading out wealth more equally. They point to the *diminishing marginal utility* of money; as we get richer, each extra dollar makes less difference to how well we live. So it would likely bring about more total good if A and B both had $5000 than if A had $9500 and B had $500. Others say that overly zealous redistribution schemes hurt everyone because they slow economic growth. The wealthy have little incentive to work harder or start new enterprises, since additional income is taken away. The poor have little incentive to work harder, since their needs are met even if they are lazy; sometimes they take advantage of the welfare system, which others pay for, to avoid working at all. Should welfare benefits be tied to willingness to work (so recipients need to seek work or be training for work)? Some object that this forces the poor to accept exploitative jobs and harms the children of those who are unable or unwilling to meet the conditions.

The gap between wealthy nations and poor nations likely will lead philosophers to think more deeply about **global** distributive justice in the coming years. *See also* BIOETHICS; BUSINESS ETHICS; CAPITAL PUNISHMENT; DISCRIMINATION; EVOLUTIONISM; IMAGINATION; ISLAMIC ETHICS; KING, MARTIN LUTHER; PUFENDORF, SAMUEL; ROUSSEAU, JEAN-JACQUES; SEXUAL ETHICS; WOLLSTONECRAFT, MARY.

PRAISEWORTHY. Well-motivated, or displaying good character. This is a different notion from "right action," which is about the external action. Consider these two cases:

- Dr. Evil, who devotes his life to torturing others, injects you with a drug he thinks will harm you. But someone switched the drugs, so instead he gives you a drug that cures your illness.
- Dr. Good, who devotes his live to helping others, injects you with a drug he thinks will cure your disease. But someone switched the drugs, so instead he gives you a drug that harms you.

Here Dr. Evil, who has an evil and blameworthy character, did the right thing for the wrong reason. Dr. Good, who has a good and praiseworthy character, did the wrong thing by mistake.

This distinction is important in practice. Suppose I think **abortion** is wrong; I need not hold that those who do such things are blameworthy, or bad people. Ignoring this distinction may lead us to think that people who disagree with us on moral issues are evil; this divides people and inhibits discussion between good people of different moral beliefs.

What kind of motivation is the best, highest, or most praiseworthy? Various possible answers include:

(1)   doing something just because it is right (acting from duty);
(2)   acting out of **benevolent** feelings toward others;
(3)   acting out of love and gratitude toward **God**;
(4)   acting to preserve one's moral self-respect;
(5)   acting to respect the intrinsic dignity of the person;
(6)   trying to be **just**, honest, grateful, a good friend, etc. (following a

mix of specific moral principles or **virtues**);

(7)   trying to find out what is right (using facts, **consistency**, **impartiality**, the **golden rule**, etc.) and then acting accordingly;

(8)   a mix of the above.

These suggest classic approaches to ethics. For example, (1) makes us think of **Immanuel Kant** while (2) makes us think of **David Hume**. Kant is sometimes seen as holding that the best motivation is to act only from duty. Critics object that it is better to act out of positive feelings; we would be insulted if our friends helped us "out of duty" rather than because they like us. Kant might answer that feelings are unstable and that we ought to treat others well even if we have no warm feelings toward them; acting from duty is thus superior. Or he might say that the highest virtue is to act from good human motives (like caring feelings) combined with a strong commitment to do the right thing that will carry the day even when these motives are absent.

Augustine holds that the proper motivation is just (3), acting out of love and gratitude toward God, and that we are to **love our neighbor** not for the neighbor's sake but for the sake of God. Some Christians disagree and say that we ought to love God's creatures for their own sake (as God loves them) as well as for the sake of showing gratitude and love toward God.

Some defend the "mix of the above" view (8); they think the best motivation is to have some personally meaningful combination of these "higher motives." In practice, they say, these higher motives link together and support each other; it is unhelpful to try to prune them or order them into a hierarchy.

These higher motives differ from "lower motives," such as acting:

(1)   out of social conformity or group pressure;

(2)   from habit, impulse, or instinct;

(3)   to avoid **punishment** or blame, or to gain reward or praise;

(4)   to gain honor or wealth or preserve one's reputation.

These motives are morally neutral. Acting to gain wealth, for example, can be good or bad; it is bad if our motivation involves lying, cheating, or **killing**. If **Lawrence Kohlberg** is correct, we all progress through a series of motivational stages, starting with punishment/obedience, progressing through self-interest, parental approval, and group approval, and then to higher motives. *See also* BUTLER, JOSEPH; RESPONSI-

BILITY; SUPEREROGATORY; WHY BE MORAL QUESTION.

PRESCRIPTIVISM. The view that moral judgments express prescriptions, or imperatives, instead of truth claims. *Universal prescriptivism* holds that moral judgments express **universalizable** prescriptions; so "You ought to do this" means something like "Do this and let everyone do the same in similar cases." Prescriptivism's most prominent defender is **R. M. Hare** (whose entry discusses the view in greater depth).

PRIMA FACIE DUTY. A duty that holds other-things-being-equal. A prima facie duty to do something becomes an actual (all-things-considered) duty whenever it is not overridden by a stronger duty. *See also* OUGHT; ROSS, W. D.

PRISONER'S DILEMMA. A much-discussed story in which two **egoistic** prisoners can do better for themselves if they cooperate instead of pursuing their own interests individually.

Bonnie and Clyde are arrested for a robbery and urged to confess their crime. Each can confess or not; and each is interested only in getting the shortest jail sentence. If neither confess, both are jailed for one year. If one confesses but the other does not, the one who confesses goes free and the other is jailed for nine years. If both confess, both are jailed for eight years.

Bonnie	Clyde	Bonnie	Clyde
silent	silent	1 year	1 year
confesses	silent	0 years	9 years
silent	confesses	9 years	0 years
confesses	confesses	8 years	8 years

You are Bonnie; what should you do? If Clyde is silent, you do better to confess (since you avoid jail). If Clyde confesses, you do better to confess (since you spend less time in jail). Either way you do better to confess; so you confess. Clyde reasons the same way; so he confesses too. So both, following the egoist strategy, get eight years in jail.

Bonnie and Clyde could have done better for themselves had both followed a policy of cooperation instead of a policy of egoism. Then each, by remaining silent, would receive only one year in jail.

This similar story suggests **Thomas Hobbes**'s approach to the state of nature and the **social contract**. The Hatfields and the McCoys are families with neighboring farms. Each can steal from the other, and each is interested only in gaining the most money. If both are honest, both produce $6000 worth of crops. If one steals and the other is honest, then the one who steals gains $10,000 and the honest one gains only $2000. If both steal, both produce only $3000 worth of crops (since each has to spend time fighting the other side):

Hatfields	McCoys	Hatfields	McCoys
honest	honest	$6000	$6000
steal	honest	$10,000	$2000
honest	steal	$2000	$10,000
steal	steal	$3000	$3000

You are the Hatfields; what should you do? If the McCoys are honest, you do better by stealing; and if the McCoys steal, then again you do better by stealing. So either way you do better by stealing; so you steal. The McCoys reason the same way; so they steal too. So both, following the egoist strategy, gain only $3000.

Again, both would do better and gain $6000 if both were honest. So the egoist strategy hurts the Hatfields and the McCoys. If we really care about promoting our self-interest, we will try to get everyone to adopt a cooperative approach and give up egoism. But, alas, the temptation to cheat would remain; if the other side is honest, we do better for ourselves by stealing. So society needs to **punish** cheaters. *See also* DECISION THEORY; FREE RIDER; MATHEMATICS; POLITICAL PHILOSOPHY; SOCIOBIOLOGY; WHY BE MORAL QUESTION.

PRIVACY. Roughly, the state of being free from intrusion by others in one's personal affairs and in information about oneself. Privacy raises issues such as: What does privacy entail? What is the value of privacy? Do persons have a **right** to privacy?

Aristotle distinguished two spheres of life: the public (political matters of the **ancient** Greek city-state) and the private (family matters); the latter sphere should be more free from intrusion. In the **modern** era, **John Locke** claimed that the property we own as well as our own lives and liberties should be protected from interference. In the **nineteenth century, John Stuart Mill** contended that society should not interfere with acts of an individual that do not harm others; individuals should be free in matters that affect only them (*see* **paternalism**).

Much of the modern discussion dates back to an 1890 article, "The Right to Privacy," by Samuel Warren and Louis Brandeis. The authors claim that U.S. law recognizes a "right to be let alone" that protects our inner self (beliefs, thoughts, desires, etc.) from public exposure, for example, by the press. Today **business ethicists** and **bioethicists** debate whether customers, patients, and employees have a right to keep personal information from being shared with others, including other businesses, hospitals, insurance companies, and the government.

Two U.S. Supreme Court cases have influenced the discussion. The 1965 *Griswold v. Connecticut* decision ruled that the state cannot prohibit the sale of contraceptives because this violates the privacy of marriage and its **sexual** relations; this established a constitutional right to privacy. The 1973 *Roe v. Wade* decision legalizing **abortion** also appealed to the right to privacy; legal scholars debate whether the Constitution does recognize such a right that would apply here.

Judith Jarvis Thomson denies that there is a separate ethical right to privacy. She argues that so-called "privacy" concerns are captured by rights about personhood and property. Imagine someone looking at a pornographic photograph that you locked in your safe. Thomson argues that this violates your property right not to have your things viewed against your will; we need not appeal to a separate right to privacy. Others think we need a separate right to privacy for some other cases.

What is the value of privacy? James Rachels argues that privacy allows us to separate our relationships. We share intimate things more with a lover than with a stranger, and we share personal matters more with friends than with professional colleagues. We cannot mark off such levels of closeness or intimacy without having privacy. Jeffrey Reiman and Joseph Kupfer argue that privacy helps us develop our own identities in a **autonomous** way. If employers or others watch us too closely, whether on the job or off, we feel pressured to conform to their expectations; so we find it more difficult to develop in a free way into the persons that we want to become. **Thomas Nagel** and Jeffery Johnson argue that privacy protects us from the judgment of others, so we need not worry so much about how other people view us. If all our actions, ideas, and feelings were public, our whole life would be subject to the criticisms of others; living in such a "fishbowl" would be unpleasant. Privacy, by shielding part of our lives from the evaluation of others, gives us a safe, hospitable environment where we can relax; this is essential to our mental well-being.

Philosophers disagree about why privacy is important, but most acknowledge that its value lies somewhere in the accounts given above. Earl Spurgin argued recently that privacy has many benefits; which benefit is most important depends on context. The value of privacy may be different for me as citizen of a country than it is for me as employee of a university. Each of the values described above may play an important role in specific contexts.

Privacy continues to provide new issues. **Computer** technology, for example, brings new ways to gather data on people and violate their privacy. And the war against **terrorism** may sometimes violate privacy rights. *See also* POLITICAL PHILOSOPHY.

PROFESSIONAL ETHICS. The study of moral issues involving professions. Much of **business ethics** is about the professional obligations of business persons, and much of **bioethics** is about the professional obligations of medical practitioners and researchers. We could investigate and debate the obligations, **rights**, and **virtues** of people of any profession—for example, authors, clergy, engineers, farmers, lawyers, police, politicians, social workers, soldiers, and teachers.

Many professions have ethical codes of conduct established by members of the profession. A code of ethics for politicians, for example, might require that they not accept gifts from lobbyists and that they not vote on funding projects without first making public any conflicts of interest (for example, their ownership of a company that may receive a government contract). Such codes help to guide members of a profession, guard against abuses, and encourage thinking about the profession's mission to society and to the individuals it serves. Many professional schools use such codes as part of a course dealing with ethics in their profession. *See also* ETHICS: APPLIED.

PROPERTY. *See* BUSINESS ETHICS; HUMAN RIGHTS DECLARATION; LOCKE, JOHN; MARX, KARL; NOZICK, ROBERT; PUFENDORF, SAMUEL; RIGHTS; ROUSSEAU, JEAN-JACQUES; SOCIALISM.

PSYCHOLOGY. Can use its experimental methods to investigate many issues involving morality, such as: Are humans by nature entirely self-interested (*see* **egoism** and **Thomas Hobbes**), or do we have some inherent attraction toward **benevolence** or duty (*see* **Joseph Butler, David Hume, John Locke, Jean-Jacques Rousseau,** and **Adam Smith**).

Are we attracted by pleasure alone (*see* **John Stuart Mill**) or by a variety of **goods**, such as knowledge, friendship, and **virtue**? What is **happiness** and what kind of life promotes it (*see* **consequentialism** and **utilitarianism**)? What is mental health? When are we **responsible** for what we do? Are our actions **determined** or free or both? Are our actions influenced more by **rational** reflection and virtuous character, or by unconscious impulses and random circumstances? Do egoism, in-**justice**, retributive thinking (*see* **punishment**), **abortions**, and promiscuous **sexual** practices have negative long-range consequences on one's life? Is **homosexuality** a mental illness? Is moral thinking determined more by genetics or by culture (*see* **anthropology, biology, Charles Darwin**, and **sociobiology**)? As we grow up, do we just internalize the moral standards of our society (*see* **cultural relativism**), or do we develop naturally toward higher stages of moral reasoning (*see* **Lawrence Kohlberg**)? Do males and females differ in their moral thinking (*see* **Carol Gilligan**)? Can **animals** have a morality? From a psychological view, how can we understand areas like **consistency** (cognitive dissonance), moral decision making (*see* **rational moral thinking**), empathy (*see* **imagination**), autonomy, **impartiality**, the **golden rule**, and **moral weakness**? What types of ethical theory (*see* **ethics: metaethics** and **ethics: normative**) are workable psychologically? While most such issues remain controversial, the experimental, **scientific** methods of psychology can contribute much to our understanding of them.

Is ethics a branch of psychology? Some **naturalistic** ethicists reduce ethical notions to psychological notions like desire (*see* **subjectivism, cultural relativism, ideal observer theory**, and **Richard Brandt**). Others contend that such analyses confuse the **normative** with the descriptive (*see* **G. E. Moore**).

Psychology began as a branch of philosophy. After emerging as a separate discipline in the 19th century, it was dominated by Sigmund Freud, and later by behaviorists. Still later, humanistic psychologists like Abraham Maslow, reacting against the prevailing reductionism and determinism, focused on promoting growth in areas like autonomy, fulfillment, and loving relationships. Today the sharp division between different schools of psychology has diminished. *See also* JOHN DEWEY; DISABILITY ETHICS; MORAL EDUCATION.

PUFENDORF, SAMUEL (1632–1694). German philosopher and historian who defended a system of **natural law**. While not a household name today, he created one of the most detailed non-**consequentialist** moral systems and was a major influence in the Enlightenment; he was studied in Protestant universities and commended by significant figures such as **John Locke** and **Jean-Jacques Rousseau**. He built on the **ancient** Stoics, **Thomas Hobbes**, and the natural-law thinker Hugo Grotius. He made little mention of **Thomas Aquinas** and tried to purge natural law of metaphysical elements such as the inherent purpose of an action. He wanted to develop moral norms that respected but did not depend on religious differences and so could appeal to Lutheran, Reformed, and Catholic elements in Germany and other nations after the Peace of Westphalia (1648), a **social contract** that recognized pluralism and brought a time of peace to Europe.

His *On the Law of Nature and Nations* (1672) and *On the Duty of Man and Citizen according to Natural Law* (1673) distinguish *natural (moral) law* from *civil law* and *religious (revealed) law*; while all three are based on the command of a superior, natural law can be known by the reason of every person and is common to all.

Pufendorf sees moral duties as actions needed for social life; "**Love your neighbor**" is another way to express the social-life norm. So moral law is inherently social; it does not cover what you do on your own without affecting others. Nor does it deal with inner motivation; that is a matter for religion. Duties are **divine commands**; we have two motives for following these commands: self-interest (since **God** rewards obedience and punishes disobedience) and respect for the rational **benevolence** of God (who understands how we must act to live together in society). Without God, natural laws would be useful rules but not *laws* or *duties*. Specific moral norms are worked out not by appealing to God but by uncovering, in a Hobbesian way, social rules needed to restrain **egoist** impulses and bring about the sort of social life that we prefer for ourselves and would agree to in the state of nature.

The most basic moral duty is that we ought to do what cultivates and preserves social life, and to keep from doing what harms social life. This leads to more detailed duties to God, oneself, and others. Because a viable society, according to Pufendorf, requires belief in a punishing but benevolent God, these two duties come first:

(1)   to believe in God (that he exists, created the universe, cares for the human race, and is perfect, and that there is just one God); and

(2)   to act in a suitable way toward God (which requires admiration, respect, worship, and obedience).

Pufendorf claims that belief in God is based on both strong rational arguments and the common consent of humanity. Those who promote atheism, unless they can prove their case, are subject to **punishment**. Since there is no **conscience** without religion, belief in God is a civil concern. (Recall that atheism in Pufendorf's time was uncommon.)

There are two duties to oneself, which oblige us so that we may better contribute to society:

(1)   to care for our bodies (which forbids **suicide** and requires things like exercise, healthy food, and avoiding excessive alcohol); and
(2)   to care for our souls (which requires things like developing our intelligence and other talents and learning job skills).

One is permitted to defend one's life when attacked by another, and one is not obliged to prefer the **good** of another to one's own good. In case of extreme necessity, it is permissible to steal food from the rich in order not to die. Pufendorf uses the case of three men in a lifeboat that can support only two; they should draw straws to decide who is thrown overboard—and anyone who refuses should be thrown overboard.

There are three basic duties toward others:

(1)   not to harm others (which forbids things like murder, beatings, robbery, and insults, and commands restitution for harm done);
(2)   to value and treat others as equals in terms of their humanity (while humans may differ in abilities, the **rights** of all are to be safeguarded equally by moral law; and what we require of others we should in similar circumstances require of ourselves); and
(3)   to promote the good of others, insofar as we can (especially in ways that are convenient and involve no great personal costs, like gifts from the wealthy to the **poor**; we should consider those in the greatest need and how our talents can contribute; and we should show gratitude for good done to us).

The duty to treat others as equals (*see* **egalitarianism**) became an important part of Enlightenment thinking and its opposition to feudal inequalities. These three basic duties are concretized in further duties about areas like promises, speech, and civil law.

Civil government is needed because without it we would be subject to attack and thus lack security; the state of nature, contrary to Hobbes, is a state not of war but of fragile peace. Government also helps to punish wrongdoing, encourage the growth of other-regarding **virtues**, and further specify rules for social cooperation. Government would be created by an agreement between the male leaders of households (*see* **sexism**) and a sovereign, whereby the sovereign would agree to rule wisely and promote the security of the people, while the people would agree to obey the sovereign. If the sovereign rules poorly and abuses his power, the people must suffer patiently; in very extreme and unusual cases they could be justified in establishing a new ruler.

In civil matters, the state is superior to the church. The state, however, ought to respect the church's authority in strictly religious matters and respect the individual's freedom of conscience.

There also are international laws; these are based either on natural law or on special agreements between states. International relations, however, are to some degree in a lawless "state of nature," and nations must strive to defend their own interests and security.

Pufendorf gives an alternative to the theory of property of John Locke and **Robert Nozick**; they claim that if you develop unused land then it becomes your possession, so you may sell it if you like. Pufendorf argues that there is no natural right to possess land. Apart from civil laws about property, the natural law says you can use land that no one else is using; but if you move away then it reverts back to the public domain (so you cannot sell it). The state may decide to make laws about property, whereby unused land that you take and improve becomes yours to possess or sell; but the state might instead keep all land in the public domain, as in nomadic societies (*see* **Karl Marx**). So, as with Rousseau, the right to property is not a natural right but rather is a civil right in most societies. *See also* MODERN ETHICS.

PUNISHMENT. A penalty imposed for wrongdoing. Penalties can be physical (prison, whipping, or death), financial (fines), or restrictive of **rights** (suspending a driver's license or imposing a curfew). Governments mete out punishments for legal wrongs such as murder, tax evasion, and speeding. Individuals also mete out punishments, usually for moral wrongs, such as a parent grounding a teen for lying.

Ethicists have developed three primary justifications of punishment. One is *deterrence* and has its roots in **utilitarian** principles. **Jeremy Bentham** argued that, since punishment is a pain, it should be meted out only in order to bring about a greater **good**. When done correctly, punishment can do that by deterring the person punished or others from committing similar wrongs in the future. When a government incarcerates thieves, the penalty gives them a reason not to commit the crime again. They and other potential thieves must weigh the expected benefits of future crime against the pains of incarceration. The punishment for a crime should inflict the amount of pain on the criminal that is necessary to deter people from committing such crimes. Punishing with too little pain will result in more pain for future victims of crimes; punishing with too much pain is cruel and unnecessary.

Many object that this approach could justify punishing an innocent person. Although Barry did not steal, if we said he did and punished him then we would deter others from stealing; the pains prevented to future victims may outweigh his suffering. Utilitarians usually respond that citizens likely will discover in time that Barry is innocent and that their unhappiness will then outweigh the gains from the deterrence.

Others argue that deterrence does not work; we still have murderers despite the death penalty and incarceration. Utilitarians respond that deterrence, even though imperfect, does work fairly well; we would have more murders if we did not punish murderers severely.

Another justification of punishment is *retribution*; this has its roots in the **Biblical** "an eye for an eye," which limited punishment to the harm the offender did to another (so one who knocks out another's eye is not to have both eyes knocked out, but just one). For retributivists, punishment is supported by **justice**. Not to inflict pain on offenders would leave affairs unbalanced; criminals would prosper and victims suffer. **Immanuel Kant** addressed *just deserts*. Criminals deserve the pain of punishment since, through their actions, they have willed the pain on themselves. The punishment, however, must fit the crime; a petty thief should not be executed and a murderer should not merely be admonished. Punishment must "balance the scales" by returning a like suffering to the criminals.

Many object that retribution is a disguise for revenge, which is neither ethically justified nor **psychologically** healthy. Retributivists respond that just deserts differ from revenge. Revenge might motivate one to execute a petty thief, while just deserts cannot support this.

The last justification is *reform*, which has its roots in **Aristotle**: punishment is justified as a way to rehabilitate criminals. The pain or threat of pain from punishment gives criminals and would-be criminals reason to rethink and change their attitudes. The goal is not just to deter crime, but, more importantly, to change the criminals' attitudes about right and wrong and about crime.

Many object that rehabilitation is impossible since our characters are fixed and cannot be changed. Aristotle and other reformists disagree and claim that our characters are, at least in part, up to us. By practicing the **virtues**, we can develop characters that habitually choose right acts over wrong acts. Punishment should give criminals a reason to practice the virtues; eventually they may avoid crime because they see it as bad, not just because they want to avoid punishment.

Others object that rehabilitation does not work in practice; most criminals who are punished commit further crimes. Reformists respond that we need to change our prisons so they do a better job in helping criminals to rehabilitate.

Some thinkers propose a view that combines rights with consequences. They say the innocent have a right not to be punished, a right that does not depend on speculation about consequences; it would be wrong to punish the innocent even if this maximizes good results (for example, by discouraging race riots). The guilty have given up the right not to be punished; society may and ought to punish them to promote deterrence and reform, in a way that maximizes good consequences.

There is much debate about **capital punishment**. Many argue that it is wrong because it inflicts more pain than is necessary or violates the **sanctity of human life** (especially since some innocent people who were wrongly convicted have been executed). Others defend it on deterrence or retributivist grounds.

There also are issues connecting punishment with our **responsibility** for our actions. Should we, as Aristotle thought, limit punishment to *voluntary* acts? Or should we adopt a *strict liability* model (*see* **business ethics**) that justifies punishment for some involuntary acts? Does just punishment assume that we have **free will**? Is it just to punish people who do not **know right from wrong** (such as the insane)? *See also* FREE RIDER.

– R –

RACISM. Wrongful difference in the treatment of people of different races. The world has seen many blatant examples of racism. Many in the U.S. —which proclaimed that all men were created equal and had the **right** to life, liberty, and the pursuit of **happiness**—enslaved blacks and proclaimed that the only good Indian was a dead Indian. American segregation and South African apartheid kept blacks from voting, attending better schools, and securing higher paying jobs. Sometimes less obvious racial differences—as between German Nazis and **Jews**, or Rwandan Hutus and Tutsis—led to massive genocidal **killing**. Even in countries that have largely eliminated blatant racism, there remain fringe neo-Nazi groups and subtle issues about quotas and busing.

Most arguments defending blatant racism follow a similar pattern. First, there is a stereotype that members of a given race have such and such characteristics (which give that race a "lower status"):

- "Indians are immoral, bloodthirsty savages."
- "Jews are immoral, greedy, and enemies of the German people."
- "Tutsis are vermin (harmful to society)."
- "Blacks are inferior."

Then there is a premise about how people with these characteristics ought to be treated. For example, such people ought to be enslaved or killed or relegated to an inferior social status (and thus kept from voting, higher education, and better jobs).

Suppose that a racist tells us that blacks ought to be treated poorly because they are inferior (where "treating X poorly" might be understood, for example, as enslaving X or giving X inferior social status). How do we respond to his argument? Should we dispute his factual premise, and say "All races are genetically equal"? Or should we counter with our own moral principle, and say "People of all races ought to be treated equally" (*see* **egalitarianism**)? Either strategy likely will lead to a stalemate, where the racist has his premises and we have ours, and neither side can convince the other.

A better strategy is to formulate the racist's argument clearly and then watch it self-destruct. His conclusion, presumably, is about how *all* blacks ought to be treated. If his conclusion uses "all" then so must his premises. So his argument would be:

> All blacks are inferior.
> All who are inferior ought to be treated poorly.
> ∴ All blacks ought to be treated poorly.

To clarify this further, we need to determine what he means by "inferior." What puts someone into the "inferior" group? Is it IQ, education, wealth, physical strength, or what? Let us suppose that he decides on an IQ criterion. For him, let us suppose, "inferior" = "of IQ less than 80." Then his argument is:

All blacks have an IQ of less than 80.
All who have an IQ of less than 80 ought to be treated poorly.
∴ All blacks ought to be treated poorly.

Once he assigns this meaning to "inferior," it becomes clear that his inferior/non-inferior division cuts across racial lines. Every race has some members with an IQ of less than 80, and some with an IQ of greater than 80. So the first premise is factually false. And we can remind the racist that his second premise also applies to whites; to be consistent, he must believe that low-IQ whites ought to be treated poorly (as blacks are treated). As a racist, he will reject these consequences of his principle, and so he will be inconsistent.

If the racist's conclusion is about how *all* blacks are to be treated, then he needs a criterion to separate the races cleanly, so all blacks will be on one side and all whites on the other. An IQ number does not do this—and neither does any other plausible criterion. These considerations of **consistency** and factual accuracy (*see* **information**) will destroy most racist arguments.

Another problem with such arguments is that race categories are vague. It is true that groups differ genetically in terms of color of skin, hair, and eyes; body shape and build; ability to digest milk; resistance to various diseases; various DNA sequences; and so forth. But these differences vary in complex and overlapping ways, and often gradually across continents; they give no clear criterion of whether two individuals are of *the same race*. Are short Pygmies and tall Maasai in Africa of the same race? What about Navaho, Inuit, and Japanese? Or Swedes, Italians, and Arabs? Are German Jews and Nazis of the same race? Where we draw racial boundaries often depends on what group we want to define as "different." In the U.S., "one drop of black blood" traditionally made a person "black"; so the offspring of white slave masters and black slave women were conveniently kept as slaves.

Different views about **knowing right from wrong** are weaker or stronger in how they enable us to criticize racist attitudes and actions. On the weak side are **cultural relativism** (which must hold that socially accepted racism is good), **subjectivism** (which must hold that racism that I like is good), extreme **emotivism** (which holds that moral judgments just express feelings and cannot be rationally criticized), and **J. L. Mackie**'s error theory (which holds that all moral judgments are equally false, whether pro-racist or anti-racist). **Intuitionism** is not much stronger since it encounters difficulties if racists think it self-evident that whites ought to be treated better than blacks.

Providing stronger ammunition against racism are *rationalized attitudes views* that insist that **rational moral thinking** must be consistent, informed, **impartial**, **imaginative**, and so forth. This family of views includes **ideal observer theory**, moderate emotivism, and **R. M. Hare**'s universal **prescriptivism**. Such views, especially ones that include the **golden rule**, give stronger ways to attack racism.

Hare suggests that we first need to help the racist to understand the facts (about race, how racist actions affect their victims, how other societies can live in racial harmony, etc.). Then we need to have him put himself in the place of his victims and imagine himself and his family being treated the same way in their place. Then we apply the golden rule: Is the racist willing that he and his family would be treated the same way if they were in the place of their victims? If not, then the racist is inconsistent and thus not rational in his moral thinking.

Hare thinks a fanatical racist could say "Yes, I am willing that I be treated that way in their place"; he describes a Nazi who so hated the idea of being Jewish that, when he found out that he had Jewish ancestry, he commanded that he and his family be put in concentration camps and killed. But perhaps such fanatics can be criticized using **Richard Brandt**'s *cognitive therapy*. We might try to help the Nazi to understand the source of this hatred (which may come from social conditioning, false beliefs, stereotypes, and so forth) and expand his knowledge and personal experience of Jews in an open way. Presumably his hatred of Jews would diminish or disappear if he did this, which would allow golden rule reasoning to work in the normal way.

Divine command theory bases ethics on religion and **God**'s will; so we would evaluate racism by determining what God wills, perhaps by applying **love your neighbor** or the golden rule. Historically, though, the **Bible** was often used to defend racism; Harriet Beecher Stowe's *Uncle Tom's Cabin* described a preacher who defended slavery on the basis of his creative interpretation of the passage (Genesis 9:25) where Noah curses his son Canaan and his descendents: "Cursed be Canaan! The lowest of slaves shall he be to his brothers."

In many ways, racism is a mirror image of **sexism**. Both **discriminate** against people because they belong to a certain group. Both typically come from false stereotypes and bad reasoning. How we approach both areas is influenced by our assumptions about ethics and how ethical reasoning works. *See also* ARENDT, HANNAH; BENEDICT, RUTH; BIOLOGY; BUSINESS ETHICS; CAPITAL PUNISHMENT;

DARWIN, CHARLES; EVOLUTIONISM; HUMAN RIGHTS DEC-
LARATION; KING, MARTIN LUTHER; MILL, JOHN STUART;
MORAL EDUCATION; RAWLS, JOHN.

RAND, AYN (1905–1982). American writer who espoused ethical **egoism**
in novels and nonfiction works. She was born in Russia and immigrated
to the U.S. in 1924. Her novels, including *The Fountainhead* (1943)
and *Atlas Shrugged* (1957), popularize the **virtues** of self-interest, individualism, and capitalism.

Even though Rand has a popular influence, professional philosophers tend to ignore her and focus instead on writers who develop the
same ideas more systematically. Her libertarian position on individual
rights is inspired by **John Locke** and formulated by **Robert Nozick**.
This is the view that society should, above all else, respect the rights of
individuals and not violate these rights in order to promote other desirable ends. She also adopts **Adam Smith**'s *invisible hand,* the theory
that society's resources are allocated most efficiently if those operating
in the market are free to promote their own interests. Rand argues that a
free market respects individual rights and leads to a more prosperous
society that benefits everyone.

At the heart of Rand's writings is ethical egoism, the view that we
ought always to do whatever maximizes **good** consequences for ourselves. Rand rejects **altruism** (*see* **benevolence** and **love your neighbor**), a view she thinks asks individuals to sacrifice themselves for the
sake of others. Since she thinks such sacrifice hurts both the individual
and society, she contends that the individual is paramount and should
not sacrifice for the sake of others. Suppose that Jane's husband
becomes ill and needs constant care for the rest of his life. Jane, out of
social pressure to promote her husband's good rather than her own,
decides to become his day-to-day caregiver rather than placing him in
an institution; so she gives up her career as a research scientist, work
she did very well and wanted to pursue. This decision harms both Jane
and society. Jane loses the financial and personal rewards that would
come from developing her research talents. Society loses the benefits
that would come from Jane's work and the institutional revenues that
would come from her husband being in an institution.

Critics say Rand presents the ethical life as a false dichotomy, as if
we must choose between pursuing only our own interests or only the
interests of others. Both interests matter; the ethical life needs to weigh
one against the other when they conflict. Jane needs to value both her

own interests and those of her husband; she needs to choose an option that as far as possible promotes both in an acceptable way. She might perhaps pursue her own career and be a part-time caregiver; even if this would not work, it should be among the options she considers.

Whether correct or not, Rand's ethical egoism challenges those who advocate extreme forms of altruism. Rand also challenges us to take seriously individual rights and the virtues of capitalism.

RATIONAL MORAL THINKING. Many philosophers believe that our moral beliefs can be more or less rational, and that this depends on how well they satisfy various *features of rational moral thinking*. These features include items such as being:

- **informed** (which includes things like understanding the situation and alternative moral viewpoints, and self-knowledge);
- **consistent** (which includes things like logical consistency of beliefs, ends-means consistency, and the **golden rule**);
- **impartial** (to make similar evaluations about similar actions, regardless of the individuals involved); and
- **imaginative** (to have a vivid and accurate awareness of the situation of another or of our own situation at another point in time).

Sometimes other features are added; for example, in forming moral beliefs we need to think for ourselves (instead of just conforming) and dialogue with others in our society and in other societies (since other people can point out our inconsistencies and make us aware of factors to which we would otherwise be blind). While we never satisfy these conditions completely, they provide an ideal to strive for and a "yardstick" for evaluating our moral thinking.

These rationality conditions are about how we ideally ought to form our moral beliefs. Most conditions are not very controversial. But we can still ask why we should follow these conditions and not others. How can we justify a set of rationality conditions? Are rationality conditions objective, self-evident truths about how we ought to do our moral thinking (*see* **intuitionism**)? Are they demands of society or of God (*see* **cultural relativism** and **divine command theory**)? Are they somehow built into the meaning of moral terms (*see* **ideal observer theory** and **prescriptivism**)? Do they just reflect our feelings (*see* **emotivism** and **subjectivism**)? Despite wide disagreement about the *status* of the conditions, there is greater agreement on their *content*.

Some suggest that we take a few rationality conditions as basic and then try to generate the other rationality conditions out of these. Suppose that we regard it as clear that we ought to be consistent in forming our moral beliefs. Then, we can ask, insofar as we are consistent in our moral thinking, what other conditions would we want ourselves and others ideally to fulfill in forming moral beliefs? Consider "Be informed." Since we demand that others try to be informed when they deliberate about how to act toward us, we will, if consistent, demand this of ourselves and hold that we and others ought to be informed. So consistency will lead us to accept "Be informed" as a rationality condition. In a similar way, consistency will lead us to accept "Be imaginative" and the other conditions. *See also* DECISION THEORY; KNOWING RIGHT FROM WRONG; ETHICS: METAETHICS; MORAL EDUCATION; RACISM; RELATIVISM; SCIENCE; SEXISM.

RATIONALISM. *See* KNOWING RIGHT FROM WRONG.

RAWLS, JOHN (1921–2002). Influential and widely discussed American **political philosopher.** His main work, *A Theory of Justice* (1971), defended liberal democratic ideas.

Rawls sees **justice** as being about the **rights,** duties, benefits, and burdens of social cooperation. Justice is the first **virtue** of social institutions, as truth is of systems of thought. Laws and institutions, regardless of their other virtues, must be changed if they are unjust. Each person has rights based on justice that cannot be overridden by usefulness to society or the individual.

How can we arrive at the basic principles of justice? Rawls's answer involves a thought experiment about a **social contract** to which we would agree under certain hypothetical conditions ("the original position"). Imagine that we are free, interested in pursuing our self-interest, and aware of all the relevant facts, but ignorant of our specific characteristics (whether wealthy or **poor,** black or white, male or female, Christian or Muslim, genius or slow-witted). This "veil of ignorance" about our particular characteristics is meant to ensure **impartiality;** if we do not know our race, for example, then we cannot manipulate the social contract to favor our race over others. These conditions express our **intuitions** about justice; they also express our nature as free and morally equal **autonomous** beings who restrict ourselves only by principles that we choose to follow—or would choose if we chose fairly. The principles of justice are the rules to which we would agree in the original position. Since the original position provides procedural fairness, Rawls calls his theory "justice as fairness."

In the original position, we do not know our own view of the **good**; but we know that we will have some such view and that promoting it requires liberty and wealth. So we desire liberty and wealth. Since we know we will have concerns of **conscience** (religious, moral, and philosophical) that we want to protect—even though we do not know which particular concerns we will have—we will support this principle:

(1)   *Equal liberty principle*: Each person is to have an equal right to the most extensive scheme of equal basic liberties compatible with a similar scheme of liberties for others.

This principle ensures things such as freedom of religion and freedom of speech; such rights are not to be violated for the sake of social usefulness or economic advantage. (**Mary Wollstonecraft** had earlier proposed a somewhat similar principle.) This first principle takes priority over the second, which addresses the distribution of wealth:

(2)   *Difference principle*: Social and economic inequalities are to be arranged so that they are both (a) to the greatest benefit of the least advantaged, consistent with the just savings principle, and (b) attached to offices and positions open to all under conditions of fair equality of opportunity.

From the original position, we might be attracted to a strictly equal distribution of wealth (*see* **egalitarianism**). But this would make society stagnate since people would have no financial incentive to do difficult things (like become doctors or inventors) that ultimately benefit everyone. So we would prefer a rule that permits financial incentives; for example, there should be just enough extra pay for doctors to ensure that we all (including the worst off) have enough quality doctors. In a Rawlsian society, the only inequalities are those that are justified as coming from incentives that ultimately benefit everyone and are open to everyone on an equal basis. The difference principle is sometimes called *maximin* (*see* **decision theory**) since has us maximize our worst possible outcome as rational agents choosing in the original position.

Rawls argues that in the original position we would not choose **utilitarianism**, that we ought always to do what maximizes the sum-total of benefits for all. Utilitarianism provides a shaky basis for our firm convictions about liberty since it could allow violations of human rights for the sake of social usefulness; we would prefer a more direct way to secure liberty even if we knew (which we do not) that utilitarianism always supports human rights. Utilitarianism could support enslaving or oppressing a minority for the sake of a greater sum-total of advantages; but we would not risk living under unacceptable conditions just because it provides a higher total of benefits. Utilitarianism does not take seriously the distinction between persons; it sees society in terms of maximizing a total instead of as a cooperative scheme for mutual advantage regulated by fairness principles.

Rawls recognizes that different ways to define the original position would lead to different principles of justice; we can derive utilitarianism if we specify that the parties act to maximize their own *expected utility*. Why pick one definition of the original position over another? Rawls's answer appeals to moral intuitions; the best evidence for a moral perspective, he thinks, is that it fits our moral intuitions as a whole after we try to achieve a *reflective equilibrium* between general principles and concrete judgments. He believes *justice as fairness* gives a systematic account of our duties that better reflects our intuitions about justice than does utilitarianism.

Rawls's ideas, while influential, have faced criticism. Some argue that the original position does not necessarily lead to the two principles of justice, or that the two principles (especially the second) are deficient. **R. M. Hare** criticizes the appeal to intuitions (which makes Rawls's view attractive to those with similar biases but gives no real argument) and the rejection of utilitarianism (which we would choose from the original position if we wanted to maximize our chances at the cost of risking a lower level of welfare). **Alasdair MacIntyre** criticizes Rawls's universalism; he argues that what is just in a society depends on that society's traditions (*see* **liberalism/communitarianism**). Rawls's Harvard colleague, **Robert Nozick**, rejects the difference principle. Nozick claims that what we earn fairly, through hard work and just agreements, is ours; schemes (like a progressive income tax) that force a redistribution of wealth are unjust because they steal from us and violate our property rights.

Rawls's *Political Liberalism* (1993) addresses justice in a pluralistic society, where people differ radically in their religious and metaphysical beliefs (for example, some believe in objective moral truths while others think morality is a matter of personal feelings). He argues for basing principles of justice on an *overlapping consensus*, where different people may accept the same principles for different reasons.

Rawls's *The Law of Peoples* (1999) examines international justice. While Rawls argues for universal human rights, restrictions on **war**, and some aid to poorer nations, he opposes applying the difference principle on an international basis; thus wealthy nations have no strong obligations toward poor nations. Many critics are unhappy with this and plead for philosophers to think more deeply about **global** distributive justice. *See also* ABORTION AND INFANTICIDE; DWORKIN, RONALD; FREE RIDER; KANT, IMMANUEL; KOHLBERG, LAWRENCE; MATHEMATICS; NAGEL, THOMAS.

REASON. *See* KNOWING RIGHT FROM WRONG; RATIONAL MORAL THINKING.

REID, THOMAS (1710–1796). Scottish philosopher who defended common sense. While serving as a Presbyterian minister, Reid studied and rejected **David Hume**'s ideas. After publishing *An Inquiry into the Human Mind on the Principles of Common Sense* (1764) against Hume, Reid followed **Adam Smith** as professor of moral philosophy at the University of Glasgow.

Reid rejects the **subjectivist** view that moral judgments are based on our feelings, that "X is good" means "I like X" or "I approve of X." For a subjectivist like Hume, moral judgments are akin to **aesthetic** judgments about novels or other works of art; our use of "bad" in morality and aesthetics just expresses how we feel. Reid claims that this view violates common sense, which sees right and wrong as objective. People who say "It is wrong to betray your spouse" intend to state an objective truth that holds for all people; the way we use moral language shows that we do not intend it just to describe our feelings. Reid thinks we know moral truths through **intuition** or reason.

Hume wrote "Reason is and ought only to be the slave of the passions, and can never pretend to any other office than to serve and obey them." He thinks reason cannot move us to act but our feelings can; he concludes that moral judgments, since they move us to act, must be based on feelings. Against Hume, Reid contends that not only feelings but also rational principles can move us to act.

Critics object to Reid's appeal to intuition; if we have intuitive insight into the basic moral principles, then why do we disagree so much about them? Many critics also insist on the parallel between aesthetic judgments and moral judgments; just as "that is a bad movie" expresses how we feel, not some objective truth, so too "that is a bad action" expresses how we feel. Despite such criticisms, Reid presented a challenge to Hume that influenced Scottish thought for some time. *See also* MACKIE, J. L.; MODERN ETHICS.

RELATIVISM. A family of views that hold that morality somehow exists only in relation to something else (like a culture or an individual).

Normative relativism (see **normative/descriptive***)* holds that "good" and similar terms apply only relative to something else. For **cultural relativism** (*cultural normative relativism*), morality is relative to culture: "X is good" means "The majority (of the society in question) approves of X." It makes no sense to ask if slavery is *right* unless you say which culture you have in mind; slavery might be *right in one culture* but *wrong in another*. In itself, apart from cultural standards, slavery is neither right nor wrong.

For **subjectivism** (*subjective normative relativism*), morality is relative to the individual. Moral judgments describe our feelings: "X is good" means "I like X." If I like X but you do not, then "X is good" is true for me but false for you. Nothing is good objectively, apart from our feelings; values exist only in the preferences of individual people.

These two forms of normative relativism are both **cognitive** theories since they hold that moral judgments are true or false; but this truth or falsity is relative, since "X is good" can be true for me (or for my culture) but false for you (or for your culture). Neither form of normative relativism is popular among philosophers for reasons provided in the cultural relativism and subjectivism entries.

Another kind of relativism is *descriptive relativism*, which holds that people differ in their basic moral beliefs. Descriptive relativism also has two forms. *Cultural descriptive relativism* holds that cultures differ in their basic moral beliefs (for example, about polygamy, infanticide, female circumcision, and penalties for adultery). *Subjective descriptive relativism* holds that individuals differ in their basic moral beliefs.

Critics object that those who differ morally need not differ in *basic moral beliefs*. Some differences come from different factual beliefs. Society A thinks it right to kill parents when they become old and feeble since they believe this enhances their welfare in the afterlife; society B thinks this is wrong since they do not share this belief. Both groups may share the more basic norm that we ought to promote the welfare of our parents, but they apply this differently because of different factual beliefs. Groups also may have different ways to implement similar basic values: Americans drive on the right and British on the left, but both agree that society ought to promote safe driving by having everyone drive on the same side. So moral differences do not prove a disagreement in *basic moral norms*. Critics of descriptive relativism contend that we would all agree on basic moral norms.

A more radical descriptive relativism holds that there is not just a minor disagreement on basic moral norms but a wide disagreement: human nature is so plastic that almost no basic values are held universally or even widely. So how much do different cultures or individuals disagree on moral issues? While some **anthropologists** stress disagreements, others stress similarities. Some hold that most cultures have fairly similar norms against **killing**, stealing, and lying, although there may be differences in detail, and that a society that diverged too much in such areas likely would not survive for long (*see* **Charles Darwin** and **David Hume**). Others point out that the **golden rule** is almost universally accepted across the world—and that the diverse cultures that make up the United Nations have agreed to an extensive **human rights declaration**. **Lawrence Kohlberg**, a **psychologist**, claims that people of all cultures go through roughly the same stages of moral thinking. So along with differences there may be deep similarities in the moral thinking of different groups.

Relativists sometimes argue that, since people disagree widely in their moral beliefs, neither side is correct; so descriptive relativism proves normative relativism. Critics object that, even if we concede the wide disagreement in moral beliefs (which focuses on only part of the picture), still the mere fact of disagreement does not show that there is no truth of the matter, that neither side is right or wrong. Cultures disagree widely about anthropology, religion, or even physics; yet there may still be a truth of the matter about these subjects.

J. L. Mackie provided a more subtle version of what he calls the *argument from relativity*. He asks us to consider the variations in moral codes between different societies, historical periods, and social classes. He claims that these variations are better explained by the hypothesis that they reflect ways of life than by the hypothesis that they express perceptions of objective values. If we directly perceive moral truths, as we perceive colors or perhaps **mathematical** axioms, then surely there would be a larger conformity in moral beliefs than what we discover when we study anthropology.

It is difficult to answer Mackie's challenge if we keep to a "perception" model of moral knowledge (*see* **intuitionism** and **knowing right**

from wrong). Perhaps we could do better with a *rationalized attitudes* model, where we can strive toward moral knowledge by taking our current attitudes (which reflect a way of life that we inherit from our society) and trying to become more rational (more **consistent, informed, impartial, imaginative,** and so forth). This model could perhaps explain the diversity of moral beliefs without giving up the claim that genuine moral knowledge is possible.

A third kind of relativism, *metaethical relativism*, claims that people would differ in their moral beliefs even if they were *ideally rational*, where "ideally rational" might be specified as being ideally consistent, informed, impartial, imaginative, and so forth. While some philosophers accept metaethical relativism, others, such as **William Frankena** and **R. M. Hare**, reject it, claiming that we would agree on all moral issues if we were ideally rational; it is difficult to resolve this issue since not even moral philosophers are ideally rational. Some, such as **Richard Brandt**, think it better to ask not whether ideally rational moral thinkers would disagree at all, but rather how much they would disagree; he believes there would be broad agreement on most moral issues but some disagreement on details, especially in areas where the initial disagreements that we inherit from social conditioning cannot be overcome by further rational reflection.

A more radical metaethical relativism would hold that there is no neutral framework for distinguishing "rational" moral judgments. But it is difficult to deny that moral beliefs that are informed and consistent, for example, tend to be more rational than those that are not.

Sometimes moral relativism is defended as a corollary from global relativism, which holds that all truth is relative (a view that is often criticized as being self-refuting). Thinkers who accept some form of moral relativism include Herodotus and Protagoras of **ancient** Greece, Zhuangzi (Chuang-Tzu) of ancient China, anthropologists **Ruth Benedict** and Edward Westermarck, and contemporary philosophers **Gilbert Harman** and David Wong. *See also* GLOBAL ETHICS.

RELIGION. *See* AUGUSTINE; AQUINAS, THOMAS; BIBLICAL ETHICS; BUDDHIST ETHICS; DAOIST ETHICS; DIVINE COMMAND THEORY; GOD; HINDU ETHICS; ISLAMIC ETHICS; JEWISH ETHICS; MORAL THEOLOGY; NATURAL LAW; POLITICAL PHILOSOPHY; RICOEUR, PAUL; RIGHTS.

RESPONSIBILITY. "Responsible" has two main senses. In the first sense, your responsibilities are your duties. So in **business ethics** we ask "Do corporations have responsibilities (duties) to the general public or just to their shareholders?" Similarly, "responsible adults" are those who can be counted on to fulfill their duties, while "irresponsible adults" regularly neglect their duties.

In the second sense, what you are responsible for is (roughly) what you caused. So "Who is responsible for the mess in the refrigerator?" means "Who caused the mess in the refrigerator?" Responsibility in this second sense relates closely to **praise**/blame and reward/**punishment**; it is not right to blame or punish Jane for making the mess unless Jane was responsible for making it (i.e., she caused it). The rest of this entry is about this second sense of "responsible."

It is widely accepted that it is right to praise/blame and reward/punish people only for what they are responsible for having done. **Aristotle** identified difficulties with this. Suppose an unpredictable gust of wind makes me fall and knock you down. Am I responsible for knocking you down in such a way that I can be rightly blamed or punished? Aristotle would say no, since my action was not *voluntary*. What caused me to knock you down was the wind, which is outside of me, and not my character, which is inside of me. He also says ignorance can lessen our responsibility if we are not responsible for the ignorance; if I give you a glass of water that I reasonably think is safe, but it contains poison that someone else secretly slipped in, then I am not responsible for **killing** you. Aristotle claims that threats do not remove responsibility; if I do a bad thing because otherwise someone would kill me, I am responsible for my action (although perhaps subject to less blame or punishment). We often use praise/blame and reward/punishment to encourage/discourage certain types of action; this presupposes that the action is voluntary in something like Aristotle's sense.

Other questions about responsibility include: Does responsibility require **free will**? Is denying responsibility for our actions (which **Simone de Beauvoir** and **Jean-Paul Sartre** called "bad faith") morally culpable? Can our responsibility be influenced by chance factors beyond our control (*see* **Thomas Nagel** and **Bernard Williams**)? Can one be responsible for harm done by product defects that did not result from negligence? How far does moral responsibility extend (*see* **moral agent**)? Can children, the retarded, **animals**, and **computers** be responsible for their actions? Can a group have a "collective responsibility" which is not just the responsibility of various individuals?

RICOEUR, PAUL (1913–2005). French philosopher who taught in France and the United States and who worked in hermeneutics (textual interpretation) from a phenomenological perspective. He wrote much about narrative, symbolism, and metaphor; he often analyzed **Biblical** texts, which slanted his work toward **moral theology**.

Ricoeur's *Oneself as Another* (1992) is about ethics but says much about narrative and personal identity. As humans, we struggle to understand ourselves; we ask "Who am I?" The best answer is a narrative where we view ourselves as another person, an embodied person in interaction with other such persons; we create part of the narrative through our actions, but much just happens to us. Values are an essential part of the narrative, including what good and bad we do and what good and bad is done to us. As **Aristotle** claims, we act for a **good**; our essential good is self-esteem. As **Immanuel Kant** claims, our actions must be regulated by **universalizable** duties that bind all and promote justice and mutual respect as persons. The heart of morality is to see the other as oneself, to feel the pain of another as if it were one's own, to act out of **benevolence** and the **golden rule**. To see the other as oneself (morality) is as important as seeing oneself as another (narrative).

In a short essay on "The Golden Rule," Ricoeur explores a passage in the gospels where this rule occurs as part of a discourse on loving one's enemies. He draws three conclusions. (1) The context rules out a self-interested interpretation of the golden rule, in which we are to treat others well because they will then treat us well in return. (2) The directive to love one's enemies is more demanding than the golden rule and is above morality; but the golden rule, which is common to humanity, serves as a more practical guide on how to live. (3) The proper Christian motivation for following both norms is gratitude to **God**, who has first superabundantly loved us.

RIGHTS. What one can demand with moral or legal justification. If you have a right, then you can demand that others treat you in certain ways.

Legal rights are rights recognized by the governing body of society; for example, in a given society we might have a legal right to sell our slaves. On the other hand, *human rights* are rights that we have, or ought to have, simply because we are human beings, and not because we belong to a specific society; for example, we all have the human right not to be enslaved. With the exception of *legal positivists* (who hold that legal validity has no connection with morality), there is a broad consensus that **political** structures are set up, at least in part, to protect human rights and that human rights ought to trump legal rights; so civil laws that violate human rights are un**just** and ought to be changed (*see* **Thomas Aquinas, John Rawls**, and **Ronald Dworkin**). This entry focuses on human (moral) rights.

We can classify rights as negative or positive. A *negative right* is a right not to be interfered with in certain ways. **John Locke** wrote of our right to life, liberty, and property. These are areas where others ought not to interfere; it is seriously wrong to take away another's life, freedom, or possessions. Other rights are often claimed, many of which could be subsumed under Locke's three. For example, we have the right to think and act for ourselves (**autonomy**), to follow our **conscience**, to express our views (freedom of speech and the press), to form and follow our religious beliefs, to vote for the officials who govern us, and to have recourse to a fair trial before being **punished**— and we ought not to be prevented from these things because of **race**, religion, political beliefs, **disabilities, sex**, or sexual orientation (*see* **homosexuality**)—nor ought we on such grounds to be insulted, brutalized, or **discriminated** against regarding educational or employment opportunities (*see* **business ethics**). Not all rights can be **exceptionless**; for example, society cannot permit people to follow religious beliefs that require **killing** those with different religious beliefs. The goal, as Rawls puts it, is that each person have an equal right to the most extensive scheme of equal basic liberties compatible with a similar scheme of liberties for others.

A *positive right* is a right to certain goods that others should help provide; when people speak of the "right to adequate housing," they are thinking that society ought to ensure that people have adequate housing. Other positive rights that are often mentioned include the right to a decent standard of living (*see* **poverty**), to education, to healthcare (*see* **biomedical ethics**), and to equality of opportunity. We all have the right to a "fair share" of society's goods.

There are many disputes about negative and positive rights. On the one extreme, *libertarians* like **Robert Nozick** and **Ayn Rand** tend to reject positive rights and favor negative ones. Libertarians hold that what we earn fairly, through hard work and just agreements, is ours; schemes that aim to redistribute wealth, like a progressive income tax, are unjust because they steal from us and violate our property rights. On the other side, **Karl Marx** and other radical **socialists** favor an **egalitarian** distribution of wealth over supposed property rights. Marx thought the poor should seize factories in order to bring about a fairer sharing of goods. Twentieth-century Marxist societies tended to distribute goods somewhat equally but had less concern with negative rights like freedom of the press and freedom of religion.

Rawls and other liberals (*see* **liberalism/communitarianism**) aim for a balance between negative and positive rights. Rawls's first principle of justice is about negative rights while his second is about a fair distribution of wealth (and thus about positive rights); but the first principle has priority over the second. Communitarians object to this, which they see as overemphasizing the rights of the individual at the expense of community interest; they too aim for a balance between negative and positive rights, but they see this balance differently.

Non-**consequentialists** often see rights as safeguards against considerations of social usefulness; they criticize **utilitarianism** for permitting human rights to be violated whenever this maximizes the sumtotal of everyone's **happiness**. Some utilitarians however, such as **John Stuart Mill**, emphatically support human rights; *rule utilitarians* defend a strong commitment to human rights on the grounds that a society with such a commitment will be happier.

There are many disputes about rights. For example, **abortion** raises questions about when the right to life begins, the right of women over their own bodies, and the right of **privacy** to make personal decisions without government interference. Business ethics asks whether employees have the right not to be fired without cause or whether employers have the right to fire without cause. **Capital punishment, euthanasia**, and **suicide** raise the question of whether only **God** has the right to take a life. There also are debates about the right to intellectual property (*see* **computer ethics**), the right to **pornography**, the right to private property (*see* **socialism**), and many other areas.

The scope of rights is also disputed. We often talk as if not only individuals but also nations (*see* **war**) and corporations can have rights; is this legitimate? Can **animals** have rights? Can the unborn have rights? Can the **environment** have rights?

Some **feminist ethicists**, such as **Carol Gilligan**, hold that men tend to think of morality more in terms of rights and justice while women tend to think more about caring and personal relationships; so the concern for rights is gendered. Others disagree and say that women have the same interest in rights as do men; many women, especially those arguing for gender equality (such as **Mary Wollstonecraft** and Elizabeth Cady Stanton), appeal strongly to rights.

What is the source of rights? Do rights come from an actual or ideal

social contract, are they given by God (*see* **divine command theory**), or are they based on self-evident truths (*see* **intuitionism**)? Virtually every approach to **knowing right from wrong** has been applied to our knowledge of rights.

Some propose that rights are reducible to duties (*see* **ought**). "Jones has a *right* to free speech" then just asserts that others have certain *duties* not to interfere with his speaking freely; we clarify the rights claim by spelling out the corresponding duties. Critics reject this equivalence, contending that others have these duties *because* Jones has a prior right to free speech—so the right is the basis for the duties.

Historically, talk about rights arose in **natural law** thinkers who spoke of "natural rights," like Francisco Suárez (1548–1617) and Hugo Grotius (1583–1645); but the root idea arguably dates back further, at least to **Aristotle** and the **ancient** Stoics. Rights became important with Enlightenment thinkers (*see* **modern ethics**) and the French and American Revolutions. Some **cultural relativists** think of rights as a Western concept that ought not to be imposed on other cultures. However, responding to Nazi atrocities, the United Nations in 1948 approved a strong **Human Rights Declaration** by a 48–0 vote (with South Africa, Saudi Arabia, and six Soviet nations abstaining); so rights are recognized across the **globe**, although not always put into practice. *See also* ISLAMIC ETHICS; MARTIN LUTHER KING.

ROSS, W. D. (1877–1971). William David Ross was a British philosopher who contributed to the study of **Aristotle** and to moral philosophy. His *The Right and the Good* (1930) defended commonsense beliefs about morality; it combined a non-**consequentialist** approach to normative ethics with **intuitionist** views on metaethics (*see* **ethics: normative** and **ethics: metaethics**).

Ross defended a system of *prima facie duties*; these are about what we **ought** to do other-things-being-equal. A prima facie duty to do something becomes an actual (all-things-considered) duty when it is not overridden by a stronger duty. Suppose you promise to do something for someone; then you have an obligation or duty (of a prima facie sort) to do as you promised. But how strong is the obligation? What would it take to justify violating it? Ross wanted to avoid these two extremes, which respectively take promises too strictly and too lightly:

- **Exceptionless duty** approach: You ought to keep a promise in every possible case, even if the promise is trivial and keeping the promise would prevent you from saving someone's life.

- **Utilitarian** approach: You ought to break a promise if doing so would have the slightest gain in good consequences.

Ross saw breaking a promise as wrong in itself; it is wrong, not just because it tends to have bad consequences, but because of the kind of act it is (breaking one's word). So keeping promises is an independent duty, not just a "rule of thumb" to promote good consequences. But it is not our only duty and stronger duties can conflict with it. So this duty can be overridden in some cases, but it is not automatically overridden if some alternative action has slightly better consequences.

Ross accepted seven basic prima facie duties:

- *Fidelity*: Keep your promises.
- *Reparation*: Make up for any harm you have done to another.
- *Gratitude*: Return **good** to those who have done good to you.
- **Justice**: Upset distributions of pleasure or **happiness** that do not accord with merit.
- *Self-improvement*: Improve your **virtue** and knowledge.
- *Beneficence*: Do good to others. (*See* **benevolence**.)
- *Non-maleficence*: Do not harm others.

Some of these are about doing good or harm. Ross accepted three main intrinsic goods: virtue, knowledge, and (with some qualification) pleasure. So to do good to another is to promote the virtue, knowledge, or pleasure of the other. To do harm is to bring vice, ignorance, or pain.

When only one duty applies, it is our actual duty. But often our duties conflict; so our fidelity duty to keep a promise may conflict with our benevolence duty to help someone in need. When duties conflict, we have to follow the stronger duty; which duty is stronger is a matter of intuitive judgment that cannot be reduced to strict rules. We can never know our actual duty with certainty, especially since our action may have further unknown consequences.

Other duties flow from these seven basic duties. When we talk, we make an implicit promise not to tell lies; so we have a duty not to tell lies. We make an implicit promise to obey the laws of our country; so we have a duty to obey the law. This duty to obey the law derives also in part from gratitude (for benefits received from our country) and beneficence (to cooperate in promoting the general good).

Ross saw some basic duties as stronger than others. Non-maleficence is normally stronger than beneficence. In general, it is not right to harm one person to help another or to promote social usefulness. One of the defects of utilitarianism, according to Ross, is that it permits any harm to the individual for the sake of maximizing good results.

Ross saw many of our duties as depending on how we relate to other people. We have special duties to X if we made a promise to X, harmed X, or were helped by X, or if X is our spouse, child, or friend. Each relationship leads to special duties. Utilitarianism sees such personal relationships as morally irrelevant; our only duty is to maximize good consequences. So utilitarianism does not adequately account for the personal and relational aspects of duty.

Ross saw these prima facie duties as objective truths that are known through moral intuition. He took our reflective commonsense beliefs to be the "hard data" to which ethical theories must conform; he rejected utilitarianism because it clashes with reflective commonsense moral beliefs. "Moral intuition" for Ross points not to some kind of perception (like sense experience) but rather to our reflective and firm but unprovable beliefs about morality.

The basic axioms of morality are self-evident, just like the basic axioms of **mathematics**. Neither is self-evident from the beginning of our lives or from the first time we consider them. Both become self-evident to us when we reach sufficient mental maturity and reflect on the concrete instances that they cover. Both are firm but incapable of proof. Both are objective; there is a real moral order just as there is a real numerical structure. Our confidence in both rests on the same basis; there is no reason to trust our basic mathematical intuitions but distrust our basic moral intuitions.

Ross used moral intuitions to determine the basic intrinsic values and prima facie duties and whether one value or duty outweighs another. Unlike some intuitionists, Ross did not think we have a moral intuition into the rightness or wrongness of a concrete action; he thought the rightness of a concrete action depends not just on moral principles but also on the empirical facts, which, insofar as we can know them at all, are a matter of empirical investigation rather than intuition.

Ross's views about the objectivity and self-evidence of basic moral principles were influenced by **G. E. Moore**'s intuitionism. Like Moore, Ross saw "good" as indefinable. Ross rejected Moore's definition of "right action" as "action that has best consequences"; instead, he saw "good" and "right" as both indefinable and as related in complex ways. He rejected Moore's *ideal utilitarianism* and instead proposed a non-consequentialist system of prima facie duties. *See also* ENDS-JUS-TIFIES-MEANS; FEMINIST ETHICS; GILLIGAN, CAROL; IM-PARTIALITY; LOVE YOUR NEIGHBOR; SIDGWICK, HENRY.

ROUSSEAU, JEAN-JACQUES (1712–1778). French philosopher, born in Geneva, who argued for direct democracy and influenced the thinking behind the French Revolution. His troubled life began with his mother's death after his childbirth, a death for which his irresponsible father blamed him. Rousseau had little formal education; but he read so widely that he was asked by Denis Diderot to write articles for the *Encyclopaedia* and he was awarded a prize by the Academy of Dijon. Rousseau moved frequently to flee perceived persecution, and for a time lived with **David Hume** (who he later believed also was persecuting him). His last works attempted self-analysis.

Rousseau's *Discourse on the Origin of Inequality* (1758) and *On the Social Contract* (1762) give his version of **social contract** theory. Against **Thomas Hobbes**, he argues that our **egoist** tendencies come not from human nature but from being corrupted by society; humans by nature are good. Society ought to be a direct democracy, where law is decided by the majority vote of all citizens. Such a society would mold us not to be purely self-interested but to cooperate as free beings. Hobbes's ideal of an absolute sovereign who is there to **punish** us encourages people to be immature and overly self-interested.

John Locke provided a *labor-mixing* theory of property and defended representative democracy. Rousseau argues that Locke's approach to property leads to "haves" and "have nots"; it promotes envy and the dependence of the **poor** on the wealthy (who own most of the land). Locke's style of government protects the wealthy and keeps the poor from rising above their conditions; government officials favor the wealthy rather than promote the common **good**. Since the wealthy control wages, the poor will not have enough money to allow them to be independent; thus the wealthy maintain control. Rousseau's view inspired **Karl Marx** and Friedrich Engels, but was rejected by **Robert Nozick, Ayn Rand**, and other libertarian philosophers.

Rousseau argues that one can be free only in a direct democracy. Only then does one have the moral freedom of living under laws that one creates. Unlike the freedom of the state of nature, where we follow animalistic responses and do as we please, this democratic freedom moves one toward the **autonomy** of living in a social world governed by one's own laws. This solves the fundamental problem of the social contract that others, such as Hobbes and Locke, failed to solve: to find a form of association by which all individuals are protected from being harmed by others and yet obey only laws of their own choosing.

While Rousseau's ideas influenced **Immanuel Kant**, they were attacked by **John Stuart Mill** who thought they could infringe on the **rights** of individuals. Mill argues that direct democracy likely would result in the *tyranny of the majority*, whereby those on the winning side of a vote violate the rights of the minority. Rousseau responds that I am not tyrannized just by losing a vote; and if society is organized correctly then people will vote **impartially** for what promotes the common good. The *general will* is the will of the political organism of which I am part; so the general will is, even if I voted the other way, *my will*—I can be "forced to be free" and to follow it as my own will. Rousseau admits that things can go wrong if society allows multiple religions and divisive associations; these could lead us to promote individual interests rather than the common good. Mill would counter that "forcing us to be free" is unjustified **paternalism** and that permitting only one civil religion violates our freedom of religion; censorship, which Rousseau also advocates, would deny our freedom of speech. Many see the debate between Rousseau and Mill as the precursor to the contemporary **liberalism/communitarianism** debate.

Others object that Rousseau's ideas are impractical since citizens in a large country would lack the knowledge and motivation to vote on every issue. Rousseau admits that his ideas would work only in a small society; a large, diverse country would not have a general will. So we cannot be truly free if we cannot live in a small society. He would add that voter apathy (which many complain about today) comes from knowing that the wealth and powerful control all the candidates; so we think it does not matter how we vote. He thinks there would be less voter apathy in a small society that was a direct democracy.

Whether they agree with Rousseau or not, many **political philosophers** today find him fascinating because he attempted to find a way that we can be just as free within society as in the state of nature. Right or wrong, his attempt is admirable. *See also* MODERN ETHICS.

– S –

SANCTITY OF LIFE. The belief that the direct **killing** of an innocent human being is seriously wrong (sometimes the "innocent" restriction is omitted). *See also* BIOETHICS; CAPITAL PUNISHMENT; EU-THANASIA; PUNISHMENT; SINGER, PETER; SUICIDE; TER-RORISM; WAR.

SARTRE, JEAN-PAUL (1905–1980). French philosopher who provided the principal philosophical formulation of existentialism. He served in the French Army during World War II and was held as a prisoner of war for a year by the Nazis. After the war, he wrote several novels and plays that popularized existentialism and brought him fame. He was awarded, but did not accept, the Nobel Prize for Literature in 1964. Although he rejected the "bourgeois" institution of marriage, he developed a life-partner relationship with **Simone de Beauvoir**.

Existentialism is a theory about being with implications for ethics. The important fact about humans is that we exist in the world and encounter each other and other things. These encounters bring a central existential question, "What is the meaning of life (our existence)?" Some existentialists think **God** predetermines the meaning of our lives: just as scissors have a purpose given by their maker, so also humans have a purpose given by God (*see* **divine command theory** and **natural law**). Sartre rejects this because he thinks it denies our **free will**. For humans, *existence precedes essence*; we exist first, and then we have to determine what to make of ourselves. There is no predetermined purpose or "human nature" that we have to fulfill since there is no God to establish it. Instead, through our own existence and actions we decide to become what we are; we have the freedom and **responsibility** to define our own nature and the meaning of our lives.

Sartre believes there are two possible responses to freedom. Determinism denies freedom; it says that, when I act, I cannot act other than how I do, given previous conditions. So I follow bad habits or socially imposed roles because I think I cannot act otherwise; I make excuses for how I live instead of taking charge of my life. Sartre rejects this as "bad faith" or "self-deception" since he believes that deep down we all believe we are free; we shirk the responsibilities of freedom and instead treat ourselves as mere things controlled by external forces. In contrast, the authentic approach embraces our freedom and responsibility. When I act, I originate the act and thus I am responsible for it; by seeing ourselves this way, we avoid treating ourselves as mere things. Instead, we form our own lives, as an artist forms a statue.

Sartre thinks free choice is inescapable: not to choose is to choose. He describes a student who had to choose between leaving Nazi-occupied France to join the Free French Forces or remaining in France to help his mother. No ethical theory was specific enough to tell the young man what to do in his concrete situation. Sartre told him: "You are free, choose, that is, invent." Freedom brings the anguish of decision and responsibility, but we can bear this.

Sartre's idea of freedom has an element of **universality**. Our choices create an image not only of what we ought to be but also of what humans in general ought to be. This heightens our responsibility; we choose not just for ourselves but for everyone.

Sartre claims that one can never choose evil; one always chooses the **good**, and a thing can be good for one only if it is good for all. Sartre seems to accept **Socrates**'s view that if we know what is best then we will do it; only ignorance can lead us to do otherwise (*see* **weakness of will**). But then, critics say, Sartre seems committed to a kind of determinism that denies our ability to choose evil.

Critics also object that Sartre gives us an "anything goes" morality in which Nazi values are objectively just as good as any others. If we choose our own values, then why cannot we choose Nazis values? Sartre's answer appeals to universality; if we will our own freedom, then we also have to will the freedom of others (*see* **Immanuel Kant**).

SCIENCE. Relates to morality in many ways. First, science can give us **information** needed to make better moral judgments. For example, rationally deciding how we ought to deal with global warming (*see* **environmental ethics**) requires the best scientific data about its extent, consequences, causes, and possible solutions. Our data would come from physical, **biological**, and social sciences, but would likely not give us certainty about the long-range consequences of alternative actions.

Second, science can help us appraise factual beliefs that are taken for granted as we theorize about ethics. Various ethical theories presuppose, for example, that only pleasure or our own good can be desired (*see* **hedonism** and **egoism**); that races and sexes are equal or unequal (*see* **racism** and **sexism**); that we have or do not have **free will**; and that mature moral beliefs come from society, intuition, or reason (*see* **cultural relativism**, **intuitionism**, and **rational moral thinking**). Various scientific theories may support or challenge these views (*see* **Lawrence Kohlberg**, **Charles Darwin**, and **sociobiology**).

Third, some believe that science can establish the basic principles of morality. The clearest way to defend this idea is to define "**good**" in empirical terms (as, for example, "in accord with evolution," "socially accepted," or "maximizing the satisfaction of human desires"—*see* **naturalism**). Given such a definition, ethical judgments become empirical judgments that can be established by scientific means. Critics, however, object that such definitions distort the meaning of "good" (*see* **G. E. Moore**) and that science thus cannot establish basic moral principles. If these objections are correct, then we must either find some rational basis for morality other than science (*see* **knowing right from wrong**) or else despair of morality as a rational enterprise (*see* **logical positivism, emotivism**, and **J. L. Mackie**).

Fourth, some believe that science itself rests on ethical, or at least evaluative, judgments—for example, that we *ought*, other things being equal, to prefer the simplest theory that adequately explains the data (*see* **epistemology** and **ethics of belief**).

Fifth, science can bring technologies (like atomic weapons, genetically altered foods, and test-tube babies) that raise new ethical issues. While **consequentialists** can apply their "Do whatever has the best consequences" norm to new issues, non-consequentialists must adapt older ethical norms or develop new norms.

Sixth, the practice of science raises ethical issues. As we consider funding for pure and applied research, for example, we must ask whether knowledge about the universe is good in itself; some answer no and say that all research ought to aim at promoting pleasure or relieving distress. Many issues arise about experimentation on humans (*see* **bioethics**) and **animals**. And many scientific societies have **professional** *codes of ethics* that regulate its members. *See also* ANTHROPOLOGY; MATHEMATICS; PSYCHOLOGY.

SELF-EVIDENT TRUTHS. Truths that are known but require no further proof or justification. *See* INTUITIONISM.

SEXISM. Wrongful difference in the treatment of men and women. In the U.S. before 1920, men could vote but women could not; given that there was no good reason for this difference, this practice was *sexist*. Women were long denied equal educational and employment opportunities. While many blatant gender inequalities have been eliminated, at least in some parts of the world, there remain subtle issues about sexism that are less clear (*see* **feminist ethics**).

The common stereotype about women until fairly recently was that they were intellectually inferior since they were less logical and appealed more to emotion and intuition. So women ought to be kept from voting, higher education, and leadership roles in government and **business**. We can put this into an argument:

> Men are more intelligent than women.
>
> All who are more intelligent, and only those, ought to be allowed to vote, participate in higher education, and assume leadership roles in government and business.
>
> ∴ Men, but not women, ought to be allowed to vote, participate in higher education, and assume leadership roles in government and business.

The first premise has been criticized in two ways. Some say that, if we empirically compare men and women with the same educational opportunities and background, both groups have equal intellectual skills; experiments with college students, for example, show no significant difference in logical skills between men and women. Another response contends that, while the intellectual skills of both groups differ, both are equally valuable. Logical skills are only one part of intelligence; woman have other qualities, such as emotional sensitivity and a more holistic intuition, that are just as important.

Others criticize the argument's clarity. What does the first premise, "Men are more intelligent than women," mean? We might take this to claim "*Every* man is more intelligent than any woman" (so there is some intelligence level such that every man is above this level and every women is below it); this universal claim is entirely implausible but is needed to derive the universal conclusion that "*Every* man ought to be allowed to vote (and so forth) but no woman ought to be allowed to do this." Or we could take the first premise to mean "The average intelligence level of men is higher than the average intelligence level of women." Even if we grant this highly doubtful statistical claim, it would not justify banning every woman from voting, participating in higher education, and assuming leadership roles in government and business; for clearly many women have greater intelligence than most men who participate in these activities. A sexist who holds the second premise ("All who are more intelligent, and only those, ought to be allowed to vote . . .") must, to be **consistent**, allow the vote to women of greater intelligence but not to men of lesser intelligence.

In many ways, sexism is a mirror image of **racism**. Both **discriminate** against people because they belong to a certain group. Both typically come from false stereotypes and bad reasoning. And how we approach both areas is influenced by our assumptions about ethics and how ethical reasoning works.

Different views about **knowing right from wrong** are weaker or stronger in how they enable us to criticize sexist attitudes and actions. On the weak side are **cultural relativism** (which must hold that socially accepted sexism is **good**), **subjectivism** (which must hold that sexism that I like is good), extreme **emotivism** (which holds that moral judgments just express feelings and cannot be rationally criticized), and **J. L. Mackie's** error theory (which holds that all moral judgments are equally false, whether sexist or anti-sexist). **Intuitionism** is not much stronger since it encounters difficulties if sexists think it self-evident that males ought to be treated better than females.

Providing stronger ammunition against sexism are rationalized *attitudes views* that insist that **rational moral thinking** must be consistent, **informed, impartial, imaginative,** and so forth. This family of views includes **ideal observer theory,** moderate emotivism, and **R. M. Hare's** universal **prescriptivism.** Such views, especially ones that include the **golden rule,** give stronger ways to attack sexism.

This entry has emphasized voting, education, and leadership roles. Sexism raises other issues about business, like job discrimination, sexual harassment, equal pay for equal work, maternity leave, and day care. There also are issues about athletics, gender roles, bodily ideals, female circumcision, sexist language, **pornography,** and **abortion**— and about the treatment of **homosexuals,** lesbians, transsexuals, and hermaphrodites. There also are males issues, such as anti-male stereotypes and laws, paternity leave, visitation rights, and sexual harassment against males; while some *masculinists* oppose feminism for going too far, others support it as an ally in their common struggle for gender equality. *See also* BEAUVOIR, SIMONE DE; BIOLOGY; HUMAN RIGHTS DECLARATION; MILL, JOHN STUART; SEXUAL ETHICS; RAWLS, JOHN; WOLLSTONECRAFT, MARY.

SEXUAL ETHICS. This entry focuses on what moral norms ought to regulate genital sexual relations.

The *conservative view,* or at least one form of it, holds that sexual relations are morally proper only if they occur between husband and wife in a form of sexual intercourse that is open to the procreation of children. So oral and anal sex are morally improper, as are premarital sex, adultery, masturbation, **homosexual** relations, bestiality, and contraception. This conservative norm is often defended on the grounds that any other use of sexual relations perverts the **natural, biological** purpose of sex organs, which are intended (by **God** or **evolution** or both) for reproduction and for strengthening the life-bond between potential parents. A common objection to this defense is that it need not be wrong to use organs for something other than their primary biological purpose—for example, to use our feet to kick a football; similarly, it need not be wrong to use sex organs for something other than their reproductive functions. Although the "natural biological function" defense often is attributed to **Thomas Aquinas, John Finnis** claims that it is better, and truer to Aquinas, to argue for the conservative norm based on the role that sexual relations play in a **good** human life; human life, and especially family life, will prosper better if sexual relations are limited (an idea that is explored later in this entry).

The *liberal view* rejects special moral norms for sexual conduct; sexual relations are to be guided only by ordinary moral norms, such as not to harm oneself or others, not to treat others only as a means to getting what one wants (*see* **Immanuel Kant**), to promote good **consequences** (including pleasure for oneself and others), to keep promises, and to respect **autonomy**. Such norms make a case against rape (which hurts others and violates autonomy) and most adultery (which hurts families and violates marriage vows). But most consensual adult sexual relations, including premarital and homosexual sex, emerge as morally acceptable, so long as these do not harm others or violate other ordinary moral norms. Liberals disagree about whether casual (uncommitted) sex is morally proper; if it is morally improper, then this must be because it harms people by trivializing sex for them, so that it serves more for immediate gratification than for building a deeper life-bond.

The *moderate view* tries to steer between these two extremes. It sees the liberal "sexual revolution" as having bad social consequences, especially on children and the breakup of families. Liberal sexual attitudes have brought massive increases in divorce, teenage pregnancy, unwed mothers, date rape, and sexually transmitted diseases. Women often are forced to bear the entire burden of raising children; and children who are brought up without a father are statistically much more likely to suffer from **psychological** problems, **poverty**, doing poorly in school and dropping out, drug abuse, criminal behavior and prison, and furthering the cycle of fatherless families. Liberal sexual attitudes in practice (although not necessarily in theory) lead people to pursue immediate gratification instead of building life-bonds that will help nurture the next generation of children. Borrowing from rule **utilitarian-**

ism, the moderate view says that people will live better if they follow fairly strict rules about sexual relations, which liberalism does not provide; without fairly strict rules about sex, people more often will talk themselves into doing foolish things that harm themselves, their loved ones, and society. On the moderate view, the basic sexual norm is to follow those rules about sexual relations that are required, in one's cultural situation, to promote the integrity of the family and the nurturing of children. Moderates, on this basis, accept many but not all of the conservative prohibitions; the challenge is to sort through the traditional probations and determine which are needed for a well-functioning society and which can be dropped. While there are many empirical studies about the negative results of broken families on children, there need to be more studies about what moral beliefs would tend to promote healthy families and well-nurtured children.

While conservatives, liberals, and moderates battle about how in general to approach sexual ethics, other issues have emerged. Disputed areas not mentioned above include decency in dress and speech, incest, polygamy, **pornography**, promiscuity, prostitution, romantic love, seduction, **sexism**, sexual abuse of children, sexual harassment in **business**, sexual identity, and sexual perversion. *See also* ABORTION; ANSCOMBE, ELIZABETH; AUGUSTINE; BEAUVOIR, SIMONE DE; BIBLICAL ETHICS; FEMINIST ETHICS; GLOBAL ETHICS; ISLAMIC ETHICS; PRIVACY.

SIDGWICK, HENRY (1838–1900). English philosopher who was one of the leaders of the 19th-century **utilitarian** movement. He argued that commonsense morality, although often vague and **inconsistent**, is at its core utilitarian. He also supported women's education and helped establish Newham College for women at Cambridge. Despite this, he was wary of the radical social reform associated with British utilitarians. His utilitarianism was linked with commonsense morality, which resists radical change.

Sidgwick's *The Methods of Ethics* (1874) examines three methods for deciding what we ought to do: **egoism**, utilitarianism, and **intuitionism**. Egoism holds that we ought always to do whatever maximizes **good** consequences for ourselves, while utilitarianism holds that we ought always to do whatever maximizes good consequences for everyone. Intuitionism holds that we should follow moral truths that are either self-evident or known by moral intuition.

Sidgwick believes that utilitarianism and intuitionism together form a coherent whole and a reasonable basis for action. It also is reasonable, however, to act according to egoism. This leads to a problem that Sidgwick leaves unresolved. Since the utilitarian/intuitional system may demand a self-sacrifice that egoism rejects, we are left with two reasonable systems that may produce contradictory obligations. Unless we find evidence for a power, such as **God**, that will reward such self-sacrifice, we cannot reconcile the two systems. Although Sidgwick thinks belief in God is natural, he does not think there is evidence to support it and he refuses to appeal to it in his philosophical works. Thus, the reconciliation problem remains.

Nevertheless, Sidgwick thinks commonsense morality essentially is the utilitarian/intuitional system. He believes several commonsense moral principles are self-evident, such as:

(1) *Prudence*: It is rational to prefer a greater good in the future to a lesser good now.

(2) *Justice* (**universalizability**): Unless there is some relevant difference between the two cases, one should judge right for another what one judges to be right for oneself.

(3) *Benevolence*: (a) the good of one person is of equal importance to the good of another person, and (b) rational beings ought to aim at the general good.

These principles, being compatible with and required by utilitarianism, demonstrate how commonsense morality is fundamentally utilitarian.

Although the appeal to self-evident principles departs sharply from previous utilitarians such as **Jeremy Bentham** and **John Stuart Mill**, Sidgwick considers himself a genuine utilitarian. He holds that the only ultimate good is desirable or pleasant states of consciousness and that the right act is the act that produces the most good. He thinks moral rules such as "Do not **kill**," "Do not lie," and "Keep your promises" are justified because they maximize the good. He evaluates character traits and motives as desirable if they tend to produce acts that maximize the good. But he differs in his metaethics (*see* **ethics: metaethics**); he bases utilitarianism on self-evident principles and rejects attempts to **define** ethical concepts such as "good" and "ought" using nonethical terms such as "pleasant."

Some critics reject the appeal to self-evident principles, while other critics, such as **W. D. Ross**, argue that utilitarianism clashes with commonsense moral intuitions. But most contemporary ethicists admire

Sidgwick's clear and systematic style and his willingness to admit that he cannot resolve all the problems of ethics.

SINGER, PETER (1946–). Controversial Australian philosopher known for his views in areas like famine relief, **animal rights**, and infanticide. He studied in England and now teaches in the U.S. at Princeton.

Singer holds preference **utilitarianism**, which he learned from his teacher, **R. M. Hare.** To think morally is to be **impartial** in considering everyone's interests. Similar interests of every being are equally important—whether the being is a next-door neighbor or a far-off stranger, black or white, male or female, human or animal. Moral thinking favors whatever maximizes the sum-total of the interests of every sentient being, where interests are gauged by desires (preferences).

Singer's main interest is applied ethics (*see* **ethics: applied**). Early on, he published a paper about famine relief (*see* **poverty**), for which he donates a fifth of his income. As a utilitarian, he holds that, when deciding how much to give to famine relief, you should consider equally your interests and those of starving individuals in a distant country; if you do this, you will help others with great generosity, even at significant cost to yourself. His paper, though, appeals not to utilitarianism but to a weaker principle that could be accepted from various approaches. He proposes that we ought to prevent very bad things from happening, if we can do so without sacrificing anything of comparable moral importance for ourselves. If the personal cost of preventing someone's starvation would be that you can afford only a small house, you should prevent the starvation.

Singer is best known for fathering the *animal liberation* movement; his 1975 book of that title sold 500,000 copies and led to the improved treatment of animals. His book describes in gory detail the animal cruelty involved in animal experiments and factory farms. It contends that **racism, sexism,** and *speciesism* all are wrong for the same reason: they give greater weight to the interests of those of one's own race, sex, or species. The moral approach is to consider equally the interests of every sentient being—to give X's suffering the same weight as an equal suffering of Y, regardless of race, gender, or species.

Singer's disciple Henry Spira (1927–1998) put these ideas into practice. Spira started by organizing protests against senseless and painful animal experiments at the New York Museum of Natural History. Then he turned to Revlon, which used animals to test the safety of cosmetics; the cruel Draize test put toxic chemicals on the eyes of rabbits. Revlon at first ignored Spira; but a full-page ad in the *New York Times* on 15 April 1980 caught their attention and threatened to hurt sales. So Revlon yielded to Spira's demand that they put some money aside to fund research into alternative tests not involving animals; besides avoiding pain to animals, these tests turned out to be more accurate and less expensive. Then Spira turned to other projects; many of these were successful, leading to better treatment of animals.

Singer's book on Spira has advice for activists. It suggests that we focus on concrete, achievable projects; "get the ball rolling" instead of trying to do everything at once. Do not divide people into saints and sinners; instead, put yourself in the place of the people you want to change and explore how they can achieve their goals without, for example, being cruel to animals. Be patient, and change your strategy if needed. Above all, do your homework and get clear on the facts.

Singer's *Practical Ethics* (1979) applied utilitarianism to various practical issues; but it is best known for what it says about infanticide. Singer holds that it is not seriously wrong to kill a lower animal, if this is done painlessly. But it is seriously wrong to kill an animal with self-awareness and strong desires about its future. The difference depends on development, not species; killing an adult pig, which has some self-awareness and desires about its future, is in itself more serious than killing a human infant, which lacks these. Infants and fetuses have very little right to life. Imagine a newborn infant called Laurie. Killing little Laurie, while not in itself seriously wrong, could be seriously wrong if it brings misery to older folks who want her. Laurie will merit a strong right to life when she develops personhood (rationality and self-awareness). Singer sees birth as morally irrelevant in the development of a human. Since he believes it can be right to **abort** a defective fetus, he similarly believes it can be right to kill a defective infant. Many object that, while killing a defective infant (e.g., by poisoning it) is wrong, it is not necessarily wrong just to let it die (e.g., by refusing to perform an extraordinary operation needed to save its life). Singer disagrees. He sees killing and letting-die as morally equivalent, since both have the same result. Many object that we should follow our moral intuitions about such matters, not some theory like utilitarianism. Singer disagrees. He thinks our moral intuitions largely mirror the norms of our culture. Rational moral principles should sometimes lead us to change our moral intuitions and take unpopular stands.

Singer has many critics among both philosophers and the larger population. When he was installed in a prestigious **bioethics** chair at

Princeton, a group of **disabled** people, many in wheelchairs, protested his appointment and accused Singer of being a neo-Nazi who rejects the sanctity of human life; they quoted his words: "Killing a disabled infant is not morally equivalent to killing a person. Very often it is not wrong at all." Many others regard Singer as a moral hero for his work on animal rights and famine relief. *See also* DOUBLE EFFECT; ENVIRONMENTAL ETHICS; EUTHANASIA; MEDIEVAL ETHICS; MORAL PATIENT; SOCIOBIOLOGY.

SKEPTICISM. *See* KNOWING RIGHT FROM WRONG.

SLAVERY. *See* RACISM.

SMITH, ADAM (1723–1790). Scottish philosopher and economist who defended capitalism. As a student at the University of Glasgow, where he later taught, he attended Francis Hutcheson's lectures. Upon moving to Edinburgh, he developed a close friendship with **David Hume**.

Smith's most famous work, *An Inquiry into the Nature and Causes of the Wealth of Nations* (1776), is better known by economists than by philosophers. Smith thought individuals pursuing their interests in a free market would, *as if by an invisible hand,* promote the public interest and prosperity since the free market would allocate resources in the most efficient way possible. Many libertarians (*see* **Robert Nozick** and **Ayn Rand**) use this "invisible hand" image against government taxes and regulations that inhibit a free market. Others point out that Smith thinks the invisible hand works only if people have a concern for others and a sense of justice and fair play; without these, some government intervention may be needed to ensure a just and fair market. Disputes about government intervention often surface in **business ethics**.

Smith's earlier *Theory of Moral Sentiments* (1759) is of more interest to philosophers. Smith's sympathy-based moral **psychology** is the centerpiece of the book. Like Hume, Smith thinks sympathy, which we all have to some degree, is the basis of our judgments of others' feelings and actions, and of **virtue**. For you to approve of how I feel (or act), means that you *sympathize* with my feelings (or actions): you believe you would feel similarly if you were in a similar position. If you do not believe you would feel similarly, then you will disapprove of how I feel (or act).

Sympathy determines the "suitableness" or "propriety" of feelings and actions in their specific context, and thus their virtue or vice. Suppose you see me throwing things around my office in a violent rage. You immediately disapprove of my behavior because you do not sympathize with my feelings. Later, you learn that I just found out that my young child was killed by a drunken driver. Your disapproval turns into approval as you come to sympathize with my feelings and behavior, and see how these are proper in this context.

Smith holds a version of **ideal observer theory**. I am to evaluate my feelings and behavior as though they were someone else's. In judging the propriety of my anger at a betrayal, I must judge from the same **impartial** position from which I would judge another's anger. Would I sympathize with another person who felt anger over a similar betrayal? If so, then I approve of my feeling; if not, then I must disapprove.

Critics object that Smith's view leads to **relativism**, since different people or **cultures** may have different emotional reactions to the same feeling or act. Because of stress or exhaustion, I cannot sympathize with the joy a colleague feels over the news that her paper will be published; but you immediately sympathize with her joy. While some thinkers are content with such relativism, Smith seems not to be. Smith argues that we have "general rules" to guide us in situations, such as when we are stressed or judging ourselves, where our sympathy might not operate properly; he suggests rules of **justice** and **benevolence**. But he does not explain what these rules involve or how they are justified. Hume appealed to the *general point of view* to deal with similar problems about relativism. Smith must argue similarly on the basis of impartiality; he must hold that if two people adopt similar impartial viewpoints, free from biases and prejudices, they will have the same judgments about the same feeling or action; but many are skeptical of such claims. Others, using **Charles Darwin**'s ideas, defend Smith by arguing that natural selection produces the similarity of emotional reactions that he needs; wildly different emotional reactions would not have promoted survival (*see* **sociobiology**).

Although Smith lived during the blossoming of **utilitarianism**, he does not base virtue on utility. You approve of my action because of its propriety or suitableness; concerns about its utility come later and may further support your approval. *See also* MODERN ETHICS.

SOCIAL CONTRACT. A concept used to justify moral and **political** authority as coming from the consent of the governed.

The classic social contract theorists (**Thomas Hobbes, John Locke,** and **Jean-Jacques Rousseau**) wanted to move away from what they saw as arbitrary justifications for government authority, such as birth-right and divine right. They reasoned that, since each person is born free and equal, no one has moral authority over any other person unless that person grants it. This raises the question: Why would free and equal people ever consent to the moral and political authority of others?

In answering this question, the classic social contract theorists use the *state of nature*, the human condition prior to government and socie-ty. Although some believe that the state of nature actually existed while others believe it is merely hypothetical, all agree that it does not pro-mote the human cooperation required to satisfy our needs; without a common authority to enforce agreements (like **business** contracts), people cannot cooperate successfully. Thus, the rational thing to do in the state of nature is to give up our natural freedom and equality and submit to the authority of a government. This is the *social contract*; we would agree to it in order to promote our own interests. The resulting authority enforces the agreements we need to cooperate successfully.

The type of government supported depends on how miserable the state of nature would be. Hobbes advocated an absolute sovereign because he saw people in the state of nature as totally **egoistic** and their lives as "solitary, poor, nasty, brutish, and short." Locke and Rousseau saw the state of nature as less miserable, with Locke describing its problems as "inconveniences." So Locke advocated representative gov-ernment and Rousseau advocated direct democracy.

John Rawls more recently has used social-contract ideas to deter-mine the basic rules of **justice** for society. Replacing the state of nature is the *original position*: a hypothetical situation from which rational and free people, behind a *veil of ignorance* (in which they do not know their place in society—their race, sex, religion, economic status, and the like), choose the guiding principles of society. Under such condi-tions, persons would choose principles that are fair to all, rather than principles that benefit just their group. Rawls thinks two principles would be chosen: (1) the *equal liberty principle* guarantees the greatest set of liberties for each person compatible with an equal set for others and (2) the *difference principle* ensures an equal distribution of wealth except for inequalities that benefit all.

. David Gauthier has pointed out that a social contract designed to promote the interests of the contractors may not protect the **rights** of the weak (including the **disabled** and **animals**). *See also* HUME, DAVID; KOHLBERG, LAWRENCE; LIBERALISM/COMMUNITA-RIANISM; MORAL PATIENT; PUFENDORF, SAMUEL.

SOCIAL DARWINISM. *See* DARWIN, CHARLES; EVOLUTIONISM; SOCIOBIOLOGY.

SOCIALISM. Communal ownership and control of organizations that provide goods or services; socialism is marked by cooperation and an **egalitarian** ideal of everyone sharing somewhat equally in the goods of society. The opposing approach is capitalism, where privately owned and operated **businesses** provide goods and services for profit; capitalism is marked by competition, free markets, and the profit motive.

Socialist systems can take many forms. Some are controlled locally and democratically, as in the Kibbutz model in Israel; others are highly centralized and autocratic, as in Stalinist Russia. Some respect individual **rights** and liberties, such as free speech and free elections, as in Sweden; others deny such rights, as in Stalinist Russia.

Socialists such as **Karl Marx** claim that socialism brings a fairer distribution of goods, a spirit of cooperation, a lessening of class divisions, and a greater self-esteem on the part of workers. Capitalism, by contrast, is based on a greedy self-interest that enriches capitalists but brings **poverty** and a dehumanized existence to workers. Capitalism also is unstable, leading to frequent recessions that bring more pain to workers than to capitalists. The root problem is the private ownership of the means of production.

Capitalists such as **Adam Smith** claim that capitalism better serves society. Individuals pursuing their self-interest in a free market will, as if by an "invisible hand," also promote the public interest since the free market will allocate resources efficiently and thus lead to prosperity. Socialism makes the economy stagnate since people do not work as hard or as creatively without the profit motive. **Robert Nozick** adds that socialism violates the rights of individuals. What we earn fairly, through **just** investments and hard work, is ours; schemes that redistribute wealth are unjust because they steal from us and violate our property rights. Inequalities naturally would arise in a strictly egalitarian society, as enterprising individuals pursue new ways to make goods; to prevent such inequalities, a socialist would have to forbid free capitalistic acts between consenting adults.

Russia embraced a form of Marxist socialism in 1917, and a similar system spread to one-third of the planet. But Marxism eventually led to economic problems and shared **poverty**. So in 1991 the Soviet Union collapsed and Russia rejected Marxism. Many saw this as the ultimate proof that socialism does not work. But others saw it as proving only the unworkability of the Russian type of socialism, whose autocratic centralized control and denial of human rights were untrue to Marx's thinking. Various political parties identified as "socialist" continue to thrive over much of the globe, except in places such as the United States, where "socialism" is used mostly as a term of abuse.

Today most countries, whether they call themselves "capitalist" or "socialist," combine elements from both approaches. So predominantly capitalist countries, aware of problems that capitalism can cause for poor workers, have established things like trade unions, a minimum wage, social security, unemployment compensation, norms about the treatment of employees, free public education, free lunches for school children, and free medical care for the poor or the elderly—with many of these being financed by inheritance taxes and a graduated income tax. And predominantly socialist countries have privatized some industries and turned to a market economy. Many countries have moved away from an ideological commitment to capitalism or socialism and are more concerned with the practical question of whether specific areas (mining, manufacturing, transportation, utilities, medical care, and so forth) would work better if nationalized or privatized.

Critics contend that the movement toward socialism has not gone far enough since there still is a large gap between rich and poor, most of which is based on the accident of birth. In the United States, the richest 20 percent of the population have a combined wealth 14 times as great as that of the poorest 20 percent; the head of a U.S. corporation often earns 50 or 100 times the salary of an ordinary worker. The richest 300 people in the world have a combined wealth greater than that of the three billion poorest people. The gap between rich nations and poor nations across the **globe** is especially acute. Critics add that the capitalistic thirst for increased consumption cannot continue indefinitely without **environmental** disaster. *See also* BIOETHICS; EVOLUTIONISM; LOCKE, JOHN; NINETEENTH-CENTURY ETHICS; POLITICAL PHILOSOPHY; RAND, AYN.

SOCIOBIOLOGY. The study of social behavior in terms of evolution.

Evolution holds that new forms of life emerge from mutation plus selection. Organisms develop random inheritable variations, and those organisms with favorable characteristics are more likely to survive and produce offspring with these same characteristics; repeating this process many millions of times leads to the emergence of radically new life forms. But how does this connect with ethics and social behavior?

In the **nineteenth century**, *Social Darwinists* saw evolution as a "dog eat dog" struggle in which the strong survive and overcome the weak (*see* **evolutionism**). Human life, they thought, follows and ought to follow this same pattern; so it accords with nature and is right that strong individuals, **businesses**, social classes, and nations struggle for supremacy and overcome the weak. **Friedrich Nietzsche** had somewhat similar ideas; he thought humans, like other animals, evolved with the *will to power* and domination as their basic motivation.

Charles Darwin applied evolution to morality in a different way. He thought that humans were social animals, like wolves, and thus have an inbred tendency to help each other—a tendency that promotes the survival of the group. While human sympathy at first was limited to people of one's own clan or tribe, in time, as our rational powers evolved and developed, we started to extend our sympathies more widely, to all humanity, including its weakest members, and even to **animals**. So Darwin saw evolution as supporting **benevolence**.

What is the unit of evolutionary selection: the individual or the group? Social Darwinists thought in terms of the individual: altruistic individuals would be weeded out because of their reduced tendency to survive and reproduce. Darwin thought in terms of the group: altruistic groups have a stronger tendency to survive. Which side is correct? Contemporary sociobiologists, such as William Hamilton, Robert Trivers, and Edward Wilson, think both sides are wrong; the unit of evolutionary selection, they contend, is the gene. Genes that are well adapted tend to be transmitted to future organisms; evolution promotes the survival of the fittest genes.

Consider a society of bees. The only female with offspring is the queen bee. But the female worker bees share the same genes (more or less) as the queen; by promoting the bee society, these female workers ensure that copies of their genes are transmitted to future organisms. Something similar holds for human society. We are biologically oriented to ensure that copies of our genes are passed into the future. We can do this by having offspring ourselves or by helping those who have genes like ours to have offspring. We tend to provide greater help to close relatives since we share more genes with them.

Besides such *kin altruism* there is also *reciprocal altruism*, sometimes between widely different species. Some small fish act as "cleaners," eating food from the gills of larger fish; both sides benefit from this practice and have developed an instinctive concern for the other side, since this promotes the survival of their genes. Other animals whose interests are connected, like humans, seem similarly to evolve an innate tendency to cooperate with and show concern for each other.

So evolution would build into us a tendency to altruism, especially toward closer relatives or cooperation partners. The explanation is genetic: such altruism promotes the survival of our genes. Some refer to "selfish genes"; evolution works as if genes promoted their survival by using the bodies of other beings. So does **egoism** rule? Some sociobiologists think this, but others hold that human **benevolence** is genuine and that "selfish genes" is just a metaphor to explain how there evolved a tendency toward benevolence.

Sociobiology becomes complicated as it tries to explain how humans developed a mix of altruism and egoism, and how this applies to how we treat close and further relatives and strangers. There is much controversy about details and the larger question of how much human behavior is innate and how much is due to socialization.

Robert Axelrod added computer simulations to the discussion. His programs play reiterated **prisoner dilemma** games against each other to see which ones (whether altruistic or selfish) do best and survive. The winner is the tit-for-tat program that cooperates on the first move (even though this hurts a little in terms of self-interest) and then will cooperate on each further move if and only if the other player cooperated on the previous move; tit-for-tat excels because it promotes the interests of both parties. Perhaps future discussions about what genetic patterns would survive will make greater use of computer simulations. The recent mapping of human genetic structures into computerized form likely will spur further interest in sociobiological issues.

Peter Singer has proposed another explanation of how morality has evolved. He sees evolution as providing us with (1) our basic desires about what we want in life and (2) the rational desire to be **consistent**, which shows itself in the distressful "cognitive dissonance" that we feel when we recognize that we are inconsistent. These two factors lead us first to believe that certain things are **good** for us, and then to generalize that what is good for us must also good for others and thus ought to be promoted for them as well (*see* **golden rule, R. M. Hare, universalizability**, and **utilitarianism**). This approach seems compatible with sociobiology. *See also* ANTHROPOLOGY; BIOLOGY; SCIENCE.

SOCRATES (c. 470–399 BC). Ancient Greek philosopher who is often considered to be the father of Western philosophy. He is featured by his student **Plato** in many of the latter's dialogues; these give us some access to Socrates's ideas and approach to philosophy. Socrates's use of questions to motivate others to explore ideas is the foundation of the argument/objection/response dialectic that philosophers employ today; this *Socratic method* has influenced teaching styles, perhaps most notably in law schools. Those who use the dialogical method test ideas by trying to derive absurdities from them and seek beliefs that can be held **consistently** after a careful examination.

When Socrates lived, ancient Greece was shifting dramatically from a monarchy to a democracy and from an agricultural to a commercial economy. Because of these changes, the Sophists questioned traditional Greek values; but the Sophists were more concerned with persuasive rhetoric than with pursuing new values. Socrates, in contrast, tried to seek the truth in a rational way and to develop new values.

Plato's *Apology* presents a vivid picture of Socrates as a person who pursued the life of reason even though it led to his death sentence, purportedly for corrupting the youth of Athens; he encouraged the youth to seek the truth rather than merely adopt commonly held views. Later thinkers would explore issues that Socrates raised, such as how to define moral terms like **"virtue"** (*see* **ethics: metaethics**) and our motivation to be moral (*see* **why be moral question**). *See also* ARISTOTLE; CONSCIENTIOUSNESS; DIVINE COMMAND THEORY; FREE WILL AND DETERMINISM; POLITICAL PHILOSOPHY.

SPECIESISM. *See* SINGER, PETER.

STATE OF NATURE. The human condition prior to government and society, seen either as an actual condition of the past or as part of a thought experiment. *See* SOCIAL CONTRACT.

STEM-CELL RESEARCH. Stem cells are generic cells that produce specialized cells. Many people hope that research on stem cells taken from embryos may someday lead to new ways to treat diseases. Such research began on mice embryos in 1981 and on human embryos in 1998. Many have similar hopes about research on human stem cells taken from other sources, including unfertilized eggs, the umbilical cord, the placenta, and the bodies of ordinary adults.

Since current methods of obtaining embryonic stem cells kill the embryo, there is much controversy about *human embryonic stem-cell research*. Is such research morally proper? Ought the law to permit it? Those who see no moral objection to very early **abortions** generally see no moral objection to **killing** human embryos for research or having laws that allow this; but some suggest going slowly on such research since it violates the moral sensitivity of many people and may lead us down a slippery slope toward dehumanizing practices. Those who believe that very early abortions are seriously wrong usually think that human embryonic stem-cell research is wrong and should be illegal; these people have no moral objection to stem-cell research that does not involve killing embryos. Two other views are possible for them.

(1) Some who think it wrong to kill a human embryo believe that such killing ought not to be against the law. The law ought to be based on consensus (which does not exist here); and it is inconsistent for the law to permit abortion for slight reasons but forbid killing human embryos for research that may help people. Scientists who see such killing as wrong may in **conscience** do research on cells taken from embryos killed by others (as they may do research on adult murder victims).

(2) Some appeal to the principle of *extraordinary means*: while direct killing is wrong, one need not take extraordinary means to prolong life. So turning off a respirator or refusing a major operation can be permissible even when these are needed for life. Most embryonic stem cells are taken from frozen embryos that are left over from *in vitro* fertilization procedures. Keeping these embryos frozen indefinitely (for centuries?) is, such people argue, an *extraordinary means* of prolonging life and thus not morally obligatory. Thus it is permissible to thaw such embryos and use some of their cells for medical purposes, even though they will die. Most who argue this way condemn the practices that led to the frozen embryos; but they see no obligation to keep the embryos alive indefinitely by extraordinary means.

As this entry was written, a medical breakthrough was announced that may end the ethical controversy: a way was discovered to convert ordinary skin cells into stem cells that may be just as useful as the controversial embryonic cells. *See also* BIOETHICS; DOUBLE EFFECT; POLITICAL PHILOSOPHY.

STOIC ETHICS. *See* ANCIENT ETHICS.

SUBJECTIVISM. The view that "X is **good**" means "I like X." Some prefer terms like "approve" or "desire"; **David Hume** wrote of the sentiment of "approbation." More broadly, subjectivism is the view that terms like "good," "bad," "right," and "wrong" describe our feelings.

Subjectivism, unlike **cultural relativism**, preserves our freedom to form our own moral beliefs. Subjectivists concede that we get our values from society, at least initially; but eventually we have to decide whether to accept or reject these values. When we say "I like it—it is good," we are talking about our own feelings; morality is **relative** to the individual, not to society. We determine our moral principles by following our feelings.

Critics object that we can ascribe badness to things we like, as in "I like smoking but it is bad." Subjectivists reply that here we shift between evaluating the immediate satisfaction and evaluating the consequences. It would be clearer to say, "I like the immediate satisfaction that I get from smoking (= the immediate satisfaction is good); but I do not like the consequences (= the consequences are bad)."

Critics object that moral judgments make an objective claim about what is true in itself, apart from our feelings. But perhaps this objectivity is an illusion that comes from objectifying our subjective reactions. We laugh at a joke and call it "funny"—as if funniness were an objective property of things. We have a feeling of strangeness about something and call it "weird"—as if weirdness were an objective property. Similarly, we like something and call it "good"—as if goodness were an objective property instead of just our subjective reaction.

A stronger objection is that if "X is good" and "I like X" meant the same thing, then this reasoning would be valid: "I like X, therefore X is good." So we could validly reason: "I like getting drunk and hurting people, therefore this is good." And Nazis could validly reason: "I like killing Jews, therefore this is good." But such reasoning seems not to be valid; the conclusion seems not to follow.

Critics object that subjectivism gives a crude approach to morality since feelings may be ignorant or biased; subjectivism does not tell us how to develop wise and responsible feelings. The view also gives a weak basis for dealing with areas like **racism** (which would be good if we liked it) and **moral education** (where children would presumably be taught to follow their feelings, which may be very immature).

Critics say that subjectivism seems plausible because what we like tends to correspond with what we think is good. Subjectivism explains this: calling something "good" just means that we like it. But other explanations are possible. For example, perhaps we tend to be motivated to like what our minds discover (through reason or religion) to be good; so other views can explain the rough connection between what we like and what we think is good. Sometimes the correspondence may fail; we may like things that we think are bad, such as hurting other people. Morality is supposed to constrain our feelings. The thought that hurting others is bad can keep us from doing it, even though we would like to do it. So we cannot identify what is good with what we like. Many philosophers today with subjectivist tendencies move to **emotivism, J. L.** Mackie's *error theory*, or **ideal observer theory.** Some use "subjectivism" in a wider sense to include views like the first two; they would call the view considered in this entry "classical subjectivism." *See also* AESTHETICS; KNOWING RIGHT FROM WRONG; MOORE, G. E.; NATURALISM; REID, THOMAS.

SUICIDE. The intentional **killing** of oneself to obtain some self-interested goal. The main issues treated here are which acts count as instances of suicide and whether suicide is morally permissible.

Clear cases of suicide include killing oneself intentionally by shooting, hanging, or poison to avoid illness, depression, shame, or capture by the police. It is not suicide if I kill myself unintentionally by negligence—perhaps by not properly mounting my bicycle's front tire, which then falls off and leads to my death. Nor is it suicide if I jump on a grenade to save my platoon; I use my body to shield others from the explosion, but I do not do this in order to bring about my own death.

Other cases are less clear. Did **Socrates** commit suicide when he drank the hemlock, which he was sentenced to do after being convicted of corrupting the youth of Athens? Some say it was suicide, though morally justified, while others say it was not suicide since Socrates did not choose to end his life. Does a person who commits a crime in order to be killed by the police commit suicide? Some look to the intention and say yes, while others look to the immediate cause and say no. Is physician-assisted suicide (whereby the patient triggers a death mechanism set up by the physician) suicide, or **euthanasia**, or both? Does a suicide bomber in time of **war** commit suicide (his goal is to destroy the enemy and not to bring about his own death)?

Many oppose suicide on religious grounds. **Medieval** philosophers such as **Augustine** and **Thomas Aquinas** see suicide as a sin, as violating the **natural law** that **God** has implanted in our minds, which tells us that human life is sacred and that the direct killing of an innocent human being (including oneself) is seriously wrong. In the **modern** era, **John Locke** adopts a similar view based on property **rights**; since God gave us life, our lives belong to him, and so suicide is wrong because it destroys God's property. Other religious people see death as the final summing up our life in faith and love, and as a purification (often through suffering) to prepare for the afterlife; suicide would violate this crucial moment of our life's journey toward God.

The **ancient** philosopher **Plato** condemns most suicides as cowardly acts that hurt the community; but in rare cases a suicide could be virtuous, as was Socrates's drinking of the hemlock or killing oneself out of shame for immoral acts. **Aristotle** similarly argues that suicide harms society, which needs our contributions, and that it is a vice to inflict such harm. These views, which emphasize the interests of the community over those of the individual, give communitarian grounds for the wrongness of suicide (*see* **liberalism/communitarianism**).

Immanuel Kant argues that suicide is immoral because it violates the *categorical imperative*. We ought to act only on a maxim that we can will to be universal law of nature. But the maxim to end our life when it brings us more pain than satisfaction could not exist as a consistent law of nature—since the very feeling that impels us to promote living would then destroy life. Also, we should treat humanity, whether in ourselves or in another, as an end-in-itself and not only as a means. But if we destroy ourselves to avoid pain, we use persons merely as a means to maintain a tolerable life; but persons must always be treated as ends-in-themselves.

Many ethicists argue that suicide is morally permissible in some or all cases. **David Hume** criticizes Aquinas's argument against suicide on two grounds. First, he argued that the existence of God, which the argument assumes, cannot be proved and is a superstition. Second, he argues that Aquinas's appeal to natural law is inconsistent; if committing suicide violates God's natural plan, then why does it not violate God's plan when we fight diseases?

Utilitarians counter the communitarian argument by pointing out that only in some cases does a suicide clearly harm the community (as when a parent's suicide leaves children as orphans); the suicide of an elderly person who is a drain on resources may not harm the community in any obvious way. Utilitarians see suicide as justified when it promotes the greatest balance of **happiness** over misery. **John Stuart Mill** goes further in his *harm principle*, which says that society is not justified in interfering with the acts of competent adults unless those acts harm someone else. To control individuals for their own good is **paternalistic**, violates our **autonomy**, and produces a less happy society. By the harm principle, society ought not to interfere with or condemn a suicide unless this suicide would harm another (for example, by leaving children as orphans).

Libertarian philosophers (*see* **Robert Nozick** and **Ayn Rand**) go further in arguing for the moral permissibility of suicide. They argue that our bodies belong to us and that we have the right to do with them what we please so long as we do not violate the rights of others. So I am morally permitted to commit suicide anytime I wish, but I cannot do so by, say, intentionally driving my car into oncoming traffic.

Some ethicists, while they think that suicide often is morally permissible, do not want to go as far as the harm principle or the libertarian view. They think that suicide is morally permissible (and should be allowed by society) for autonomous people, but that society should discourage people from killing themselves in cases where, for example, they are less than rational in their thinking (perhaps because of temporary pain or depression) or because they are pressured by family members (who want to avoid the burden of caring for a sick person).

There are many attitudes about suicide in the West, and many more in the non-Western world. These reveal much about wider differences on religion, duties, individual **rights**, and community interests. *See also* BIOETHICS; DOUBLE EFFECT.

SUPEREROGATORY. Beyond what duty requires. To act in a supererogatory fashion is to do more than what one is required to do. Such acts often are more **praiseworthy** than those that merely conform to duty. One who walks down the street without killing others does not receive much praise; however, one who risks life and limb by rushing into a burning building to save a trapped person is praised as a hero. Supererogatory acts can come at great risk to life, as in the previous example, but they need not; for example, one who takes the "first step" to reconcile with a former friend who has acted wrongly acts in a supererogatory fashion. Act **utilitarianism** is sometimes criticized as leaving no room for supererogatory actions; on this view, our duty is always to do what has the best results.

SUPERNATURALISM. *See* DIVINE COMMAND THEORY; NATURAL LAW.

SUPERVENIENCE. Dependence. To say that "**good**" *supervenes* on non-moral properties means that whether something is good depends on its non-moral properties; so we cannot judge A to be good and B not to be good unless we think A and B differ in their non-moral properties. We arrive at the **universalizability** principle if we add that these non-moral properties must be "universal" in the sense of being expressible without proper names (like "Gensler," "Chicago," or "IBM") or pointer words (like "I," "this," or "now").

Some areas besides ethics use the notion of supervenience. Many say that mental qualities (like feeling warm) *supervene* on the physical state of one's body; this claim need not involve a reduction of mental concepts or properties to physical concepts or properties. Other supervenience claims involve beauty, causality, probability, or entailment.

– T –

TAOIST ETHICS. *See* DAOIST ETHICS.

TELEOLOGICAL ETHICS. Sometimes this term is used as equivalent to **consequentialism**, the view that we ought always to do whatever maximizes **good** consequences. Sometimes it is used more broadly to cover any view that bases our duty on some good to be achieved, such as the view, sometimes attributed to **Aristotle**, that we ought always to do whatever would most promote our **virtue**.

TERRORISM. Violence against property or persons which uses fear and intimidation to achieve political, social, or religious goals. While there is some unclarity about the concept, terrorism is usually distinguished from **war**; the latter involves a more widespread battle between armies, navies, or air forces.

Some say that terrorism must involve *unjustified* violence or goals; this makes terrorism wrong by definition. On this usage, we call "terrorist" only what we disapprove of; but then, as political pundits sometimes quip, "one person's terrorist is another person's freedom fighter." Many Americans saw Osama Bin Laden as a "freedom fighter" when he tried to drive the Soviets out of Afghanistan but as a "terrorist" when he engineered the 11 September 2001 attack on New York and Washington to drive the U.S. out of Saudi Arabia. Similarly, our moral attitudes may influence whether we label as "terrorist" the bombing of a clinic that performs **abortion**s, suicide bombers in a Baghdad market filled with U.S. personnel, or the 1995 bombing of the Federal Building in Oklahoma City to protest the growing reach of federal government.

Some say that terrorism by definition must target *innocent civilians*. On this definition, the 11 September attack on the (civilian) World

Trade Center was terrorism while the attack on the (military) Pentagon was not. Complications can arise about who is considered "innocent." People who worked at the World Trade Center might be considered as collaborators with the U.S. government, even if they oppose that government's activities; and people who work at a clinic that performs abortions might be thought to collaborate in the abortions, even if they personally oppose abortion. Critics object that this strategy would make almost everyone into a "collaborator" of some sort and thus excuse violations of human **rights** on flimsy grounds.

For the rest of this entry, we will assume a morally neutral definition of terrorism that does not assume that the violence or goals are unjustified. So defined, is terrorism ever morally permissible?

Utilitarians and other **consequentialists** hold that terrorist acts are morally permissible if they maximize the total balance of good consequences; a terrorist **killing** of innocent civilians might topple an oppressive regime and thus maximize good consequences. But many utilitarians object that such cases rarely, if ever, exist; either the imagined gains will not outweigh the loss of innocent life, or there will be less brutal alternatives that would bring about the desirable goals.

Many non-consequentialists see terrorism that kills innocent persons as always wrong (*see* **double effect, end-justifies-means**, and **exceptionless duties**). Following **Immanuel Kant**, they might argue that such terrorism treats people as mere means rather than as ends-in-themselves. Or they might see such terrorism as violating personal **autonomy**, the **golden rule**, the **sanctity of human life**, or the basic human right to life.

Some non-consequentialists see terrorism, even of a kind that kills innocent human life, as morally permissible when needed to avoid disaster in extreme and unusual cases. Imagine a case where the Nazi genocide of six million Jews could have been prevented by killing the young and still innocent Adolph Hitler (whom we foresee will become an evil dictator) or by killing some of the adult Hitler's children and threatening to kill the others unless the genocide is stopped. Some non-consequentialists would approve of killing the innocent in such cases since the gain to humanity would be so great. But critics object that killing the innocent to promote some good often backfires (and does not bring about the intended good) and may instead lead us down a slippery slope into a moral chaos, where routinely killing innocent people becomes a way to promote political goals.

While ethicists universally reject the great majority of the terrorism that occurs in the world today, they differ in the principles and arguments to which they appeal. *See also* GLOBAL ETHICS; PRIVACY.

THEOLOGICAL VOLUNTARISM. *See* DIVINE COMMAND THEORY.

TRUTH, MORAL. *See* COGNITIVISM/NON-COGNITIVISM.

TWENTIETH-CENTURY ETHICS. The analytic tradition in 20th-century ethics divides instructively, but with some oversimplification, into three periods. The first period, from about 1903 to 1936, focused on **intuitionism** and normative ethics (*see* **ethics: normative**). The second, from about 1936 to 1971, narrowed ethics to a discussion of moral language. The third, since about 1971, has been very diverse. There also are other traditions, most notably the continental tradition.

(1) Most analytic accounts begin 20th-century ethics with **G. E. Moore**'s *Principia Ethica* (1903). Moore argued that traditional ethics was flawed by attempts to define "**good**" in empirical or **metaphysical** terms; such definitions commit the *naturalistic fallacy* of confusing evaluative with non-evaluative notions. "Good" is not the same as "desired" or "pleasant" or "socially accepted"; instead, "good" is one of the many ideas that cannot be defined using other ideas. Since ethics is not analyzable empirically, its basic principles must be known by intuition; it is self-evident that various kinds of things (not just pleasure) are intrinsically good and that our duty is to do what maximizes the intrinsic goodness in the world (**utilitarianism**).

While most British ethicists for a time followed Moore's intuitionism, many came to disagree with his utilitarianism. H. A. Prichard's "Does Moral Philosophy Rest on a Mistake?" (1912) argued that duties can be as self-evident as the goodness of consequences. **W. D. Ross**'s *The Right and the Good* (1930) argued that we sometimes ought to keep a promise even when it has slightly better total consequences to break it; he defended a set of self-evident **prima facie duties**.

Over time, Moore's clarity and originality were questioned; his intuitionism was seen as part of a long trend in British ethics and similar to that of **modern** and **nineteenth-century** thinkers such as **Thomas Reid** and **Henry Sidgwick**. In the U.S., which was slow to join the analytic camp, empirical ethics still dominated, as with the pragmatists William James, **John Dewey**, **C. I. Lewis**, and Ralph Perry; Perry's *General Theory of Value* (1926) defined "good" as "the object of a positive interest (desire)" and "right action" as "action that promotes a harmony of interests." Bertrand Russell gave up Moore's intuitionism when the American George Santayana criticized its absolutizing of moral intuitions. As time passed, many thinkers became increasingly skeptical about moral intuitions, which seemed to vary so much. (2) **A. J. Ayer**'s *Language, Truth and Logic* (1936) saw ethics as emotional: "X is good" means "Hurrah for X!" There is no ethical truth or ethical knowledge; there are only ethical feelings. The sole function of moral philosophy is to tell us that moral concepts are unanalyzable pseudo-concepts; so moral philosophy was narrowed to moral language, an emphasis that dominated for decades. Charles Stevenson's *Ethics and Language* (1944) later gave a more detailed analysis of ethical language from the **emotivist** perspective.

Ayer accepted **logical positivism**, a "**science** is everything" view that claimed that any genuine truth claim has to be either analytic (true by definition) or empirically testable. This eliminated Moore's self-evident ethical principles, which were neither analytic nor empirically testable. Even though logical positivism has long since died, abandoned even by Ayer, anti-rationalism in ethics remains strong and few appeal to considerations that are not either analytic or empirical.

Ludwig Wittgenstein, although not an ethicist, deeply influenced 20th-century ethics. At first, he had a narrow view of language: only **mathematical** and scientific language was legitimate. While this led him to a mystical view of ethics (which is said to be transcendental and beyond language), it led the positivists to emotivism. Wittgenstein later came to see as legitimate a wide variety of "language games." This led several ethicists to go beyond emotivism and to see ethical language as part of its own language game, with its own rules:

- Stephen Toulmin's *An Examination of the Place of Reason in Ethics* (1950) gave a rule-utilitarian analysis of moral language;
- **R. M. Hare**'s *The Language of Morals* (1952) saw moral judgments as prescriptions or imperatives (like "Do this");
- Roderick Firth's "Ethical Absolutism and the Ideal Observer" (1952) gave an **ideal-observer** analysis of moral predicates;
- **Philippa Foot**'s "Moral Arguments" (1958) argued for naturalistic constraints on what could count as "good" or "moral";
- Kurt Baier's *The Moral Point of View* (1958) gave a *rationalized attitudes* approach to moral beliefs (*see* **knowing right from wrong**); and
- **William Frankena**'s *Ethics* (1963) moderated emotivism with

Baier's ideas and claimed that ideally rational individuals would agree on all their moral beliefs.

So moral language came to be seen as having its own logic, which was more complex than a simple "Boo!" or "Hurrah!" Nazi moral atrocities committed during this period had little impact on analytic moral philosophy, which focused narrowly on moral language. But eventually philosophers broadened their interests to substantive moral issues. Hare's *Freedom and Reason* (1963) pointed in the new direction. While ethics was still about analyzing language, its goal was to give us tools to think better about moral issues, tools like **universalizability** and the **golden rule**, which Hare applied to **racism** (which **Martin Luther King** was then confronting too).

(3) Two events in 1971 pointed to an expansion of interest. First, **John Rawls**'s *A Theory of Justice* used **social contract** notions to attack utilitarianism and defend **liberal** ideas about human **rights** and the distribution of wealth. Rawls's Harvard colleague **Robert Nozick** soon published an opposing libertarian view. Then **Alasdair MacIntyre** and other communitarians criticized both for overemphasizing individual rights. Since then, there has been much discussion of **justice, political philosophy**, and rights (*see* **Ronald Dworkin**).

That same year, the first volume of *Philosophy and Public Affairs* appeared, with articles on **applied ethics** by ethicists such as **Richard Brandt**, Baruch Brody, R. M. Hare, **Thomas Nagel, Peter Singer**, and Judith Jarvis Thomson. Applied ethics grew quickly, covering areas like **abortion, animal rights, bioethics, business ethics, environmental ethics, killing, moral education, poverty, sexism**, and **war**.

There also was a renewed interest in utilitarianism. Richard Brandt's *Ethical Theory* (1959) introduced the terms "act utilitarianism" and "rule utilitarianism." J. J. C. Smart and **Bernard Williams**'s *Utilitarianism: For and Against* (1973) debated the view. Peter Singer's *Animal Liberation* (1972) and *Practical Ethics* (1979) applied utilitarianism to many practical issues, including animal rights and infanticide. R. M. Hare's *Moral Thinking* (1981) defended *preference utilitarianism* and a higher synthesis between act and rule utilitarianism. Utilitarianism continues to be widely defended and widely criticized.

Lawrence Kohlberg, a **psychologist** unhappy with the **relativism** of many social scientists (see **Ruth Benedict** and **cultural relativism**), did research to support the idea that humans naturally develop toward higher forms of moral reasoning. He concluded that people, regardless of culture, develop in their moral thinking through a series of six stages; we all as young children begin thinking of morality in terms of **punishment** and reward, and we gradually move toward a purer justice perspective. On the other hand, **Carol Gilligan**'s *In a Different Voice* (1982) claimed, against Kohlberg, that there are *two* mature ways to think about morality: justice and caring. Men tend to think of morality in terms of justice, principles, rights, and duties; women tend instead to appeal to caring, feelings, personal relationships, and responsibilities. This launched much debate and the rapid growth of **feminist ethics**.

J. L. Mackie's *Ethics: Inventing Right and Wrong* (1977) encouraged the rethinking of questions about the nature of value. While admitting that moral language asserts independent moral facts, Mackie argued that there are no such moral facts; so all moral judgments are false. That same year, **Gilbert Harman**'s *The Nature of Morality* attacked moral facts on the grounds that we need not assume them to explain people's experiences and moral beliefs. There followed much debate about **moral realism** and the existence of moral facts. Some accepted moral facts while others rejected them; still others argued that moral facts exist in a manner of speaking. Richard Brandt's *A Theory of the Good and the Right* (1979) contended that moral concepts were confused and need replacement rather than analysis; he proposed a definition of "rational desire" that would replace "good" and not presuppose any preexisting moral facts.

Elizabeth Anscombe's "Modern Moral Philosophy" (1958), Philippa Foot's *Virtues and Vices* (1978), and Alasdair MacIntyre's *After Virtue* (1981) promoted an "ethics of **virtue**" that defined itself in opposition to an "ethics of duty." While this new movement at first tended to follow **Aristotle** closely, later authors included elements from **Immanuel Kant, David Hume**, or **Frederich Nietzsche**.

Issues of **global ethics** grew in importance because of increasing globalization and because the solution to many problems (such as global warming, war, **terrorism**, international business, and the regulation of the Internet) was seen to depend on a wide cooperation between people from all over the globe. A central issue is whether it is possible to have a consensus across the globe about core values.

Other frequently addressed topics include (among many others):

- social cooperation, especially between **egoists** (*see* **Kenneth Arrow, prisoner's dilemma**, and **Ayn Rand**);
- the evolutionary origins of ethics in **sociobiology** (investigated by

thinkers such as Robert Trivers and Edward Wilson);
- Kantian approaches (Harry Gensler, Alan Gewirth, Barbara Herman, Christine Korsgaard, and Onora O'Neill);
- **natural law** approaches (Elizabeth Anscombe, Alan Donagan, **John Finnis**, and Peter Geach);
- **divine command** approaches (Robert Adams, John Hare, George Mavrodes, and Philip Quinn);
- ethical implications of Humean views of the self (**Darek Parfit**);
- the Humean idea that **ought**-judgments are inherently motivational (a view called "motivational internalism");
- conceptions of the good; and
- how to understand and justify **rationality** and **impartiality**, which many held to be central to moral beliefs.

These issues often connect in complex ways. This book's bibliography and chronology give a more detailed picture of current interests.

This dictionary emphasizes the analytic tradition that has been dominant in English-speaking countries in the 20th century. Continental philosophy, dominant on the continent of Europe, also has produced much ethical thinking; here are a few examples:

- Phenomenologists **Franz Brentano**, Nicolai Hartmann, and Max Scheler based ethics on emotions, which they saw as being correct or incorrect in a basic, unanalyzable way; something is intrinsically good if it is correct to have positive emotions toward it for its own sake. Like Moore, these thinkers rejected naturalistic definitions of "good" and claimed that we know facts about what is intrinsically good by intuition, not by proof.
- Atheistic existentialists Albert Camus, **Simone de Beauvoir**, and **Jean-Paul Sartre** rejected moral facts and struggled about how to live in an absurd world devoid of inherent moral significance. Like non-**cognitivists** of the analytic tradition, they thought we must create our own values.
- Jewish thinkers **Martin Buber** and Emmanuel Levinas based ethics on our encounter with the Other: the *finite Thou* of our neighbor and the *infinite Thou* of **God**. With Buber, we can have either an *I-It* relationship with our neighbor (where we regard the other as a thing to be used) or an *I-Thou* relationship (where we enter into deeper communication and appreciation).
- The Christian thinker **Paul Ricoeur** focused on the interpretation

of texts. His *Oneself as Another* connects our self-identity with the narratives we create about ourselves, where we see ourselves as if we were another person. The heart of morality is to see another as oneself, which involves the golden rule.

- Political thinkers **Simone Weil** and **Hannah Arendt** reflected on the evils of Nazi totalitarianism. Weil based values on God and claimed that every human being is sacred and deserves respect. Arendt wrote of the "banality of evil": Nazis committed atrocities not out of hatred but in an unthinking, conformist way, whereby they isolated themselves from thinking morally about the human significance of their actions.

- **Jürgen Habermas** and other critical theorists gave an interdisciplinary analysis of society, economics, and culture, often using **Karl Marx**. Habermas criticized views that reject ethical truths and ethical rationality; he based ethics on Kantian rational discourse, whereby people discuss issues in an **informed**, impartial, **consistent**, and free manner. This is a social version of the *rationalized attitudes* approach used by many analytic thinkers.

The rigid wall separating the analytic and continental traditions in ethics is beginning to break down.

– U –

UNIVERSAL LAW, FORMULA OF. *See* KANT, IMMANUEL.

UNIVERSALIZABILITY. The principle that what is right (wrong, **good**, bad, etc.) in one case is also right (wrong, good, bad, etc.) in any exactly or relevantly similar case, regardless of the individuals involved.

While universalizability is widely accepted, some think it useless. They complain that (1) in the actual world, no two acts are exactly similar in all their properties; (2) universalizability lets us appeal to trivial differences between cases (as in "It is permissible for me to steal from you, but wrong for you to steal from me, because I have six toes and you do not"); and (3) universalizability lets any properties be morally relevant (as in "Everyone with black skin ought to be enslaved").

Defenders see universalizability as useful in testing our **consistency** and **impartiality**, and this in three ways. (1) While admitting that no two acts in the actual world are *exactly similar*, they suggest that we consider exactly similar *hypothetical cases* where we switch in our **imagination** the roles that the individuals play. By universalizability, if I ought to enslave X, then in the exactly reversed situation X ought to enslave me. I am inconsistent and violate impartiality if I accept the former but reject the latter. For the "exactly reversed situation," I could switch all the properties in my imagination, or just the morally relevant properties, or just those that I think are or might be morally relevant.

(2) If you say "It is permissible for me to steal from you because I have six toes," you need to imagine a hypothetical case where someone else has six toes and you do not; in this case, would it be permissible for the other person to steal from you? It is not so easy to invent relevant differences. We can appeal only to factors of which we are aware; and a factor claimed to be morally relevant must be regarded as such regardless of which side has it or is imagined to have it.

(3) If you say "Everyone with black skin ought to be enslaved," you need to imagine a hypothetical case where *you* have black skin; do you think *you* ought to be enslaved in this case? You might consider **R. M. Hare**'s story about the germ that switches everyone's skin color permanently. And you might see if you believe that Caucasians with dark tans ought to be enslaved—and that Albino blacks ought to be free.

Philosophers disagree about how to justify universalizability. Perhaps this principle is built into the meaning of "**ought**" and other moral terms (Hare), or is self-defeating to violate if we want to influence the feelings of others (the **emotivist** Charles Stevenson). Or perhaps it and the corresponding duty to be impartial are based on social conventions (**cultural relativism**), God's will (**divine command theory**), the will of an **ideal observer**, or our own feelings (**subjectivism** or emotivism). Or perhaps universalizability and impartiality help society by promoting a more neutral standpoint for settling disputes (**utilitarianism**).

We can formulate universalizability as the claim that the moral status of an act depends on the act's *universal properties*; if act A ought to be done, then act A has some set of universal properties S, such that any act with set S of properties, even in hypothetical cases, also ought to be done. Here a "universal property" is a non-evaluative property expressible without proper names (like "Gensler," "Chicago," or "IBM") or pointer words (like "I," "this," or "now"). Suppose I am tempted to steal Earl's new notebook computer. The possible act of my stealing Earl's computer has several properties or characteristics; for example, it is *wrong* (evaluative term), an act of stealing *Earl's* computer (proper name), and something *I* would be doing (pointer word).

These properties are not universal since they involve evaluative terms, proper names, or pointer words. But the act also has properties that are universal; for example, it is an act of stealing a new computer from one's neighbor, an act whose agent has blue eyes, and an act that would greatly distress the computer's owner. Universalizability holds that the morality of an act depends on its universal properties—like those of the second group—properties expressible without evaluative terms, proper names, or pointer words. *See also* BIBLICAL ETHICS; GOLDEN RULE; KANT, IMMANUEL; INFORMATION; KNOWING RIGHT FROM WRONG; LOGIC; NAGEL, THOMAS; SIDGWICK, HENRY; SOCIOBIOLOGY; SUPERVENIENCE.

UTILITARIANISM. The general view that we **ought** always to do whatever maximizes the sum-total of **good** consequences for everyone. Utilitarianism differs from **egoism**, another **consequentialist** approach, by having us consider the sum-total of everyone's good, not just our own good. Much practical thinking, especially in areas like politics and economics, is broadly utilitarian in nature.

Classical (hedonistic) utilitarianism, the simplest and historically most important form of utilitarianism, holds that we ought always to do whatever maximizes the balance of pleasure over pain for everyone affected by our action. Classical utilitarians accept a hedonistic theory of value, that the only thing good in itself is pleasure and the avoidance of pain; they often use "**happiness**" as synonymous with "pleasure." They defend utilitarianism in various ways—as, for example, being **intuitively** self-evident or based on **benevolent** feelings (*see* **emotivism**) or God's will (*see* **divine command theory**). They think their view gives a simple and flexible way to determine all our duties, accords with enlightened and benevolent moral thinking, and corrects the vagueness and inconsistencies of commonsense ethics.

While utilitarians seek to maximize the total good, they often argue that this is more likely to be achieved by spreading out wealth more equally. The reason for this is the *diminishing marginal utility* of money; as we get richer, each extra dollar makes less difference to how well we live. So it would likely bring about more total good if A and B both had $5000 than if A had $9500 and B had $500.

Classical utilitarians apply their view in two ways, either directly or indirectly. To apply the view *directly*, first determine your options; suppose you could do A or B. Then estimate, as best you can, the likely pleasure-and-pain consequences of each option on each of the affected parties. If we could put pleasures and pains into numerical units, using positive numbers for pleasure and negative numbers for pains, we could put the result into a table and then go with the highest total:

	Option A	Option B
Tom	+1	−3
Dick	−3	+1
Harry	+4	+5
Total	+2	+3

Utilitarianism says to do B.

In practice, since we do not know how to put numbers on pleasure and pain, we just weigh them in our minds and judge intuitively which option maximizes the balance of pleasure over pain. Since it is so difficult to know future consequences, some suggest we formulate utilitarianism in terms of what *probably* would maximize good consequences.

Reasoning through every choice in this direct way would be impractical and would not produce good consequences. For routine choices, it is more useful to apply utilitarianism *indirectly*, by using "rules of thumb" about what kinds of action tend to have good or bad results. Stealing, for example, tends to have bad results; so, unless circumstances are peculiar, it is best to assume that we ought not to steal. Direct utilitarian calculations are useful when we make important decisions, when the ordinary rules conflict (as when we can help a needy person only by breaking a promise), when we decide which rules to use, or when circumstances are so unusual that we doubt that following the ordinary rules will lead to the best consequences. Any moral rule should be broken when it has better consequences to do so.

Critics say classical utilitarianism is difficult or impossible to apply. Beliefs about future consequences are mostly guesswork, and we cannot really measure and sum pleasures and pains. So the view easily leads to rationalizations where we talk ourselves into thinking that some self-serving action has "the best consequences for everyone."

Critics also say classical utilitarianism has implications that are so bizarre that the view is difficult to hold **consistently**. The view entails, for example, that we are justified in **killing** an innocent person whenever this even slightly maximizes the balance of pleasure over pain. Imagine cases where you could do this by (1) secretly killing your wealthy but sickly father and donating his money to buy a park for poor children, or (2) sentencing an innocent person to death for a crime in order to discourage **terrorism**, or (3) lynching an innocent person to promote the pleasure of the coliseum crowd. Utilitarianism goes against our intuitions by permitting any harm to the individual that even slightly maximizes the balance of pleasure over pain.

Classical utilitarians respond to such cases in three ways. (1) They might deny that such cases are possible; they might claim that bad remote consequences (for example, the encouragement of future killings that do not maximize good consequences) always make it wrong to kill the innocent in cases like those described above. (2) They might "bite the bullet" and accept the implausible implications of their view; they might add that utilitarianism's implications seem implausible only because they go against arbitrary, traditional rules that we have been taught and that structure our moral intuitions. (3) They might try to modify utilitarianism to avoid the objections; perhaps a rule-utilitarian approach (explained later) with a non-hedonistic theory of value would give us a more credible form of utilitarianism.

Philosophers have developed many varieties of utilitarianism. **G. E. Moore**'s *ideal utilitarianism* holds that we ought to maximize good consequences, but it takes "good consequences" in a non-hedonistic way; various things—like knowledge, **virtue**, friendship, freedom, life, achievement, the experience of beauty, and perhaps the unexperienced existence of beautiful things—are good in themselves and ought to be promoted. **John Stuart Mill**'s approach is intermediate between this and classical utilitarianism; he thought that, while only pleasures are intrinsically good, higher pleasures (like those of poetry) count more than lower pleasures (like those of the mindless pushpin game). **R. M. Hare** and **Peter Singer** hold *preference utilitarianism*, that we ought to maximize as far as possible the satisfaction of everyone's desires. Utilitarians often use the generic terms "utility" or "interests" for what is to be maximized (which varies between theories).

Some propose that we try to maximize the *average* instead of the *total* utility. They object that "maximize total utility" could support adding millions of minimally happy individuals to get a higher total happiness, but that this would be undesirable. Critics object that "maximize average utility" could support killing individuals who are less happy than average, which would increase the average happiness, but that this would be immoral.

When we try to maximize good consequences for everyone, does this "everyone" include just humans, or does it also include **animals** (*see* **moral patient**)? If we include just humans, then our utilitarianism could approve of any cruelty to animals so long as this did not negatively impact humans. But if we include both humans and animals, then the pain of a mouse would count as much as an equal pain of a human being. Both alternatives seem extreme.

So far, we have considered various forms of *act utilitarianism*, that we ought to do the ACT with the best consequences for everyone. This contrasts with *rule utilitarianism*, which in its perhaps most plausible form says we ought to do the act that would be prescribed by the RULES with the best consequences for people to accept. Rule utilitarianism takes a two-step approach to determining our duty. First, we ask which rules (or policies) would have the best consequences for people, with their imperfections and limitations, to accept. Second, we apply these rules to our action. Consider the example of killing innocent human beings. Act utilitarianism, as noted above, holds that this is permissible in individual cases where it would bring about slightly better consequences. Rule utilitarianism, in contrast, asks what rules about killing would have the best consequences for people to accept. Consider these two possible rules about killing:

(1)   Killing another human being is strictly wrong, with perhaps exceptions for a few carefully defined cases (like self-defense).
(2)   Killing another human being is right if it has the best consequences.

Rule utilitarians would be afraid to live in a society that followed rule (2), where people could kill whenever they speculated that this would have better results; people would sometimes apply this in irresponsible ways with disastrous effects. They say it would have much better results if society followed a strict rule against killing, like (1). So they hold that rule utilitarianism brings guidelines about killing that are stricter and harmonize better with common sense.

Act utilitarians accuse rule utilitarianism of rule worship; why, they ask, should we follow a rule when violating it would have better consequences? Rule utilitarians respond that a society that followed strict rules against killing, like rule (1) above, would prosper better than a society where people followed a looser "rule of thumb" about killing, like rule (2) above, which lets people kill whenever they speculate that killing would have better consequences.

Rule utilitarians argue that their view gives a good synthesis of consequentialism and non-consequentialism and could incorporate many non-consequentialist principles like those of **W. D. Ross**. But some non-consequentialists object that rule utilitarianism, even if it generally leads to the right judgments, does so for the wrong reasons. They contend that killing innocent people is *wrong in itself*, and not just wrong because it happens to be socially useful to have a rule against it. While the various forms of utilitarianism sketched here apply to the rightness and wrongness of *actions*, similar forms apply to **virtue**. An act-utilitarian approach might describe a *virtuous person* as one who habitually acts to maximize good consequences for society and who takes moral rules as rules of thumb; and a rule-utilitarian approach might describe a *virtuous person* as one who seriously follows those moral habits about specific areas (like killing and telling the truth) that are most socially useful for people to have. Thus we can have act and rule forms of *trait utilitarianism*.

There is much more to be said for and against these various views. Utilitarianism has been much debated over several centuries and will continue to be debated in the future.

Important utilitarians not mentioned earlier in this entry include **Jeremy Bentham**, **Richard Brandt**, Richard Cumberland, John Gay, Francis Hutcheson, **James Mill**, Marcus Singer, J. J. C. Smart, and **Henry Sidgwick**. Critics include **Ronald Dworkin**, **Immanuel Kant**, David Lyons, **Derek Parfit**, **John Rawls**, W. D. Ross, and **Bernard Williams**. *See also* ABORTION; CAPITAL PUNISHMENT; DECISION THEORY; DOUBLE EFFECT; END-JUSTIFIES-MEANS; EXCEPTIONLESS DUTIES; FEMINIST ETHICS; GILLIGAN, CAROL; GOLDEN RULE; HUME, DAVID; IMPARTIALITY; JUSTICE; KOHLBERG, LAWRENCE; LOVE YOUR NEIGHBOR; MATHEMATICS; NATURAL LAW; POVERTY; PUNISHMENT; RIGHTS; SOCIOBIOLOGY; SUICIDE; SUPEREROGATORY; UNIVERSALIZABILITY; WAR.

UTILITY. *See* DECISION THEORY; GOOD; UTILITARIANISM.

– V –

VALUE. *See* GOOD.

VEIL OF IGNORANCE. *See* RAWLS, JOHN.

VIRTUE. A good habit (or disposition) to act and feel in certain ways. While virtue was important from ancient times, it has received a new emphasis with the recent "virtue ethics" movement.

Socrates began Western moral philosophy with questions like "What is virtue?"; he taught people to seek virtue and wisdom above self-interest. **Plato** thought the **good** life was characterized by four cardinal virtues: *wisdom* is excellence in thought and reason, *temperance* is control of appetites and impulses, *courage* is control of spirit and will, and *justice* is the correct ordering of the parts of the soul, whereby thought and reason guide the other parts.

Aristotle saw a virtue as an excellence of our rational powers; there are *intellectual virtues* (about thinking) and *moral virtues* (about acting). A virtue is a mean between vices of excess and deficiency; for example, bravery falls between the vices of foolhardiness (too much confidence) and cowardice (too little confidence). The mean is determined by practical reason, which determines the proper means to our end of **happiness**. The good and happy life is to live according to the virtues, which are instilled by practice. The **ancient** Stoics agreed that the good and happy life is one of virtue, which they saw as the following of the **natural moral law** that is accessible to human reason.

Thomas Aquinas, the great **medieval** thinker, built his ethics on Aristotle, with additions from Christianity. Aquinas distinguished *natural virtues* (which promote our natural happiness) from *supernatural virtues* (which promote our supernatural happiness of eternal life with **God**). The natural virtues are wisdom (prudence), courage, temperance, and justice (fairness). The supernatural virtues are faith (believing in God and in what he revealed), hope (emotionally trusting in God and his promises), and love (unselfishly striving to serve God and do good and not harm to his creatures); the greatest of these is love.

David Hume thought that to call an act or character trait "virtuous" was to express toward it feelings of approval, especially **benevolent** feelings, which he thought were natural to humans. He distinguished *natural virtues* like benevolence, which directly promote the good of others, from *artificial virtues* like keeping promises, where a social practice promotes good.

Immanuel Kant thought the highest virtue is good will, which involves acting for the sake of duty and not, for example, for the sake of self-interest; he saw that skeptics would doubt that such "true virtue" exists in the real world. The virtue of good will is to be valued for itself, and not for the sake of what it produces. Happiness is not identical with good will since we can conceive of a bad person being happy; but good will makes us worthy of happiness. The greatest good is a combination of happiness and virtue.

John Stuart Mill thought virtue was to be valued not for its own sake but because it leads to happiness; **utilitarians** praise virtue because of its usefulness. But he admitted that once we take pleasure in virtue, as it is useful to do, virtue can become part of our happiness and thus part of the utilitarian goal. Mill emphasized the difference between virtue (which is about motivation) and the rightness of an act (which is about consequences); we can do the wrong action out of virtuous (but misguided) motives, or the right action out of bad motives.

W. D. Ross, who is a good example of a non-**consequentialist**, accepted three main intrinsic goods: virtue, knowledge, and pleasure. In accepting that virtue is of value in itself, he agreed with Kant and disagreed with Mill. Several of Ross's **prima facie duties** which are about promoting goods have implications about virtue: self-improvement has us cultivate our own virtue, beneficence has us promote virtue in others, and non-maleficence has us not lead others into vice.

Virtue received a new emphasis with **Elizabeth Anscombe**'s "Modern Moral Philosophy" (1958) and **Alasdair MacIntyre**'s *After Virtue* (1981). Both thinkers criticized the "ethics of duty" approach that focuses on moral principles and which they saw as dominating moral philosophy since the Enlightenment; they were especially critical of "duty" thinkers like Kant and Mill and their contemporary followers. They thought such views were too legalistic and ignored important aspects of the moral life such as virtues, emotions, moral character, **moral education**, and moral wisdom. They favored returning to an "ethics of virtue," which was popular in ancient and medieval thinkers, especially Aristotle and Aquinas.

Soon virtue ethics became popular among many ethicists. At first it tended to have a largely Aristotelian slant, as in the work of **Philippa Foot**, but later it became more diverse. Rosalind Hursthouse's *On Virtue Ethics* (1999), while Aristotelian, incorporates ideas from Kant. Michael Slote's *Morals from Motives* (2001) defends a virtue ethics based on Hume. Some others base their virtue ethics on **Friedrich Nietzsche**. By now, "virtue ethics" describes a diverse collection of approaches. This has encouraged a debate about the role of virtue in ethics, which includes three issues (among others).

(1) Is it historically accurate to divide figures into "duty" ethicists

(like Kant and Mill) and "virtue" ethicists (like Plato, Aristotle, and Aquinas)? Barbara Herman objects that the cold, duty-bound Kant that many virtue ethicists complain about is based on a misunderstanding and that Kant has a positive approach to virtue. Similarly, Rosalind Hursthouse argues that Kant is much closer to Aristotle than many have thought and has much to contribute to our understanding of virtue.

Others contend that practically all ethicists talk about both duty and virtue, even though their emphasis may vary, and so it is an oversimplification to divide thinkers into "duty" thinkers and "virtue" thinkers. It is enlightening to see how often five thinkers in their major works use the main words for virtue and duty; here are the word counts:

	Plato's *Republic*	Aristotle's *Nic Ethics*	Aquinas's *Summa 1a*	Kant's *Groundwork*	Mill's *Utilitarianism*
"virtue" & "virtuous"	90	263	1581	12	48
"ought," "duty," & "obligation"	119	105	176	129	89

Aquinas refers much more to virtue than to duty; but his natural-law views on duty are significant (and have been developed by followers such as **John Finnis**) and he does not denigrate the importance of duty. Kant refers much more to duty than to virtue; but his view about the intrinsic value of the virtue of good will is an integral part of his ethics and he does not denigrate the importance of virtue. Aristotle is moderately virtue-oriented, as Mill is moderately duty-oriented. Plato refers slightly more to duty than to virtue, despite the common stereotype that all ancient Greek ethicists were concerned more about virtue.

(2) Is virtue reducible to duty, or vice versa? Some say "**ought**" is more basic and "virtuous" can be **defined** in terms of "ought":

(V)   A *virtuous* person can be defined as one who has internalized the correct principles about how one ought to live. (More concretely: an *honest* person can be defined as one who has internalized the correct principles of duty about cheating.)

A defender of virtue ethics could contend that "virtue" is more basic and that "ought" can be defined in terms of "virtuous":

(O) How one *ought* to live can be defined as how a virtuous person
would live, when acting in character and with a correct understanding of the situation.

A third view is that virtue and duty are interdefinable (so both definitions work) and that neither idea is more basic. Then virtue and duty
are different sides of the same moral coin, so moral perspectives can be
expressed either as principles of action or as good character traits.

(3) Is virtue ethics a third approach to normative ethics (*see* **ethics:
normative**) besides **consequentialism** and non-consequentialism? Many
claim that (a) there are duty and virtue approaches to normative ethics,
(b) the duty approach divides into consequentialism and non-consequentialism, (c) both duty approaches are too rigid, and (d) the virtue
approach is preferable because it is more flexible.

William Frankena claims that, far from virtue ethics presenting a
third approach to normative ethics, practically any ethical belief
(including consequentialist and non-consequentialist) can be put into
either a duty or a virtue format—as either a principle about how we
ought to live or as a good character trait. Here are examples:

Duty		Virtue
One ought *always* to keep a promise.	rigid	A virtuous person *always* tries to keep a promise.
One ought to keep one's promises, other things equal.	flexible	A virtuous person tries to keep a promise unless doing so strongly conflicts with virtues like caring about what happens to others.
We ought to oppress those of other races when necessary.	**racist**	Race-pride is a virtue and should lead us to oppress other races when necessary.
One ought always to do whatever maximizes good consequences for everyone.	utilitarian	A virtuous person habitually acts to maximize good consequences for everyone, regardless of what this involves.
One ought always to do whatever maximizes good consequences for oneself.	**egoist**	A virtuous person habitually acts to maximize good consequences for oneself, regardless of what this involves.

The last example is inspired by the title of Ayn Rand's book, *The Vir-*

tue of Selfishness. We can draw a similar parallel with metaethical views (*see* **ethics: metaethics**):

Duty		Virtue
"You ought to do A" means "Hurrah for your doing A!"	**emotivism**	"A is a virtuous character trait" means "Hurrah for character trait A!"
The basic truths about duties are self-evident or somehow based on moral intuitions.	**intuitionism**	The basic truths about virtues are self-evident or somehow based on moral intuitions.
Social conventions determine right and wrong.	**cultural relativism**	Social conventions determine virtue and vice.
God's will determines right and wrong.	**divine command**	God's will determines virtue and vice.

Frankena sees duty and virtue not as rivals but as complementary aspects of morality. Principles of duty correspond to good character traits; to influence our lives, duties have to be internalized as virtues.

Despite disagreements about the relative priority of duty and virtue, recent work in the area of virtue has been invigorating for many ethicists. *See also* PRAISEWORTHY.

– W –

WAR. Armed conflict between **political** groups (either between nations or between different factions within a nation).

Is war ever morally justified? *Pacifists* say no. Most pacifists object to **killing** generally, even in self-defense, and are especially concerned about war's widespread killing. Some argue on **consequentialist** grounds that war's costs, especially in human lives, always exceed its benefits. Others argue that war violates our duty to treat others **justly** and to respect their dignity as ends-in-themselves (*see* **Immanuel Kant**). Still others object to war on religious grounds, often seeing it as violating the sanctity of human life. Pacifists believe that war's alleged benefits can be achieved better through nonviolent means, such as diplomacy and the **civil disobedience** employed by **Martin Luther King** and Mahatma Gandhi (*see* **Hindu ethics**).

Some critics object that pacifists are **free-riders** who reap society's benefits without bearing one of its greatest burdens, namely, participating in war. But many pacifists arguably bear an equivalent burden by being imprisoned, beaten, or killed for their nonviolent resistance. Many critics argue that extreme pacifism is unrealistic, since war is sometimes needed to defeat evils like Nazism.

The so-called *realism* view holds that nations do, and should, wage war when it promotes their self-interest, regardless of moral considerations. Nations exist in a lawless *state of nature* (*see* **social contract**), as described by **Thomas Hobbes**. War is inevitable since nations have competing interests but no common authority over them. Moral considerations should not factor into decisions about whether to go to war or how to wage war; so anything is permissible in war.

The influential *just war theory*, with roots in **Augustine** and **Thomas Aquinas**, discriminates between just and unjust wars, and just and unjust ways of conducting war. A just war requires several conditions. First, a *just cause* must motivate a nation's decision to go to war. This generally involves defending the rights of persons or nations; examples include resisting an attack from another nation, defending other nations from attack, or aiding those who suffer under brutal regimes. In addition, war must bring about a good *proportional* to the harm done and must be a *last resort* (no other options for ending the evil will work).

Must an actual attack occur for just cause to be present? Some say no, arguing that it is enough to have good evidence that an attack is coming; so a nation can act before its citizens suffer the harm of an attack. Others disagree, saying that waging war before an actual attack is like **punishing** people for crimes not yet committed.

Wars must be waged in a moral manner, so not just anything is permissible. Only military targets, including industries that support the war, are legitimate. Innocent civilians cannot be targeted directly, although it is not immoral if some civilians die as an unintended result of attacking a legitimate military target (*see* **double effect**). Most just-war theorists reject weapons of mass destruction, including nuclear bombs (which the U.S. used against Hiroshima and Nagasaki in Japan), chemical and biological weapons, and saturation bombing against cities (which the Allies used against Dresden in Germany); such attacks do not discriminate between military and civilian targets, and they cause too much harm to satisfy the proportionality test. In addition, prisoners of war must be treated humanely. This excludes torturing, killing, or raping prisoners, or using them for cruel experiments; international law regulates such matters. Some **utilitarian** critics, however, try to justify targeting civilians, using nuclear weapons against cities, or torturing prisoners when such methods would end a war earlier and thus save lives. Other critics say that whatever the enemy does to us is right for us to do to them. Just-war theorists reject such ideas.

Finally, peace agreements must be fair. Peace treaties should reform corrupt institutions and bring conquered countries back into the community of nations; treaties should not excessively punish conquered nations or innocent civilians. Leaders and soldiers on both sides who are suspected of war crimes should be brought to trial.

Does **terrorism** count as war? Some say yes since it is an armed conflict between political groups. Others believe terrorism is not war since it does not involve conventional armed forces. Whether or not terrorism is war, do the usual just-war considerations apply? For example, must suspected terrorists be treated humanely as prisoners of war?

Other new issues are arising. Is it right to attack an irresponsible nation that is thought to be on the verge of developing nuclear weapons (the U.S. attacked Iraq on this basis in 2003)? Is it right to attack an irresponsible nation that is committing massive genocide on its own citizens (the world did not step in to stop the 1994 genocide in Rwanda)? Many argue that greater **global** cooperation is needed for dealing with such problems. *See also* ARENDT, HANNAH; BIBLICAL ETHICS; ISLAMIC ETHICS.

WEAKNESS OF WILL (also called akrasia). Knowing what is best but choosing to do otherwise. Suppose that Cathy knows that the best thing for her to do tonight is to study for tomorrow's exam, but her friend asks her to go to a party instead. If Cathy chooses to go to the party, she suffers from weakness of will. She knows what is best, but does not have the fortitude to choose it.

Not all ethicists believe in weakness of will. **Socrates** argues that anyone who fails to do what is best suffers from ignorance. If Cathy chooses to go to the party, then she does not truly understand that studying is best. She may not understand how important the midterm is or how partying will affect her performance on the exam. Socrates thinks we cannot have full knowledge and then be controlled by forces other than knowledge.

R. M. Hare's **prescriptivism** claims that our sincere assent to "I **ought** to do A" logically requires that we act to do A if we can. This has been criticized as making weakness of will impossible. Hare responds that if we do not do A, but believe that we ought to do A, then either we are incapable (perhaps psychologically) of doing A or else we are taking "ought" to describe demands of society instead of to express our own evaluation. *See also* ARISTOTLE; CONSCIENCE.

WEIL, SIMONE (1909–1943). **Jewish** social philosopher and mystic who later gravitated toward Christianity. She had a high moral sense of the dignity of the human person, who is to be treated as an end-in-itself and not just as a means or a thing (*see* **Immanuel Kant**); on this basis, she criticized the treatment of workers, both in Western capitalistic countries and in the Soviet Union. From age five, when she would not take sugar because French soldiers in World War I did not have any, she thought it important to experience the sufferings of others. So she later worked in a factory to appreciate better the dehumanization that this brought. After serving with anarchist forces during the Spanish Civil War, she had a series of mystical experiences. After this, she wrote much about Christian themes, such as Christ's incarnation and the need for renunciation and forgiveness, and she came to base values and the dignity of the person on **God**. After the Nazi takeover of France, she went to London to work in the French Resistance. She limited her food to what the French were permitted under Nazi rule, which harmed her health and perhaps hastened her death from tuberculosis. In her last years, as part of her opposition to Nazism, she developed a comprehensive statement on the obligations that humans owe to each other. Every human being is sacred and deserving of respect; this is the basis of obligation, which is concerned with human needs, of both the body and the soul. Weil avoided the notion of human **rights**, which she saw as overly legalistic. Her many writings, most of which were published after her death, became influential in French and English social thought; they deal with themes such as social **justice**, religious life, the spiritual dehumanization of industrial society, and the terrors of the totalitarian state.

WELL-BEING. *See* GOOD.

WHY BE MORAL QUESTION. A centuries-old challenge to identify the motivation for us to act morally. Suppose we determine what is right and wrong (*see* **ethics: normative** and **ethics: metaethics**). Why should we be concerned to do what is right and avoid doing what is wrong? Why should we be moral? Often this challenge is understood as asking how being moral promotes our own **good**.

The first classic attempt to state and answer this challenge was by **Plato** in *The Republic*. Glaucon challenged **Socrates**'s views on **justice** (morality) by claiming that it is in one's interest to act unjustly (immorally) when one can do so without being discovered and punished. Glaucon used the example of the ring of Gyges, which renders the wearer invisible. Glaucon argued that there is no reason for one to act justly while wearing the ring since one can reap the benefits of unjust acts without being discovered and penalized. Socrates responded by claiming that unjust acts, whether discovered or not, damage the health of one's soul. Since it is in everyone's interest to have a healthy soul, we all have a motivation to act justly.

Many philosophers believe that Socrates's response fails since it does not explain why immoral acts damage one's soul and why it is in one's interest to have a healthy soul. **Medieval** philosophers such as **Thomas Aquinas** tried to solve these problems by appealing to **God**. One should act morally because one will be rewarded by God in the afterlife; even if others do not discover and **punish** one's unjust acts in this world, God will punish them later. **Buddhist** and **Hindu** thinkers would similarly appeal to *karma*, the idea that the good or evil that we do to others will come back upon us, now or in a future reincarnation.

Such other-worldly views fell out of favor in the West with the birth of **modern ethics** and its more worldly focus. The medieval response provided a motivation only for those who believe in God; but many are skeptical of God's existence. So many looked for a motivation to act morally that would appeal to atheists and agnostics as well.

Thomas Hobbes's *Leviathan* attempted to show that reason provides the motivation. Hobbes described "the fool" (**free rider**) as one who is prepared to act unjustly if this can be done without being discovered and without damaging society. Both conditions are important since Hobbes believed it is in one's interest to be part of a functioning society rather than the state of nature (*see* **social contract**). Hobbes argued that the fool is making an irrational gamble with little chance of success; the fool risks returning to the state of nature (which would harm everyone, including the fool) or being discovered and punished. Since we are relatively equal in mental capacities, it is unrealistic to think we will outwit everyone else.

Many reject Hobbes's response because it relies on the kind of society that he advocates: one that is governed by an absolute sovereign.

Only under such an authoritarian regime does the fool's gamble seem so likely to be discovered and severely punished. Few today, however, would advocate that kind of regime.

In *An Enquiry Concerning the Principles of Morals*, **David Hume** appealed to our feelings. He argued that most people care about their characters and cannot feel good about themselves if they act immorally. For most of us, the gains from immoral acts do not provide us with such good feelings that they override the bad feelings we would have.

Many philosophers reject Hume's response because it does not provide motivation to act morally for those who do not care about their characters. Hume admits that he cannot provide motivation to such people; some contemporary Humeans argue that it is sufficient if we can provide a motivation to act morally that holds for most people.

Many contemporary ethicists discuss this question, often from a somewhat Hobbesian or Humean perspective. **William Frankena** interprets "Why be moral?" as something like "Would we choose the moral way of life if we were *rational* in the sense of being factually **informed, consistent**, and clearheaded?" He argues that most (or perhaps all) would choose to be moral under such conditions, assuming that most (or perhaps all) have desires that are not purely **egoistic**. Even though acting morally is not always in our self-interest (since it may call upon us to make sacrifices), still it may be that we would choose it if we were rational in the required sense. *See also* CONSCIENCE; FOOT, PHILIPPA; KANT, IMMANUEL; OUGHT.

WILLIAMS, BERNARD (1929–2003). English philosopher who rejected attempts to put ethics into a systematic theory. He became Knightbridge Chair of Philosophy at Cambridge at only 38, and he served on several government committees, including one on obscenity and censorship. In protest of Margaret Thatcher's government, he left Great Britain for Berkeley in 1987. In 1990, he returned to Britain and became White's Professor of Moral Philosophy at Oxford.

Many know Williams for his *Utilitarianism: For and Against* (1973), coauthored with J. J. C. Smart. Williams rejects **utilitarianism** in part because it tries to place ethics into one systematized theory, an effort that oversimplifies and is destined to fail. Our theories ignore how humans tend to value different things, how even one person's own values can conflict, how the ethical situations we face are often beyond our control (matters of luck), and how emotions influence ethical choices. Williams is especially critical of **Kantianism**, since it tests the rightness of an action by asking whether we can will its guiding principle to become a universal law; but this abstracts from the emotions and values of the agent.

Utilitarianism faces another problem: it prescribes actions that are contrary to our **intuitions** about how we should act. Williams describes an unemployed chemist who must decide whether to accept a job in a laboratory that researches chemical weapons, which he opposes. Utilitarianism, by directing us to maximize the sum-total of good consequences for everyone, requires the scientist to take the position despite personal qualms. Since someone else will take the position if he does not, his refusal will not lessen chemical weapons research. Moreover, this job would help his family. Williams also describes a tourist who tries to stop a government official who wants to **kill** 20 inhabitants of a village to discourage political protest. The official makes this offer to the tourist: if you kill one of the villagers yourself, then the other 19 will live; if you refuse, I will kill all 20. Utilitarianism demands that the tourist kill one of the villagers since this will produce more good than refusing (only one death versus 20). Williams argues that both cases show that utilitarianism does not account for our moral intuition that we are especially **responsible** for what we do rather than for what others do. The scientist and tourist are responsible for choosing to live well through their own actions, not for choosing in ways that account for the wrongs of other scientists or government officials. Utilitarianism ignores the importance of personal integrity and often prescribes actions that conflict with our values.

Some argue that Williams's stories ignore remote psychological effects on the agents. If we count how bad the scientist and tourist will feel if they act as described, then the good produced by the actions may be outweighed by the bad consequences of these long-term feelings. But if utilitarianism is a correct theory, Williams asks, then what do they have to feel bad about? If their duty is to maximize good consequences, then they should feel good about what they do. The reason they have for feeling bad is that utilitarian calculations do not make sense of our moral intuitions and the ethical life. Others argue that the acts of the scientist and the tourist may set a bad precedent for others to follow. But if utilitarianism is a correct theory, Williams argues, then these acts set a good precedent and we should want others to act likewise in similar circumstances (*see* **consistency**).

Williams introduced the paradoxical term "moral luck," which refers to how random, unintended factors can affect moral praise or blame (*see* **Thomas Nagel**). We commonly assume that people are responsible only for what is under their control. Suppose a university president decided to hold graduation indoors because weather forecasters predicted a storm; but the storm never came. We would deem it unfair to blame the president for the decision since the president had no control over the weather or the forecast. Yet sometimes moral responsibility seems influenced by matters of luck beyond our control. Consider a man who tried to strangle a woman but was prevented from doing so by his sudden epileptic seizure. Although we would **punish** the man, we would not punish him as harshly as we would if he succeeded in killing the woman. This seems counterintuitive since the only reason he did not kill the woman was a seizure beyond his control.

Such cases in part lead Williams to conclude that ethical theories cannot deal with the complexities of life; they have trouble sorting through matters of luck and assigning responsibility. So in *Ethics and the Limits of Philosophy* (1985) he encourages ethicists to abandon attempts to systematize the ethical life. He pushes us to return to the question "How do I live well?" that occupied **ancient** Greek philosophers. He believes such an approach accounts for the complexities of human life and answers the practical questions we face. Ethics makes its mark on society by addressing practical questions in ways that move us toward solutions, not by failed attempts to produce ethical theories.

WISDOM. *See* RATIONAL MORAL THINKING.

WOLLSTONECRAFT, MARY (1759–1797). English **feminist ethicist** who argued for the social equality of women. She was part of a group of English **political** radicals who promoted the ideals of the French Revolution (but not its later abuses), including the abolition of slavery and the end of special privileges for the upper classes and aristocracy.

Wollstonecraft's *A Vindication of the Rights of Man* (1790) attacked Edmund Burke's negative *Reflections on the French Revolution* (1790). She criticized Burke for being inconsistent, relying on what was traditional instead of what was prescribed by reason, and portraying England (with its **poverty** and rigid class system) as a better model than that of the French revolutionaries. One's birthright as a rational being, she argues, is to have "such a degree of liberty, civil and religious, as is compatible with the [same] liberty of every individual with whom he is united in a **social compact**" (*see* **John Rawls**); as rational creatures, we inherit such **rights** from **God**. She laments that these rights had not yet been put into political practice anywhere on the globe. Her work raised a stir, both because of what it said and because it was written by a woman at a time when women did not engage much in politics. Her *A Vindication of the Rights of Woman* (1792) extended her argument to the treatment of women. If our rights depend on our rationality, and women are as rational as men, then women should have the same rights as men; there is no excuse for denying to women the educational, political, and employment rights given to men. She realized, however, that the disputed point here was her claim that women are as rational as men. She admitted, as a matter of fact, that men excelled over women in almost every area that involved reason; but she claimed this was due to the oppressive education and social conditioning to which women were subjected. Men were educated to think for themselves in a rational way, while women were trained to be frivolous, submissive, and emotional. So she called for political changes that would bring an equal education to both men and women. Boys and girls were to be taught the same subjects in the same classrooms; there were not to be "boy subjects" and "girl subjects." She contended that the inherent rationality of both sexes was basically equal and the same.

Some feminists, while appreciative of Wollstonecraft's pioneering work against **sexism**, are critical of her belief that the rationality of both sexes is basically the same; they claim that the rational and emotional nature of the sexes is significantly different, though of equal value (*see* **Carol Gilligan**). Other feminists support Wollstonecraft against such criticisms. *See also* MODERN ETHICS.

Bibliography

Much has been written on ethics over the last 25 centuries. This bibliography attempts to cover the classics (broadly construed) and a representative sample of everything else. It lists only works in English. It emphasizes Western ethics but includes some non-Western works; regrettably there are fewer non-Western materials in English. The thousand or so items listed here cover a wide range of topics within ethics.

The materials are divided into six main groups (1–6), with subgroups indicated by a letter after the digit (1A, 1B, etc.):

While most items fit neatly into just one category, some items overlap categories. Imagine a book entitled *Christian Bioethics, Aristotle, and*

Recent Biology. With some arbitrariness, the authors would likely put this book under World Religions and Non-Western Ethics (4B) instead of under Applied Ethics (5), Ancient Ethics (3B), or Science and Ethics (4A). Please try related sections when looking for materials.

General Ethics Textbooks (2A) covers textbooks for general introductory courses about ethical theories or thinkers; textbooks on business or medical ethics or moral problems are under Applied Ethics (5). History of Ethics (3) covers materials by, or mostly about, pre-1900 Western moral philosophers; the remaining categories (4–6) are post-1900 (except that 4B has all religious and non-Western materials regardless of date). Science and Ethics (4A) covers areas like anthropology, biology, game theory, and psychology, including views about moral development and moral education. World Religions and Non-Western Ethics (4B) covers various religious and quasi-religious traditions (such as Confucian ethics), including materials on applied ethics written from a religious framework. Websites are included with written materials; all websites mentioned were accessed on 4 August 2007, so this is not repeated in the bibliography.

Since so much has been written about ethics, this bibliography is highly selective. While some choices were obvious, others were not. Subjective factors affected the choices, especially those involving what readings the authors happen to have found and what topics they happen to have found interesting. If your writings are not included here, please do not take it as an affront or as a negative evaluation of your work. And bear in mind that many works included here have further bibliographies; most people find readings by combining suggestions from various sources.

Reading suggestions for some of the sections may be helpful. Under 1A (Philosophy Reference Works), the authors suggest the *Encyclopedia of Philosophy* and *Encyclopædia Britannica*; for longer articles, they suggest the *Routledge Encyclopedia of Philosophy*, *Internet Encyclopedia of Philosophy*, and *Stanford Encyclopedia of Philosophy*. Under 1B (Ethics Reference Works), they suggest the *Encyclopedia of Ethics*. Under 1C (Ethics Journals), they suggest *Ethics*, *Mind*, *American Philosophical Quarterly*, and *Journal of Philosophy*.

Under 2A (General Ethics Textbooks) the authors suggest Brandt and Frankena (which are older classics), Pojman (*Discovering Right and Wrong*), and Gensler (which is very basic). For anthologies, they suggest Sher and Shafer-Landau (both have classic and contemporary readings), Timmons (contemporary), and Gensler-Spurgin-Swindal (which has easy readings mostly on contemporary theory).

Under 3A (General History of Ethics), the authors suggest Arrington.

Under 3B (Ancient Ethics), they suggest Plato's *Republic* and Aristotle's *Nicomachean Ethics*. Under 3C (Medieval Ethics), they suggest Augustine's *On Free Choice of the Will* and Aquinas's *Treatise on Law*. Under 3D (Modern Ethics), they suggest Hobbes's *Leviathan*, Hume's *Treatise of Human Nature* and *Enquiry Concerning the Principles of Morals*, and Kant's *Groundwork of the Metaphysic of Morals* and *Critique of Practical Reason*. Under 3E (Nineteenth-Century Ethics), they suggest Mill's *Utilitarianism* and Sidgwick's *The Methods of Ethics*.

Under 4B (World Religions and Non-Western Ethics), the authors suggest Gustafson's *Can Ethics Be Christian?* (Protestant), Wadell (Catholic), Gupta (for Eastern and Western selections), Confucius's *Analects* (which may be the most influential book on ethics ever written), and Laozi's *Dao De Jing* (for an opposing Chinese perspective). The books in this Historical Dictionaries series on world religions (Buddhism, Hinduism, Islam, Jainism, Shinto, Taoism) would also be useful. Under 4C (Logic and Ethics), the authors suggest von Wright's "Deontic Logic," any of Castañeda's essays, and Gensler's *Formal Ethics* and *Introduction to Logic*.

Under 5 (Applied Ethics), the authors suggest the Pojman-Beckwith anthology on abortion, Singer's controversial *Practical Ethics*, Boatright's business ethics text, the DeJardins-McCall business ethics anthology, the Regan-Singer anthology on animal rights, Sterba's environmental ethics anthology, the Beauchamp-Childress bioethics text, Pence's bioethics text and his book of cases, and the Mappes-DeGrazia bioethics anthology.

Under 6 (Ethical Theory), the authors suggest Moore's *Principia Ethica*; Ross's *The Right and the Good*; Ayer's *Language, Truth and Logic*; Hare's *Freedom and Reason*; Rawls's *A Theory of Justice*; Nozick's *Anarchy, State, and Utopia*; MacIntyre's *After Virtue*; Sartre's *Existentialism and Human Emotions*; and Habermas's *Moral Consciousness and Communicative Action*. Someone needs to write a short book about 20th-century continental ethics that is designed for analytic philosophers.

The best ethics website is http://ethics.sandiego.edu, *Ethics Updates* by Lawrence M. Hinman at the University of San Diego.

1. General Materials

1A. Philosophy Reference Works

Alexander, Dey, ed. *Philosophy in Cyberspace*. 2nd ed. Bowling Green, Ohio:

Philosophy Documentation Center, 1998.

Angeles, Peter Adam, ed. *The HarperCollins Dictionary of Philosophy*. 2nd ed. New York: HarperPerennial, 1992.

Audi, Robert, ed. *The Cambridge Dictionary of Philosophy*. 2nd ed. Cambridge: Cambridge Univ. Pr., 1999.

Bertman, Martin A. *Research Guide in Philosophy*. Morristown, N.J.: General Learning Pr., 1974.

Blackburn, Simon, ed. *The Oxford Dictionary of Philosophy*. Oxford: Oxford Univ. Pr., 1994.

Borchert, Donald M., ed. *Encyclopedia of Philosophy*. 2nd ed. Detroit, Mich.: Macmillan, 2006. [The first edition appeared in 1967.]

Copleston, Frederick C. *A History of Philosophy*. 5 vols. Westminster, Md.: Newman Bookshop, 1946–1975.

Craig, Edward, ed. *Routledge Encyclopedia of Philosophy*. 10 vols. London: Routledge, 1998.

EpistemeLinks. http://www.epistemelinks.com/Main/MainText.aspx [public domain writings]

EServer. http://eserver.org/philosophy [public domain writings]

Flew, Antony, ed. *A Dictionary of Philosophy*. 2nd ed. New York: St. Martin's, 1984.

Free Online Dictionary of Philosophy. http://www.swif.it/foldop

Guerry, Herbert. *A Bibliography of Philosophical Bibliographies*. Westport, Conn.: Greenwood, 1977.

Gutenberg Project. http://www.gutenberg.org/catalog [public domain writings]

Honderich, Ted, ed. *Oxford Companion to Philosophy*. Oxford: Oxford Univ. Pr., 1995.

Iannone, A. Pablo. *Dictionary of World Philosophy*. London: Routledge, 2001.

Internet Encyclopedia of Philosophy. http://www.utm.edu/research/iep

Lacey, Alan Robert. *A Dictionary of Philosophy*. 3rd ed. London: Routledge, 1996.

Lineback, R. H., ed. *The Philosopher's Index*. Bowling Green, Ohio: Philosophy Documentation Center, 1967–.

Mautner, Thomas. *A Dictionary of Philosophy*. Oxford: Blackwell, 1996.

Online Books Page. http://digital.library.upenn.edu/books/authors.html [public domain writings]

Pappas, Theodore, ed. *Encyclopædia Britannica*. Chicago: Encyclopædia Britannica, 2008. [on DVD]

Reese, William L. *Dictionary of Philosophy and Religion: Eastern and Western Thought*. 2nd ed. Atlantic Highlands, N.J.: Humanities, 1996.

Runes, Dagobert D., ed. *Dictionary of Philosophy*. Rev. ed. New York: Philosophical Library, 1983.

Stanford Encyclopedia of Philosophy. http://plato.stanford.edu/contents.html

Urmson, J. O., and Jonathan Rée. *The Concise Encyclopedia of Western Philosophy and Philosophers*. Rev. ed. London: Unwin Hyman, 1989.

1B. Ethics Reference Works

Becker, Lawrence C., and Charlotte B. Becker, eds. *Encyclopedia of Ethics*. 2nd ed. New York: Routledge, 2001.

Chadwick, Ruth, ed. *Encyclopedia of Applied Ethics*. New York: Academic, 1998.

Childress, James F., and John Macquarrie, eds. *The Westminster Dictionary of Christian Ethics*. Philadelphia: Westminster, 1986.

Clarke, Paul Barry, and Andrew Linzey. *Dictionary of Ethics, Theology and Society*. London: Routledge, 1996.

Grenz, Stanley, and Jay T. Smith. *Pocket Dictionary of Ethics*. Downers Grove, Ill.: InterVarsity, 2003.

Harrison, R. K., ed. *Encyclopedia of Biblical and Christian Ethics*. Nashville, Tenn.: T. Nelson, 1992.

Hester, Joseph P. *Encyclopedia of Values and Ethics*. Oxford: ABC-CLIO, 1996.

Hinman, Lawrence M. *Ethics Updates*. http://ethics.sandiego.edu

LaFollette, Hugh, ed. *The Blackwell Guide to Ethical Theory*. Malden, Mass.: Blackwell, 2000.

Post, Stephen G., ed. *Encyclopedia of Bioethics*. New York: Macmillan, 2004.

Roth, John K. *Ethics*. Englewood Cliffs, N.J.: Salem, 1994.

Terkel, Susan Neiburg, and R. Shannon Duval, eds. *Encyclopedia of Ethics*. New York: Facts on File, 1999.

Werhane, Patricia H., and R. Edward Freeman, eds. *The Blackwell Encyclopedic Dictionary of Business Ethics*. Cambridge, Mass.: Blackwell, 1997.

1C. Ethics Journals

Agriculture and Human Values. Gainesville: Center for Applied Philosophy and Ethics in the Professions, Univ. of Florida.

American Journal of Bioethics. Cambridge, Mass.: MIT.

Business and Professional Ethics Journal. Troy, N.Y.: Human Dimensions Center, Rensselaer Polytechnic Institute.

Business and Society Review. Darien, Conn.: Management Reports, Inc.

Business Ethics Quarterly. Bowling Green, Ohio: Society for Business Ethics.

Business Ethics: A European Review. Oxford: Blackwell.

Christian Bioethics. Lisse, Netherlands: Swets & Zeitlinger.

Environmental Ethics. Albuquerque: John Muir Institute for Environmental Studies, Univ. of New Mexico.

Ethical Theory and Moral Practice. Dordrecht: Springer.

Ethics. Chicago: Univ. of Chicago Pr. [formerly *International Journal of Ethics*]

Ethics and Behavior. Hillsdale, N.J.: Lawrence Erlbaum Associates.

Ethics and Education. Durham, England: Taylor & Francis.

Ethics and Information Technology. Dordrecht: Springer.

Ethics and International Affairs. New York: Carnegie Council on Ethics and International Affairs.

Ethikos: Examining Ethical Issues in Business. New York: Ethikos.

International Journal of Applied Philosophy. Fort Pierce, Fla.: H. A. Heise.

International Journal of Value-based Management. Dordrecht: Springer.

Journal of Academic Ethics. Dordrecht: Springer.

Journal of Agricultural and Environmental Ethics. Dordrecht: Springer.

Journal of Applied Philosophy. Oxford: Blackwell.

Journal of Bioethical Inquiry. Netherlands: Springer.

Journal of Business Ethics. Dordrecht: Springer.

Journal of Ethics. Dordrecht: Springer.

Journal of Global Ethics. Birmingham, England: Taylor & Francis.

Journal of Human Values. Thousand Oaks, Calif.: Sage.

Journal of Law, Medicine, and Ethics. Boston: American Society of Law, Medicine, and Ethics.

Journal of Mass Media Ethics. Mahwah, N.J.: L. Erlbaum.

Journal of Medicine and Philosophy. Dordrecht: D. Reidel.

Journal of Military Ethics. Philadelphia: Taylor & Francis.

Journal of Moral Philosophy. London: Continuum.

Journal of Philosophy. New York: W.T. Bush. [important general journal that also publishes in ethics]

Journal of Religious Ethics. Atlanta, Ga.: Scholars.

Journal of the Society of Christian Ethics. Baltimore, Md.: Georgetown Univ. Pr.

Journal of Value Inquiry. Dordrecht: Springer.

Medicine, Health Care, and Philosophy. Dordrecht: Springer.

Mind. Oxford: Blackwell. [important general journal that also publishes in ethics]

Philosopher's Index. Bowling Green, Ohio: Philosophy Documentation Center, Bowling Green State Univ. [index of most philosophy journals]

Philosophy and Public Affairs. Princeton, N.J.: Princeton Univ. Pr.

Professional Ethics. Dexter, Mich.: Thomsan-Shore.

Public Affairs Quarterly. Bowling Green, Ohio: Philosophy Documentation Center, Bowling Green State Univ.

Research in Ethical Issues in Organizations. Stamford, Conn.: JAI.

Social Philosophy and Policy. New York: Cambridge Univ. Pr.

Social Philosophy Today. Lewiston, N.Y.: E. Mellen.

Theoretical Medicine and Bioethics. Dordrecht: Springer.

1D.   Ethics Organizations

These are some organizations that have a significant role in ethical discussions.

American Academy of Medical Ethics. http://www.ethicalhealthcare.org/organizations.html [This has links to other bioethics organizations.]

American Catholic Philosophical Association. http://www.acpaweb.org
American Philosophical Association. http://www.apa.udel.edu
Association for Practical and Professional Ethics. http://www.indiana.edu/~appe
Center for the Study of Ethics in the Professions. http://ethics.iit.edu/codes/
  resources.html [This has much about professional ethics codes.]
Council for a Parliament of the World's Religions. http://www.cpwr.org [See
  especially http://www.cpwr.org/resource/ethic.pdf.]
Feminists for Life. http://feministsforlife.org
Global Ethics Foundation. http://www.weltethos.org/dat_eng/index_e.htm [See es-
  pecially http://www.weltethos.org/pdf_decl/Decl_english.pdf.]
International Society of Business, Economics, and Ethics. http://www.isbee.org
Markkula Center for Applied Ethics. http://www.scu.edu/ethics
National Organization for Women. http://now.org
National Right to Life Organization. http://www.nrlc.org [See especially http://
  www.nrlc.org/abortion/wdlb/wdlb.html.]
Not Dead Yet. http://www.notdeadyet.org/docs/about.html
People for the Ethical Treatment of Animals. http://www.peta.com
Society for Business Ethics. http://www.societyforbusinessethics.org
Society for Ethics. http://www-rohan.sdsu.edu/faculty/corlett/se.html
Society for Phenomenology and Existential Philosophy. http://www.spep.org
Society of Christian Ethics. http://www.scethics.org
Society of Christian Philosophers. http://www.siu.edu/~scp
UNESCO Report on Global Ethics. http://kvc.minbuza.nl/uk/archive/report/
  chapter1_3.html
United Nations. http://www.ohchr.org or http://www.un.org [See especially
  http://www.unhchr.ch/udhr/lang/eng.htm.]

2. Teaching Materials

2A. General Ethics Textbooks

Blackburn, Simon. *Being Good*. Oxford: Oxford Univ. Pr., 2001.
Bonevac, Daniel, ed. *Today's Moral Issues*. 5th ed. New York: McGraw-Hill, 2006.
Boss, Judith A., ed. *Ethics for Life*. 2nd ed. New York: McGraw-Hill, 2002.
———. *Perspectives on Ethics*. Mountain View, Calif.: Mayfield, 1998.
Brandt, Richard B. *Ethical Theory*. Englewood Cliffs, N.J.: Prentice Hall, 1959.
Cahn, Steven M., and Peter Markie, eds. *Ethics: History, Theory, and Contemporary Issues*. Oxford: Oxford Univ. Pr., 2006.
Denise, Theodore C., Nicholas P. White, and Sheldon P. Peterfreund, eds. *Great Traditions in Ethics*. 11th ed. Belmont, Calif.: Wadsworth, 2005.

Ellin, Joseph. *Morality and the Meaning of Life: An Introduction to Ethical Theory.* Fort Worth, Tex.: Harcourt Brace, 1995.

Ewing, Alfred C. *Ethics.* London: English Universities Pr., 1953.

Fagothey, Austin, and Milton A. Gonsalves. *Right and Reason.* 9th ed. Columbus, Ohio: Merrill, 1989.

Frankena, William K. *Ethics.* 2nd ed. Englewood Cliffs, N.J.: Prentice Hall, 1973.

Frankena, William K., and John T. Granrose, eds. *Introductory Readings in Ethics.* Englewood Cliffs, N.J.: Prentice Hall, 1974.

Gensler, Harry J. *Ethics: A Contemporary Introduction.* London: Routledge, 1998.

Gensler, Harry J., Earl W. Spurgin, and James C. Swindal, eds. *Ethics: Contemporary Readings.* New York: Routledge, 2004.

Gómez-Lobo, Alfonso. *Morality and the Human Goods: An Introduction to Natural Law Ethics.* Washington, D.C.: Georgetown Univ. Pr., 2002.

Grisez, Germain G., and Russell Shaw. *Beyond the New Morality: The Responsibilities of Freedom.* 3rd ed. Notre Dame, Ind.: Univ. of Notre Dame Pr., 1988.

Johnson, Oliver A., and Andrews Reath, eds. *Ethics: Selections from Classical and Contemporary Writers.* 9th ed. Belmont, Calif.: Wadsworth, 2004.

Kagan, Shelly. *Normative Ethics.* Boulder, Colo.: Westview, 1998.

Moore, Brooke Noel, and Robert Michael Stewart, eds. *Moral Philosophy: A Comprehensive Introduction.* Mountain View, Calif.: Mayfield, 1994.

Pahel, Kenneth, and Marvin Schiller. *Readings in Contemporary Ethical Theory.* Englewood Cliffs, N.J.: Prentice-Hall, 1970.

Percesepe, Gary, ed. *Introduction to Ethics: Personal and Social Responsibility in a Diverse World.* Englewood Cliffs, N.J.: Prentice Hall, 1995.

Pojman, Louis P. *Ethics: Discovering Right and Wrong.* 5th ed. Belmont, Calif.: Wadsworth, 2006.

———, ed. *Ethical Theory: Classical and Contemporary Readings.* 5th ed. Belmont, Calif.: Wadsworth, 2007.

Pojman, Louis P., and Lewis Vaughn, eds. *The Moral Life: An Introductory Reader in Ethics and Literature.* 3rd ed. New York: Oxford Univ. Pr., 2007.

Rachels, James, ed. *Ethical Theory.* 2 vols. Oxford: Oxford Univ. Pr., 1998.

Rachels, James, and Stuart Rachels. *The Elements of Moral Philosophy.* 5th ed. Boston: McGraw-Hill, 2006.

———, eds. *The Right Thing to Do: Basic Readings in Moral Philosophy.* 4th ed. Boston: McGraw-Hill, 2007.

Sellars, Wilfred, and John Hospers, eds. *Readings in Ethical Theory.* 2nd ed. New York: Appleton Century Crofts, 1970.

Shafer-Landau, Russ, ed. *Ethical Theory: An Anthology.* Malden, Mass.: Blackwell, 2007.

Shafer-Landau, Russ, and Terence Cuneo, eds. *Foundations of Ethics: An Anthology.* 3rd ed. Malden, Mass.: Blackwell, 2007.

Sher, George, ed. *Moral Philosophy: Selected Readings.* 2nd ed. Fort Worth, Tex.: Harcourt Brace, 1996.

Singer, Peter. *Practical Ethics*. 2nd ed. Cambridge: Cambridge Univ. Pr., 1993.
———, ed. *Ethics*. Oxford: Oxford Univ. Pr., 1994.
Thomson, Judith Jarvis, and Gerald Dworkin, eds. *Ethics*. New York: Harper & Row, 1968.
Timmons, Mark, ed. *Disputed Moral Issues: A Reader*. Oxford: Oxford Univ. Pr., 2007.
Weston, Anthony. *Creative Problem-solving in Ethics*. Oxford: Oxford Univ. Pr., 2007.
Williams, Bernard. *Morality: An Introduction to Ethics*. New York: Harper & Row, 1972.

2B. Ethics Videos and Software

Unless a Web address is given, these are VCR video tapes or DVDs.

Alkemade, Monique. *The Examined Life*. Pasadena, Calif.: Intelecom, 1998. [a series of tapes]
Baldwin, Alec. *Meet Your Meat*. http://www.meat.org or http://www.petatv.com
Childress, James F., et al. *What Does it Mean to be Human? Religion and Bioethics*. Princeton, N.J.: Princeton Univ., 2001.
Doyle, Michael W., et al. *Business Ethics: To Tell the Truth*. Princeton, N.J.: Princeton Univ., 1997.
Dworkin, Ronald, and Kwame Anthony Appiah. *Great Ideas of Philosophy: Political Philosophy*. Princeton, N.J.: Films for the Humanities and Sciences, 2004.
Ethical Issues on DVD and Video Tape. New York: Insight Media. [a large series of video tapes and DVDs]
Gensler, Harry J. *Web Exercises on Ethics*. http://www.jcu.edu/philosophy/gensler/exercise.htm [runs on Web browser or independently in Windows]
Goodpaster, Kenneth E., and Scott D. Cook. *Ethics in Management*. Boston: Harvard Business School, 1985. [a series of tapes]
Hare, Richard M., and Bryan Magee. *Moral Philosophy*. Princeton, N.J.: Films for the Humanities and Sciences, 1997.
Hinman, Lawrence M. *Ethics Updates Videos*. http://ethics.sandiego.edu/video
Hsieh, Shan-Yuan. *Life and Thought of Confucius*. San Jose, Calif.: Cupertino Community Television De Anza College TV Center, 1985.
Jacoby, Frank, et al. *Beyond Borders: Ethics in International Business*. Washington, D.C.: Ethics Resource Center, 1992.
———. *Marketplace Ethics: Issues in Sales & Marketing*. Washington, D.C.: Ethics Resource Center, 1990.
———. *A Matter of Judgment*. Washington, D.C.: Ethics Resource Center, 1986.
———. *Tough Decisions: Ethics Issues in Government Contracting*. Washington, D.C.: Ethics Resource Center, 1987.
Jankowski, Laurence J. *Some Ethical Considerations in Journalism*. Maumee,

Ohio: Instructional Video, 1989.

Kamm, Frances, Larry Temkin, and Richard Sorabji. *Ethics: What Is Right?* Princeton, N.J.: Films for the Humanities & Sciences, 2004.

Lehrer, Jim. *Ethics in Corporate America*. Princeton, N.J.: Films for the Humanities and Sciences, 2003.

McGee, Bryan. *Great Philosophers* Series. Princeton, N.J.: Films for the Humanities and Sciences. [BBC videos on Plato, Aristotle, Hume, Hegel and Marx, Kant, Marxist Philosophy, Nietzsche, etc.]

Mertzman, Robert. *Ethics, the Environment, and Professionals*. Lincoln, Neb.: GPN, 1993.

Mertzman, Robert, and Peter Madsen. *Ethics and Financial Professionals*. Lincoln, Neb.: GPN, 1993.

Philosopher's Magazine Morality Play. http://www.philosophersnet.com/games/morality_play.htm

Rodriguez, Bert, et al. *Ethics for the Mental Health Professional*. Dallas, Tex.: Bert Rodriguez Video Education, 1997.

Santa Clara University Markkula Center for Applied Ethics. *The Ethics Outlook: A National Ethics Agenda*. Santa Clara, Calif.: The Center, 2004–.

Shapiro, Harold, et al. *The Ethics of Cloning*. Princeton, N.J.: Films for the Humanities & Sciences, 1997.

Singer, Peter. *Peter Singer: A Dangerous Mind*. Princeton, N.J.: Films for the Humanities & Sciences, 2003.

Smith, Janet E. *Contraception: Why Not?* Dayton, Ohio: One More Soul, 1995.

3. History of Ethics

3A. General History of Ethics

Arrington, Robert L. *Western Ethics: An Historical Introduction*. Malden, Mass.: Blackwell, 1998.

Ashby, Warren. *A Comprehensive History of Western Ethics*. Amherst, N.Y.: Prometheus, 1997.

Becker, Lawrence C., and Charlotte B. Becker, eds. *A History of Western Ethics*. New York: Garland, 1992.

Bourke, Vernon Joseph. *History of Ethics*. Garden City, N.Y.: Doubleday, 1968.

Brinton, Crane. *A History of Western Morals*. New York: Harcourt Brace, 1959.

MacIntyre, Alasdair C. *A Short History of Ethics*. 2nd ed. London: Routledge, 1998.

Maritain, Jacques. *Moral Philosophy: An Historical and Critical Survey of the Great Systems*. London: G. Bles, 1964.

Rogers, Reginald A. P. *A Short History of Ethics: Greek and Modern*. London:

Macmillan, 1965.

Sidgwick, Henry. *Outlines of the History of Ethics for English Readers*. 6th ed. London: Macmillan, 1931.

3B. Ancient Ethics

Ackrill, J. L. *Essays on Plato and Aristotle*. New York: Clarendon, 1997.

Annas, Julia. *The Morality of Happiness*. New York: Oxford Univ. Pr., 1995.

Aristotle. *The Complete Works of Aristotle*. 2 vols. Ed. Jonathan Barnes. Princeton, N.J.: Princeton Univ. Pr., 1984.

———. *Nicomachean Ethics*. Trans. Terence Irwin. Indianapolis, Ind.: Hackett, 1985.

———. *The Politics*. Trans. Carnes Lord. Chicago: Univ. of Chicago Pr., 1984.

Aurelius, Marcus. *Meditations*. Trans. George Long. Chicago: Henry Regnery, 1956.

Bobonich, Christopher. *Plato's Utopia Recast: His Later Ethics and Politics*. Oxford: Clarendon, 2002.

Bryant, Joseph M. *Moral Codes and Social Structure in Ancient Greece*. Albany, N.Y.: SUNY, 1996.

Carrick, Paul. *Medical Ethics in the Ancient World*. Washington, D.C.: Georgetown Univ. Pr., 2001.

Cicero, Marcus Tullius. *On the Good Life*. Trans. Michael Grant. London: Penguin, 1971.

Cooper, John M. *Reason and Emotion: Essays on Ancient Moral Psychology and Ethical Theory*. Princeton, N.J.: Princeton Univ. Pr., 1999.

———. *Reason and Human Good in Aristotle*. Cambridge, Mass.: Harvard Univ. Pr., 1975.

Didymos, Arius. *Epitome of Stoic Ethics*. Ed. Arthur J. Pomeroy. Atlanta, Ga.: Society of Biblical Literature, 1999.

Edelstein, Ludwig. *The Hippocratic Oath: Text, Translation and Interpretation*. Baltimore: Johns Hopkins Pr., 1943.

Epictetus. *Discourses*. Ed. Christopher Gill, trans. Robin Hard. Rutland, Vt.: C. E. Tuttle, 1995.

Epicurus. *Works*. Trans. Cyril Bailey. Oxford: Clarendon, 1926.

Freeman, Kathleen. *Ancilla to Pre-Socratic Philosophers: A Complete Translation of the Fragments*. Cambridge, Mass.: Harvard Univ. Pr., 1948.

Gadamer, Hans Georg. *The Idea of the Good in Platonic-Aristotelian Philosophy*. Trans. P. Christopher Smith. New Haven, Conn.: Yale Univ. Pr., 1986.

———. *Plato's Dialectical Ethics*. Trans. Robert M. Wallace. New Haven, Conn.: Yale Univ. Pr., 1991.

Gómez-Lobo, Alfonso. *The Foundations of Socratic Ethics*. Indianapolis, Ind.: Hackett, 1994.

Gosling, Justin C. B., and Christopher C. W. Taylor. *The Greeks on Pleasure*.

Oxford: Clarendon, 1982.

Grene, David. *Greek Political Theory: The Image of Man in Thucydides and Plato.* Chicago: Univ. of Chicago Pr., 1950.

Hare, Richard M. *Plato.* Oxford: Oxford Univ. Pr., 1982.

Hertzler, Joyce O. *The Social Thought of the Ancient Civilizations.* New York: McGraw-Hill, 1936.

Huby, Pamela M. *Greek Ethics.* London: Macmillan, 1967.

Inwood, Brad. *Ethics and Human Action in Early Stoicism.* Oxford: Clarendon, 1985.

Irwin, Terence, ed. *Aristotle's Ethics.* New York: Garland, 1995.

———. *Plato's Ethics.* New York: Garland, 1995.

Kenny, Anthony. *Aristotelian Ethics: A Study of the Relationship between the Eudemian and Nicomachean Ethics of Aristotle.* Oxford: Clarendon, 1978.

Koen, Avraam. *Atoms, Pleasure, Virtue: The Philosophy of Epicurus.* New York: P. Lang, 1995.

Kraut, Richard. *Aristotle on the Human Good.* Princeton, N.J.: Princeton Univ. Pr., 1989.

Kraut, Richard, ed. *Plato's Republic: Critical Essays.* Lanham, Md.: Rowman & Littlefield, 1997.

Laertius, Diogenes. *Lives of Eminent Philosophers.* Trans. R. D. Hicks. Cambridge, Mass.: Harvard Univ. Pr., 1925.

Long, A. A. *Hellenistic Philosophy: Stoics, Epicureans, Sceptics.* Berkeley: Univ. of California Pr., 1986.

Lucretius. *The Nature of Things.* Trans. Frank Copley. New York: Norton, 1977.

Mitsis, Phillip. *Epicurus' Ethical Theory.* Ithaca, N.Y.: Cornell Univ. Pr., 1988.

Nussbaum, Martha C. *The Fragility of Goodness: Luck and Ethics in Greek Tragedy and Philosophy.* Cambridge: Cambridge Univ. Pr., 1986.

———. *The Therapy of Desire: Theory and Practice in Hellenistic Ethics.* Princeton, N.J.: Princeton Univ. Pr., 1994.

Panichas, George Andrew. *Epicurus.* New York: Twayne, 1967.

Plato. *The Collected Dialogues of Plato, Including the Letters.* Ed. Edith Hamilton and Huntington Cairns. Princeton, N.J.: Princeton Univ. Pr., 1961.

———. *Five Dialogues.* Trans. G. M. A. Grube. Indianapolis, Ind.: Hackett, 1981. [contains the *Euthyphro, Apology, Crito, Meno,* and *Phaedo*]

———. *Gorgias.* Trans. W. C. Helmbold. New York: Macmillan, 1985.

———. *The Republic.* Trans. G. M. A. Grube. Indianapolis, Ind.: Hackett, 1974.

Plotinus. *The Enneads.* Trans. Stephen MacKenna. Burdett, New York: Larson, 1992.

Preus, Anthony. *Historical Dictionary of Ancient Greek Philosophy.* Lanham, Md.: Scarecrow, 2007.

Preuss, Peter. *Epicurean Ethics.* Lewiston, N.Y.: E. Mellen, 1994.

Prior, William J. *Virtue and Knowledge: An Introduction to Ancient Greek Ethics.* London: Routledge, 1991.

Rice, Daryl H. *A Guide to Plato's Republic.* New York: Oxford Univ. Pr., 1998.

Rorty, Amélie Oksenberg, ed. *Essays on Aristotle's Ethics.* Berkeley: Univ. of California Pr., 1980.

Ross, William D. *Aristotle.* London: Methuen, 1923.

Rowe, Christopher J. *An Introduction to Greek Ethics.* New York: Barnes & Noble, 1977.

Seneca, Lucius Annaeus. *Moral and Political Essays.* Trans. John M. Cooper and J. F. Procopé. Cambridge: Cambridge Univ. Pr., 1995.

Seung, Thomas K. *Plato Rediscovered: Human Value and Social Order.* Lanham, Md.: Rowman & Littlefield, 1996.

Sharples, R. W. *Stoics, Epicureans and Sceptics: An Introduction to Hellenistic Philosophy.* London: Routledge, 1996.

Sherman, Nancy. *The Fabric of Character: Aristotle's Theory of Virtue.* Oxford: Clarendon, 1989.

———. *Making a Necessity of Virtue: Aristotle and Kant on Virtue.* Cambridge: Cambridge Univ. Pr., 1997.

———, ed. *Aristotle's Ethics: Critical Essays.* Lanham, Md.: Rowman & Littlefield, 1999.

Striker, Gisela, ed. *Essays on Hellenistic Epistemology and Ethics.* Cambridge: Cambridge Univ. Pr., 1996.

Urmson, J. O. *Aristotle's Ethics.* Oxford: Blackwell, 1988.

Vlastos, Gregory, ed. *The Philosophy of Socrates: A Collection of Critical Essays.* Garden City, N.Y.: Anchor, 1971.

———. *Plato, A Collection of Critical Essays II: Ethics, Politics, and Philosophy of Art and Religion.* Garden City, N.Y.: Anchor, 1971.

White, Nicholas P. *A Companion to Plato's Republic.* Indianapolis, Ind.: Hackett, 1979.

3C. Medieval Ethics

Abelard, Peter. *Ethical Writings.* Trans. Paul Vincent Spade. Indianapolis, Ind.: Hackett, 1995.

Aquinas, Thomas. *Selected Writings of St. Thomas Aquinas.* Trans. Robert P. Goodwin. Englewood Cliffs, N.J.: Prentice Hall, 1965.

———. *Summa Theologica.* 3 vols. Trans. Fathers of the English Dominican Province. New York: Benziger Brothers, 1947–1948.

———. *Treatise on Law.* Chicago: Henry Regnery, 1970. [contains questions 90–97 of part I–II of the *Summa Theologica*]

Aristides. *The Apology of Aristides on Behalf of the Christians.* Piscataway, N.J.: Gorgias, 2004.

Augustine of Hippo. *Confessions.* Trans. R. S. Pine-Coffin. London: Penguin, 1982.

———. *On Free Choice of the Will.* Trans. Thomas Williams. Indianapolis, Ind.:

Hackett, 1993.

Babcock, William S., ed. *The Ethics of St. Augustine*. Atlanta, Ga.: Scholars, 1991.

Boethius. *The Consolations of Philosophy*. Trans. W. V. Cooper. London: J. M. Dent, 1902.

Brown, Stephen F., and Juan Carlos Flores. *Historical Dictionary of Medieval Philosophy and Theology*. Lanham, Md.: Scarecrow, 2007.

Finnis, John M. *Aquinas: Moral, Political, and Legal Theory*. Oxford: Oxford Univ. Pr., 1998.

Flannery, Kevin L. *Acts Amid Precepts: The Aristotelian Logical Structure of Thomas Aquinas's Moral Theory*. Washington, D.C.: Catholic Univ. of America Pr., 2001.

Irenaeus of Lyons. *St. Irenaeus of Lyons against the Heresies*. Trans. Dominic J. Unger and John J. Dillon. New York: Paulist, 1992.

Kaye, Sharon M., and Robert M. Martin. *On Ockham*. Belmont, Calif.: Wadsworth, 2001.

Kaye, Sharon M., and Paul Thomson. *On Augustine*. Belmont, Calif.: Wadsworth, 2001.

Keenan, James F. *Goodness and Rightness in Thomas Aquinas's Summa Theologiae*. Washington, D.C.: Georgetown Univ. Pr., 1992.

MacDonald, Scott, and Eleonore Stump, eds. *Aquinas's Moral Theory: Essays in Honor of Norman Kretzmann*. Ithaca, N.Y.: Cornell Univ. Pr., 1999.

Maimonides, Moses. *The Commandments*. Trans. Charles B. Chavel. London: Soncino, 1967.

McInerny, Ralph M. *Ethica Thomistica: The Moral Philosophy of Thomas Aquinas*. Washington, D.C.: Catholic Univ. of America Pr., 1997.

O'Connor, Daniel J. *Aquinas and Natural Law*. London: Macmillan, 1968.

Ockham, William of. *Philosophical Writings of William of Ockham*. Trans. Philotheus Boehner. Indianapolis, Ind.: Bobbs-Merrill, 1957.

Potts, Timothy C., ed. *Conscience in Medieval Philosophy*. Cambridge: Cambridge Univ. Pr., 1980.

Scotus, John Duns. *Duns Scotus on the Will and Morality*. 2nd ed. Trans. Allan B. Wolter, ed. William A. Frank. Washington, D.C.: Catholic Univ. of America Pr., 1997.

Tornay, Stephen C. *Ockham: Studies and Selections*. La Salle, Ill.: Open Court, 1938.

3D. Modern Ethics

Burke, Edmund. *Reflections on the Revolution in France*. Ed. L. G. Mitchell. Oxford: Oxford Univ. Pr., 1993.

Burt, Edwin A., ed. *The English Philosophers from Bacon to Mill*. New York: Random House, 1939.

Butler, Joseph. *Five Sermons Preached at the Rolls Chapel and A Dissertation*

Upon the Nature of Virtue. Ed. Stephen L. Darwall. Indianapolis, Ind.: Hackett, 1983.

Chappell, Vere C., ed. *Hume: A Collection of Critical Essays*. Garden City, N.Y.: Anchor Books, 1966.

Clarke, Samuel. *A Discourse Concerning the Unchangeable Obligations of Natural Religion*. London: W. Botham, 1706.

Cudworth, Ralph. *Treatise Concerning Eternal and Immutable Morality*. Ed. Sarah Hutton. Cambridge: Cambridge Univ. Pr., 1996.

Cumberland, Richard. *A Treatise of the Laws of Nature*. New York: Garland, 1978.

Diderot, Denis, ed. *The Encyclopedia: Selections*. Ed. and trans. Stephen J. Gendzier. New York: Harper & Row, 1969.

Edwards, Jonathan. *Freedom of the Will*. Ed. Arnold S. Kaufman and William K. Frankena. New York: Irvington, 1982.

———. *The Nature of True Virtue*. Ann Arbor: Univ. of Michigan Pr., 1966.

Flew, Antony. *David Hume: Philosopher of Moral Science*. Oxford: Blackwell, 1986.

Forbes, Duncan. *Hume's Philosophical Politics*. Cambridge: Cambridge Univ. Pr., 1975.

Gay, John. *Dissertation Concerning the Fundamental Principle and Immediate Criterion of Virtue*. New York: Garland, 1978.

Grotius, Hugo. *The Rights of War and Peace, Including the Law of Nature and of Nations*. Trans. A. C. Campbell. London: M. W. Dunne, 1901.

Guyer, Paul, ed. *Kant's Groundwork of the Metaphysics of Morals: Critical Essays*. Lanham, Md.: Rowman & Littlefield, 1998.

Haakonssen, Knud. *Natural Law and Moral Philosophy from Grotius to the Scottish Enlightenment*. Cambridge: Cambridge Univ. Pr., 1996.

Hampton, Jean. *Hobbes and the Social Contract Tradition*. Cambridge: Cambridge Univ. Pr., 1986.

Harrison, Jonathan. *Hume's Moral Epistemology*. Oxford: Clarendon, 1976.

———. *Hume's Theory of Justice*. Oxford: Clarendon, 1981.

Hill, Thomas E., Jr. *Dignity and Practical Reason in Kant's Moral Theory*. Ithaca, N.Y.: Cornell Univ. Pr., 1992.

Hobbes, Thomas. *Leviathan*. Ed. Michael Oakeshott. New York: Macmillan, 1962.

Holzhey, Helmut, and Vilem Mudroch. *Historical Dictionary of Kant and Kantianism*. Lanham, Md.: Scarecrow, 2005.

Hume, David. *Enquiries Concerning Human Understanding and Concerning the Principles of Morals*. 3rd ed. Ed. L. A. Selby-Bigge. Oxford: Clarendon, 1975.

———. *Hume's Moral and Political Philosophy*. Ed. Henry D. Aiken. New York: Hafner, 1948.

———. *A Treatise of Human Nature*. 2nd ed. Ed. L. A. Selby-Bigge. Oxford: Clarendon, 1978.

Hunt, Lynn, ed. and trans. *The French Revolution and Human Rights: A Brief Documentary History*. Boston: St. Martin's, 1996.

Hutcheson, Francis. *A System of Moral Philosophy*. 2 vols. London: Continuum, 2005.

Jacobson, Anne Jaap, ed. *Feminist Interpretations of David Hume*. University Park: Pennsylvania State Univ. Pr., 2000.

Kant, Immanuel. *Critique of Practical Reason*. Trans. L. W. Beck. New York: Library of Liberal Arts, 1956.

———. *The Doctrine of Virtue*. Trans. M. J. Gregor. New York: Harper & Row, 1964. [contains Part II of the *Metaphysics of Morals*]

———. *Groundwork of the Metaphysic of Morals*. Trans. H. J. Paton. New York: Harper & Row, 1948. [Kant's book sometimes goes by other titles, such as "Fundamental Principles of the Metaphysics of Morals."]

———. *Lectures on Ethics*. Ed. Peter Heath and J. B. Schneewind, trans. Peter Heath. Cambridge: Cambridge Univ. Pr., 1997.

———. *The Metaphysical Elements of Justice*. Trans. John Ladd. New York: Macmillan, 1965.

Korsgaard, Christine M. *Creating the Kingdom of Ends*. Cambridge: Cambridge Univ. Pr., 1996.

Locke, John. *An Essay Concerning Human Understanding*. New York: Dover, 1959.

———. *Of Civil Government: Two Treatises*. London: J.M. Dent, 1924.

Machiavelli, Niccolò. *The Prince*. Trans. George Bull. London: Penguin, 1961.

Mackie, John L. *Hume's Moral Theory*. London: Routledge, 1980.

Monro, David H., ed. *A Guide to the British Moralists*. London: Fontana, 1972.

Morris, Christopher W., ed. *The Social Contract Theorists: Critical Essays on Hobbes, Locke, and Rousseau*. Lanham, Md.: Rowman & Littlefield, 1999.

O'Neill, Onora. *Constructions of Reason: Explorations of Kant's Practical Philosophy*. Cambridge: Cambridge Univ. Pr., 1989.

Paton, Herbert J. *The Categorical Imperative: A Study in Kant's Moral Philosophy*. Chicago: Univ. of Chicago Pr., 1948.

Pufendorf, Samuel. *On the Duty of Man and Citizen according to Natural Law*. Ed. James Tully, trans. Michael Silverthorne. Cambridge: Cambridge Univ. Pr., 1991.

———. *Of the Law of Nature and Nations*. 4th ed. Trans. Basil Kennett. Clark, N.J.: Lawbook Exchange, 2005.

Raphael, David D., ed. *British Moralists, 1650–1800*. Oxford: Clarendon, 1969.

Reid, Thomas. *An Inquiry Into the Human Mind: On the Principles of Common Sense*. Glasgow, Scotland: Gray, 1804.

Rousseau, Jean-Jacques. *The Basic Political Writings*. Trans. Donald A. Cress. Indianapolis, Ind.: Hackett, 1987. [contains the *Discourses on the Sciences and Arts*, *The Origin of Inequality*, *Political Economy*, and *The Social Contract*]

Schneewind, Jerome B. *The Invention of Autonomy: A History of Modern Moral Philosophy*. Cambridge: Cambridge Univ. Pr., 1998.

———, ed. *Moral Philosophy from Montaigne to Kant: An Anthology*. Cambridge: Cambridge Univ. Pr., 1990.

Shaftesbury, Earl of (Anthony Ashley Cooper). *Characteristics of Men, Manners, Opinions, Times, Etc.* Ed. John Robertson. Gloucester, Mass.: P. Smith, 1963.

Sherman, Nancy. *Making a Necessity of Virtue: Aristotle and Kant on Virtue.* Cambridge: Cambridge Univ. Pr., 1997.

Smith, Adam. *An Inquiry into the Nature and Causes of the Wealth of Nations.* Ed. Kathryn Sutherland. Oxford: Oxford Univ. Pr., 1993.

————. *The Theory of Moral Sentiments.* Ed. D. D. Raphael and A. L. Macfie. Oxford: Clarendon, 1976.

Snare, Francis. *Morals, Motivation, and Convention: Hume's Influential Doctrines.* Cambridge: Cambridge Univ. Pr., 1991.

Starrett, Vincent., ed. *Three Great Documents on Human Liberties: Magna Charta, Declaration of Independence, Constitution of the United States.* Canton, Ohio: Timken Roller Bearing, 1942.

Stroud, Barry. *Hume.* London: Routledge, 1977.

Suárez, Francisco. *Selections.* Trans. Gladys L. Williams. Oxford: Clarendon, 1944.

Sullivan, Roger J. *Immanuel Kant's Ethical Theory.* Cambridge: Cambridge Univ. Pr., 1989.

Tuck, Richard. *Natural Rights Theories: Their Origin and Development.* Cambridge: Cambridge Univ. Pr., 1979.

Wolff, Robert Paul, ed. *Kant: A Collection of Critical Essays.* Garden City, N.Y.: Anchor, 1967.

Wollstonecraft, Mary. *Political Writings.* Ed. Janet Todd. Toronto: Univ. of Toronto Pr., 1993. [contains *A Vindication of the Rights of Men, A Vindication of the Rights of Woman,* and *An Historical and Moral View of the French Revolution*]

Wood, Allen W. *Kant's Ethical Thought.* Cambridge: Cambridge Univ. Pr., 1999.

3E.   Nineteenth-Century Ethics

Avineri, Shlomo. *Hegel's Theory of the Modern State.* Cambridge: Cambridge Univ. Pr., 1972.

Bakunin, Mikhail Aleksandrovich. *The Basic Bakunin: Writings, 1869–1871.* Trans. Robert M. Cutler. Buffalo, N.Y.: Prometheus, 1992.

Bentham, Jeremy. *An Introduction to the Principles of Morals and Legislation.* Ed. J. H. Burns and H. L. A. Hart. London: Athlone, 1970.

Blondel, Maurice. *Action.* Trans. Olivia Blanchette. Notre Dame, Ind.: Univ. of Notre Dame Pr., 1984.

Bradley, Francis Herbert. *Ethical Studies.* Oxford: Clarendon, 1927.

Brentano, Franz C. *The Origin of the Knowledge of Right and Wrong.* Trans. Cecil Hague. Westminster, England: A. Constable, 1902.

Burbidge, John W. *Historical Dictionary of Hegel.* Lanham, Md.: Scarecrow, 2001.

Chisholm, Roderick M. *Brentano and Intrinsic Value.* Cambridge: Cambridge

Univ. Pr., 1986.

Clifford, William K. *The Ethics of Belief, and Other Essays*. Ed. Leslie Stephen and Sir Frederick Pollock. London: Watts, 1947.

Darwin, Charles. *Descent of Man*. 2nd ed. Chicago: Montgomery Ward, 1874.

Diethe, Carol. *Historical Dictionary of Nietzscheanism*. 2nd ed. Lanham, Md.: Scarecrow, 2007.

Dworkin, Gerald, ed. *Mill's On Liberty: Critical Essays*. Lanham, Md.: Rowman & Littlefield, 1997.

Emerson, Ralph Waldo. *Emerson's Antislavery Writings*. Ed. Len Gougeon and Joel Myerson. New Haven, Conn.: Yale Univ. Pr., 1995.

———. *Five Essays on Man and Nature*. Ed. Robert E. Spiller. New York: Appleton-Century-Crofts, 1954.

Fichte, Johann Gottlieb. *The Foundations of Natural Right*. Ed. Frederick Neuhouser, trans. Michael Baur. Cambridge: Cambridge Univ. Pr., 2000.

———. *The Vocation of Man*. Ed. Roderick M. Chisholm. New York: Liberal Arts, 1956.

Green, Thomas H. *Works of Thomas Hill Green*. 5 vols. Ed. R. L. Nettleship. Bristol, England: Thoemmes, 1997. [Vol. 4 has his *Prolegomena to Ethics* and vol. 5 (pages 108–82) has his "Lectures on Moral and Political Philosophy."]

Hegel, G. W. F. *Philosophy of Right*. Trans. T. M. Knox. Oxford: Oxford Univ. Pr., 1952.

Huxley, Thomas Henry. *Evolution and Ethics, and Other Essays*. New York: D. Appleton, 1896.

James, William. *Essays on Faith and Morals*. New York: Longmans Green, 1947.

Kierkegaard, Søren. *The Essential Kierkegaard*. Eds. Howard V. Hong and Edna H. Hong. Princeton, N.J.: Princeton Univ. Pr., 2000.

Lowance, Mason, ed. *Against Slavery: An Abolitionist Reader*. New York: Penguin, 2000.

Lyons, David, ed. *Mill's Utilitarianism: Critical Essays*. Lanham, Md.: Rowman & Littlefield, 1997.

Mackintosh, James. *Dissertation on the Progress of Ethical Philosophy*. Edinburgh: Adam and Charles Black, 1836.

Marx, Karl, and Friedrich Engels. *Basic Writings on Politics and Philosophy*. Ed. Lewis S. Feuer. New York: Anchor, 1989.

———. *The Communist Manifesto*. Ed. Samuel H. Beer. Arlington Heights, Ill.: Harlan Davidson, 1955.

———. *The Marx-Engels Reader*. 2nd ed. Ed. Robert C. Tucker. New York: W. W. Norton, 1978.

Mill, James. *Political Writings*. Ed. Terence Ball. Cambridge: Cambridge Univ. Pr., 1992.

———. *The Principles of Toleration*. New York: B. Franklin, 1971.

Mill, John Stuart. *Considerations on Representative Government*. New York: Harper, 1862.

————. *On Liberty*. Ed. Elizabeth Rapaport. Indianapolis, Ind.: Hackett, 1978.

————. *On the Subjection of Women*. Greenwich, Conn.: Fawcett, 1971.

————. *Utilitarianism*. Ed. Oskar Piest. New York: Macmillan, 1957.

Mill, John Stuart, and Harriet Taylor Mill. *Essays on Sex Equality*. Ed. Alice S. Rossi. Chicago: Univ. of Chicago Pr., 1970.

Nietzsche, Friedrich W. *Beyond Good and Evil: Prelude to a Philosophy of the Future*. Trans. Walter Kaufmann. New York: Vintage, 1966.

————. *On the Genealogy of Morals and Ecce Homo*. Ed. and trans. Walter Kaufmann. New York: Vintage, 1967.

————. *Thus Spake Zarathustra*. Trans. Thomas Common and H. James Birx. Buffalo, N.Y.: Prometheus, 1993.

————. *The Will to Power*. Trans. Walter Kaufmann and R. J. Hollingdale. New York: Vintage, 1967.

Postema, Gerald J. *Bentham and the Common Law Tradition*. Oxford: Clarendon, 1986.

Proudhon, Pierre-Joseph. *What is Property?* Ed. and trans. Donald R. Kelley and Bonnie G. Smith. Cambridge: Cambridge Univ. Pr., 1993.

Schneewind, Jerome B. *Sidgwick's Ethics and Victorian Moral Philosophy*. Oxford: Clarendon, 1977.

————, ed. *Mill: A Collection of Critical Essays*. Garden City, N.Y.: Anchor, 1968.

Schopenhauer, Arthur. *The Basis of Morality*. Trans. Arthur Brodrick Bullock. London: Allen, 1915.

————. *Essay on the Freedom of the Will*. Trans. Konstantin Kolenda. Indianapolis, Ind.: Bobbs-Merrill, 1960.

————. *The World as Will and Representation*. Trans. E. F. J. Payne. New York: Dover, 1969.

Sidgwick, Henry. *Essays on Ethics and Method*. Ed. Marcus G. Singer. Oxford: Clarendon, 2000.

————. *The Methods of Ethics*. London: Macmillan, 1901.

————. *Outlines of the History of Ethics for English Readers*. 6th ed. London: Macmillan, 1931.

Spencer, Herbert. *The Data of Ethics*. New York: D. Appleton, 1879.

————. *The Principles of Ethics*. 2 vols. New York: D. Appleton, 1902–1904.

Stephen, Leslie. *The Science of Ethics*. London: Smith Elder, 1882.

Stowe, Harriet Beecher. *Uncle Tom's Cabin*. New York: Harper & Row, 1965.

Taylor, Charles. *Hegel and Modern Society*. Cambridge: Cambridge Univ. Pr., 1979.

Walsh, W. H. *Hegelian Ethics*. London: Macmillan, 1967.

Whately, Richard. *Introductory Lessons on Morality*. Cambridge, Mass.: John Bartlett, 1857.

Whewell, William. *The Elements of Morality*. London: J. W. Parker, 1845.

Wood, Allen W. *Hegel's Ethical Thought*. Cambridge: Cambridge Univ. Pr., 1990.

————. *Karl Marx*. New York: Routledge, 2004.

4. Interdisciplinary

4A.   Science and Ethics

Axelrod, Robert M. *The Evolution of Cooperation*. New York: Basic, 1984.

Badcock, Christopher R. *Evolution and Individual Behavior: An Introduction to Human Sociobiology*. Cambridge, Mass.: Blackwell, 1991.

————. *Evolutionary Psychology*. Malden, Mass.: Blackwell, 2000.

————. *The Problem of Altruism: Freudian-Darwinian Solutions*. New York: Blackwell, 1986.

Benedict, Ruth. *An Anthropologist at Work: Writings of Ruth Benedict*. Ed. Margaret Mead. Boston: Houghton Mifflin, 1959.

————. "Anthropology and the Abnormal." *The Journal of General Psychology* 10, no. 2 (Jan. 1934): 59–82.

Binmore, Ken G. *Game Theory and the Social Contract*. Cambridge, Mass.: MIT, 1994.

Braithwaite, Richard B. *Theory of Games as a Tool for the Moral Philosopher*. Cambridge: Cambridge Univ. Pr., 1955.

Brandt, Richard B. *Hopi Ethics: A Theoretical Analysis*. Chicago: Univ. of Chicago Pr., 1954.

————. "The Psychology of Benevolence and Its Implications for Philosophy." *Journal of Philosophy* 73, no. 14 (12 Aug. 1976): 429–53.

Carr, David, and Jan Steutel, eds. *Virtue Ethics and Moral Education*. London: Routledge, 1999.

Clark, Stephen R. L. *The Nature of the Beast: Are Animals Moral?* Oxford: Oxford Univ. Pr., 1982.

Dawkins, Richard. *The Selfish Gene*. New York: Oxford Univ. Pr., 1976.

Dewey, John. *Human Nature and Conduct: An Introduction to Social Psychology*. New York: Modern Library, 1950.

Doris, John M. *Lack of Character: Personality and Moral Behavior*. Cambridge: Cambridge Univ. Pr., 2002.

Erikson, Erik H. *Insight and Responsibility: Lectures on the Ethical Implications of Psychoanalytic Insight*. New York: W. W. Norton, 1964.

Festinger, Leon. *A Theory of Cognitive Dissonance*. Stanford, Calif.: Stanford Univ. Pr., 1957.

Freud, Sigmund. *Civilization and its Discontents*. Trans. James Strachey. New York: Norton, 1989.

Gilligan, Carol. *In a Different Voice*. Cambridge, Mass.: Harvard Univ. Pr., 1982.

Haidt, Jonathan. "The Emotional Dog and Its Rational Tail." *Psychological Review*

108, no. 4 (October 2001): 814–34.

Hamilton, William D. "The Genetic Evolution of Social Behavior I and II." *Journal of Theoretical Biology* 7, no. 1 (July 1964): 1–52.

Hoffman, Martin L. "Conscience, Personality, and Socialization Techniques." *Human Development* 13, no. 2 (Mar.-Apr. 1970): 90–126.

———. *Empathy and Moral Development*. Cambridge: Cambridge Univ. Pr., 2000.

———. "Is Altruism Part of Human Nature?" *Journal of Personality and Social Psychology* 40, no. 1 (Jan. 1981): 121–37.

Houck, Lynne D., and Lee C. Drickamer. *Foundations of Animal Behavior: Classic Papers with Commentaries*. Chicago: Univ. of Chicago Pr., 1996.

Katz, Robert L. *Empathy: Its Nature and Uses*. London: Collier-Macmillan, 1963.

Kohlberg, Lawrence. "The Claim to Moral Adequacy of the Highest Stage of Moral Judgment." *Journal of Philosophy* 70, no. 18 (25 Oct. 1973): 630–48.

———. "A Cognitive-Developmental Approach to Moral Education." *Humanist* 32, no. 6 (November-December 1972): 13–16.

———. *Essays on Moral Development* (*The Philosophy of Moral Development* and *The Psychology of Moral Development*). 2 vols. San Francisco: Harper & Row, 1981 and 1984.

Krebs, Dennis L. "Psychological Approaches to Altruism: An Evaluation." *Ethics* 92, no. 3 (April 1982): 447–58.

Kuhn, H. W., and A. W. Tucker, eds. *Contributions to the Theory of Games*. 4 vols. Princeton, N.J.: Princeton Univ. Pr., 1950–1959.

Ladd, John. *The Structure of a Moral Code: A Philosophical Analysis of Ethical Discourse Applied to the Ethics of the Navaho Indians*. Cambridge, Mass.: Harvard Univ. Pr., 1957.

Lombardi, Frances G., and Gerald Scott Lombardi, eds. *Circle Without End: A Sourcebook of American Indian Ethics*. Happy Camp, Calif.: Naturegraph, 1982.

Martin, Mike W. *From Morality to Mental Health: Virtue and Vice in a Therapeutic Culture*. Oxford: Oxford Univ. Pr., 2006.

Maslow, Abraham H. *Toward a Psychology of Being*. Princeton, N.J.: Van Nostrand, 1962.

May, Larry, Marilyn Friedman, and Andy Clark, eds. *Mind and Morals: Essays on Cognitive Science and Ethics*. Cambridge, Mass.: MIT, 1996.

Méro, László. *Moral Calculations: Game Theory, Logic, and Human Frailty*. Trans. Anna C. Gosi-Greguss, ed. David Kramer. New York: Copernicus, 1998.

Murphy, Jeffrie G. *Evolution, Morality, and the Meaning of Life*. Totowa, N.J.: Rowman & Littlefield, 1982.

Pfaff, Donald W. *The Neuroscience of Fair Play: Why We (Usually) Follow the Golden Rule*. New York: Dana Pr., 2007.

Piaget, Jean. *The Moral Judgment of the Child*. Trans. Marjorie Gabain. Glencoe, Ill.: Free Pr., 1948.

Poundstone, William. *Prisoner's Dilemma*. New York: Doubleday, 1992.

Rachels, James. *Created from Animals: The Moral Implications of Darwinism*. Oxford: Oxford Univ. Pr., 1991.

Rapoport, Anatol, and Albert M. Chammah. *Prisoner's Dilemma*. Ann Arbor: Univ. of Michigan Pr., 1965.

Ridley, Matt. *The Origins of Virtue: Human Instincts and the Evolution of Cooperation*. New York: Viking, 1997.

Rimland, B. "The Altruism Paradox." *Psychological Reports* 51, no. 2 (Oct. 1982): 521–22.

Rushton, J. Philippe, and Richard M. Sorrentino, eds. *Altruism and Helping Behavior: Social, Personality, and Developmental Perspectives*. Hillsdale, N.Y.: Lawrence Erlbaum, 1981.

Schulman, Michael, and Eva Mekler. *Bringing Up a Moral Child*. 2nd ed. New York: Doubleday, 1994.

Sumner, William G. *Folkways*. Boston: Ginn, 1911.

Taylor, Alan D. *Mathematics and Politics: Strategy, Voting, Power and Proof*. New York: Springer-Verlag, 1995.

Trivers, Robert L. "The Evolution of Reciprocal Altruism." *Quarterly Review of Biology* 46, no. 1 (March 1971): 35–57.

———. *Natural Selection and Social Theory: Selected Papers of Robert Trivers*. Oxford: Oxford Univ. Pr., 2002.

———. *Social Evolution*. Menlo Park, Calif.: Benjamin/Cummings, 1985.

Turnbull, Colin. *The Mountain People*. New York: Simon & Schuster, 1972.

Von Neumann, John, and Oskar Morgenstern. *Theory of Games and Economic Behavior*. Princeton, N.J.: Princeton Univ. Pr., 1947.

Westermarck, Edward. *Ethical Relativity*. New York: Harcourt Brace, 1932.

———. *The Origin and Development of the Moral Ideas*. 2 vols. London: Macmillan, 1906–1908.

White, Douglas J. *Decision Theory*. Chicago: Aldine, 1969.

Wilson, Edward O. *Sociobiology: The New Synthesis*. 25th anniversary ed. Cambridge, Mass.: Harvard Univ. Pr., 2000.

Wren, Thomas E. *Caring about Morality: Philosophical Perspectives in Moral Psychology*. Cambridge, Mass.: MIT, 1991.

Wright, Robert. *The Moral Animal: Evolutionary Psychology and Everyday Life*. New York: Pantheon, 1994.

4B.   World Religions and Non-Western Ethics

Adamec, Ludwig W. *Historical Dictionary of Islam*. Lanham, Md.: Scarecrow, 2001.

Allinson, R. E. "The Golden Rule as the Core Value in Confucianism and Christianity." *Asian Philosophy* 2, no. 2 (1992): 173–85.

Apostles. "Didache." In *Readings in Christian Ethics: A Historical Sourcebook*, ed.

J. Philip Wogaman and Douglas M. Strong, 13–14. Louisville, Ky.: Westminster John Knox, 1996.

Becker, Gerhold K., ed. *Ethics in Business and Society: Chinese and Western Perspectives*. New York: Springer, 1996.

Bernardin, Joseph L. *A Moral Vision for America*. Ed. John P. Langan. Washington, D.C.: Georgetown Univ. Pr., 1998.

Borowitz, Eugene B., and Frances Weinman Schwartz. *The Jewish Moral Virtues*. Philadelphia: Jewish Publication Society, 1999.

Brockopp, Jonathan E., ed. *Islamic Ethics of Life: Abortion, War, and Euthanasia*. Columbia: Univ. of South Carolina Pr., 2003.

Browne, Lewis. *The World's Great Scriptures*. New York: Macmillan, 1946.

Cahill, Lisa Sowle. *Love Your Enemies: Discipleship, Pacifism, and Just War Theory*. Minneapolis, Minn.: Fortress, 1994.

———. *Sex, Gender, and Christian Ethics*. Cambridge: Cambridge Univ. Pr., 1996.

Chan, Wing T. "The Evolution of the Confucian Concept Jên." *Philosophy East and West* 4, no. 4 (January 1955): 295–319.

———. *A Source Book in Chinese Philosophy*. Princeton, N.J.: Princeton Univ. Pr., 1963.

Chilton, Bruce, and James I. H. McDonald. *Jesus and the Ethics of the Kingdom*. Grand Rapids, Mich.: W.B. Eerdmans, 1987.

Collinge, William J. *Historical Dictionary of Catholicism*. 2nd ed. Lanham, Md.: Scarecrow, 2001.

Confucius. *The Analects*. Trans. Simon Leys. New York: W. W. Norton, 1997.

Cua, Antonio S. *Moral Vision and Tradition: Essays in Chinese Ethics*. Washington, D.C.: Catholic Univ. of America Pr., 1998.

Curran, Charles E. *Christian Morality Today*. Notre Dame, Ind.: Fides, 1966.

———, ed. *Contraception: Authority and Dissent*. New York: Herder and Herder, 1969.

Curran, Charles E., Margaret A. Farley, and Richard A. McCormick. *Feminist Ethics and the Catholic Moral Tradition*. New York: Paulist, 1996.

Curran, Charles E., and Richard A. McCormick, eds. *Dialogue about Catholic Sexual Teaching*. New York: Paulist, 1993.

Daly, Robert J., ed. *Christian Biblical Ethics*. New York: Paulist, 1984.

Dan, Joseph. *Jewish Mysticism and Jewish Ethics*. 2nd ed. Northvale, N.J.: J. Aronson, 1996.

Dasgupta, Surama. *Development of Moral Philosophy in India*. 2nd ed. New Delhi: Munshiram Manoharlal, 1994.

Dykstra, Craig. *Vision and Character: A Christian Educator's Alternative to Kohlberg*. New York: Paulist, 1981.

Engelhardt, H. Tristram. *The Foundations of Christian Bioethics*. Exton, Pa.: Swets & Zeitlinger, 2000.

Freund, Richard A. *Understanding Jewish Ethics*. San Francisco: EM Text, 1990.

Fuchs, Josef. *Christian Ethics in a Secular Arena*. Trans. Bernard Hoose and Brian McNeil. Washington, D.C.: Georgetown Univ. Pr., 1984.

Fung, Yu-Lan. *A History of Chinese Philosophy*. 2 vols. Trans. Derk Bodde. Princeton: Princeton Univ. Pr., 1952–1953.

Gill, Robin. *A Textbook of Christian Ethics*. Edinburgh: T&T Clark, 1995.

Graham, Angus C. *Disputers of the Tao: Philosophical Argument in Ancient China*. La Salle, Ill.: Open Court, 1989.

Grisez, Germain G., and Russell Shaw. *Fulfillment in Christ: A Summary of Christian Moral Principles*. Notre Dame, Ind.: Univ. of Notre Dame Pr., 1991.

Gupta, Bina, ed. *Ethical Questions: East and West*. Lanham, Md.: Rowman & Littlefield, 2002.

Gustafson, James M. *Can Ethics be Christian?* Chicago: Univ. of Chicago Pr., 1975.

———. *Christ and the Moral Life*. New York: Harper & Row, 1968.

———. *Theology and Christian Ethics*. Philadelphia: United Church, 1974.

Hall, David L., and Roger T. Ames. *Thinking through Confucius*. Albany, N.Y.: SUNY, 1987.

Hallett, Garth L. *Christian Moral Reasoning: An Analytic Guide*. Notre Dame, Ind.: Univ. of Notre Dame Pr., 1983.

———. *Greater Good: The Case for Proportionalism*. Washington, D.C.: Georgetown Univ. Pr., 1995.

———. *Priorities and Christian Ethics*. Cambridge: Cambridge Univ. Pr., 1998.

Hamilton, Sue. *Indian Philosophy: A Very Short Introduction*. Oxford: Oxford Univ. Pr., 2001.

Häring, Bernhard. *Toward a Christian Moral Theology*. Notre Dame, Ind.: Univ. of Notre Dame Pr., 1966.

Harrington, Daniel J., and James F. Keenan. *Jesus and Virtue Ethics: Building Bridges between New Testament Studies and Moral Theology*. Lanham, Md.: Sheed & Ward, 2002.

Harvey, Peter. *An Introduction to Buddhist Ethics*. Cambridge: Cambridge Univ. Pr., 2000.

Höchsmann, Hyun. *On Philosophy in China*. Belmont, Calif.: Wadsworth, 2004.

Holmes, Arthur F., ed. *War and Christian Ethics: Classic and Contemporary Readings on the Morality of War*. Grand Rapids, Mich.: Baker Academic, 2005.

Hoyt, Robert G., ed. *The Birth Control Debate*. Kansas City, Mo.: National Catholic Reporter, 1968.

Hughes, Gerard J. *Authority in Morals: An Essay in Christian Ethics*. Washington, D.C.: Georgetown Univ. Pr., 1984.

Hume, Robert Ernest. *The World's Living Religions*. 2nd ed. New York: Scribner, 1959.

Inada, Kenneth K. *Guide to Buddhist Philosophy*. Boston: G. K. Hall, 1985.

Ivanhoe, Philip J. *Confucian Moral Self-Cultivation*. 2nd ed. Indianapolis, Ind.: Hackett, 2000.

Jensen, Joseph. *Ethical Dimensions of the Prophets*. Collegeville, Minn.: Liturgical Pr., 2006.

Keenan, James F. *Moral Wisdom: Lessons and Texts from the Catholic Tradition*. Lanham, Md.: Rowman & Littlefield, 2004.

———. *Virtues for Ordinary Christians*. Kansas City, Mo.: Sheed & Ward, 1996.

Kelsay, John. *Islam and War: A Study in Comparative Ethics*. Louisville, Ky.: Westminster, 1993.

Kraemer, Hendrik. *The Bible and Social Ethics*. Philadelphia: Fortress, 1965.

Küng, Hans. *A Global Ethic for Global Politics and Economics*. Trans. John Bowden. New York: Oxford Univ. Pr., 1998.

———. *Global Responsibility: In Search of a New World Ethic*. New York: Continuum, 1993.

———, ed. *Yes to a Global Ethic*. New York: Continuum, 1996.

Küng, Hans, and Karl-Josef Kuschel, eds. *A Global Ethic: The Declaration of the Parliament of the World's Religions*. New York: Continuum, 1993.

Küng, Hans, and Jürgen Moltmann, eds. *The Ethics of World Religions and Human Rights*. London: SCM, 1990.

Küng, Hans, and Helmut Schmidt, eds. *A Global Ethic and Global Responsibilities: Two Declarations*. London: SCM, 1998.

Laozi. *Dao De Jing: the Book of the Way*. Trans. Moss Roberts. Berkeley: Univ. of California Pr., 2001.

Linzey, Andrew. *Christianity and the Rights of Animals*. New York: Crossroad, 1987.

Little, David, and Sumner B. Twiss. *Comparative Religious Ethics*. San Francisco: Harper and Row, 1978.

Mahoney, John. *The Making of Moral Theology: A Study of the Roman Catholic Tradition*. Oxford: Clarendon, 1990.

Marmura, Michael E., ed. *Islamic Theology and Philosophy*. Albany, N.Y.: SUNY, 1984.

Matthews, Victor H., and Don C. Benjamin. *Old Testament Parallels: Laws and Stories from the Ancient Near East*. New York: Paulist, 1997. [contains the Code of Hammurabi and similar ancient codes]

Mattuck, Israel I. *Jewish Ethics*. New York: Hutchinson's Univ. Library, 1953.

May, William E. *Contraception: "Humanae Vitae" and Catholic Moral Thought*. Chicago: Franciscan Herald Pr., 1984.

McCormick, Richard A., and Paul Ramsey, eds. *Doing Evil to Achieve Good: Moral Choice in Conflict Situations*. Chicago: Loyola Univ. Pr., 1978.

McGovern, Arthur F. *Liberation Theology and Its Critics*. Maryknoll, N.Y.: Orbis, 1989.

———. *Marxism: An American Christian Perspective*. Maryknoll, N.Y.: Orbis, 1980.

McInerny, Ralph M. *The Question of Christian Ethics*. Washington, D.C.: Catholic Univ. of America Pr., 1993.

Meeks, Wayne A. *The Origins of Christian Morality: The First Two Centuries.* New Haven: Yale Univ. Pr., 1993.

Miller, Richard B. *Interpretations of Conflict: Ethics, Pacifism, and the Just-War Tradition.* Chicago: Univ. of Chicago Pr., 1991.

Munro, Donald J. *A Chinese Ethics for the New Century.* Hong Kong: Chinese Univ. Pr., 2005.

———, ed. *Individualism and Holism: Studies in Confucian and Taoist Values.* Ann Arbor: Univ. of Michigan Pr., 1985.

Murray, John Courtney. *We Hold These Truths: Catholic Reflections on the American Proposition.* New York: Sheed & Ward, 1960.

Neusner, Jacob, ed. *How the Golden Rule Figures in World Religions.* London: Continuum, 2008.

Newman, Louis E. *Past Imperatives: Studies in the History and Theory of Jewish Ethics.* Albany, N.Y.: SUNY, 1998.

Niebuhr, H. Richard. *Christ and Culture.* New York: Harper, 1951.

Niebuhr, Reinhold. *Love and Justice: Selections from the Shorter Writings of Reinhold Niebuhr.* Ed. D. B. Robertson. Cleveland, Ohio: World, 1957.

———. *Moral Man and Immoral Society: A Study of Ethics and Politics.* New York: Scribner, 1932.

Nivison, David S. *The Ways of Confucianism: Investigations in Chinese Philosophy.* Ed. Bryan W. Van Norden. Chicago: Open Court, 1996.

Novak, David. *Jewish Social Ethics.* New York: Oxford Univ. Pr., 1992.

———. *Natural Law in Judaism.* Cambridge: Cambridge Univ. Pr., 1998.

Ng, On-cho. *Historical Dictionary of Confucianism.* Lanham, Md.: Scarecrow, forthcoming.

Nygren, Anders. *Agape and Eros.* Trans. Philip S. Watson. Philadelphia: Westminster, 1953.

Odozor, Paulinus Ikechukwu, ed. *Sexuality, Marriage, and Family: Readings in the Catholic Tradition.* Notre Dame, Ind.: Univ. of Notre Dame Pr., 2001.

Outka, Gene H. *Agape: An Ethical Analysis.* New Haven, Conn.: Yale Univ. Pr., 1972.

Outka, Gene H., and Paul Ramsey, eds. *Norm and Context in Christian Ethics.* New York: Scribner, 1968.

Parliament of the World's Religions. "Declaration of a Global Ethics." Center for Global Ethics: 1993. http://astro.ocis.temple.edu/~dialogue/geth.htm

Pas, Julian F. *Historical Dictionary of Taoism.* Lanham, Md.: Scarecrow, 1998.

Picken, Stuart D. B. *Historical Dictionary of Shinto.* Lanham, Md.: Scarecrow, 2002.

Pogge, Thomas W. *World Poverty and Human Rights.* Cambridge: Polity, 2002.

Prebish, Charles S. *The A to Z of Buddhism.* Lanham, Md.: Scarecrow, 2001.

Rae, Scott B., and Kenman L. Wong, eds. *Beyond Integrity: A Judeo-Christian Approach to Business Ethics.* Grand Rapids, Mich.: Zondervan, 2004.

Richards, Glyn. *The Philosophy of Gandhi.* Totowa, N.J.: Barnes & Noble, 1982.

Roetz, Heiner. *Confucian Ethics of the Axial Age*. Albany, N.Y.: SUNY, 1993.

Rosner, Fred. *Biomedical Ethics and Jewish Law*. Hoboken, N.J.: KTAV, 2001.

Rost, H. T. D. *The Golden Rule*. Oxford: G. Ronald, 1986.

Rousseau, Richard W., ed. *Human Dignity and the Common Good: The Great Papal Social Encyclicals from Leo XIII to John Paul II*. Westport, Conn.: Greenwood, 2002.

Rowley, Harold H. "The Chinese Sages and the Golden Rule." *Bulletin of the John Rylands Library* 24 (1940): 321–52.

Sachedina, Abdulaziz A. *The Islamic Roots of Democratic Pluralism*. Oxford: Oxford Univ. Pr., 2001.

Schubeck, Thomas L. *Liberation Ethics*. Minneapolis, Minn.: Fortress, 1993.

———. *Love that Does Justice*. Maryknoll, N.Y.: Orbis, 2007.

Scrunton, Roger. *Animal Rights and Wrongs*. London: Metro and Demos, 2000.

Shanahan, Timothy, and Robin Wang, eds. *Reason and Insight: Western and Eastern Perspectives on the Pursuit of Moral Wisdom*. Belmont, Calif.: Wadsworth, 1996.

Shannon, William H. *The Lively Debate: Response to Humanae Vitae*. New York: Sheed & Ward, 1970.

Sherwin, Byron L. *Jewish Ethics for the Twenty-first Century*. Syracuse, N.Y.: Syracuse Univ. Pr., 2000.

Shun, Kwong-loi, and David B. Wong, eds. *Confucian Ethics*. Cambridge: Cambridge Univ. Pr., 2004.

Silver, Daniel Jeremy. *Judaism and Ethics*. New York: KTAV, 1970.

Smith, Janet E. "Natural Law and Sexual Ethics." In *Common Truths: New Perspectives on Natural Law*, ed. Edward B. McLean, 193–218. Wilmington, Del.: ISI, 2000.

———, ed. *Why Humanae Vitae Was Right: A Reader*. San Francisco: Ignatius, 1993.

Solomon, Norman. *Historical Dictionary of Judaism*. 2nd ed. Lanham, Md.: Scarecrow, 2007.

Spohn, William C. *What Are They Saying about Scripture and Ethics?* New York: Paulist, 1995.

Sullivan, Bruce M. *The A to Z of Hinduism*. Lanham, Md.: Scarecrow, 2001.

Sullivan, William M., and Will Kymlicka, eds. *The Globalization of Ethics: Religious and Secular Perspectives*. Cambridge: Cambridge Univ. Pr., 2007.

Svarverud, Rune. *Methods of the Way: Early Chinese Ethical Thought*. Boston: Brill, 1998.

Tillich, Paul. *Morality and Beyond*. New York: Harper & Row, 1963.

Twiss, Sumner B., and Bruce Grelle. *Explorations in Global Ethics: Comparative Religious Ethics and Interreligious Dialogue*. Boulder, Colo.: Westview, 1998.

UNESCO. Report on Global Ethics. http://kvc.minbuza.nl/uk/archive/report/chapter1_3.html

Unger, Peter. *Living High and Letting Die*. New York: Oxford Univ. Pr., 1996.

United Nations. "Declaration of Human Rights." http://www.un.org/Overview/
rights.html

Wadell, Paul J. *Happiness and the Christian Moral Life: An Introduction to Christian Ethics*. Lanham, Md.: Rowman & Littlefield, 2008.

Westermarck, Edward. *Christianity and Morals*. New York: Macmillan, 1939.

Wiley, Kristi L. *Historical Dictionary of Jainism*. Lanham, Md.: Scarecrow, 2004.

Wogaman, J. Philip. *Christian Ethics: A Historical Introduction*. Louisville, Ky.:
Westminster John Knox, 1993.

Wogaman, J. Philip, and Douglas M. Strong, eds. *Readings in Christian Ethics: A
Historical Sourcebook*. Louisville, Ky.: Westminster John Knox, 1996.

Zhuangzi. *Chuang Tzu: Mystic, Moralist, and Social Reformer*. 2nd ed. Trans.
Herbert A. Giles. Shanghai, China: Kelley & Walsh, 1926.

4C. Logic and Ethics

Anderson, Alan Ross. "The Formal Analysis of Normative Systems." In *The Logic
of Decision and Action*, ed. Nicholas Rescher, 147–213. Pittsburgh, Pa.: Univ.
of Pittsburgh Pr., 1966.

———. "The Logic of Norms." *Logique et Analyse* 1, no. 2 (April 1958): 84–91.

Åqvist, Lennart. "Choice-Offering and Alternative-Presenting Disjunctive Commands." *Analysis* 25, no. 5 (April 1965): 182–84.

Beardsley, Elizabeth Lane. "Imperative Sentences in Relation to Indicatives."
Philosophical Review 53, no. 2 (March 1944): 175–85.

Castañeda, Hector-Neri. "Actions, Imperatives, and Obligations." *Proceedings of
the Aristotelian Society* 68 (1967–1968): 25–48.

———. "Ethics and Logic: Stevensonian Emotivism Revisited." *Journal of Philosophy* 64, no. 20 (Oct. 1967): 671–83.

———. "Imperative Reasonings." *Philosophy and Phenomenological Research*
21, no. 1 (September 1960): 21–49.

———. "On the Semantics of the Ought-to-Do." *Synthese* 21, no. 4 (December
1970): 449–68.

———. "Outline of a Theory on the General Logical Structure of the Language of
Action." *Theoria* 26, no. 3 (1960): 151–82.

Chisholm, Roderick M. "Contrary-to-Duty Imperatives and Deontic Logic." *Analysis* 24, no. 2 (December 1963): 33–36.

———. "The Ethics of Requirement." *American Philosophical Quarterly* 1, no. 2
(April 1964): 147–53.

———. "Supererogation and Offense: A Conceptual Scheme for Ethics." *Ratio* 5
(old series), no. 1 (June 1963): 1–14.

Clarke, D. S., Jr. "The Logical Form of Imperatives." *Philosophia* 5, no. 4 (October 1975): 417–27.

———. "Mood Consistency in Mixed Inferences." *Analysis* 30, no. 3 (January
1970): 100–103.

Dahl, Norman O. " ' "Ought" Implies "Can" ' and Deontic Logic." *Philosophia* 4, no. 4 (October 1974): 485–511.

Feldman, Fred. *Doing the Best We Can: An Essay in Informal Deontic Logic.* Dordrecht: D. Reidel, 1986.

Fisher, Mark. "A Logical Theory of Commanding." *Logique et Analyse* 4, no. 15–16 (October 1961): 154–69.

———. "Strong and Weak Negation of Imperatives." *Theoria* 28, no. 2 (1962): 196–200.

———. "A System of Deontic-Alethic Modal Logic." *Mind* 71, no. 282 (May 1962): 231–36.

Forrester, James W. *Being Good and Being Logical: Philosophical Groundwork for a New Deontic Logic.* Armonk, N.Y.: M.E. Sharpe, 1996.

Geach, Peter T. "Imperative and Deontic Logic." *Analysis* 18, no. 3 (January 1958): 49–56.

———. "Imperative Inference." *Analysis Supplement* 23 (1963): 37–42.

Gensler, Harry J. "Acting Commits One to Ethical Beliefs." *Analysis* 43, no. 1 (January 1983): 40–43.

———. "Ethical Consistency Principles." *Philosophical Quarterly* 35, no. 139 (April 1985): 156–70.

———. "How Incomplete is Prescriptivism?" *Mind* 93, no. 369 (January 1984): 103–107.

———. *Formal Ethics.* London: Routledge, 1996.

———. *Introduction to Logic.* London: Routledge, 2002. [chapters 9–11]

———. "The Prescriptivism Incompleteness Theorem." *Mind* 85, no. 340 (October 1976): 589–96.

Gombay, Andre. "What *Is* Imperative Inference?" *Analysis* 27, no. 5 (April 1967): 145–52.

Greenspan, P. S. "Conditional Oughts and Hypothetical Imperatives." *Journal of Philosophy* 72, no. 10 (22 May 1975): 259–66.

Hare, Richard M. *The Language of Morals.* Oxford: Clarendon, 1952. [Chapters 1–4 address imperative logic.]

———. *Practical Inferences.* Berkeley: Univ. of California, 1972.

Hilpinen, Risto, ed. *Deontic Logic: Introductory and Systematic Readings.* Dordrecht: D. Reidel, 1971.

———. *New Studies in Deontic Logic: Norms, Actions, and the Foundations of Ethics.* Dordrecht: D. Reidel, 1981.

Hofstadter, Albert, and J. C. C. McKinsey. "On the Logic of Imperatives." *Philosophy of Science* 6 (1939): 446–57.

Kamp, Hans. "Free Choice Permission." *Proceedings of the Aristotelian Society* 74 (1973–1974): 57–74.

Kenny, A. J. "Practical Inference." *Analysis* 26, no. 3 (January 1966): 65–75.

Körner, Stephan, ed. *Practical Reason: Papers and Discussions.* New Haven, Conn.: Yale Univ. Pr., 1974.

Lappin, Shalom. "Moral Judgments and Identity across Possible Worlds." *Ratio* 20, no. 1 (June 1978): 69–74.

MacKay, Alfred F. "Inferential Validity and Imperative Inference Rules." *Analysis* 29, no. 5 (April 1969): 145–56.

———. "The Principle of Mood Consistency." *Analysis* 31, no. 3 (January 1971): 91–96.

Prior, Arthur N. *Logic and the Basis of Ethics*. Oxford: Clarendon, 1949.

———. *Papers in Logic and Ethics*. Ed. P. T. Geach and A. J. Kenny. Amherst: Univ. of Massachusetts Pr., 1976.

Rescher, Nicholas. "An Axiom System for Deontic Logic." *Philosophical Studies* 9, no. 1–2 and 4 (January-February and June 1958): 24–30 and 64.

———. *The Logic of Commands*. London: Routledge & Kegan Paul, 1966.

———, ed. *The Logic of Decision and Action*. Pittsburgh, Pa.: Univ. of Pittsburgh Pr., 1966.

Roberts, Colin. "Zellner and Imperative Inferences." *Mind* 84, no. 333 (January 1975): 111–13.

Ross, Alf. "Imperatives and Logic." *Philosophy of Science* 11 (1944): 30–46.

Schueler, G. F. "*Modus Ponens* and Moral Realism." *Ethics* 98, no. 3 (April 1988): 492–500.

Sosa, Ernest. "The Logic of Imperatives." *Theoria* 32, no. 3 (1966): 224–35.

———. "On Practical Inference and the Logic of Imperatives." *Theoria* 32, no. 3 (1966): 211–23.

———. "On Practical Inference with an Excursus on Theoretical Inference." *Logique et Analyse* 13, no. 49–50 (March-June 1970): 213–30.

———. "The Semantics of Imperatives." *American Philosophical Quarterly* 4, no. 1 (January 1967): 57–64.

Turnbull, Robert G. "Imperatives, Logic, and Moral Obligation." *Philosophy of Science* 27 (1960): 374–90.

Williams, Bernard A. O. "Consistency and Realism." *Aristotelian Society Supplement* 45 (1966): 1–22.

———. "Imperative Inference." *Analysis Supplement* 23 (1963): 30–36.

Wright, Georg Henrik von. "Deontic Logic." *Mind* 60, no. 237 (January 1951): 1–15.

———. *An Essay in Deontic Logic and the General Theory of Action*. Amsterdam: North-Holland, 1968.

———. *The Logic of Preference*. Edinburgh: Edinburgh Univ. Pr., 1963.

———. *Norm and Action: A Logical Enquiry*. New York: Humanities, 1963.

———. *Practical Reason*. Ithaca, N.Y.: Cornell Univ. Pr., 1983.

Zellner, Harold. "A Note on R. M. Hare and the Paradox of the Good Samaritan." *Mind* 82, no. 326 (April 1973): 281–82.

5. Applied Ethics

Aiken, William, and Hugh LaFollette, eds. *World Hunger and Morality*. 2nd ed. Upper Saddle River, N.J.: Prentice Hall, 1996.

Alora, Angeles Tan, and Josephine M. Lumitao, eds. *Beyond a Western Bioethics: Voices from the Developing World*. Washington, D.C.: Georgetown Univ. Pr., 2001.

Alpern, Kenneth D., ed. *The Ethics of Reproductive Technology*. New York: Oxford Univ. Pr., 1992.

Anderson, Elizabeth. *Value in Ethics and Economics*. Cambridge, Mass.: Harvard Univ. Pr., 1993.

Arras, John D., and Bonnie Steinbock. *Ethical Issues in Modern Medicine*. 4th ed. Mountain View, Calif.: Mayfield, 1995.

Arthur, John. *Morality and Moral Controversies*. 7th ed. Upper Saddle River, N.J.: Pearson Prentice Hall, 2005.

Atiyah, Patrick S. *Promises, Morals, and Law*. Oxford: Oxford Univ. Pr., 1981.

Attfield, Robin. *The Ethics of Environmental Concern*. 2nd ed. Athens: Univ. of Georgia Pr., 1991.

Baird, Robert M., Reagan Ramsower, and Stuart E. Rosenbaum, eds. *Cyberethics: Social and Moral Issues in the Computer Age*. Amherst, N.Y.: Prometheus, 2000.

Baird, Robert M., and Stuart E. Rosenbaum, eds. *The Ethics of Abortion*. 2nd ed. Buffalo, N.Y.: Prometheus, 1993.

Barry, Vincent, ed. *Moral Issues in Business*. Belmont, Calif.: Wadsworth, 1979.

Battin, Margaret Pabst. *The Least Worst Death: Essays in Bioethics on the End of Life*. New York: Oxford Univ. Pr., 1994.

Bayertz, Kurt. *GenEthics: Technological Intervention in Human Reproduction as a Philosophical Problem*. Trans. Sarah L. Kirkby. Cambridge: Cambridge Univ. Pr., 1994.

Beauchamp, Tom L. *Case Studies in Business, Society, and Ethics*. 5th ed. Upper Saddle River, N.J.: Pearson Prentice Hall, 2004.

Beauchamp, Tom L., and Norman Bowie, eds. *Ethical Theory and Business*. 6th ed. Upper Saddle River, N.J.: Prentice Hall, 2001.

Beauchamp, Tom L., and James F. Childress. *Principles of Biomedical Ethics*. 5th ed. New York: Oxford Univ. Pr., 2001.

Beauchamp, Tom L., and LeRoy Walters, eds. *Contemporary Issues in Bioethics*. 6th ed. Belmont, Calif.: Wadsworth, 2003.

Bedau, Hugo Adam, ed. *The Death Penalty in America: Current Controversies*. New York: Oxford Univ. Pr., 1997.

Benjamin, Martin, and Joy Curtis. *Ethics in Nursing*. 3rd ed. New York: Oxford Univ. Pr., 1992.

Berlow, Lawrence H. *Sports Ethics: A Reference Handbook*. Santa Barbara, Calif.: ABC-CLIO, 1994.

Bird, Frederick, and Manuel Velasquez, eds. *Just Business Practices in a Diverse and Developing World: Essays on International Business and Global Responsibilities*. New York: Palgrave Macmillan, 2006.

Blackstone, William T., ed. *Philosophy and Environmental Crisis*. Athens: Univ. of Georgia Pr., 1974.

Blake, Nigel, and Kay Pole, eds. *Objections to Nuclear Defence*. London: Routledge, 1984.

Blustein, Jeffrey. *Parents and Children: The Ethics of the Family*. New York: Oxford Univ. Pr., 1982.

Boatright, John R. *Ethics and the Conduct of Business*. 5th ed. Upper Saddle River, N.J.: Prentice Hall, 2007.

————. *Ethics in Finance*. Malden, Mass.: Blackwell, 1999.

————, ed. *Cases in Ethics and the Conduct of Business*. Englewood Cliffs, N.J.: Prentice Hall, 1995.

Bok, Sissela. *A Strategy for Peace: Human Values and the Threat of War*. New York: Pantheon, 1989.

Bowie, Norman E. *Business Ethics: A Kantian Perspective*. Malden, Mass.: Blackwell, 1999.

————. *Ethical Issues in Government*. Philadelphia: Temple Univ. Pr., 1981.

————, ed. *The Blackwell Guide to Business Ethics*. Malden, Mass.: Blackwell, 2002.

Boxill, Bernard R. *Blacks and Social Justice*. 2nd ed. Lanham, Md.: Rowman & Littlefield, 1992.

Boylan, Michael, ed. *Business Ethics*. Upper Saddle River, N.J.: Prentice Hall, 2001.

Brody, Baruch A. *Abortion and the Sanctity of Human Life: A Philosophical View*. Cambridge, Mass.: MIT, 1975.

Broome, John. *Counting the Cost of Global Warming*. Cambridge: White Horse, 1992.

————. *Weighing Lives*. Oxford: Oxford Univ. Pr., 2004.

Brown, Peter G., and Henry Shue. *Food Policy: The Responsibility of the United States in the Life and Death Choices*. New York: Free Pr., 1977.

Bryan, Willie V. *In Search of Freedom: How Persons with Disabilities Have Been Disenfranchised from the Mainstream of American Society*. Springfield, Ill.: C.C. Thomas, 1996.

Burleigh, Michael. *Ethics and Extermination: Reflections on Nazi Genocide*. Cambridge: Cambridge Univ. Pr., 1997.

Burley, Justine, and John Harris, eds. *A Companion to Genethics*. Malden, Mass.: Blackwell, 2002.

Cahn, Steven M., ed. *Morality, Responsibility, and the University: Studies in Academic Ethics*. Philadelphia: Temple Univ. Pr., 1990.

————. *Saints and Scamps: Ethics in Academia*. Lanham, Md.: Rowman & Littlefield, 1994.

Calhoun, Cheshire. *Feminism, the Family, and the Politics of the Closet: Lesbian and Gay Displacement.* Oxford: Oxford Univ. Pr., 2000.

Callahan, Sidney Cornelia. "Abortion and the Sexual Agenda: A Case for Pro-life Feminism." *Commonweal* 113, no. 8 (25 April 1986): 232–38.

Callahan, Sidney Cornelia, and Daniel Callahan, eds. *Abortion: Understanding Differences.* New York: Plenum, 1984.

Callicott, J. Baird. *Beyond the Land Ethic: More Essays in Environmental Philosophy.* Albany, N.Y.: SUNY, 1999.

———. *In Defense of the Land Ethic: Essays in Environmental Philosophy.* Albany, N.Y.: SUNY, 1989.

Carr, Albert Z. "Is Business Bluffing Ethical?" *Harvard Business Review* 46, no. 1 (Jan.-Feb. 1968): 143–53.

Carruthers, Peter. *The Animals Issue: Moral Theory in Practice.* Cambridge: Cambridge Univ. Pr., 1992.

Carson, Rachel. *Silent Spring.* Boston: Houghton Mifflin, 1962.

Childress, James F. *Practical Reasoning in Bioethics.* Bloomington: Indiana Univ. Pr., 1997.

Cohen, Carl, and Tom Regan. *The Animal Rights Debate.* Lanham, Md.: Rowman & Littlefield, 2001.

Cohen, Elliot D., and Michael Davis, eds. *AIDS: Crisis in Professional Ethics.* Philadelphia: Temple Univ. Pr., 1994.

Cohen, Elliot D., and Deni Elliott, eds. *Journalism Ethics: A Reference Handbook.* Santa Barbara, Calif.: ABC-CLIO, 1997.

Copp, David, and Susan Wendell, eds. *Pornography and Censorship.* Buffalo, N.Y.: Prometheus, 1983.

Daniels, Norman. *Just Health Care.* Cambridge: Cambridge Univ. Pr., 1985.

De George, Richard T. *Business Ethics.* 2nd ed. New York: Macmillan, 1986.

———. *Competing with Integrity in International Business.* New York: Oxford Univ. Pr., 1993.

Degrazia, David. *Animal Rights: A Very Short Introduction.* Oxford: Oxford Univ. Pr., 2002.

———. *Taking Animals Seriously: Mental Life and Moral Status.* Cambridge: Cambridge Univ. Pr., 1996.

DesJardins, Joseph R. *An Introduction to Business Ethics.* 2nd ed. Boston: McGraw-Hill, 2006.

DesJardins, Joseph R., and John J. McCall, eds. *Contemporary Issues in Business Ethics.* Belmont, Calif.: Wadsworth, 2005.

Dewey, John. *Experience and Education.* New York: Collier, 1938.

———. *Moral Principles in Education.* Carbondale: Southern Illinois Univ. Pr., 1975.

———. *The School and Society.* Ed. Jo Ann Boydston. Carbondale: Southern Illinois Univ. Pr., 1980.

Donagan, Alan. *Morality, Property and Slavery.* Lawrence: Univ. of Kansas, 1981.

Donaldson, Thomas. *The Ethics of International Business*. New York: Oxford Univ. Pr., 1989.

Donaldson, Thomas, and Thomas W. Dunfee. *Ties that Bind: A Social Contracts Approach to Business Ethics*. Boston: Harvard Business School Pr., 1999.

Donaldson, Thomas, Patricia H. Werhane, and Margaret Cording, eds. *Ethical Issues in Business: A Philosophical Approach*. 7th ed. Upper Saddle River, N.J.: Prentice Hall, 2002.

Durkheim, Emile. *Moral Education: A Study in the Theory and Application of the Sociology of Education*. Trans. Everett K. Wilson and Herman Schnurer, ed. Everett K. Wilson. Glencoe, Ill.: Free Pr., 1961.

———. *Professional Ethics and Civic Morals*. Trans. Cornelia Brookfield. Glencoe, Ill.: Free Pr., 1958.

Duska, Ronald, and Mariellen Whelan. *Moral Development: A Guide to Piaget and Kohlberg*. New York: Paulist, 1975.

Dworkin, Gerald, Gordon Bermant, and Peter G. Brown, eds. *Markets and Morals*. Washington, D.C.: Hemisphere, 1977.

Dworkin, Gerald, R. G. Frey, and Sissela Bok. *Euthanasia and Physician-Assisted Suicide*. Cambridge: Cambridge Univ. Pr., 1998.

Dworkin, Ronald. *Life's Dominion: An Argument about Abortion, Euthanasia, and Individual Freedom*. New York: Knopf, 1993.

Ehrlich, Paul R. *The Population Bomb*. New York: Ballantine, 1968.

Elliot, Robert, ed. *Environmental Ethics*. Oxford: Oxford Univ. Pr., 1995.

Ellos, William J. *Ethical Practice in Clinical Medicine*. London: Routledge, 1990.

Engelhardt, H. Tristram. *Bioethics and Secular Humanism: The Search for a Common Morality*. London: SCM, 1991.

———. *The Foundations of Bioethics*. New York: Oxford Univ. Pr., 1986.

Erwin, Edward, Sidney Gendin, and Lowell Kleiman, eds. *Ethical Issues in Scientific Research*. New York: Garland, 1994.

Ezorsky, Gertrude, ed. *Moral Rights in the Workplace*. Albany, N.Y.: SUNY, 1987.

———. *Philosophical Perspectives on Punishment*. Albany, N.Y.: SUNY, 1972.

———. *Racism and Justice: The Case for Affirmative Action*. Ithaca, N.Y.: Cornell Univ. Pr., 1991.

Feinberg, Joel. *Doing and Deserving: Essays in the Theory of Responsibility*. Princeton, N.J., Princeton Univ. Pr., 1970.

———. *Harm to Others*. Oxford: Oxford Univ. Pr., 1984.

———. *Harm to Self*. Oxford: Oxford Univ. Pr., 1986.

———, ed. *The Problem of Abortion*. 2nd ed. Belmont, Calif.: Wadsworth, 1984.

Feinberg, Joel, and Hyman Gross, eds. *Philosophy of Law*. 5th ed. Belmont, Calif.: Wadsworth, 1995.

Finnis, John M., Joseph M. Boyle, Jr., and Germain Grisez. *Nuclear Deterrence, Morality, and Realism*. Oxford: Clarendon, 1987.

Fletcher, Joseph F. *Morals and Medicine*. Princeton, N.J.: Princeton Univ. Pr.,

1954.

Ford, Norman M. *The Prenatal Person: Ethics from Conception to Birth.* Malden, Mass.: Blackwell, 2002.

Foucault, Michel. *The History of Sexuality.* 3 vols. Trans. Robert Hurley. New York: Pantheon, 1978.

Fox, Michael Allen. *The Case for Animal Experimentation: An Evolutionary and Ethical Perspective.* Berkeley: Univ. of California Pr., 1986.

Fox, Stephen R. *The American Conservation Movement: John Muir and His Legacy.* Madison: Univ. of Wisconsin Pr., 1985.

Frederick, Robert E., ed. *A Companion to Business Ethics.* Oxford: Blackwell, 2002.

Freeman, R. Edward. *Strategic Management: A Stakeholder Approach.* Boston: Pitman, 1984.

———, ed. *Business Ethics: The State of the Art.* New York: Oxford Univ. Pr., 1991.

French, Peter A. *Collective and Corporate Responsibility.* New York: Columbia Univ. Pr., 1984.

———. *Ethics and College Sports.* Lanham, Md.: Rowman & Littlefield, 2004.

———, ed. *Individual and Collective Responsibility: Massacre at My Lai.* Cambridge, Mass.: Schenkman, 1972.

Frey, Raymond G. *Rights, Killing, and Suffering: Moral Vegetarianism and Applied Ethics.* Oxford: Blackwell, 1983.

Fried, Charles. *Contract as Promise: A Theory of Contractual Obligation.* Cambridge, Mass.: Harvard Univ. Pr., 1981.

Friedlander, Henry. *The Origins of Nazi Genocide: From Euthanasia to the Final Solution.* Chapel Hill: Univ. of North Carolina Pr., 1995.

Friedman, Milton. *Capitalism and Freedom.* Chicago: Univ. of Chicago Pr., 1962.

———. "The Social Responsibility of Business Is to Increase Its Profits." *New York Times Magazine* 119, no. 41 (Sept. 13, 1970): 32–33, 122–26.

Gabard, Donald L., and Mike W. Martin, eds. *Physical Therapy Ethics.* Philadelphia: F.A. Davis, 2003.

Garner, Robert, ed. *Animal Rights: The Changing Debate.* New York: New York Univ. Pr., 1996.

Gensler, Harry J. "A Kantian Argument against Abortion." *Philosophical Studies* 49, no. 1 (Jan. 1986): 83–98.

Gillon, Raanan, and Ann Lloyd Ba, eds. *Principles of Health Care Ethics.* New York: John Wiley & Sons, 1994.

Glover, Jonathan. *Causing Death and Saving Lives.* New York: Penguin, 1977.

———. *Humanity: A Moral History of the Twentieth Century.* London: J. Cape, 1999.

———. *What Sort of People Should There Be?* New York: Penguin, 1984.

Godlovitch, Roslind and Stanley, and John Harris, eds. *Animals, Men and Morals: An Inquiry into the Maltreatment of Non-humans.* London: Gollancz, 1971.

Goldman, Alan H. *Justice and Reverse Discrimination*. Princeton, N.J.: Princeton Univ. Pr., 1979.

———. *The Moral Foundations of Professional Ethics*. Totowa, N.J.: Rowman & Littlefield, 1980.

Goodpaster, Kenneth E., and Laura L. Nash. *Policies and Persons: A Casebook in Business Ethics*. 3rd ed. New York: McGraw-Hill, 1998.

Gordon, Lewis R. *Bad Faith and Antiblack Racism*. Atlantic Highlands, N.J.: Humanities, 1995.

Gorman, Robert F., and Edward S. Mihalkanin. *Historical Dictionary of Human Rights and Humanitarian Organizations*. 2nd ed. Lanham, Md.: Scarecrow, 2007.

Gorovitz, Samuel. *Drawing the Line: Life, Death, and Ethical Choices in an American Hospital*. New York: Oxford Univ. Pr., 1991.

Grisez, Germain G. *Abortion: The Myths, the Realities, and the Arguments*. New York: Corpus, 1970.

Grisez, Germain G., and Joseph M. Boyle, Jr. *Life and Death with Liberty and Justice: A Contribution to the Euthanasia Debate*. Notre Dame, Ind.: Univ. of Notre Dame Pr., 1979.

Griswold, Charles L. *Forgiveness: A Philosophical Exploration*. Cambridge: Cambridge Univ. Pr., 2007.

Gross, Barry R. *Discrimination in Reverse: Is Turnabout Fair Play?* New York: New York Univ. Pr., 1978.

Grovier, Trudy. *Forgiveness and Revenge*. New York: Routledge, 2002.

Gunn, Alastair S. *Environmental Ethics for Engineers*. Chelsea, Mich.: Lewis, 1986.

Haas, Peter J. *Morality after Auschwitz*. Philadelphia: Fortress, 1988.

Haber, Joram Graf. *Forgiveness*. Savage, Md.: Rowman & Littlefield, 1991.

Hardin, Garrett James. *The Limits of Altruism: An Ecologist's View of Survival*. Bloomington: Indiana Univ. Pr., 1977.

Hare, Richard M. "Abortion and the Golden Rule." *Philosophy and Public Affairs* 4, no. 3 (Spring 1975): 201–22.

———. *Essays on Bioethics*. Oxford: Clarendon, 1993.

———. *Essays on Political Philosophy*. Oxford: Clarendon, 1989.

———. *Essays on Religion and Education*. Oxford: Clarendon, 1992.

———. "A Kantian Approach to Abortion." *Social Theory and Practice* 15 (Spring 1989): 1–14, 25–32.

Hargrove, Eugene C. *Foundations of Environmental Ethics*. Englewood Cliffs, N.J.: Prentice Hall, 1989.

Hart, H. L. A. *The Concept of Law*. Oxford: Clarendon, 1961.

———. *Punishment and Responsibility: Essays in the Philosophy of Law*. New York: Oxford Univ. Pr., 1968.

Heilbroner, Robert L. *The Worldly Philosophers: The Lives, Times, and Ideas of the Great Economic Thinkers*. 7th ed. New York: Touchstone, 1999.

Hester, D. Micah, and Paul J. Ford. *Computers and Ethics in the Cyberage.* Upper Saddle River, N.J.: Prentice Hall, 2001.

Heyd, David. *Genethics: Moral Issues in the Creation of People.* Berkeley: Univ. of California Pr., 1992.

Hinman, Lawrence, ed. *Contemporary Moral Issues.* 2nd ed. Upper Saddle River, N.J.: Prentice Hall, 2000.

Höchsmann, Hyun. *On Peter Singer.* Belmont, Calif.: Wadsworth, 2002.

Hoekema, David A. *Campus Rules and Moral Community: In Place of Loco Parentis.* Lanham, Md.: Rowman & Littlefield, 1994.

Holmes, Helen Bequaert, ed. *Issues in Reproductive Technology: An Anthology.* New York: Garland, 1992.

Hook, Sidney. *Academic Freedom and Academic Anarchy.* New York: Cowles, 1970.

————. *In Defense of Academic Freedom.* New York: Pegasus, 1971.

Hook, Sidney, Paul Kurtz, and Miro Todorovich, eds. *The Ethics of Teaching and Scientific Research.* Buffalo: Prometheus, 1977.

Houlgate, Laurence D. *Child and the State: A Normative Theory of Juvenile Rights.* Baltimore, Md.: Johns Hopkins Pr., 1980.

————. *Morals, Marriage, and Parenthood: An Introduction to Family Ethics.* Belmont, Calif.: Wadsworth, 1999.

House, H. Wayne, and John Howard Yoder. *The Death Penalty Debate.* Dallas, Tex.: Word, 1991.

Hull, N. E. H., and Peter Charles Hoffer. *Roe v. Wade: The Abortion Rights Controversy in American History.* Lawrence: Univ. Pr. of Kansas, 2001.

Hursthouse, Rosalind. "Virtue Theory and Abortion." *Philosophy and Public Affairs* 20, no. 3 (Summer 1991): 223–46.

Jamieson, Dale. *A Companion to Environmental Philosophy.* Malden, Mass.: Blackwell, 2001.

Jecker, Nancy S., Albert R. Jonsen, and Robert A. Pearlman, eds. *Bioethics.* Boston: Jones and Bartlett, 1997.

Johnson, Deborah G. *Computer Ethics.* 3rd ed. Englewood Cliffs, N.J.: Prentice Hall, 2001.

————, ed. *Ethical Issues in Engineering.* Englewood Cliffs, N.J.: Prentice Hall, 1991.

Johnson, Deborah G., and Helen Nissenbaum, eds. *Computers, Ethics and Social Values.* Englewood Cliffs, N.J.: Prentice Hall, 1995.

Johnson, Lawrence E. *A Morally Deep World: An Essay on Moral Significance and Environmental Ethics.* Cambridge: Cambridge Univ. Pr., 1991.

Jokic, Aleksandar, ed. *War Crimes and Collective Wrongdoing.* Malden, Mass.: Blackwell, 2001.

Kamm, Frances Myrna. *Morality, Mortality.* 2 vols. New York: Oxford Univ. Pr., 1993 and 1996.

Kass, Leon, and James Q. Wilson. *The Ethics of Human Cloning.* Washington,

D.C.: AEI, 1998.

Kavka, Gregory S. *Moral Paradoxes of Nuclear Deterrence*. Cambridge: Cambridge Univ. Pr., 1987.

King, Martin Luther, Jr. *A Testament of Hope: The Essential Writings of Martin Luther King, Jr.* Ed. James Melvin Washington. San Francisco: Harper & Row, 1986.

Klotzko, Arlene Judith, ed. *The Cloning Sourcebook*. 2nd ed. Oxford: Oxford Univ. Pr., 2003.

Kohl, Marvin, ed. *Infanticide and the Value of Life*. Buffalo, N.Y.: Prometheus, 1978.

Kuhse, Helga, and Peter Singer, eds. *Bioethics: An Anthology*. Oxford: Blackwell, 1999.

LaFollette, Hugh, ed. *Ethics in Practice*. 3rd ed. Malden, Mass.: Blackwell, 2007.

LaFollette, Marcel C. *Stealing into Print: Fraud, Plagiarism, and Misconduct in Scientific Publishing*. Berkeley: Univ. of California Pr., 1992.

Langford, Duncan, ed. *Internet Ethics*. New York: St. Martin's, 2000.

Lapides, Frederick R., and David J. Burrows, eds. *Racism: A Casebook*. New York: Crowell, 1971.

Lappé, Frances Moore. *Diet for a Small Planet*. New York: Ballantine, 1971.

Larson, Andrea, and R. Edward Freeman. *Women's Studies and Business Ethics*. New York: Oxford Univ. Pr., 1997.

Lee, Patrick. *Abortion and Unborn Human Life*. Washington, D.C.: Catholic Univ. of America Pr., 1996.

Leopold, Aldo. *For the Health of the Land: Previously Unpublished Essays and Other Writings*. Ed. J. Baird Callicott and Eric T. Freyfogle. Washington, D.C.: Island, 1999.

―――. *A Sand County Almanac, and Sketches Here and There*. New York: Oxford Univ. Pr., 1949.

Levy, Peter B. *100 Key Documents in American Democracy*. Westport, Conn.: Greenwood, 1994. [documents such as the Roe v. Wade decision and civil rights speeches of Abraham Lincoln, Martin Luther King, and John Kennedy]

Lichtenberg, Judith, ed. *Democracy and the Mass Media*. Cambridge: Cambridge Univ. Pr., 1990.

Lippke, Richard. *Radical Business Ethics*. Lanham, Md.: Rowman & Littlefield, 1995.

List, Peter C., ed. *Environmental Ethics and Forestry: A Reader*. Philadelphia: Temple Univ. Pr., 2000.

Machan, Tibor R., ed. *Business Ethics in the Global Market*. Stanford, Calif.: Hoover Institution Pr., 1999.

Mahajan, Gurpreet, ed. *Democracy, Difference, and Social Justice*. New York: Oxford Univ. Pr., 1998.

Mappes, Thomas A., and David DeGrazia. *Biomedical Ethics*. 6th ed. New York: McGraw-Hill, 2006.

Marquis, Don. "Why Abortion Is Immoral." *Journal of Philosophy* 86, no. 4 (April 1989): 183–202.

Martin, Mike W., and Roland Schinzinger. *Ethics in Engineering*. New York: McGraw-Hill, 1989.

Matthews, Gareth B. *The Philosophy of Childhood*. Cambridge, Mass.: Harvard Univ. Pr., 1994.

May, Larry. *Masculinity & Morality*. Ithaca, N.Y.: Cornell Univ. Pr., 1998.

———. *The Morality of Groups: Collective Responsibility, Group-based Harm, and Corporate Rights*. Notre Dame, Ind.: Univ. of Notre Dame Pr., 1987.

May, Larry, Eric Rovie, and Steve Viner, eds. *The Morality of War: Classical and Contemporary Readings*. Upper Saddle River, N.J.: Pearson Education, 2006.

May, Larry, and Robert A. Strikwerda, eds. *Rethinking Masculinity: Philosophical Explorations in Light of Feminism*. Lanham, Md.: Littlefield Adams, 1992.

McCloskey, Deirdre N. *The Bourgeois Virtues: Ethics for an Age of Commerce*. Chicago: Univ. of Chicago Pr., 2006.

McCloskey, Henry J. *Ecological Ethics and Politics*. Totowa, N.J.: Rowman & Littlefield, 1983.

McCorvey, Norma, and Andy Meisler. *I Am Roe: My Life, Roe v. Wade, and Freedom of Choice*. New York: HarperCollins, 1994.

McGary, Howard. *Race and Social Justice*. Malden, Mass.: Blackwell, 1999.

Midgley, Mary. *Animals and Why They Matter*. Athens: Univ. of Georgia Pr., 1983.

Miller, Peter, and Laura Westra, eds. *Just Ecological Integrity: The Ethics of Maintaining Planetary Life*. Lanham, Md.: Rowman & Littlefield, 2002.

Morgan, William J., Klaus V. Meier, and Angela Schneider, eds. *Ethics in Sport*. Champaign, Ill.: Human Kinetics, 2001.

Murphy, Jeffrie G., and Jean Hampton. *Forgiveness and Mercy*. Cambridge: Cambridge Univ. Pr., 1988.

Murphy, Liam, and Thomas Nagel. *The Myth of Ownership: Taxes and Justice*. New York: Oxford Univ. Pr., 2002.

Næss, Arne. *Ecology, Community, and Lifestyle*. Trans. David Rothenberg. Cambridge: Cambridge Univ. Pr., 1989.

———. "The Shallow and the Deep, Long-Range Ecology Movement." *Inquiry* (Oslo) 16, no. 95 (Spring 1973): 95–100.

Nagel, Thomas. *Concealment and Exposure*. New York: Oxford Univ. Pr., 2002.

———. *Mortal Questions*. Cambridge: Cambridge Univ. Pr., 1979.

Nelson, Hilde Lindemann, ed. *Feminism and Families*. New York: Routledge, 1997.

Nussbaum, Martha C. *Sex and Social Justice*. New York: Oxford Univ. Pr., 1999.

O'Neill, Onora. *Faces of Hunger: An Essay on Poverty, Justice, and Development*. London: G. Allen and Unwin, 1986.

Okin, Susan Moller. *Justice, Gender, and the Family*. New York: Basic, 1989.

Ozar, David T., and David J. Sokol. *Dental Ethics at Chairside: Professional*

Principles and Practical Applications. St. Louis, Mo.: Mosby, 1994.

Parens, Erik, and Adrienne Asch, eds. *Prenatal Testing and Disability Rights*. Washington, D.C.: Georgetown Univ. Pr., 2000.

Parker, David. *Ethics, Theory, and the Novel*. Cambridge: Cambridge Univ. Pr., 1994.

Passmore, John. *Man's Responsibility for Nature*. 2nd ed. London: Duckworth, 1980.

Pence, Gregory E. *Classic Cases in Medical Ethics*. 5th ed. New York: McGraw-Hill, 2008.

———. *The Elements of Bioethics*. New York: McGraw Hill, 2007.

———. *Who's Afraid of Human Cloning?* Lanham, Md.: Rowman & Littlefield, 1998.

Piderit, John J. *The Ethical Foundations of Economics*. Washington, D.C.: Georgetown Univ. Pr., 1993.

Pinches, Charles, and Jay B. McDaniel, ed. *Good News for Animals? Christian Approaches to Animal Well-Being*. Maryknoll, N.Y.: Orbis, 1993.

Pojman, Louis P. *Life and Death*. London: Jones and Bartlett, 1992.

———, ed. *Environmental Ethics: Readings in Theory and Application*. 5th ed. Belmont, Calif.: Wadsworth, 2008.

Pojman, Louis P., and Francis J. Beckwith, eds. *The Abortion Controversy*. 2nd ed. Belmont, Calif.: Wadsworth, 1998.

Pojman, Louis P., and Jeffrey Reiman. *The Death Penalty: For and Against*. Lanham, Md.: Rowman & Littlefield, 1998.

Powell, John. *Abortion: The Silent Holocaust*. Allen, Tex.: Argus, 1981.

Raphael, David D. *Problems of Political Philosophy*. New York: Praeger, 1970.

Reeder, John P., Jr. *Killing and Saving: Abortion, Hunger, and War*. University Park: Pennsylvania State Univ. Pr., 1996.

Regan, Tom. *The Case for Animal Rights*. Berkeley: Univ. of California Pr., 1983.

———, ed. *Matters of Life and Death*. 3rd ed. New York: McGraw-Hill, 1993.

Regan, Tom, and Peter Singer, eds. *Animal Rights and Human Obligations*. 2nd ed. Englewood Cliffs, N.J.: Prentice Hall, 1989.

Reidy, David A., and Mortimer N. S. Sellers, eds. *Universal Human Rights: Moral Order in a Divided World*. Lanham, Md.: Rowman & Littlefield, 2005.

Reynolds, George Walter. *Ethics in Information Technology*. Boston: Thomson, 2007.

Richards, David A. J. *Identity and the Case for Gay Rights: Race, Gender, Religion as Analogies*. Chicago: Univ. of Chicago Pr., 1999.

Rolston, Holmes. *Philosophy Gone Wild: Environmental Ethics*. Buffalo, N.Y.: Prometheus, 1988.

Rosenthal, Joel H., ed. *Ethics & International Affairs: A Reader*. Washington, D.C.: Georgetown Univ. Pr., 1999.

Routley (now Sylvan), Richard. "Is There a Need for a New, an Environmental, Ethic?" *Proceedings of the 15th World Congress of Philosophy*, vol. 1. (Sophia,

Bulgaria: Sophia Press, 1973): 205–10.

Sagoff, Mark. *The Economy of the Earth.* Cambridge: Cambridge Univ. Pr., 1988.

Sartre, Jean-Paul. *Anti-Semite and Jew.* Trans. George J. Becker. New York: Schocken, 1965.

Satris, Stephen, ed. *Taking Sides: Clashing Views on Controversial Moral Issues.* 10th ed. New York: McGraw-Hill, 2005.

Schmidtz, David. *The Limits of Government: An Essay on the Public Goods Argument.* Boulder, Colo.: Westview, 1991.

Schwarz, Stephen D. *The Moral Question of Abortion.* Chicago: Loyola Univ. Pr., 1990.

Schweickart, David. *After Capitalism.* Lanham, Md.: Rowman & Littlefield, 2002.

———. *Against Capitalism.* Cambridge: Cambridge Univ. Pr., 1993.

———. *Capitalism or Worker Control?* New York: Praeger, 1980.

Sen, Amartya. *On Economic Inequality.* Oxford: Clarendon, 1997.

Sherwin, Susan. *No Longer Patient: Feminist Ethics and Health Care.* Philadelphia: Temple Univ. Pr., 1992.

Shue, Henry. *Basic Rights: Subsistence, Affluence, and U.S. Foreign Policy.* Princeton, N.J.: Princeton Univ. Pr., 1980.

———. *Nuclear Deterrence and Moral Restraint: Critical Choices for American Strategy.* Cambridge: Cambridge Univ. Pr., 1989.

Sikora, R. I., and Brian Barry, eds. *Obligations to Future Generations.* Philadelphia: Temple Univ. Pr., 1978.

Silver, Lee M. *Remaking Eden: How Genetic Engineering and Cloning Will Transform the American Family.* New York: Avon, 1998.

Silvers, Anita, David Wasserman, and Mary B. Mahowald. *Disability, Difference, Discrimination: Perspectives on Justice in Bioethics and Public Policy.* Lanham, Md.: Rowman & Littlefield, 1998.

Simon, Robert L., ed. *Neutrality and the Academic Ethic.* Lanham, Md.: Rowman & Littlefield, 1994.

Singer, Peter. *Animal Liberation.* 2nd ed. New York: Avon, 1990.

———. *Ethics into Action: Henry Spira and the Animal Rights Movement.* Lanham, Md.: Rowman & Littlefield, 2000.

———. "Famine, Affluence, and Morality." *Philosophy and Public Affairs* 1, no. 3 (Spring 1972): 229–43.

———. *One World: The Ethics of Globalization.* 2nd ed. New Haven, Conn.: Yale Univ. Pr., 2004.

———. *Practical Ethics.* 2nd ed. Cambridge: Cambridge Univ. Pr., 1993.

———. *Unsanctifying Human Life.* Ed. Helga Kuhse. Oxford: Blackwell, 2002.

Singer, Peter, and others. *Singer and His Critics.* Ed. Dale Jamieson. Oxford: Blackwell, 1999.

———. *Singer Under Fire.* Ed. Jeffrey Schaler. Chicago: Open Court, 2008.

Snow, Nancy E. *Stem Cell Research: New Frontiers in Science and Ethics.* Notre Dame, Ind.: Univ. of Notre Dame Pr., 2003.

Soble, Alan. *The Philosophy of Sex and Love: An Introduction.* St. Paul, Minn.: Paragon House, 1998.

————, ed. *Philosophy of Sex: Contemporary Readings.* 4th ed. Lanham, Md.: Rowman & Littlefield, 2002.

Spinello, Richard A. *Ethical Aspects of Information Technology.* Englewood Cliffs, N.J.: Prentice Hall, 1994.

Spinello, Richard A., and Herman T. Tavani, eds. *Readings in Cyberethics.* 2nd ed. Sudbury, Mass.: Jones and Bartlett, 2004.

Spurgin, Earl W. "Do Shareholders Have Obligations to Stakeholders?" *Journal of Business Ethics* 33, no. 4 (October 2001): 287–97.

————. "The End of Romance and the Value of Privacy." *Public Affairs Quarterly* 20, no. 3 (July 2006): 247–65.

————. "Hume, Broken Promises, and the Reactions of Promisees." *Southwest Philosophy Review* 12, no. 1 (January 1996): 21–31.

————. "Looking for Answers in All the Wrong Places." *Business Ethics Quarterly* 14, no. 2 (April 2004): 293–313.

————. "Occupational Safety and Paternalism: Machan Revisited." *Journal of Business Ethics* 63, no. 2 (January 2006): 155–73.

————. "The Problem with 'Dead Peasants' Insurance." *Business and Professional Ethics Journal* 22, no. 1 (Spring 2003): 19–36.

————. "What's So *Special* About a Special Ethics for Business?" *Journal of Business Ethics* 24, no. 4 (April 2000): 273–81:

————. "What's Wrong with Computer-Generated Images of Perfection in Advertising?" *Journal of Business Ethics* 45, no. 3 (July 2003): 257–68.

————. "What Was Wrong with Abercrombie & Fitch's 'Magalog'?" *Business and Society Review* 111, no. 4 (Winter 2006): 387–408.

Steffen, Lloyd, ed. *Abortion: A Reader.* Cleveland, Ohio: Pilgrim, 1996.

Steinbock, Bonnie, and Alastair Norcross, eds. *Killing and Letting Die.* New York: Fordham Univ. Pr., 1994.

Sterba, James P., ed. *Earth Ethics: Introductory Readings on Animal Rights and Environmental Ethics.* Saddle River, N.J.: Prentice Hall, 2000.

Stewart, Robert M., ed. *Philosophical Perspectives on Sex and Love.* New York: Oxford Univ. Pr., 1995.

Sumner, L. W. *Abortion and Moral Theory.* Princeton, N.J.: Princeton Univ. Pr., 1981.

Thomson, Judith Jarvis. "A Defense of Abortion." *Philosophy and Public Affairs* 1, no. 1 (Fall 1971): 47–66.

Timmons, Mark, ed. *Disputed Moral Issues: A Reader.* Oxford: Oxford Univ. Pr., 2007.

Tooley, Michael H. *Abortion and Infanticide.* Oxford: Oxford Univ. Pr., 1983.

————. "Abortion and Infanticide." *Philosophy and Public Affairs* 2, no. 1 (Fall 1972): 37–65.

United States National Commission for the Protection of Human Subjects of

Biomedical and Behavioral Research. *The Belmont Report*. Washington, D.C.: The Commission, 1978.

United Nations. *Universal Declaration of Human Rights*. Adopted by the General Assembly on 10 December 1948. http://www.un.org/Overview/rights.html

Varner, Gary E. *In Nature's Interests? Interests, Animal Rights, and Environmental Ethics*. New York: Oxford Univ. Pr., 1998.

Velasquez, Manuel G. *Business Ethics: Concepts & Cases*. 6th ed. Upper Saddle River, N.J.: Pearson Prentice Hall, 2006.

Walker, Margaret Urban. *Moral Repair: Reconstructing Moral Relations after Wrongdoing*. Cambridge: Cambridge Univ. Pr., 2006.

Walzer, Michael. *Arguing about War*. New Haven, Conn.: Yale Univ. Pr., 2004.

———. *Just and Unjust Wars*. 4th ed. New York: Basic, 2006.

Warren, Karen, ed. *Ecological Feminist Philosophies*. Bloomington: Univ. of Indiana Pr., 1996.

Warren, Samuel D., and Louis D. Brandeis. "The Right to Privacy." *Harvard Law Review* 4, no. 5 (December 1890): 193–220.

Weinstein, Bruce D., ed. *Dental Ethics*. Philadelphia: Lea & Febiger, 1993.

Weir, Robert F., ed. *Physician-assisted Suicide*. Bloomington: Indiana Univ. Pr., 1997.

Werhane, Patricia H. *Adam Smith and His Legacy for Modern Capitalism*. New York: Oxford Univ. Pr., 1991.

———. *Persons, Rights, and Corporations*. Englewood Cliffs, N.J.: Prentice Hall, 1985.

Werhane, Patricia H., A. R. Gini, and David T. Ozar, eds. *Philosophical Issues in Human Rights: Theories and Applications*. New York: Random House, 1986.

Westphal, Dale, and Fred Westphal, eds. *Planet in Peril: Essays in Environmental Ethics*. Fort Worth, Tex.: Harcourt Brace, 1994.

White, James E. *Contemporary Moral Problems*. 8th ed. Belmont, Calif.: Wadsworth, 2005.

Wiener, Norbert. *The Human Use of Human Beings: Cybernetics and Society*. Boston: Houghton Mifflin, 1950.

Witoszek, Nina, and Andrew Brennan, eds. *Arne Næss and the Progress of Ecophilosophy*. Lanham, Md.: Rowman & Littlefield, 1999.

Woodward, Paul A., ed. *The Doctrine of Double Effect*. Notre Dame, Ind.: Univ. of Notre Dame Pr., 2001.

Worthington, Everett L., ed. *Handbook of Forgiveness*. New York: Routledge, 2005.

Zack, Naomi. *Race and Mixed Race*. Philadelphia: Temple Univ. Pr., 1993.

———. *Thinking about Race*. Belmont, Calif.: Wadsworth, 1998.

Zimmerman, Michael E., ed. *Environmental Philosophy: From Animal Rights to Radical Ecology*. Upper Saddle River, N.J.: Prentice Hall, 1998.

6. Ethical Theory

Adamson, Jane, Richard Freadman, and David Parker, eds. *Renegotiating Ethics in Literature, Philosophy and Theory*. Cambridge: Cambridge Univ. Pr., 1998.

Adorno, Theodor W. *Problems of Moral Philosophy*. Ed. Thomas Schroder, trans. Rodney Livingstone. Stanford, Calif.: Stanford Univ. Pr., 2000.

Anscombe, Elizabeth. *Ethics, Religion, and Politics*. Minneapolis: Univ. of Minnesota Pr., 1981.

———. *Intention*. Ithaca, N.Y.: Cornell Univ. Pr., 1963.

———. "Modern Moral Philosophy." *Philosophy* 33, no. 124 (January 1958): 1–19.

Apel, Karl-Otto. *The Response of Discourse Ethics to the Moral Challenge of the Human Situation as Such and Especially Today*. Leuven, Belgium: Peeters, 2001.

Arendt, Hannah. *Eichmann in Jerusalem: A Report on the Banality of Evil*. New York: Viking, 1964.

———. *The Origins of Totalitarianism*. New York: Harcourt Brace, 1951.

———. *The Portable Hannah Arendt*. Ed. Peter Baehr. New York: Penguin, 2000.

Arrington, Robert L. *Rationalism, Realism, and Relativism: Perspectives in Contemporary Moral Epistemology*. Ithaca, N.Y.: Cornell Univ. Pr., 1989.

Arrow, Kenneth J. *Social Choice and Individual Values*. 2nd ed. New Haven, Conn.: Yale Univ. Pr., 1973.

Avineri, Shlomo, and Avner de-Shalit, eds. *Communitarianism and Individualism*. Oxford: Oxford Univ. Pr., 1992.

Ayer, Alfred J. *Language, Truth and Logic*. 2nd ed. London: V. Gollancz, 1946.

Baier, Annette C. *Moral Prejudices: Essays on Ethics*. Cambridge, Mass.: Harvard Univ. Pr., 1994.

———. *Postures of the Mind: Essays on Mind and Morals*. Minneapolis: Univ. of Minnesota Pr., 1985.

Baier, Kurt. *The Moral Point of View*. Ithaca, N.Y.: Cornell Univ. Pr., 1958.

———. *The Rational and the Moral Order*. Chicago: Open Court, 1994.

Baron, Marcia. *Kantian Ethics Almost without Apology*. Ithaca, N.Y.: Cornell Univ. Pr., 1995.

Barry, Brian M. *The Liberal Theory of Justice: A Critical Examination of the Principal Doctrines in A Theory of Justice by John Rawls*. Oxford: Clarendon, 1973.

———. *Theories of Justice*. Berkeley: Univ. of California Pr., 1989.

Beauvoir, Simone de. *The Coming of Age*. Trans. Patrick O'Brian. New York: Putnam, 1972.

———. *The Ethics of Ambiguity*. Trans. Bernard Frechtman. New York: Citadel, 1976.

———. *The Second Sex*. Trans. H. M. Parshley. New York: Knopf, 1952.

Becker, Lawrence C. *Reciprocity*. London: Routledge, 1986.

Benhabib, Seyla. *Critique, Norm, and Utopia: A Study of the Foundations of Critical Theory.* New York: Columbia Univ. Pr., 1986.

Benhabib, Seyla, and Fred Dallmayr, eds. *The Communicative Ethics Controversy.* Cambridge, Mass.: MIT, 1990.

Bernauer, James W. *Michel Foucault's Force of Flight: Toward an Ethics for Thought.* Atlantic Highlands, N.J.: Humanities Pr. International, 1990.

Bittner, Rüdiger. *What Reason Demands.* Trans. Theodore Talbot. Cambridge: Cambridge Univ. Pr., 1989.

Blackburn, Simon. *Essays in Quasi-Realism.* Oxford: Oxford Univ. Pr., 1993.

———. *Ruling Passions: A Theory of Practical Reasoning.* Oxford: Clarendon, 1998.

———. *Spreading the Word.* Oxford: Clarendon, 1984.

Blum, Lawrence A. *Friendship, Altruism, and Morality.* London: Routledge, 1980.

———. *Moral Perception and Particularity.* Cambridge: Cambridge Univ. Pr., 1994.

Brandt, Richard B. "The Concept of Rational Action." *Social Theory and Practice* 9 (1983): 143–65.

———. "The Definition of an 'Ideal Observer' Theory in Ethics" and "Some Comments on Professor Firth's Reply." *Philosophy and Phenomenological Research* 15, no. 3 (March 1955): 407–13 and 422–23.

———. "Rational Desires." *Proceedings and Addresses of the American Philosophical Association* 43 (1970): 43–64.

———. "Rationality, Egoism, and Morality." *Journal of Philosophy* 69, no. 20 (9 Nov. 1972): 681–97.

———. *A Theory of the Good and the Right.* Oxford: Clarendon, 1979.

———. "Toward a Credible Form of Utilitarianism." In *Morality and the Language of Conduct*, ed. Hector-Neri Castañeda and George Nakhnikian, 107–43. Detroit, Mich.: Wayne State Univ. Pr., 1965.

Braybrooke, David. *Natural Law Modernized.* Toronto: Univ. of Toronto Pr., 2001.

Brink, David O. *Moral Realism and the Foundations of Ethics.* New York: Cambridge Univ. Pr., 1989.

Broad, Charlie D. *Five Types of Ethical Theory.* New York: Harcourt Brace, 1930.

———. "Imperatives, Categorical and Hypothetical." *Philosopher* 2 (1950): 62–75.

Buber, Martin. *Good and Evil.* Trans. Ronald Gregor Smith and Michael Bullock. New York: Scribner, 1958.

———. *I and Thou.* Trans. Ronald Gregor Smith. New York: Scribner, 1958.

Cadoux, A. T. "The Implications of the Golden Rule." *International Journal of Ethics* 22, no. 3 (April 1912): 272–87.

Calarco, Matthew, and Peter Atterton, eds. *The Continental Ethics Reader.* New York: Routledge, 2003.

Callahan, Sidney Cornelia. *In Good Conscience: Reason and Emotion in Moral Decision Making.* San Francisco: Harper, 1991.

Camus, Albert. *The Myth of Sisyphus and Other Essays.* Trans. Justin O'Brien. New York: Random House, 1955.

———. *The Stranger.* Trans. Stuart Gilbert. New York: Vintage, 1946.

Caputo, John D. *Against Ethics: Contributions to a Poetics of Obligation with Constant Reference to Deconstruction.* Bloomington: Indiana Univ. Pr., 1993.

Card, Claudia, ed. *Adventures in Lesbian Philosophy.* Bloomington: Indiana Univ. Pr., 1994.

———. *On Feminist Ethics and Politics.* Lawrence: Univ. Pr. of Kansas, 1999.

Carritt, Edgar F. *Ethical and Political Thinking.* Oxford: Clarendon, 1947.

———. *The Theory of Morals: An Introduction to Ethical Philosophy.* London: Oxford Univ. Pr., 1928.

Carson, Thomas L. *The Status of Morality.* Dordrecht: D. Reidel, 1984.

———. *Value and the Good Life.* Notre Dame, Ind.: Univ. of Notre Dame Pr., 2000.

Carson, Thomas L., and Paul K. Moser, eds. *Morality and the Good Life.* New York: Oxford Univ. Pr., 1997.

Castañeda, Hector-Neri. *The Structure of Morality.* Springfield, Ill.: Thomas, 1974.

Castañeda, Hector-Neri, and George Nakhnikian, eds. *Morality and the Language of Conduct.* Detroit, Mich.: Wayne State Univ. Pr., 1965.

Cavell, Stanley. *The Claim of Reason: Wittgenstein, Skepticism, Morality, and Tragedy.* Oxford: Clarendon, 1979.

Chappell, Timothy D. J. *Understanding Human Goods: A Theory of Ethics.* Edinburgh: Edinburgh Univ. Pr., 1999.

Cohen, Mitchell, and Nicole Fermon. *Princeton Readings in Political Thought: Essential Texts since Plato.* Princeton, N.J.: Princeton Univ. Pr., 1996.

Coleman, Jules L., ed. *Rights and Their Foundations.* New York: Garland, 1994.

Crisp, Roger, ed. *How Should One Live? Essays on the Virtues.* Oxford: Clarendon, 1996.

Crisp, Roger, and Michael Slote. *Virtue Ethics.* Oxford: Oxford Univ. Pr., 1997.

Daly, Cahal B. *Moral Philosophy in Britain: From Bradley to Wittgenstein.* Portland, Ore.: Four Courts, 1996.

Dancy, Jonathan. *Ethics without Principles.* Oxford: Clarendon, 2004.

———. *Moral Reasons.* Oxford: Blackwell, 1993.

———. *Practical Reality.* Oxford: Oxford Univ. Pr., 2000.

Daniels, Norman, ed. *Reading Rawls: Critical Studies on Rawls' A Theory of Justice.* New York: Basic, 1975.

Darwall, Stephen L. *Impartial Reason.* Ithaca, N.Y.: Cornell Univ. Pr., 1983.

———, ed. *Deontology.* Malden, Mass.: Blackwell, 2003.

———, ed. *Virtue Ethics.* Malden, Mass.: Blackwell, 2003.

Darwall, Stephen L., Allan Gibbard, and Peter Railton, eds. *Moral Discourse and Practice: Some Philosophical Approaches.* New York: Oxford Univ. Pr., 1997.

Davion, Victoria, and Clark Wolf, eds. *The Idea of a Political Liberalism: Essays on Rawls.* Lanham, Md.: Rowman & Littlefield, 2000.

Delaney, Cornelius F., ed. *The Liberalism-Communitarianism Debate: Liberty and*

Community Values. Lanham, Md.: Rowman & Littlefield, 1994.

DePaul, Michael, and Linda Zagzebski Trinkaus. *Intellectual Virtue: Perspectives from Ethics and Epistemology.* Oxford: Clarendon, 2003.

Derrida, Jacques. *Ethics, Institutions, and the Right to Philosophy.* Trans. Peter Pericles Trifonas. Lanham, Md.: Rowman & Littlefield, 2002.

Dewey, John. *The Moral Writings of John Dewey.* 2nd ed. Ed. James Gouinlock. Amherst, N.Y.: Prometheus, 1994.

———. *The Public and its Problems.* Athens, Ohio: Swallow, 1954.

Dewey, John, and James H. Tufts. *Ethics.* New York: H. Holt, 1908.

Dombrowski, Daniel A. *Rawls and Religion: The Case for Political Liberalism.* Albany, N.Y.: SUNY, 2001.

Donagan, Alan. *The Theory of Morality.* Chicago: Univ. of Chicago Pr., 1977.

Downie, Robert S., and Elizabeth Telfer. *Respect for Persons.* New York: Schocken, 1969.

Durkheim, Emile. *On Morality and Society: Selected Writings.* Ed. Robert N. Bellah. Chicago: Univ. of Chicago Pr., 1973.

Dworkin, Gerald. *The Theory and Practice of Autonomy.* Cambridge: Cambridge Univ. Pr., 1988.

Dworkin, Ronald. *Law's Empire.* Cambridge, Mass.: Harvard Univ. Pr., 1986.

———. *A Matter of Principle.* Cambridge, Mass.: Harvard Univ. Pr., 1985.

———. *Taking Rights Seriously.* Cambridge, Mass.: Harvard Univ. Pr., 1977.

Edel, Abraham. *In Search of the Ethical: Moral Theory in Twentieth-Century America.* New Brunswick, N.J.: Transaction, 1992.

———. *Method in Ethical Theory.* Indianapolis, Ind.: Bobbs-Merrill, 1963.

Edgley, Roy. *Reason in Theory and Practice.* London: Hutchinson, 1969.

Edwards, Paul. *The Logic of Moral Discourse.* Glencoe, Ill.: Free Pr., 1955.

Ellos, William J. *Narrative Ethics.* Aldershot, England: Avebury, 1994.

Etzioni, Amitai. *New Communitarian Thinking: Persons, Virtues, Institutions, and Communities.* Charlottesville: Univ. Pr. of Virginia, 1995.

Ewing, Alfred C. *The Definition of Good.* New York: Macmillan, 1947.

Finnis, John M. *Fundamentals of Ethics.* Washington, D.C.: Georgetown Univ. Pr., 1983.

———. *Moral Absolutes.* Washington, D.C.: Catholic Univ. of America Pr., 1991.

———. *Natural Law and Natural Rights.* Oxford: Clarendon, 1980.

Firth, Roderick. "Ethical Absolutism and the Ideal Observer." *Philosophy and Phenomenological Research* 12, no. 3 (March 1952): 317–45.

———. "Reply to Professor Brandt." *Philosophy and Phenomenological Research* 15, no. 3 (March 1955): 414–21.

Fischer, John M. *Responsibility and Control: A Theory of Moral Responsibility.* Cambridge: Cambridge Univ. Pr., 1998.

Flanagan, Owen J. *Self Expressions: Mind, Morals, and the Meaning of Life.* New York: Oxford Univ. Pr., 1996.

———. *Varieties of Moral Personality: Ethics and Psychological Realism.* Cambridge, Mass.: Harvard Univ. Pr., 1991.

Flanagan, Owen J., and Amélie Oksenberg Rorty, eds. *Identity, Character, and Morality: Essays in Moral Psychology.* Cambridge, Mass.: MIT, 1990.

Fletcher, Joseph F. *Situation Ethics: The New Morality.* London: SCM Pr., 1966.

Flew, Antony. *Evolutionary Ethics.* London: Macmillan, 1967.

Foot, Philippa. "Moral Arguments." *Mind* 67, no. 268 (October 1958): 502–13.

———. "Moral Beliefs." *Proceedings of the Aristotelian Society* 59 (1958–1959), 83–104.

———. *Moral Dilemmas and Other Topics in Moral Philosophy.* Oxford: Clarendon, 2002.

———. "Morality as a System of Hypothetical Imperatives." *Philosophical Review* 81, no. 3 (July 1972): 305–16.

———. *Natural Goodness.* Oxford: Clarendon, 2001.

———. *Virtues and Vices and Other Essays in Moral Philosophy.* Berkeley: Univ. of California Pr., 1978.

———, ed. *Theories of Ethics.* London: Oxford Univ. Pr., 1967.

Foucault, Michel. *Ethics: Subjectivity and Truth.* Ed. Paul Rabinow, trans. Robert Hurley. New York: New Pr., 1997.

———. *Politics, Philosophy, Culture.* Ed. Lawrence D. Kritzman, trans. Alan Sheridan. New York: Routledge, 1988.

Frankena, William K. "The Naturalistic Fallacy." *Mind* 48, no. 192 (October 1939): 464–77.

———. *Perspectives on Morality: Essays.* Ed. K. E. Goodpaster. Notre Dame, Ind.: Univ. of Notre Dame Pr., 1976.

———. *Thinking about Morality.* Ann Arbor: Univ. of Michigan Pr., 1980.

Frankfurt, Harry G. *The Importance of What We Care About.* Cambridge: Cambridge Univ. Pr., 1988.

———. *Necessity, Volition, and Love.* Cambridge: Cambridge Univ. Pr., 1999.

Frazer, Elizabeth, Jennifer Hornsby, and Sabina Lovibond, eds. *Ethics: A Feminist Reader.* Oxford: Blackwell, 1992.

Freeman, Samuel. *The Cambridge Companion to Rawls.* Cambridge: Cambridge Univ. Pr., 2003.

French, Peter A. *The Scope of Morality.* Minneapolis: Univ. of Minnesota Pr., 1979.

Frey, Raymond G. *Utility and Rights.* Minneapolis: Univ. of Minnesota Pr., 1984.

Friedman, Marilyn. *Autonomy, Gender, Politics.* Oxford: Oxford Univ. Pr., 2003.

———. *What Are Friends for? Feminist Perspectives on Personal Relationships and Moral Theory.* Ithaca, N.Y.: Cornell Univ. Pr., 1993.

Gadamer, Hans Georg. *Hermeneutics, Religion, and Ethics.* Trans. Joel Weinsheimer. New Haven, Conn.: Yale Univ. Pr., 1999.

Gauthier, David P. *Morals by Agreement.* Oxford: Clarendon, 1986.

———, ed. *Morality and Rational Self-Interest.* Englewood Cliffs, N.J.: Prentice-Hall, 1970.

Geach, Peter T. *The Virtues*. Cambridge: Cambridge Univ. Pr., 1977.

Gensler, Harry J. "Ethical Consistency Principles." *Philosophical Quarterly* 35, no. 139 (April 1985): 156–70.

———. "Ethics Is Based on Rationality." *Journal of Value Inquiry* 20, no. 4 (Dec. 1986): 251–64.

———. *Formal Ethics*. London: Routledge, 1996.

———. "Gold or Fool's Gold? Ridding the Golden Rule of Absurd Implications." In *Analyzing the Golden Rule*, ed. Jacob Neusner. Lanham, Md.: University Press of America, 2008.

———. "The Prescriptivism Incompleteness Theorem." *Mind* 85, no. 340 (October 1976): 589–96.

———. "Singer's Unsanctity of Human Life: A Critique." In *Singer Under Fire*. Ed. Jeffrey Schaler. Chicago: Open Court, 2008.

George, Robert P. *In Defense of Natural Law*. Oxford: Clarendon, 1999.

———, ed. *Natural Law Theory: Contemporary Essays*. Oxford: Clarendon, 1992.

Gert, Bernard. *Morality: A New Justification of the Moral Rules*. New York: Oxford Univ. Pr., 1989.

———. *Morality: Its Nature and Justification*. New York: Oxford Univ. Pr., 1998.

Gewirth, Alan. *Human Rights: Essays on Justification and Applications*. Chicago: Chicago Univ. Pr., 1982.

———. *Reason and Morality*. Chicago: Chicago Univ. Pr., 1978.

———. *Self-Fulfillment*. Princeton, N.J.: Princeton Univ. Pr., 1998.

Gibbard, Allan. *Thinking How to Live*. Cambridge, Mass.: Harvard Univ. Pr., 2003.

———. *Wise Choices, Apt Feelings*. Cambridge, Mass.: Harvard Univ. Pr., 1990.

Glover, Jonathan. *Responsibility*. New York: Humanities, 1970.

Goldman, Alan H. *Moral Knowledge*. London: Routledge, 1988.

———. *Practical Rules: When We Need Them and When We Don't*. Cambridge: Cambridge Univ. Pr., 2002.

Goldman, Alvin I. "Ethics and Cognitive Science." *Ethics* 103, no. 2 (January 1993): 337–60.

Goldman, Alvin I., and Jaegwon Kim, eds. *Values and Morals: Essays in Honor of William Frankena, Charles Stevenson, and Richard Brandt*. Dordrecht: D. Reidel, 1978.

Gormally, Luke, ed. *Moral Truth and Moral Tradition: Essays in Honour of Peter Geach and Elizabeth Anscombe*. Dublin: Four Courts, 1994.

Gosling, Justin C. B. *Weakness of the Will*. London: Routledge, 1990.

Grice, Geoffrey R. *The Grounds of Moral Judgement*. Cambridge: Cambridge Univ. Pr., 1967.

Griffin, James. *Well-Being: Its Meaning, Measurement, and Moral Importance*. New York: Oxford Univ. Pr., 1986.

Griffiths, A. Phillips, ed. *Ethics*. Cambridge: Cambridge Univ. Pr., 1993.

Gutting, Gary, ed. *The Cambridge Companion to Foucault*. Cambridge: Cambridge Univ. Pr., 1994.

Haber, Joram Graf, ed. *Absolutism and its Consequentialist Critics*. Lanham, Md.: Rowman & Littlefield, 1994.

Habermas, Jürgen. *Between Facts and Norms*. Trans. William Rehg. Cambridge, Mass.: MIT, 1996.

———. *Justification and Application: Remarks on Discourse Ethics*. Trans. Ciaran Cronin. Cambridge, Mass.: MIT, 1994.

———. *Legitimation Crisis*. Trans. Thomas McCarthy. Boston: Beacon, 1975.

———. *Moral Consciousness and Communicative Action*. Trans. Christian Lenhardt and Shierry Weber Nicholsen. Cambridge, Mass.: MIT, 1990.

———. *Toward a Rational Society*. Trans. J. J. Shapiro. Boston: Beacon, 1970.

Hampshire, Stuart. *Thought and Action*. New York: Viking, 1959.

———, ed. *Public and Private Morality*. Cambridge: Cambridge Univ. Pr., 1978.

Hare, John E. *God and Morality: A Philosophical History*. Oxford: Blackwell, 2007.

———. *God's Call: Moral Realism, God's Commands, and Human Autonomy*. Grand Rapids, Mich.: W.B. Eerdmans, 2001.

Hare, Richard M. *Essays in Moral Theory*. Oxford: Clarendon, 1989.

———. *Freedom and Reason*. Oxford: Clarendon, 1963.

———. *The Language of Morals*. Oxford: Clarendon, 1952.

———. *Moral Thinking*. Oxford: Clarendon, 1981.

———. "Rawls' Theory of Justice." *Philosophical Quarterly* 23, nos. 91 and 92 (April and July 1973): 144–55 and 241–52.

———. *Sorting Out Ethics*. Oxford: Clarendon, 1997.

Hare, Richard M., and others. *Hare and Critics*. Ed. Douglas Seanor and N. Fotion. Oxford: Oxford Univ. Pr., 1988.

Harman, Gilbert. *Explaining Value and Other Essays in Moral Philosophy*. Oxford: Clarendon, 2000.

———. *The Nature of Morality*. New York: Oxford Univ. Pr., 1977.

Harman, Gilbert, and Judith Jarvis Thomson. *Moral Relativism and Moral Objectivity*. Cambridge, Mass.: Blackwell, 1996.

Harris, George W. *Agent-Centered Morality: An Aristotelian Alternative to Kantian Internalism*. Berkeley: Univ. of California Pr., 1999.

———. *Dignity and Vulnerability: Strength and Quality of Character*. Berkeley: Univ. of California Pr., 1997.

Harsanyi, John C. *Essays on Ethics, Social Behavior, and Scientific Explanation*. Dordrecht: D. Reidel, 1976.

———. "Ethics in Terms of Hypothetical Imperatives." *Mind* 67, no. 267 (July 1958): 305–16.

Hartland-Swann, John. *An Analysis of Morals*. London: Allen & Unwin, 1960.

Hartmann, Nicolai. *Ethics*. 3 vols. London: Allen & Unwin, 1932.

Heidegger, Martin. *Being and Time*. Trans. Joan Stambaugh. Albany, N.Y.: SUNY, 1996.

Held, David. *Introduction to Critical Theory: Horkheimer to Habermas*. Berkeley:

Univ. of California Pr., 1980.

Held, Virginia. *The Ethics of Care: Personal, Political, and Global*. Oxford: Oxford Univ. Pr., 2006.

———. *Feminist Morality: Transforming Culture, Society and Politics*. Chicago: Univ. of Chicago Pr., 1993.

———, ed. *Justice and Care: Essential Readings in Feminist Ethics*. Boulder, Colo.: Westview, 1995.

Herman, Barbara. *The Practice of Moral Judgment*. Cambridge, Mass.: Harvard Univ. Pr., 1993.

Hertzler, Joyce O. "On Golden Rules." *International Journal of Ethics* 44, no. 4 (July 1934): 418–36.

Hill, Thomas E., Jr. *Autonomy and Self-Respect*. Cambridge: Cambridge Univ. Pr., 1991.

———. *Human Welfare and Moral Worth: Kantian Perspectives*. Oxford: Clarendon, 2002.

Hittinger, Russell. *A Critique of the New Natural Law Theory*. Notre Dame, Ind.: Univ. of Notre Dame Pr., 1987.

Hofstadter, Richard. *Social Darwinism in American Thought*. New York: G. Braziller, 1955.

Hooker, Brad, ed. *Rationality, Rules, and Utility: New Essays on the Moral Philosophy of Richard B. Brandt*. Boulder, Colo.: Westview, 1993.

Horkheimer, Max. *Eclipse of Reason*. New York: Seabury, 1974.

Horkheimer, Max, and Theodor W. Adorno. *Dialectic of Enlightenment*. Trans. John Cumming. New York: Herder & Herder, 1972.

Horton, John, and Susan Mendus, eds. *After MacIntyre: Critical Perspectives on the Work of Alasdair MacIntyre*. Notre Dame, Ind.: Univ. of Notre Dame Pr., 1994.

Hudson, William D. *Modern Moral Philosophy*. London: Macmillan, 1970.

———, ed. *The Is-Ought Question: A Collection of Papers on the Central Problem in Moral Philosophy*. London: Macmillan, 1969.

Hursthouse, Rosalind. *On Virtue Ethics*. Oxford: Oxford Univ. Pr., 1999.

———, ed. *Virtues and Reasons: Philippa Foot and Moral Theory: Essays in Honour of Philippa Foot*. Oxford: Clarendon, 1995.

Jaggar, Alison M. *Feminist Politics and Human Nature*. Totowa, N.J.: Rowman & Allanheld, 1983.

———, ed. *Living with Contradictions: Controversies in Feminist Social Ethics*. Boulder, Colo.: Westview, 1994.

Jaggar, Alison M., and Iris Marion Young, eds. *A Companion to Feminist Philosophy*. Malden, Mass.: Blackwell, 1998.

Jones, Greta. *Social Darwinism and English Thought*. Atlantic Highlands, N.J.: Humanities, 1980.

Kaczor, Christopher R. *Proportionalism and the Natural Law Tradition*. Washington, D.C.: Catholic Univ. of America, 2002.

Kagan, Shelly. *The Limits of Morality*. Oxford: Clarendon, 1989.

Kamenka, Eugene. *The Ethical Foundations of Marxism*. New York: Praeger, 1962.

―――. *Marxism and Ethics*. London: Macmillan, 1969.

Kaye, Sharon M., and Harry J. Gensler. "Is God the Source of Morality?" In *God Matters: Readings in the Philosophy of Religion*, ed. Raymond Martin and Christopher Bernard, 481–87. New York: Longman, 2003.

Kearney, Richard, and Mark Dooley. *Questioning Ethics: Contemporary Debates in Philosophy*. London: Routledge, 1999.

Kekes, John. *Against Liberalism*. Ithaca, N.Y.: Cornell Univ. Pr., 1997.

―――. *A Case for Conservatism*. Ithaca, N.Y.: Cornell Univ. Pr., 1998.

Korsgaard, Christine M., et. al. *The Sources of Normativity*. Cambridge: Cambridge Univ. Pr., 1996.

Larrabee, Mary Jeanne, ed. *An Ethic of Care: Feminist and Interdisciplinary Perspectives*. New York: Routledge, 1993.

Lévinas, Emmanuel. *Alterity and Transcendence*. Trans. Michael B. Smith. New York: Columbia Univ. Pr., 1999.

―――. *Ethics and Infinity*. Trans. Richard A. Cohen. Pittsburgh, Pa.: Duquesne Univ. Pr., 1985.

―――. *On Thinking-of-the-Other*. Trans. Michael B. Smith and Barbara Harshav. New York: Columbia Univ. Pr., 1998.

Lewis, Clarence I. *An Analysis of Knowledge and Valuation*. La Salle, Ill.: Open Court, 1962.

―――. *The Ground and Nature of the Right*. New York: Columbia Univ. Pr., 1955.

―――. *Our Social Inheritance*. Bloomington: Indiana Univ. Pr., 1957.

―――. *Values and Imperatives: Studies in Ethics*. Stanford, Calif.: Stanford Univ. Pr., 1969.

Lewis, Clive Staples. *Mere Christianity*. London: Geoffrey Bles, 1952. [The first part argues for basing morality on religion.]

Lukes, Steven. *Marxism and Morality*. Oxford: Clarendon, 1985.

Lyons, David. *Forms and Limits of Utilitarianism*. Oxford: Clarendon, 1965.

―――, ed. *Rights*. Belmont, Calif.: Wadsworth, 1979.

MacIntyre, Alasdair C. *After Virtue*. 2nd ed. Notre Dame, Ind.: Univ. of Notre Dame Pr., 1984.

―――. *Dependent Rational Animals*. Chicago: Open Court, 1999.

―――. *Three Rival Versions of Moral Inquiry*. Notre Dame, Ind.: Univ. of Notre Dame Pr., 1990.

―――. *Whose Justice? Which Rationality?* Notre Dame, Ind.: Univ. of Notre Dame Pr., 1988.

Mackie, John L. *Ethics: Inventing Right and Wrong*. London: Penguin, 1977.

Marcel, Gabriel. *Being and Having*. New York: Harper & Row, 1965.

Marcuse, Herbert. *One-Dimensional Man: Studies in the Ideology of Advanced*

Industrial Society. Boston: Beacon, 1964.

Maritain, Jacques. *Natural Law: Reflections on Theory and Practice.* Ed. William Sweet. South Bend, Ind.: St. Augustine's Pr., 2001.

———. *The Person And The Common Good.* Trans. John J. Fitzgerald. New York: Scribner, 1947.

———. *The Rights of Man and Natural Law.* Trans. Doris C. Anson. New York: Scribner, 1943.

Martin, Mike W. *Love's Virtues.* Lawrence: Univ. Pr. of Kansas, 1996.

———. *Self-deception and Morality.* Lawrence: Univ. Pr. of Kansas, 1986.

McCloskey, Henry J. *Metaethics and Normative Ethics.* The Hague: Nijhoff, 1969.

McDowell, John H. *Mind and World.* Cambridge, Mass.: Harvard Univ. Pr., 1994.

———. *Mind, Value, and Reality.* Cambridge, Mass.: Harvard Univ. Pr., 1998.

McNaughton, David. *Moral Vision: An Introduction to Ethics.* Oxford: Blackwell, 1988.

Melden, A. I. *Rights and Persons.* Oxford: Blackwell, 1977.

Michelman, Stephen. *Historical Dictionary of Existentialism.* Lanham, Md.: Scarecrow, 2008.

Midgley, Mary. *Beast and Man: The Roots of Human Nature.* 2nd ed. London: Routledge, 1995.

———. *Can't We Make Moral Judgments?* New York: St. Martin's, 1991.

———. *The Ethical Primate: Humans, Freedom, and Morality.* London: Routledge, 1994.

Millgram, Elijah, ed. *Varieties of Practical Reasoning.* Cambridge, Mass.: MIT, 2001.

Milo, Ronald D., ed. *Egoism and Altruism.* Belmont, Calif., Wadsworth, 1973.

Monro, David H. *Empiricism and Ethics.* Cambridge: Cambridge Univ. Pr., 1967.

Moore, George E. *Ethics.* Oxford: Oxford Univ. Pr., 1912.

———. *Principia Ethica.* Cambridge: Cambridge Univ. Pr., 1903.

Morgan, Michael L., ed. *Classics of Moral and Political Theory.* 4th ed. Indianapolis, Ind.: Hackett, 2005.

Mulhall, Stephen, and Adam Swift. *Liberals and Communitarians.* Cambridge, Mass.: Blackwell, 1996.

Murdoch, Iris. *The Nice and the Good.* London: Chatto & Windus, 1968.

———. *The Sovereignty of Good over Other Concepts.* London: Cambridge Univ. Pr., 1967.

Murphy, Mark C. *An Essay on Divine Authority.* Ithaca, N.Y.: Cornell Univ. Pr., 2002.

———. *Natural Law and Practical Rationality.* Cambridge: Cambridge Univ. Pr., 2001.

Nagel, Thomas. *Equality and Partiality.* New York: Oxford Univ. Pr., 1991.

———. *The Possibility of Altruism.* Oxford: Clarendon, 1970.

———. *The View From Nowhere.* New York: Oxford Univ. Pr., 1986.

———. *What Does It All Mean?* New York: Oxford Univ. Pr., 1987.

Narveson, Jan. *Morality and Utility*. Baltimore, Md.: Johns Hopkins Pr., 1967.

Nelson, Leonard. *System of Ethics*. Trans. Norman Guterman. New Haven, Conn.: Yale Univ. Pr., 1956.

Neusner, Jacob, ed. *Analyzing the Golden Rule*. Lanham, Md.: University Press of America, 2008.

Nielsen, Kai. *Ethics without God*. Amherst, N.Y.: Prometheus, 1990.

———. *Marxism and the Moral Point of View: Morality, Ideology, and Historical Materialism*. Boulder, Colo.: Westview, 1988.

Noddings, Nel. *Caring: A Feminine Approach to Ethics and Moral Education*. 2nd ed. Berkeley: Univ. of California Pr., 2003.

Nowell-Smith, Patrick H. *Ethics*. Oxford: Blackwell, 1957.

Nozick, Robert. *Anarchy, State, and Utopia*. New York: Basic, 1974.

———. *The Nature of Rationality*. Princeton, N.J.: Princeton Univ. Pr., 1993.

O'Neill, Onora. *Acting on Principle: An Essay on Kantian Ethics*. New York: Columbia Univ. Pr., 1975.

———. *Towards Justice and Virtue: A Constructive Account of Practical Reasoning*. Cambridge: Cambridge Univ. Pr., 1996.

Oakeshott, Michael J. *On Human Conduct*. Oxford: Clarendon, 1975.

Ogden, Charles K., and Ivor A. Richards. *The Meaning of Meaning: A Study of the Influence of Language Upon Thought and of the Science of Symbolism*. New York: Harcourt Brace, 1925.

Olafson, Frederick A. *Ethics and Twentieth Century Thought*. Englewood Cliffs, N.J.: Prentice Hall, 1973.

———. *Principles and Persons: An Ethical Interpretation of Existentialism*. Baltimore: Johns Hopkins Pr., 1967.

Outka, Gene H., and John P. Reeder, Jr., eds. *Prospects for a Common Morality*. Princeton, N.J.: Princeton Univ. Pr., 1993.

Parfit, Derek. *Reasons and Persons*. Oxford: Clarendon, 1984.

———. *Climbing the Mountain*. Oxford: Oxford Univ. Pr., forthcoming.

Perry, Ralph B. *General Theory of Value*. Cambridge, Mass.: Harvard Univ. Pr., 1926.

———. *Realms of Value*. New York: Greenwood, 1954.

Pettit, Philip, ed. *Consequentialism*. Brookfield, Vt.: Dartmouth, 1993.

Plumwood, Val. *Feminism and the Mastery of Nature*. London: Routledge, 1993.

Pollock, Lansing. *The Free Society*. Boulder, Colo.: Westview, 1996.

Popper, Karl. *The Open Society and Its Enemies*. 8th ed. London: Routledge, 2002.

Potter, Nelson T., and Mark Timmons, eds. *Morality and Universality*. Dordrecht: D. Reidel, 1985.

Prichard, Harold A. "Does Moral Philosophy Rest on a Mistake?" *Mind* 21, no. 81 (Jan. 1912): 21–37.

———. *Moral Obligation*. Ed. W. D. Ross. Oxford: Clarendon, 1949.

Quinn, Philip L. *Divine Commands and Moral Requirements*. New York: Oxford Univ. Pr., 1978.

Raffoul, François, and David Pettigrew. *Heidegger and Practical Philosophy.* Albany, N.Y.: SUNY, 2002.

Railton, Peter. *Facts, Values and Norms.* Cambridge: Cambridge Univ. Pr., 2003.

Rand, Ayn. *Capitalism: The Unknown Ideal.* New York: New American Library, 1966.

———. *For the New Intellectual: The Philosophy of Ayn Rand.* New York: Random House, 1961.

———. *The Virtue of Selfishness.* New York: New American Library, 1964.

Rawls, John. *Collected Papers.* Ed. Samuel Freeman. Cambridge, Mass.: Harvard Univ. Pr., 1999.

———. *Justice as Fairness: A Restatement.* Ed. Erin Kelly. Cambridge, Mass.: Harvard Univ. Pr., 2001.

———. *The Law of Peoples.* Cambridge, Mass.: Harvard Univ. Pr., 1999.

———. *Lectures on the History of Moral Philosophy.* Ed. Barbara Herman. Cambridge, Mass.: Harvard Univ. Pr., 2000.

———. *Political Liberalism.* New York: Columbia Univ. Pr., 1993.

———. *A Theory of Justice.* 2nd ed. Cambridge, Mass.: Harvard Univ. Pr., 1999.

Raz, Joseph. *The Authority of Law.* Oxford: Clarendon, 1979.

———. *Engaging Reason: On the Theory of Value and Action.* Oxford: Oxford Univ. Pr., 1999.

———. *The Morality of Freedom.* Oxford: Clarendon, 1986.

———. *Practical Reason and Norms.* London: Hutchinson, 1975.

Rehg, William. *Insight and Solidarity: A Study in the Discourse Ethics of Jürgen Habermas.* Berkeley: Univ. of California Pr., 1994.

Reiman, Jeffrey. *Critical Moral Liberalism: Theory and Practice.* Lanham, Md.: Rowman & Littlefield, 1997.

Reiner, Hans. *Duty and Inclination: The Fundamentals of Morality Discussed and Redefined with Special Regard to Kant and Schiller.* Boston: Nijhoff, 1983.

Rescher, Nicholas. *Distributive Justice.* Indianapolis, Ind.: Bobbs-Merrill, 1967.

———. *Fairness: Theory & Practice of Distributive Justice.* New Brunswick, N.J.: Transaction, 2002.

———. *Introduction to Value Theory.* Englewood Cliffs, N.J.: Prentice Hall, 1969.

———. *Unselfishness.* Pittsburgh, Pa.: Univ. of Pittsburgh Pr., 1975.

Rice, Philip Blair. *On the Knowledge of Good and Evil.* New York: Random House, 1955.

Richards, David A. J. *A Theory of Reasons for Action.* Oxford: Clarendon, 1971.

Richardson, Henry S. *Practical Reasoning about Final Ends.* Cambridge: Cambridge Univ. Pr., 1994.

Ricoeur, Paul. "The Golden Rule." *New Testament Studies* 36 (1990): 392–97.

———. *The Just.* Trans. David Pellauer. Chicago: Univ. of Chicago Pr., 2000.

———. *Oneself as Another.* Trans. Kathleen Blamey. Chicago: Univ. of Chicago Pr., 1992.

———. *The Symbolism of Evil.* Trans. E. Buchanan. Boston: Beacon, 1969.

Rist, John M. *Real Ethics: Rethinking the Foundations of Morality.* Cambridge: Cambridge Univ. Pr., 2002.

Rønnow-Rasmussen, Toni. *Logic, Facts, and Representation: An Examination of R. M. Hare's Moral Philosophy.* Lund, Sweden: Lund Univ. Pr., 1993.

Ross, Alf. *Directives and Norms.* New York: Humanities, 1968.

Ross, William D. *The Foundations of Ethics.* Oxford: Clarendon, 1939.

———. *The Right and the Good.* Oxford: Clarendon, 1930.

Royce, Josiah. *The Philosophy of Loyalty.* New York: Macmillan, 1908.

———. *Studies of Good and Evil.* Hamden, Conn.: Archon, 1964.

———. *World and the Individual: Nature, Man, and the Moral Order.* New York: Dover, 1959.

Russell, Bertrand. *Russell on Ethics: Selections from the Writings of Bertrand Russell.* Ed. Charles R. Pigden. London: Routledge, 1999.

Sandel, Michael J. *Liberalism and the Limits of Justice.* Cambridge: Cambridge Univ. Pr., 1998.

———, ed. *Liberalism and Its Critics.* New York: New York Univ. Pr., 1984.

Sartre, Jean-Paul. *Being and Nothingness.* Trans. Hazel E. Barnes. New York: Philosophical Library, 1956.

———. *Existentialism and Human Emotions.* Trans. Bernard Frechtman and Hazel E. Barnes. New York: Philosophical Library, 1957.

———. *Notebooks for an Ethics.* Trans. David Pellauer. Chicago: Univ. of Chicago Pr., 1992.

Sayre-McCord, Geoffrey, ed. *Essays on Moral Realism.* Ithaca, N.Y.: Cornell Univ. Pr., 1988.

Scanlon, Thomas M. *What We Owe to Each Other.* Cambridge, Mass.: Harvard Univ. Pr., 1998.

Scheffler, Samuel. *The Rejection of Consequentialism.* Oxford: Clarendon, 1994.

———, ed. *Consequentialism and Its Critics.* Oxford: Oxford Univ. Pr., 1988.

Scheler, Max. *On Feeling, Knowing, and Valuing: Selected Writings.* Ed. Harold J. Bershady. Chicago: Univ. of Chicago Pr., 1992.

———. *Formalism in Ethics and Non-Formal Ethics of Values.* Trans. Manfred S. Frings and Roger L. Funk. Evanston, Ill.: Northwestern Univ. Pr., 1973.

———. *The Nature of Sympathy.* Trans. Peter Heath. New Haven, Conn.: Yale Univ. Pr., 1954.

Schlick, Moritz. *Problems of Ethics.* Trans. David Rynin. New York: Prentice Hall, 1939.

Sen, Amartya, and Bernard Williams, eds. *Utilitarianism and Beyond.* Cambridge: Cambridge Univ. Pr., 1982.

Shafer-Landau, Russ. *Moral Realism: A Defence.* Oxford: Clarendon, 2003.

———. *Whatever Happened to Good and Evil?* New York: Oxford Univ. Pr., 2004.

Sharp, F. C. *Ethics.* New York: Century, 1928.

Singer, Marcus G. *Generalization in Ethics*. New York: Knopf, 1961.

Sinnott-Armstrong, Walter, and Mark Timmons, eds. *Moral Knowledge? New Readings in Moral Epistemology*. New York: Oxford Univ. Pr., 1996.

Slote, Michael A. *Beyond Optimizing: A Study of Rational Choice*. Cambridge, Mass.: Harvard Univ. Pr., 1989.

———. *Common-sense Morality and Consequentialism*. London: Routledge, 1985.

———. *From Morality to Virtue*. New York: Oxford Univ. Pr., 1992.

———. *Goods and Virtues*. New York: Oxford Univ. Pr., 1983.

———. *Morals from Motives*. Oxford: Oxford Univ. Pr., 2001.

Smart, J. J. C., and Bernard Williams. *Utilitarianism: For and Against*. Cambridge: Cambridge Univ. Pr., 1973.

Smith, Michael A. *The Moral Problem*. Oxford: Blackwell, 1995.

Sokolowski, Robert. *Moral Action: A Phenomenological Study*. Bloomington: Indiana Univ. Pr., 1985.

Sommers, Christina Hoff. *The War against Boys: How Misguided Feminism Is Harming Our Young Men*. New York: Touchstone, 2000.

———. *Who Stole Feminism? How Women Have Betrayed Women*. New York: Simon & Schuster, 1994.

Statman, Daniel, ed. *Moral Luck*. Albany, N.Y.: SUNY, 1993.

———. *Virtue Ethics*. Washington, D.C.: Georgetown Univ. Pr., 1997.

Sterba, James P., ed. *Ethics: Classical Western Texts in Feminist and Multicultural Perspectives*. New York: Oxford Univ. Pr., 2000.

Stevenson, Charles L. *Ethics and Language*. New Haven, Conn.: Yale Univ. Pr., 1944.

———. *Facts and Values*. New Haven, Conn.: Yale Univ. Pr., 1963.

Stocker, Michael A. G. *Plural and Conflicting Values*. Oxford: Clarendon, 1989.

Stratton-Lake, Philip, ed. *Ethical Intuitionism: Re-evaluations*. Oxford: Clarendon, 2002.

Sumner, L. W. *Welfare, Happiness, and Ethics*. Oxford: Clarendon, 1996.

Swanton, Christine. *Virtue Ethics: A Pluralistic View*. Oxford: Oxford Univ. Pr., 2003.

Swindal, James C. *Reflection Revisited: Jürgen Habermas's Emancipative Theory of Truth*. New York: Fordham Univ. Pr., 1999.

Taylor, Charles. *The Ethics of Authenticity*. Cambridge, Mass.: Harvard Univ. Pr., 1991.

———. *Sources of the Self: The Making of the Modern Identity*. Cambridge, Mass.: Harvard Univ. Pr., 1989.

Taylor, Michael. *The Possibility of Cooperation*. Cambridge: Cambridge Univ. Pr., 1987.

Taylor, Richard. *Good and Evil*. Amherst, N.Y.: Prometheus, 2000.

Thomson, Judith Jarvis. *The Realm of Rights*. Cambridge, Mass.: Harvard Univ. Pr., 1990.

————. *Rights, Restitution, and Risk: Essays in Moral Theory.* Ed. William Parent. Cambridge, Mass.: Harvard Univ. Pr., 1986.

Toulmin, Stephen E. *An Examination of the Place of Reason in Ethics.* Cambridge: Cambridge Univ. Pr., 1950.

Urmson, J. O. *The Emotive Theory of Ethics.* London: Hutchinson, 1968.

Veatch, Henry B. *For an Ontology of Morals: A Critique of Contemporary Ethical Theory.* Evanston, Ill.: Northwestern Univ. Pr., 1971.

Walker, David M. and Daniel Gray. *Historical Dictionary of Marxism.* Lanham, Md.: Scarecrow, 2007.

Wallace, James D. *Ethical Norms, Particular Cases.* Ithaca, N.Y.: Cornell Univ. Pr., 1996.

————. *Virtues and Vices.* Ithaca, N.Y.: Cornell Univ. Pr., 1978.

Warnock, Geoffrey J. *Contemporary Moral Philosophy.* London: Macmillan, 1967.

————. *The Object of Morality.* London: Methuen, 1971.

Wattles, Jeffrey. *The Golden Rule.* New York: Oxford Univ. Pr., 1996.

Weil, Simone. *Simone Weil: An Anthology.* Ed. Siân Miles. New York: Grove, 1986.

Weithman, Paul J. ed. *Reasonable Pluralism.* New York: Garland, 1999.

Wellman, Carl. *A Theory of Rights: Persons Under Laws, Institutions, and Morals.* Totowa, N.J.: Rowman & Allanheld, 1985.

Wiggins, David. *Needs, Values, Truth: Essays in the Philosophy of Value.* Oxford: Blackwell, 1987.

Williams, Bernard. *Ethics and the Limits of Philosophy.* Cambridge, Mass.: Harvard Univ. Pr., 1985.

————. *Moral Luck: Philosophical Papers, 1973–1980.* Cambridge: Cambridge Univ. Pr., 1981.

Wittgenstein, Ludwig. "A Lecture on Ethics." In *Philosophical Occasions: 1912–1951.* Ed. James C. Klagge and Alfred Nordmann. Indianapolis, Ind.: Hackett, 1993.

————. *Philosophical Investigations.* Trans. G. E. M. Anscombe. Oxford: Blackwell, 1958

————. *Tractatus Logico-Philosophicus.* Trans. C. K. Ogden. London: Routledge, 1922.

Wong, David B. *Moral Relativity.* Berkeley: Univ. of California Pr., 1984.

Wright, Georg H. von. *The Varieties of Goodness.* London: Routledge, 1963.

Zagzebski, Linda Trinkaus. *Divine Motivation Theory.* Cambridge: Cambridge Univ. Pr., 2004.

————. *Virtues of the Mind: An Inquiry into the Nature of Virtue and the Ethical Foundations of Knowledge.* Cambridge: Cambridge Univ. Pr., 1996.